AN EXPLORER'S GUIDE

Colorado

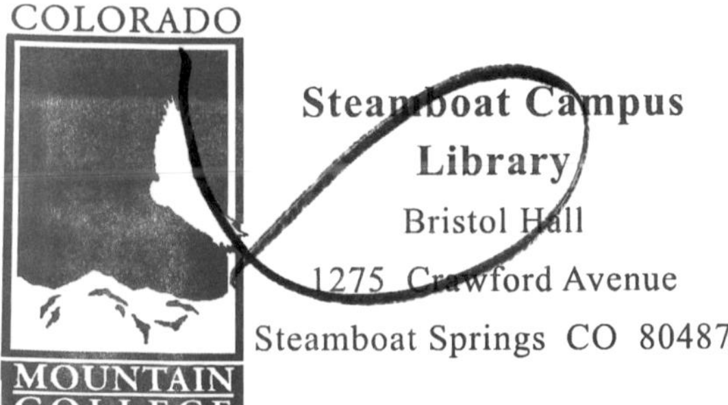

Colorado

Matt Forster

with photographs by Matt & Kim Forster

FIRST EDITION

The Countryman Press ✸ Woodstock, Vermont

First Edition

ISBN 978-0-88150-745-4

Cover photo © Barbara Magnuson & Larry Kimball
Interior photos by Matt and Kim Forster
Book design by Bodenweber Design
Page composition by PerfecType, Nashville, TN
Maps by Mapping Specialists Ltd., © 2008 The Countryman Press

Published by The Countryman Press, P.O. Box 748, Woodstock, Vermont 05091

Distributed by W.W. Norton & Company, Inc., 500 Fifth Avenue, New York, NY 10110

Printed in the United States of America

10 9 8 7 6 5 4 3 2 1

DEDICATION

To my wife, Kim, and our brand new, bouncing baby girl, Abby.

EXPLORE WITH US!

Welcome to the first edition of *Colorado: An Explorer's Guide*, the definitive guide to the Centennial State. From the expansive eastern plains to the Rocky Mountains, this guide covers the best there is to see and do in Colorado. Travelers will find important information on where to stay, where to eat, what attractions to see, and what activities are available in every region of the state. Like the other titles in the Explorer's Guides series, this book covers the usual worthwhile attractions as well as some out-of-the-way local favorites.

WHAT'S WHERE

In the beginning of the book you'll find an alphabetical listing of important information and state highlights—everything from avalanches and altitude to wildlife and wineries.

LODGING

The hotels, B&Bs, cabins, and campgrounds in this book have been included because they have a proven reputation for being great places to stay—no one pays to be listed in these pages. From season to season, rates across Colorado fluctuate greatly; so a range of rates is included with each listing. For accurate travel planning, it's essential to call ahead. Every attempt has been made to provide the most current lodging rates, but the old saying holds true that the only constant is that everything changes. A scan of room taxes across the state in 2007 revealed that state and local municipalities added an extra 10 and 16 percent to the bill.

RESTAURANTS

The eateries in this book have been separated out into two sections: Dining Out and Eating Out. Dining Out listings are typically (though not always) the most expensive. These are where you find fine cuisine. Eating Out listings are typically cheaper, family dining establishments—where you find good grub. A range of prices is included for each entry. Colorado is one of a growing number of states that have enacted a statewide ban on smoking in bars and restaurants.

KEY TO SYMBOLS

- ✎ **Child friendly.** The crayon indicates that a place or event is family-friendly and welcomes children. Most upscale restaurants do not do a good job of accommodating children, and many B&Bs restrict kids (especially kids under 12).
- ♿ **Handicapped access.** The wheelchair icon denotes a place that has indicated they have access that complies with the Americans with Disabilities Act (ADA) standards.

Liquor. This symbol indicates that the restaurant in question has a bar.

Pets. The dog's paw icon identifies lodgings that allow pets. Be sure to make arrangements in advance. Most lodgings will charge extra for pets and will often restrict certain breeds.

Rainy day. The umbrella icon points out places where you can entertain yourself but still stay dry in bad weather.

Wedding friendly. The wedding rings icon denotes places and establishments that are good venues for weddings.

Wi-Fi. This symbol indicates that a lodging, restaurant, or coffeehouse offers free wireless Internet access.

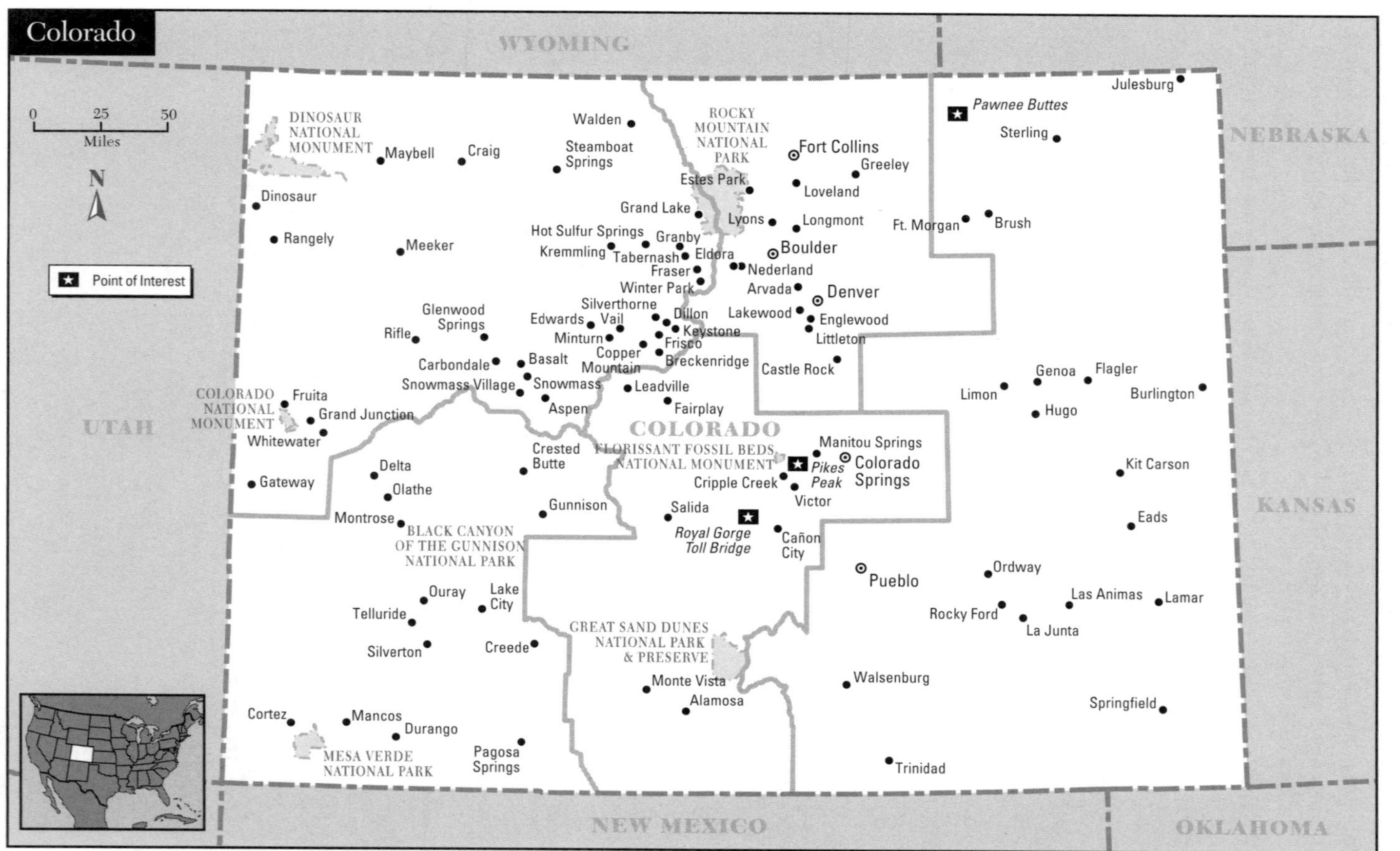
Colorado
WYOMING
NEBRASKA
KANSAS
OKLAHOMA
NEW MEXICO
UTAH
COLORADO
0 25 50
Miles
N
Point of Interest
DINOSAUR NATIONAL MONUMENT
ROCKY MOUNTAIN NATIONAL PARK
COLORADO NATIONAL MONUMENT
FLORISSANT FOSSIL BEDS NATIONAL MONUMENT
BLACK CANYON OF THE GUNNISON NATIONAL PARK
GREAT SAND DUNES NATIONAL PARK & PRESERVE
MESA VERDE NATIONAL PARK
Pawnee Buttes
Pikes Peak
Royal Gorge Toll Bridge
Julesburg
Sterling
Fort Collins
Greeley
Loveland
Longmont
Ft. Morgan
Brush
Boulder
Denver
Arvada
Lakewood
Englewood
Littleton
Castle Rock
Nederland
Eldora
Lyons
Estes Park
Grand Lake
Granby
Tabernash
Fraser
Winter Park
Hot Sulfur Springs
Kremmling
Walden
Steamboat Springs
Craig
Maybell
Dinosaur
Rangely
Meeker
Rifle
Glenwood Springs
Carbondale
Basalt
Snowmass Village
Snowmass
Aspen
Edwards
Vail
Minturn
Silverthorne
Dillon
Keystone
Frisco
Copper Mountain
Breckenridge
Leadville
Fairplay
Fruita
Grand Junction
Whitewater
Gateway
Delta
Olathe
Montrose
Crested Butte
Gunnison
Salida
Cripple Creek
Victor
Manitou Springs
Colorado Springs
Cañon City
Pueblo
Limon
Genoa
Flagler
Burlington
Hugo
Kit Carson
Eads
Ordway
Rocky Ford
La Junta
Las Animas
Lamar
Walsenburg
Springfield
Trinidad
Monte Vista
Alamosa
Ouray
Lake City
Telluride
Silverton
Creede
Cortez
Mancos
Durango
Pagosa Springs

CONTENTS

ACKNOWLEDGMENTS

Many books begin with the author's grateful acknowledgment of those who helped in some way to bring the project to fruition. Until I began work on this book, I had no idea how grateful those authors must truly feel, for without certain individuals this book would not exist as it does today. First, I would like to thank the staff I talked with at chambers of commerce and visitor bureaus across the state. Their often fanatical love of the towns and cities they represent is not only a great asset to their constituents but also to people like me, who come to see a place through their eyes. In particular, I would like to thank Mary Jo Coulehan in Pagosa Springs and Vicky Nash in Glenwood Springs for introducing me to the best their towns have to offer. Others whose help was especially appreciated include Kim Farin in Boulder, Cathy Jones in Fort Collins, and Dena Morrisey in Durango. Of all the people I met while researching the book, many stand out for their generous hospitality, and I would like to express my special appreciation to Lynn and Paul Gardner in Estes Park, Sandy Schrawder in Buena Vista, and Ron and Leeann Unfred in Grand Junction for making me feel at home in their homes.

While in Colorado, I often rely on family to pick me up, drop me off, and put me up, not to mention answer my endless questions. My parents-in-law, Lynn and Carol Chester, have always been extremely gracious with their time. Together with Carol's parents, Lawrence and Darlene Halvorson, and my sister and brother-in-law, Nikki and Mark MacLeay, they have taught me a lot about the state, and I have enjoyed listening to stories about life on the eastern plains and the Front Range. The family has deep roots here, and that kind of knowledge and experience cannot be grasped from a book.

My family back home made huge contributions to this project as well. Not only did my dad and sister each spend time with me on the road, the entire family pitched in when we needed help holding down the fort. My parents, Jim and Cathy Forster, helped more than I could imagine. My sister and her husband, Becky and Sergio Platero, contributed their time, helping with various parts of this project.

Lastly, my wife Kim deserves special recognition. Our daughter, Abigail, was born just days after I returned from my first research trip. Not only did Kim play the role of single parent during the many weeks I was away, she kept our lives moving forward while I spent hours locked in the study. Though the photos in this book were taken by the two of us, the *best* photos are hers, and without her support, I am sure there would be no book at all. When we were first dating, many years ago now, she brought me to Colorado and introduced me to her state. Her passion for the mountains, for hiking, biking, and climbing are contagious, and she brings so much excitement to everything she does, all I can ever do is hope to keep up.

INTRODUCTION

My fascination with Colorado began as a boy, listening to *An Evening with John Denver* on my parents' record player. Though the album isn't all about Colorado, per se, songs like *Rocky Mountain High* and *Take Me Home, Country Roads* left indelible impressions about Colorado in general and the Rocky Mountains in particular. Growing up in the Midwest, trips that took us west of the Mississippi were rare, but greatly enjoyed. And though I found myself in the Rockies several times, Colorado was somewhat elusive. By the time I was in college, my only experience with the state was an ill-fated road trip that left me stranded for a week north of Dotsero. It wasn't until I moved to Denver to marry my wife, Kim, a fourth-generation Colorado native, that I truly got a chance to appreciate all the state has to offer. Over the years, that appreciation has continued to grow.

Like all travel guides, this one divvies the state up into regions. Determining

A MOOSE IN COLORADO'S HIGH COUNTRY

A MOUNTAIN MAN TENDING HIS WARES

what cities and towns fit into each region is a bit tricky. Do you group towns by activity—all the ski towns in this group, and all the rest over here? Or do you do it by terrain—all the mountain towns in one group, the plains in another? You could divide them up by culture in a sense, with agricultural towns separated from industrial and college towns. Soon, however, all these classifications run into an inevitable obstacle. As you begin to examine the people, activities, and culture, you soon discover that each town, village, and hamlet should have its own region. They are all too different to be lumped together.

Consider the chapter "Southwest Colorado." Durango has a distinct Old West feel. The historic downtown, the narrow-gauge railroad, and the annual Cowboy Gathering all feed into the town's vibe. Just an hour or so west is Pagosa Springs. It's a relaxed place, with easy-going people, and the entire town evokes a strong Southwest feel—like a mini Santa Fe. Head north of Durango, and you have a touristy mountain town like Silverton, and just over the mountain from there is Telluride, one of the state's chicest ski resorts.

In the end, I decided to create five regions that loosely follow the six already established by the state Tourism Office. Maybe this will help you avoid some confusion when juggling guide book and travel brochures as you head down the road.

To research this book, I jumped in the car and traveled all over the state. I visited hotels, B&Bs, lodges, and resorts. I ate in fine Italian restaurants, roadside barbeque joints, old-school diners, and, of course, steakhouses. I visited the zoos, explored the caves, hiked trails to hidden falls, and jumped on every train I could. In the end, it really is impossible to do everything and eat everywhere—in Denver alone you could eat at a new place every meal for over two years—so I talked to people too. Lots of people. Folks who live in Colorado are more than happy to tell you about their favorite restaurants, the ones where they take their own out-of-town guests. They are also more than happy to tell you about the places that aren't so good. The input provided by hundreds of strangers gave me excellent leads and confirmed much of what I learned on my own. None of the businesses mentioned in the book paid for their inclusion. They're here because they have a proven reputation for providing a great experience.

One of the things I like best about Colorado is the sense of the state's unique history, which is very evident as you travel from town to town. This history doesn't just add to the tourist experience, it *is* the tourist experience. Even before Colorado was part of the Union, tourists made their way here. As early as 1854, men came west to what is now Colorado with large hunting parties, set on seeing how many grizzly bears, bison, antelope, and deer they could mow down in a month. This early form of "recreational tourism" might not seem quite kosher today, but it illustrates how quickly people came to appreciate this mountainous region on the country's frontier. Ever since the 19th century, tourists have been enticed to Colorado for the mountains, which offer opportunities for recreation, scenery for contemplation, and a climate conducive to good health.

The city of Colorado Springs was established in 1871 as a resort community. Not only did the town cater to tourists looking to explore the local natural wonders, but thousands of people suffering ailments like tuberculosis and rheumatism came to take the waters in Manitou Springs or simply sit on a wide shady porch and breathe that dry, fresh mountain air. Soon after the turn of the century, Pikes Peak had a road to its summit, paving the path, so to speak, for the millions who subsequently rode and eventually drove to the top.

In the mountains, the story is much the same. In 1860, the first American to "discover" Glenwood Springs was followed less than 20 years later by the first permanent settler. By the 1880s, the town's legendary Hot Springs Pool had been established, complete with a sandstone lodge and the world-class Hotel Colorado across the street.

The turn of the century brought continued development to the state's tourism industry. Mesa Verde National Park was established in 1906. Seven years later, Rocky Mountain National Park (RMNP) was created near Estes Park. Visitors making their way to Estes Park not soon after would have been able to stay at the luxurious Stanley Hotel, which F. O. Stanley built in 1909. In fact, the way

A FARM IN EASTERN COLORADO

up through the Big Thompson Canyon had been significantly improved by Stanley, allowing him to eventually offer an early motorized shuttle to his resort.

Much of this growth was driven by the wealth pouring out of the mountains in the latter portion of the 19th century. Gold, silver, and other precious metals fueled an economic boom that is evident by the number of Victorian buildings throughout the state. When mining fell off, the state's mining towns struggled. The smaller towns soon became ghosts, with a few dilapidated structures left to indicate that people once lived there. The towns that served as mining centers—Leadville, Aspen, Breckenridge—somehow continued on.

In 1912, a Norwegian skier by the name of Carl Howelsen moved to Steamboat. He brought with him a passion for cross-country skiing and ski jumping. By 1913, Steamboat had a ski jump, and soon a ski hill. Howelsen is credited with bringing skiing to Colorado. By 1937, Berthoud Pass became the state's first ski area with a tow-lift. The rope was hauled uphill by a Ford V-8 engine. Other ski areas were eventually built, and by the 1960s and '70s, the ski industry in Colorado was booming.

As you explore Colorado, there are countless opportunities to learn more about the state's rich history. From the Ute and other Native American Indians who called this region home and the mountain men and French trappers who scouted the frontier to the farmers, ranchers, and prospectors who followed, the story of this land is complex and compelling.

The book begins with a "What's Where in Colorado" section. This highlights some of the unique things you can find in Colorado. It also points the way to other sources of information. The remainder of the book describes Colorado, region by region. No individual section of the book can tell the whole story of this wide and varied state. It is my hope, however, that as a whole the book paints a pretty decent picture of what travelers can expect to find here.

I imagine you reading this book sometime in the future while planning a trip to Mesa Verde to see the cliff dwellings, or maybe on a ski vacation in Vail, or just pulling into Estes Park after the first leg of your trip, looking for a place to eat. No matter what the scenario, I envy you. As soon as I return home after exploring some new part of Colorado, I begin to look forward to the next trip. My hope is that this book will be helpful in your own travels and will open up new vistas for you and your family in Colorado.

WHAT'S WHERE IN COLORADO

ALTITUDE West of I-25, altitude is everywhere. When travelers come from lower altitudes, they often do not understand the effect it can have on their bodies. Dehydration and sunburn are easy enough to deal with—drink plenty of water, wear a hat, and use sunscreen. But no matter how healthy you are, altitude can affect anyone, and altitude sickness is something emergency rooms see a lot of here. Watch for symptoms like dizziness and headaches, and head to a lower elevation (and continue to drink water) until they disappear. If symptoms do not go away, seek medical attention.

AMUSEMENT PARKS The most popular amusement park in Colorado is **Elitch Gardens** (303-595-4386, park info or 303-595-4386 guest relations; www.elitchgardens.com), 2000 Elitch Cir. This used to be a Six Flags until it changed ownership in 2007. Located right in downtown Denver, the park has a mess of roller coasters and other rides. On hot days, their water park is a nice way to cool off. The water rides, however, are no match for those at **Water World** (303-427-7873; www.waterworldcolorado.com), 1800 W. 89th Ave. Located north of Denver, this water park has acres of slides, wave pools, and a relaxing Lazy River.

ART MUSEUMS The **Denver Art Museum** (720-913-0000; www.denverartmuseum.org), 100 W. 14th Ave., is one of the finest in the country. For western art, consider the **A. R. Mitchell Memorial Museum and Gallery** (719-846-4224; www.mitchellmuseum.com), 150 E. Main St., in Trinidad. Most major Colorado cities have some art museums. Those in Colorado Springs, Boulder, and Fort Collins are worth a visit. In the mountains, Aspen also has a noncollecting museum that features contemporary art, the **Aspen Art Museum** (970-925-8050; www.aspenartmuseum.org), 590 N. Mill St.

AVALANCHES Every year avalanches close sections of road in the mountains. Nearly 70 people will be caught in an avalanche in an average year; of those about six will die. In order to prevent avalanche disasters, the Colorado Department of Transportation does avalanche control along the major highways. This involves identifying and stopping potential avalanches. In extreme cases, explosives are used to create a controlled avalanche. Within the ski resorts, ski patrols do the same kind of work. In backcountry areas, it's up to individuals to understand the dangers and take necessary steps to protect themselves and their travel partners. The Colorado Avalanche Information Center (www.avalanche.state.co.us) is an organization that provides up-to-date avalanche forecasts, educates the public on avalanche safety, and looks into avalanche fatalities.

BED & BREAKFASTS Colorado has amazing B&Bs. With few exceptions, the innkeepers here are incredibly hospitable. Those listed throughout the book come highly recommended. For a complete listing of B&Bs throughout the state you might want to look online at **Colorado Bed & Breakfast, "On the Web"** (www.colorado-bnb.com) or **Bed & Breakfast Innkeepers of Colorado** (1-800-265-7696; www.innsofcolorado.org).

BREWERIES Even before actor Mark Harmon walked beside a mountain stream in winter, proclaiming the Rocky Mountain purity of Coors, beer has been a big deal in Colorado. This is even truer today, following a decade of growing appreciation for microbrews. California may boost more breweries (Colorado is a close second), but Colorado has more people employed in brewing beer than anywhere else, over 5,000. Most breweries offer people a chance to tour their facilities and taste the end product. Some of the better tours will be noted throughout this guide. Denver has over 90 kinds of beer brewed locally, and Fort Collins has created its own brewery culture, with the visitor center offering a brochure that outlines a day of brewery-hopping.

CANTALOUPE Over the years, Rocky Ford in southeast Colorado has built up quite a reputation for growing the world's best cantaloupe. When the fruit is in season, in August, you can find growers selling their cantaloupe and watermelon on the side of the road. Just look for handmade signs and pick-up trucks loaded with fresh melons.

CANYONS Colorado has some of the most scenic canyons in the world. The **Colorado National Monument** (970-858-3617; www.nps.gov/colm) just south of Grand Junction has many unique geological features, including rocky towers jutting up from the canyon floor. The **Black Canyon of the Gunnison National Park** (970-641-2337; www.nps.gov/blca), west of Gunnison, has stunningly tall walls and a relatively narrow span. For centuries the canyon was considered impenetrable, and even today those who want to get to the canyon floor must have plenty of experience hiking and climbing and must blaze their own trail. The most popular canyon, however, must be the Royal Gorge west of Cañon City. The **Royal Gorge Bridge and Park** (719-275-7507 or 1-888-333-5597; www.royalgorgebridge.com) has the highest suspension bridge in the world and offers great perspective on the gorge itself.

CLIFF DWELLINGS Many stop by the Manitou Cliff Dwellings in Manitou Springs to get an idea of what cliff dwellings are like. For the true experience, you must visit **Mesa Verde National Park** (970-529-4465; www.nps.gov/meve) west of Cortez in the southwest corner of the state. There you can climb down to the famous Balcony House and Cliff Palace. If you want more, a side trip to **Chimney Rock Archaeological Area** (970-883-5359; www.chimneyrockco.org) west of Pagosa Springs has several structures that you can visit on a walking tour of their mountain. Archaeological ruins aside, the scenery from the mountain is fantastic.

COLORADO TRAIL The Colorado Trail stretches across the state from Denver to Durango. Two books by the **Colorado Trail Foundation** (www.coloradotrail.org) are necessary for those inspired to walk all or part of the trail. They are *The Colorado Trail: The Official Guidebook* and *The Colorado Trail: The Trailside Databook*. The former gives an overview of each section of the trail, pointing out landmarks and giving advice from those who have walked this terrain before. The latter has detailed GPS data that will help keep your path straight.

COWBOY MUSIC Two ranches in Colorado offer chuckwagon suppers and quality cowboy entertainment. The **Flying W Ranch** (719-598-4000 or 1-800-232-3599; www.flyingw.com) in Colorado Springs features the Flying W Wranglers. Out west in Durango, you will find the Bar D Wranglers playing regularly at the **Bar D Chuckwagon Suppers** (970-247-5753 or 1-888-800-5753; www.bardchuckwagon.com).

DAMS Throughout Colorado, various rivers have been dammed to control flooding and provide water for the state. Often what is called a lake is in fact a reservoir—and as you drive around these reservoirs, you will often find yourself driving across the top of a dam. Since 9/11, the Department of Homeland Security has tightened security around the nation's dams, and parking on dams is not permitted. Therefore, if you stop on a dam to take a picture or enjoy the view, it will not be long before someone in an official-looking vehicle pulls up and asks you to move along.

DUDE RANCHES Dozens of dude ranches around the state provide guests with all sorts of prepackaged vacations. The more traditional ranches have guests riding horses and helping with the daily running of a ranch, everything from roping calves to driving cattle. More and more ranches have become like summer camps for the whole family. Horseback trail riding and fly-fishing are common activities, as are whitewater rafting, swimming, and nightly cowboy dinners and bonfires. Then there are the more upscale ranches that have a chef on hand to provide fine dining; there are wine tastings and gourmet cooking classes, and large outdoor pools and hot tubs. Very few ranches are covered in this book, but you can still find a ranch vacation that's right for you by checking with the **Colorado Dude Ranch Association** (www.coloradoranch.com). They have a list of most of the ranches in the state, along with information on what they offer.

ELK Many people come to Colorado with expectations of seeing wildlife. If prairie dogs are your idea of wildlife, you won't even have to head to the mountains—just drive by an empty lot in metro Denver. If bigger game is what you're into, however, you may have to be a little purposeful. For elk, Estes Park is the spot. Elk wander freely through town—especially in the fall, winter, and spring, when herds literally stop traffic.

FISHING Rivers and lakes all across the state are great for fishing, and every angler has a favorite spot. Whether you choose one of the reservoirs on the plains like Lake Pueblo State Park or a fast-moving stream in the mountains like Chalk Creek southwest of Buena Vista, if you are over 16 you need a fishing license. These are readily available at sporting good stores. Check out the state wildlife Web site for more information: www.wildlife.state.co.us/fishing.

FOREST SERVICE CABINS AND LOOKOUTS The U.S. Forest Service has nearly 20 cabins and fire lookouts throughout Forest Service land in Colorado's Rocky Mountains—and they are available for rent. Roberts Cabin near Como in South Park, for example, is a rustic cabin built for the railroad back in 1880. It's a two-story log cabin that sleeps six. A complete list of accommodations and rates can be found on the Forest Service Web site: www.fs.fed.us/r2/recreation/rentals/index.shtml.

FOUR-WHEEL DRIVING Many companies in Colorado take passengers on four-wheel-drive trips for sightseeing in the mountains. **Switzerland of America Tours** (970-325-4484 or 1-800-432-5337; www.soajeep.com) works out of Ouray and has a number of tour schedules. In the fall, Cripple Creek, in the mountains above Colorado Springs, celebrates **Fall Aspen Leaf Tours** (719-689-2169). For about three weeks, folks can come up to Cripple Creek to celebrate fall, and the town offers free Jeep rides into the mountains to see the aspens change color.

GEOLOGY Colorado is defined by its geology more than anything else. The Colorado Rocky Mountains are home to all of the range's highest peaks, those over 14,000 feet. A dozen fossil sites speak to the region's deep geological history. To fully appreciate Colorado's natural history, begin by learning a bit more about its geology. I found *Messages in Stone: Colorado's Colorful Geology* and *Roadside Geology of Colorado* particularly informative. The first book has great photographs; the second illustrates the geology you will find as you're driving from one part of the state to another.

HIGHWAYS Travel in the mountains, and across the plains, can be dramatically affected by the weather. Storms in Colorado have been known to shut down highways. The **Colorado Department of Transportation** maintains a Web site that tracks road conditions across the state, www.cotrip.org, so you can make adequate preparations before you leave.

MELODRAMA I am not sure what it is about the mountains, but there's nothing like visiting an old mining town that gets you geared up for a melodrama. Several theater companies in the state put on an exceptional show. All include audience participation—hooting and hollering, booing and hissing is accepted. The shows typically begin with a sing-along and end with an olio. What's an olio you ask? It's a hodgepodge of Vaudeville-style singing, dancing, and comedy. In Manitou Springs, shows are regularly scheduled at the **Iron Springs Chateau** (719-685-5104 or 719-685-5572). Farther up in Cripple Creek, where a melodrama seems to make even more sense, the **Thin Air**

Theatre (www.thinairtheatre.com) puts on shows at the **Butte Opera House** (www.butteoperahouse.com).

MOUNTAIN BIKING CAPITALS Driving through Colorado, you will hear the phrase "mountain biking capital" tossed around quite a bit. The moniker has been tagged to Durango, Crested Butte, and Fruita, and Winter Park recently had the title printed on banners that were hung on nearly every lamppost in town. So what to make of it all? Durango holds a special place in bikers' hearts because it was the site of the first professional UCI Mountain Bike & Trials World Championships in 1990. It also is surrounded by more than 2,000 miles of trails—hundreds of miles of singletrack. Crested Butte, on the other hand, has a mountain biking lineage that goes back even further to the legendary Pearl Pass-to-Aspen ride in 1976. The ride is commemorated annually with a repeat of the tour and stands as the oldest mountain bike event in the world. Mountain bike fanatics in Fruita have worked for years to create miles and miles of excellent singletrack that have earned the respect and admiration of riders from all over the country. Winter Park is a newcomer to the list, but its 600 miles of mountain singletrack are not to be taken lightly. It also enjoys the benefit of being a short drive from Denver. Check out the Outdoor Activities section in each of these town's respective chapters for more information on finding the best trails.

PARKS, MONUMENTS, AND NATIONAL HISTORIC SITES The list of National Parks in Colorado is impressive. The most popular remain **Rocky Mountain National Park** (970-586-1206; www.nps.gov/romo) west of Estes Park and **Mesa Verde National Park** (970-529-4465; www.nps.gov/meve) near Cortez. The **Dinosaur National Monument** (970-374-3000; www.nps.gov/dino) in northwest Colorado and the **Great Sand Dunes National Park and Preserve** (719-378-6300; www.nps.gov/grsa) near Alamosa, are both a little off the beaten track, but well worth the visit. **Bent's Old Fort National Historic Site** (719-383-5010; www.nps.gov/beol) is not particularly known for its scenery, but rather for its hands-on view of history, allowing visitors to really feel what life might have been like on the plains.

PARKS, STATE The **Colorado Department of Natural Resources** (www.parks.state.co.us) operates over 40 state parks. These parks are often home to some of the state's best recreational lakes. Many have campground facilities. Day passes cost $6 (at most parks); annual park passes $60. Passes can be purchased at all state parks and regional offices. They are also available at the Denver and Littleton offices.

PEACHES Start talking about peaches with Coloradoans, and they get a certain gleam in their eyes. Many childhood memories feature trips out to Grand Junction or Palisade to load up on bushels of fresh peaches, followed by weeks of peach pie, peaches and cream, and peach cobbler. Whatever was left over got canned for winter. While in Palisade, stop by **Herman Produce** (970-464-0420), 753 Elberta St. They sell the region's succulent peaches as well as other Colorado gourmet foodstuff.

RAILROADS For a time, railroads were the lifeline for many towns across Colorado. Fortunes could be made if the railroad came to town. This fact was not lost on the railroad companies themselves, who would often build a town of their own for a depot, several miles down the track from a neighbor. Today, trains offer passengers a unique vantage point for enjoying Colorado's stunning landscape. Colorado's most popular train may be either the **Royal Gorge Route** (303-569-1000 or 1-888-724-5748; www.royalgorgeroute.com) that takes passengers into the towering canyon walls of the Royal Gorge or the **Durango & Silverton Narrow-Gauge Railroad** (970-247-2733 or 1-877-872-4607; www.durangotrain.com), which follows the Animas River to Silverton. Other trains to ride are highlighted throughout the book.

ROCKY MOUNTAIN OYSTERS Not many visitors to Colorado are adventurous enough to tackle this uniquely western culinary experience. If you see them on a menu, be advised: Rocky Mountain Oysters are bull testicles. Either pounded flat or sliced into ovals, they are then deep-fried and served up with hot sauce. People who like 'em, like 'em—that's all the insight I can offer. They are so popular a dish that Bruce's Bar in Severance (now closed) used to serve up 20 tons of the delicacy every year. You might also find them called Prairie Oysters, Montana Tendergroins, and Swinging Sirloin. You can find them on menus across the state, including at **Taste Buds Restaurant** in Calhan (719-347-2490, 520 Colorado Ave.) and **Kaltenberg Castle Royal Bavarian Brewhouse** in Vail (970-479-1050, 600 Lionshead Mall). To try them fancy, call ahead to the **Briarhurst Manor** in Manitou Springs (719-685-1864, 404 Manitou Ave.).

ROCKY MOUNTAINS Many newcomers driving in from the east stop at the WELCOME TO COLORADO sign on I-70 or I-76 and stare in disbelief. Dreary hours in the car have been spent yearning for the mountains, and all they see is flat, all the way to the horizon. Don't get discouraged, Colorado isn't likely to run out of mountains anytime soon. However, they only fill two-thirds of the state map, and you have a few more hours of driving before the mighty Rockies rise from the plains.

SKIING There's plenty of skiing in Colorado. In fact, there is probably more skiing than you can imagine. Of course, the stellar ski areas like Vail offer alpine (aka downhill) skiing. And every town in the mountains seems to have a Nordic center that focuses on cross-country skiing. But don't forget the renegade sports like freeskiing and snowboarding. Vail, for example, has ski-biking. Several Nordic centers have trails set aside for skijoring (pulled on your skis by a dog), and Steamboat has an interesting variation with people pulled by horses.

SNOW Skiing is all about the snow. Several Web sites provide current snow reports on all of Colorado's ski areas. **Colorado: Ski Country USA** (www.coloradoski.com) is a good place to start. Just click on the "Snow Report" link.

SOUTH PARK If you watch a lot of Comedy Central, you might expect to find the town of South Park nestled somewhere in Colorado's mountains. You won't. South Park is a grassland basin, located in the Rockies, southwest of Denver. The largest town in South Park is Fairplay, along the Mosquito Range. Driving from Denver, west on US 285, you will climb about 5,000 feet through the mountains. The road is full of twists and turns, and mountains rise on either side. Suddenly, the landscape seems to recede and the horizon expands dramatically. Stretched out in front of you is grassland—nearly 1,000 square miles of it—edged in by distant peaks. This is South Park—and a drive through the valley is not soon forgotten.

TOURISM For a ton of information on traveling to Colorado, there's no better resource than the **Colorado Tourism Office**'s Web site, www.colorado.com. They have a directory of nearly every attraction, restaurant,

and hotel in the state. They also post numerous itineraries and advertise different promotions.

WATERFALLS Cascading water is strangely inspiring. No two waterfalls in Colorado are the same. Many Rocky Mountain towns have waterfalls within view of Main Street. Idaho Springs has a small waterfall visible high up across I-70. Telluride has Bridal Falls. In Ouray, just blocks from downtown, there are two waterfalls. One is seen from town; the other, the compact and powerful Box Canyon Falls, is within walking distance. In Steamboat, drive out Fish Creek Road and make the short hike to Fish Creek Falls, which plummets over 280 feet. Finally, one of the most photographed falls in the state is right off the highway west of Creed in the San Juans, North Clear Creek Falls. Visitors will notice signs pointing out various waterfalls as they tour the state. Be sure to stop at as many as you can.

WHITE-WATER RAFTING Though there are plenty of rivers for rafting in Colorado, Salida remains the state's white-water capital. Area outfitters like **Dvorak's Rafting & Kayak** (719-539-6851 or 1-800-824-3795; www.dvorakexpeditions.com) in Nathrop, take paddlers down the Arkansas River. Every June Salida throws the **Blue Paddle FIBArk Whitewater Festival** (www.fibark.com). FIBArk stands for "First in Boating the Arkansas," and the festival has all sorts of water events. Farther in the mountains, white-water outfitters guide trips down the Colorado and other regional waters—check relevant chapters for outfitter info.

WILDLIFE (THE SCARY KIND) There are no tigers in Colorado, except at the zoos, but the mountains are home to mountain lions and black bears, as well as other wildlife. In most cases, you will never see a mountain lion as you are hiking or biking along the trails. In most cases, you don't want to. If you come face to face with a lion or bear there are a few rules that will help keep you and your family safe: 1) Do not run, scream, or turn your back; 2) make yourself look as large as possible; 3) put children between adults; 4) speak firmly and back away slowly; and 5) if attacked, fight back. For more information on mountain safety, see the U.S. Parks Web site: www.us-parks.com/rocky/high_country_hazards.html.

WINERIES AND VINEYARDS Colorado's regional wine industry has been growing by leaps and bounds over the past decade. The **Colorado Wine Industry Development Board** (www.coloradowine.com) has a list of state wineries and a helpful locator map. They have also organized a series of wine trails, giving travelers a handy itinerary for visiting wineries. Most of Colorado's grapes are grown in the Grand Valley (the Grand Junction/Palisade area). The **Grand Junction Visitor and Convention Bureau** (www.visitgrandjunction.com) has a list of area wineries and vineyards, many of which offer tours.

The Front Range 1

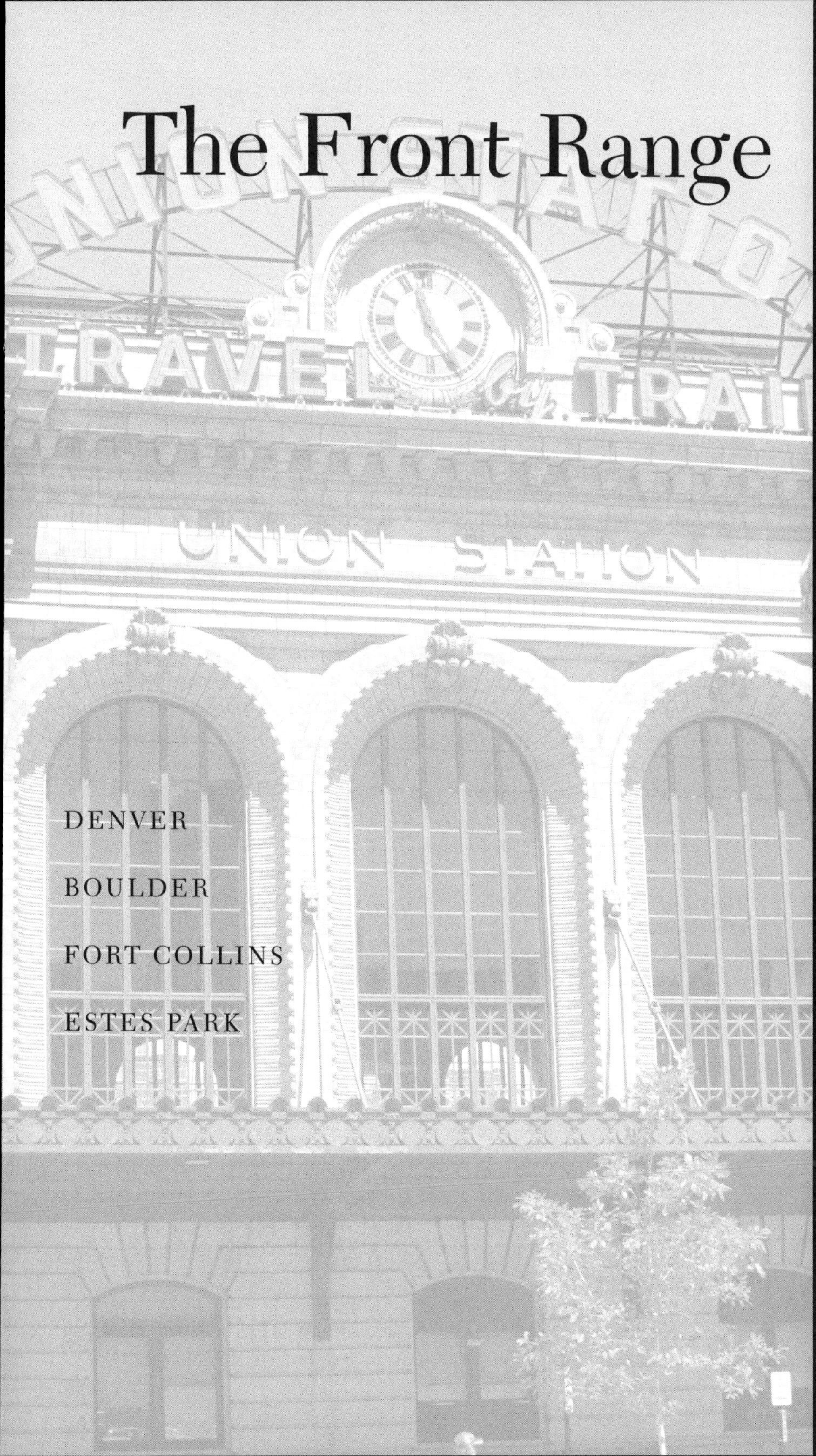

DENVER

BOULDER

FORT COLLINS

ESTES PARK

DENVER

As you come across the plains from the east, the skyline of Denver rises dramatically against the backdrop of the Front Range. Though centrally located, Denver is the gateway to Colorado, securely settled on the plains within reach of the mountains. Sitting at an altitude of 5,280 feet, Denver is quite literally the Mile High City.

Located at the confluence of Cherry Creek and the South Platte River, the site was once a seasonal campground for Ute, Arapaho, and Cheyenne tribes. In the 1850s, gold was found in the waters. As the news spread, tens of thousands of prospectors headed west to make their fortune. Various settlements sprang up and faded on both sides of the South Platte River. The mining settlement of Auraria was doing quite well when Gen. William Larimer staked a claim on the opposite side of the river. He named the new settlement Denver City in hopes that James Denver, the governor of the Kansas Territory, would make it the county seat. Ironically, Governor Denver had already submitted his resignation and would never step foot in the town that bears his name.

The gold that drew thousands, however, ran out before they started panning, and the promise of riches didn't materialize for most prospectors. In 1859, when gold was discovered in the mountains, the miners again packed up and headed west, nearly emptying the town overnight. Denver was quickly transformed into a trade center, and in time it became the requisite stop for everyone and everything heading in and out of the mountains.

The Colorado Territory was formed in 1861, and in 1865, Denver City became the territorial capital. Denver City was shortened to Denver, and in 1876 when the state was admitted into the Union, Denver became the state capital.

Throughout its history, Denver has grown in spurts, and this growth has not always been welcomed with open arms. The rejection of the Olympics in 1972 by state voters sent the message that residents were hesitant to see the state, and by default Denver, lose its uncrowded, easy-going character in exchange for unbridled expansion.

Growth, however, has come to Denver. A mild climate with 300 days of sunshine, great job opportunities, and the possibility of living close to the great outdoors are just some of the factors that have fueled the incredible jump in

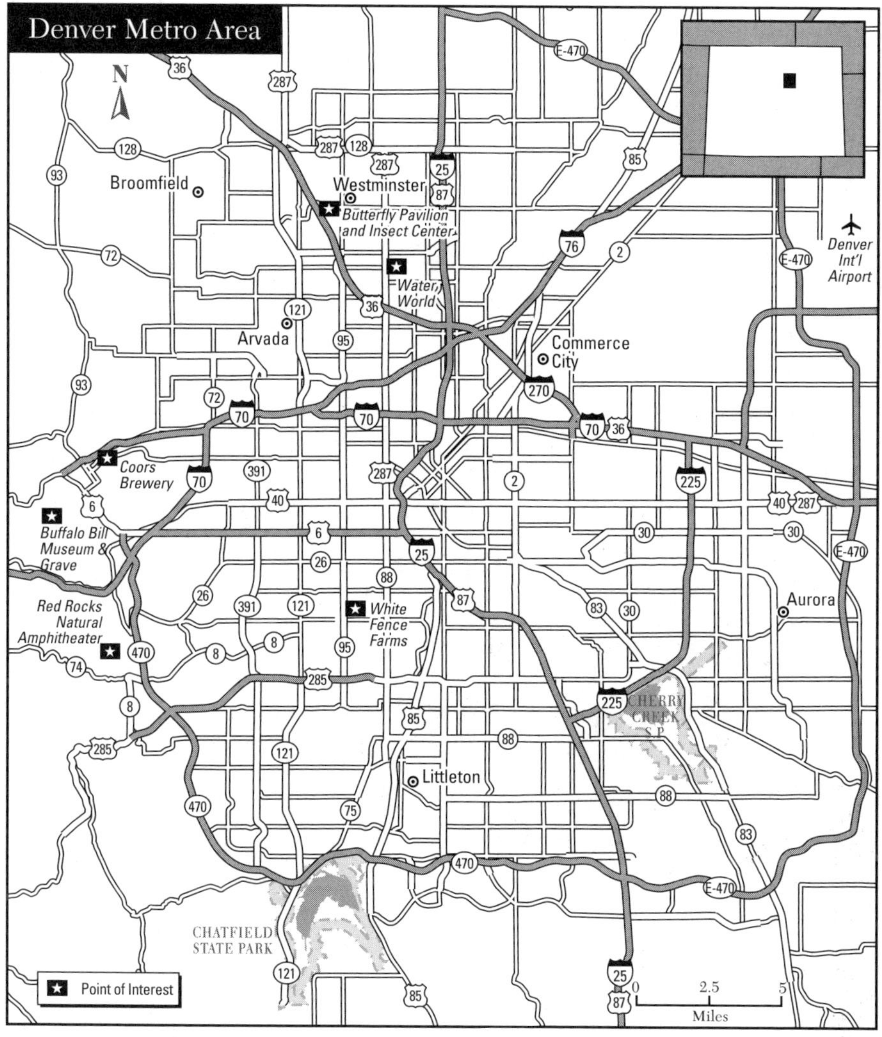

population that Denver has seen, to some extent, since the 1950s. For a decade now, the city has seen over 2 percent growth every year. With nearly three million residents in the Denver-Aurora metro area, it's no surprise that Denver has become one of the country's leading metropolitan centers.

With this growth, Denver has developed into a world-class city. Within walking distance, the city has the Elitch Gardens, the Pepsi Center, Coors Field, and the INVESCO Stadium at Mile High. In 1997, President Clinton invited the Summit of Eight to meet in Denver, and in 2008, the Democratic National Convention will be held at the Pepsi Center.

In 1995, the Denver International Airport opened northeast of Denver. With 53 square miles of property, it's the largest international airport in the United

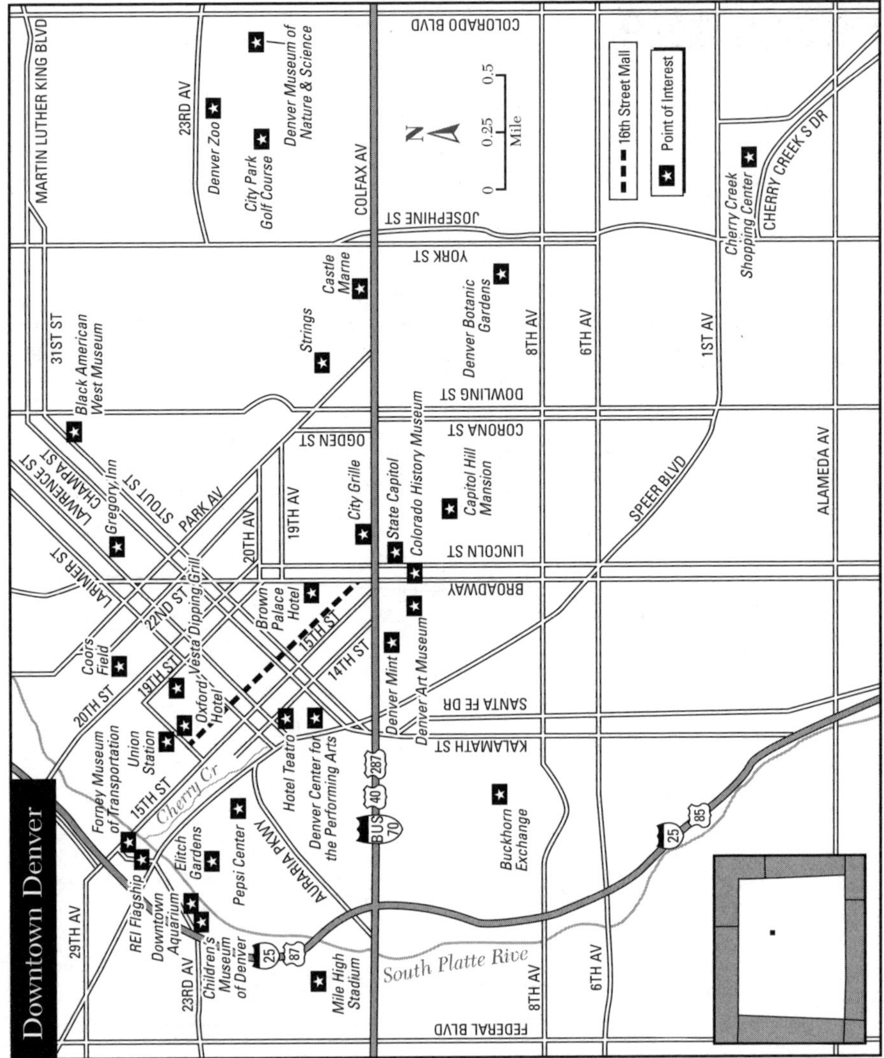

States. Catering especially to the thousands of guests who pour into the state bound for ski vacations in the mountains, the airport has special ski and snowboard conveyors for quick gathering of winter sports gear.

In little over a decade, what was Denver's skid row has become the city's central business and shopping district. With the creation of the 16th Street Mall in LoDo (Lower Downtown), people from all over the metro area drive into the city for fine dining, shopping, and theatre. Real estate prices have skyrocketed, and older industrial areas have been transformed into hip condos and shopping centers. With eight professional sports teams and numerous intercollegiate rivalries, Denver can boast more sporting events than almost any city in the country.

Every year, thousands move to Denver from outside the state. The city's Hispanic population has surpassed 30 percent and serves to highlight just one facet of the area's diverse ethnic landscape. This diversity continually adds vitality to the city's cultural offerings.

With all this urban development, the city has not neglected its connection with the great outdoors. The city maintains 155 parks, and this does not include the area's county and state parks or the city's mountain parks. Just 15–20 miles from the mountains, residents take their outdoor recreation seriously. Denver is continually listed as one of the nation's thinnest cities.

From Old West mining town to 21st-century metropolis, Denver is no longer just a stage stop on the way to the mountains. It is a destination in its own right. When you visit Denver, I hope you will take the time to soak in its unique character, a character that is firmly rooted in its history but changing and adapting with a new sense of urban sophistication.

GUIDANCE **Denver Metro Convention and Visitors Bureau** (303-892-1505 or 1-800-233-6837; www.denver.org), 1555 California St., Ste. 300. In addition to maintaining a Denver Visitor Information Center at the airport, the Visitors Bureau also has a nice location right downtown on the 16th Street Mall at 1600 California St.—the **Official Visitor Information Center–Downtown** (303-892-1505). The helpful staff is a great resource for getting directions, dining suggestions, or simply introducing you to their city.

More Web sites: www.colorado.com

GETTING THERE *By car:* In Colorado, all roads lead to Denver. East and west you have I-70; north and south, I-25. From the northeast, I-76 comes down from

DOWNTOWN DENVER

1-80 in Nebraska. As you can imagine, all these interstates converging in downtown Denver can make for a lot of traffic. On weekday afternoons, rush hour is in full swing by three and doesn't let up until after seven.

By air: The **Denver International Airport** (303-342-2000 or 1-800-AIR2DEN; www.flydenver.com) northeast of town is one of the most beautiful airports in the country—its white tension fabric roof echoes the profile of the Rockies, visible in the distance. It is also one of the busiest airports in the country, with nearly 50 million passengers served every year. **SuperShuttle** (303-444-0808; www.supershuttle.com) can take passengers from DIA to Denver. **SkyRide** (303-299-6000; www.rtd-denver.com/skyRide), which is operated by the DIA, also offers affordable transportation to and from the airport.

By train: **AMTRAK's** (1-800-872-7245; www.amtrak.com) California Zephyr, which travels from Chicago to San Francisco, makes a key stop at Union Station (1701 Wynkoop St.) in downtown Denver.

By bus: The **Greyhound** (303-293-6555; www.greyhound.com) station is located at 1055 19th St.

GETTING AROUND *By car:* Getting around Denver by car can be difficult, but not impossible. There are plenty of parking lots and structures downtown that charge anywhere from $5 to $25 per day. The streets downtown run diagonally, parallel with the Platte River—contrary to the rest of the metro area, where streets run east and west, north and south. Add in the number of one-way streets, and a newcomer can get turned around rather quickly. Bring a good map, and you will be fine.

By bus: The **Denver Regional Transportation District** (303-299-6000 or 1-800-366-7433; www.rtd-denver.com) maintains an extensive bus system that can get you anywhere in the metro area. See their Web site for a complete schedule and route information. Fares $1.50–3.75.

By bus (in LoDo): Denver's free bus service, **RTD's MallRide** (303-299-6000 or 1-800-366-7433; www.rtd-denver.com), runs the length of the 16th Street Mall. On weekdays, buses come by every five minutes or so from 5 AM (5:30 and 7 on Sat. and Sun., respectively) to 1:35 in the morning.

By light rail: The light rail system operated by the **Denver Regional Transportation District** (303-299-6000 or 1-800-366-7433; www.rtd-denver.com) connects downtown Denver with the Denver Tech Center south of town and various suburbs. Most people taking the light rail into town either take a bus to the station or park and ride. One way is $1.50–3.75.

MEDICAL EMERGENCIES **Presbyterian/St. Luke's Medical Center** (303-839-6000; www.pslmc.com), 1719 E. 19th Ave., Denver. Located close to downtown, they offer 24-hour emergency medical treatment.

Swedish Medical Center (303-788-5000; www.swedishhospital.com), 501 E. Hampton Ave., Englewood. For 24-hour emergency medical treatment in south metro Denver.

University of Colorado Hospital (720-848-4011; www.uch.edu), 12605 E.

16th Ave., Aurora. Located on the east side of the greater metro area, the hospital offers 24-hour emergency medical treatment.

✷ To See & Do

GUIDED TOURS ☂ ♿ **Colorado State Capitol** (303-866-2604; www.colorado.gov), 200 E. Colfax Ave. Historic tours are available Mon.–Fri. 9:15–2:30 (Sept.–May) and Mon.–Fri. 9–3:30 (June–Aug.). Tours take about 45 minutes. Legislative tours are available Jan.–May, when the legislature is in session; call the number above to make reservations.

☂ ♿ **Coors Brewery** (303-277-2337 or 1-866-2337; www.coors.com), 13th and Ford streets, Golden. Tours available Mon.–Sat. 10–4. The Coors brewing plant in Golden is the world's largest single-site brewery. Sitting on 2,000 acres, it produces nearly 2 million barrels of beer per day. This may seem to be an incredible claim, until you take the tour. For guests over 21 (with an ID), there is beer tasting at the end of the tour as well as a gift shop to pick up Coors memorabilia. Tours are free.

☂ ♿ **Denver Mint** (303-405-4761; www.usmint.gov), 320 W. Colfax Ave. Take a look at a penny, and you will see a small letter stamped beneath the year. West of the Mississippi, more and more of those pennies have a small "D," which means they were minted here in Denver. Tours of the Denver Mint are available Mon.–Fri. on the hour 8–2. Reservations are required and can be made online or at the reservation booth at the U.S. Mint Visitor Center on Cherokee Street (between 14th Avenue and Colfax Avenue). Try to schedule your tour early in your trip as spots tend to fill up quickly. Tours are free.

COLORADO STATE CAPITOL

MUSEUMS ☂ **Black America West Museum & Heritage Center** (303-292-2566; www.blackamericanwestmuseum.com), 3091 California St. Open June–Aug., Tues.–Sat. 10–5 and Sept.–May, Tues.–Sat. 10–2. Since 1971, the museum has commemorated the contribution of blacks in the Old West. You can learn about famous black cowboys and pioneers—O. T. Jackson, for example, founded the black pioneer town of Dearfield, which thrived east of Greeley from 1910 until the Great Depression—or see exhibits that tell the story of the Buffalo Soldiers or the Tuskegee airmen. This museum offers a unique and necessary perspective on the region's history. Adult admission $8, seniors $7, and children 12 and under $6.

☂ ♿ **The Children's Museum of Denver** (303-433-7444; www.cmdenver.org), 2121 Childrens Museum Dr. Open Mon.–Fri. 9–4 and Sat. and Sun. 10–5. The museum caters to children from birth to eight years old, using creative play experiences to help kids learn and prepare for life. This of course means that this place is a blast for kids. They can climb all over a real fire truck, put on a puppet show or perform a song, or learn about nutrition as they "shop" at My Market. Admission ages 2–59 is $7.50, age 60 and over $5.50, age 1 $5.50, and children under 1 free.

☂ ♿ **Colorado History Museum** (303-866-3670; www.coloradohistory.org), 1300 Broadway. Open Mon.–Sat. 10–5 and Sun. noon–5. As the name suggests, this museum strives to preserve and educate guests on Colorado history. You can learn about women and their role as settlers and pioneers. There is an exhibit on the creation of the 10th Mountain Division and their contribution to the United States' efforts in World War II. The museum has numerous pieces of mining equipment, and they have an original Conestoga wagon—the "prairie schooner" used by countless settlers on their westward journey. (I think you will be surprised by the size of this wagon up close. It can carry eight tons of cargo!) Adult admission is $7, seniors and students $6, children (6–12) $5 (but free on Sat.), and children under 6 free.

DENVER ART MUSEUM

Denver Art Museum (720-913-0000; www.denverartmuseum.org), 100 W. 14th Ave. Open Tues.–Thurs. 10–5, Fri. 10–10, Sat. 10–5, and Sun. noon–5. The Art Museum has housed Denver's finest collection of paintings and sculpture since 1893. More recently, the museum itself has become a piece of art. In 2006, an addition was completed that houses the museum's Modern & Contemporary and Western American Art collections. Designed by Daniel Libeskind, the building's radical lines and titanium exterior raised a few eyebrows. The city has come to terms with the newcomer, which really is a fantastic space in which to view art. Colorado residents: adult admission $10, seniors $8, youth (6–18) free in the summer, children under 6 free. Nonresidents: adult admission $13, seniors $10, youth (6–18) $5 and children under 6 free.

Denver Museum of Nature & Science (303-322-7009; www.dmns.org), 2001 Colorado Blvd. Open daily 9–5. Located down the street from the Denver Zoo in Denver's City Park, the Museum of Nature & Science covers everything from Egyptian mummies to North American Indian cultures. You can explore human biology from DNA to organs in the Hall of Life exhibit, and kids can tackle hands-on activities in the Discovery Zone. In addition, the museum has an IMAX theater and Planetarium with regular shows. Adult admission $10, juniors (3–18) and seniors $6; does not include IMAX or the Planetarium.

Forney Museum of Transportation (303-297-1113; www.forneymuseum.com), 4303 Brighton Blvd. Open Mon.–Sat. 9–5. The museum began as a private collection of antique cars. Today there are over 500 exhibits celebrating all sorts of transportation, from trains to automobiles—as they say, "anything on wheels." You can see Amelia Earhart's "Gold Bug" Kissel and one of the last remaining Big Boy locomotives. Adult admission $7, seniors $6, youth (11–15) $4.50, children (5–10) $3.50, and children under 5 free.

Molly Brown House Museum (303-832-4092; www.mollybrown.org), 1340 Pennsylvania St. Open Mon.–Sat. 9–4 and Sun. 10–4 in the summer. Otherwise Tues.–Sat. 10–3:30 and Sun. noon–3:30. Few characters in Colorado history have continued to intrigue the public like Molly Brown. Born in Hannibal, Missouri, Molly Brown made her way to Leadville, Colorado, where she married J. J. Brown. They grew wealthy in Leadville, primarily due to J. J.'s hard work and ingenuity. As their family grew, they moved to Denver where they hoped to enjoy more social opportunities, eventually setting up home at 1340 Pennsylvania. Tours of the home are given throughout the day. The hours above indicate when the last tour begins. Exhibits include items that belonged to Molly Brown and artifacts dating from the turn of the century when the Browns lived in the home. Adult admission $6.50, seniors $5, and children (6–12) $3.

Wings over the Rockies Air and Space Museum (303-360-5360; www.wingsmuseum.org), 7711 E. Academy Blvd. #1. Open Mon.–Sat. 10–5., Sun. 12–5. Located in a hangar in the old Lowry Air Force Base, the museum exhibits over three dozen airplanes and space vehicles. They have everything from small civilian planes and military fighter planes to a 16-foot model of the Titan II launch vehicle. Adult admission $9, seniors $8, children (4–12) $6, and children under 4 free.

♿ **Buffalo Bill Museum and Grave** (303-526-0744; www.bufallobill.org), 987½ Lookout Mountain Rd. Open May–Oct. daily 9–5; Nov.–April daily 9–4. According to his wife, Buffalo Bill always wanted to be buried on Lookout Mountain when he died, much to the chagrin of the folks in Cody, Wyoming, the town Buffalo Bill founded. The top of Lookout Mountain affords great panoramic views of Denver, and the trail to the gravesite is free. The museum, however, charges admission. Adults $3, seniors $2, children (6–15) $1, and children under 6 free.

✐ ♿ **Colorado Railroad Museum** (303-279-4591; www.crrm.org), 17155 W. 44th Ave., Golden. Open daily 9–5. If you like trains, there is a lot for you to like here. Driving into the parking lot, you are surrounded by trains—engines, cars, cabooses. Inside, there are exhibits illustrating the history of the railroad in Colorado. Outside, tons of railroad equipment has been preserved from around the state, like narrow-gauge locomotives that once served the mining industry up in the mountains and observation cars that once catered to tourists. Adult admission $8, seniors $7, children (2–6) $5, and children under 2 free.

THEME PARKS ✐ ♿ **Elitch Gardens** (303-595-4386 for park info or 303-595-4386 for guest relations; www.elitchgardens.com), 2000 Elitch Cir. Open May–Oct. daily 10–9. Early and late in the season, they are closed most weekdays; see Web site for complete schedule. Elitch Gardens has been a Denver institution since 1890. Originally located at 38th Avenue. and Tennyson Street northwest of town, the park opened at its present location in downtown Denver in 1995. From 1998 to 2007, it was branded Six Flags Elitch Gardens, but "Six Flags" was dropped after a recent change in ownership. This is a compact little amusement park that packs in more rides and attractions than its 70 acres would

FUN AT ELITCH GARDENS

suggest is possible. The park has everything from a classic wooden roller coaster to the Flying Roller Coaster, which has guests hanging beneath the tracks sprawled out like Superman. General admission, which includes access to the Island Kingdom Water Park, is $44.99 at the gate (only $34.99 if you order online). Guests under 48 inches tall have limited access to rides and only pay $22.99.

✐ ♿ **Water World** (303-427-7873; www.waterworldcolorado.com), 1800 West 89th Ave. Open late May–early Sept., daily 10–6. This 64-acre water park is not to be missed. With 43 water attractions and 12,300 feet of water slides, there is enough here to keep you and the family busy all day. You can spend hours just floating around the Lazy River in your inner tube or try the Lost River of the Pharoahs, the first water ride to combine white-water rafting with a themed animatronic attraction. Plenty of wave pools, places to sunbathe, and heart-pounding slides. Lines can get pretty long in the afternoon, so be sure to bring sandals as the ground gets hotter and hotter as the day drags on. General admission $29.95, children under 47 inches tall $24.95, and seniors $5. After two o'clock, sunset pricing goes into effect and tickets are half price.

✐ ♿ **Heritage Square** (303-279-2789; www.heritagesquare.info), 18301 W. Colfax Ave., Golden. Open year-round Mon.–Sat. 10–8 and Sun. noon–8. Not so much an amusement park as a collection of tourist attractions, Heritage Square has a number of shops and plenty of amusement park food. They also have an alpine slide (303-279-1661), go-carts (www.fishandfarm.com), a haunted house (www.spidermansion.com), a zip line (303-738-9844), and a little railroad (303-279-4500; www.heritagerailroad.com). Admission is free, though once you are in, everything costs money.

WINERIES & WINE TASTING **Balistreri Winery** (303-287-5156 or 1-866-896-9620; www.balistreriwine.com), 1946 E. 66th Ave. Open daily for winery tours and wine tasting noon–5. Close to the intersection of I-25 and I-76, Balistreri Winery is a short drive from downtown. The winery is located on a nice stretch of property that includes a patio for guests and greenhouses.

♿ **Creekside Cellars** (303-674-5460; www.creeksidecellars.net), 28036 CO 74, Evergreen. Open daily 11–5. The café at Creekside serves food until 4. Located along Bear Creek, about 30 miles west of Denver, Creekside Cellars makes for a great day trip. The café serves food inside or on the deck overlooking the water, and the Italian Antipasto Platter, a collection of cheeses, deli meat, and vegetables and olives, is the perfect snack after wine tasting.

ZOOS & NATURE EXHIBITS ✐ ♿ **Denver Zoo** (303-376-4800; www.denverzoo.org), 2300 Steele St. Open Oct.–Mar., daily 10–4; Apr.–Sept., daily 9–6. Located in City Park, this 80-acre zoo receives over 1.5 million visitors every year. Guests come to walk the zoo's shady paths and see the impressive collection of animals from around the world. The zoo is home to a three-ton rhinoceros named Mshindi that paints pictures—they are on display in the Pachyderm House. Every day in the summer, at 11, zookeepers bring out the elephants for a demonstration. They talk about the animals and field questions from the crowd.

A DAY IN THE MOUNTAINS

Though the mountains are right there for all to see, they are still 15–20 miles from downtown Denver. A great day trip is to head west on I-70 to the small towns of Idaho Springs and Georgetown. On the way, you can pull off at exit 254 to see the city's buffalo herd at Genesee Park.

Idaho Springs is familiar to thousands of Denverites who have stopped there on the way home after a day on the slopes. Many have made it a tradition to stop at **Beau Jo's Pizza** (303-567-4376; www.beaujos.com), 1517 Miner St., for dinner on their way home. This pizzeria is a Colorado institution. Chicago has deep dish; New York has thin crust; and Colorado has the legendary mountain pie. Pizzas here have a tall crust to hold the piles of toppings. Beau Jo's may be the first pizza place to stock tables with honey to drizzle on the remaining crust—sort of a dessert.

For a day in Idaho Springs, consider a hard-rock mine tour at the **Phoenix Mine** (www.phoenixmine.com). Just west of town on Trail Creek Road, this mine was first discovered in 1871. The tour takes around an hour, and the path

BUFFALO HERD AT GENESEE PARK

THE PHOENIX MINE IN IDAHO SPRINGS

is an even walk. There are no ladders to climb, so wheelchairs and strollers can make the trip with a little finagling.

A little farther up the interstate is Georgetown, a quaint mountain town full of shops and restaurants catering to day-trippers. **Railroad Art by Scotty** (1-800-571-5701; www.railroadart.com), 507 Sixth St., recently opened and features original prints—many recapturing the spirit of the early art deco posters. Right next door is **Georgetown Rock Shop** (303-569-2750), 501 Sixth St. At the back of the rock shop is the Russian Room, selling authentic antique icons and samovars from Eastern Europe.

A nice afternoon activity is a ride on the **Georgetown Loop Railroad: Historic Mining & Railroad Park** (1-888-456-6777; www.georgetownlooprr.com), P.O. Box 249, Georgetown, CO 80444. This railroad makes a round-trip to the old mining town of Silver Plume. On the way, the train stops at the Lebanon Silver Mine, where guests can get a guided tour.

For more information on Idaho Springs and Georgetown, visit the Clear Creek County Chamber of Commerce online at www.clearcreekcounty.org.

Also be sure to check out Bear Mountain, which when it was built in 1918, was the first exhibit in North America that tried to replicate an animals' natural habitat. It has since been placed on the National Register of Historic Places. Adult admission $11, seniors $9, children (3–11) $7, and children under 3 free. Admission rates are all $2 cheaper Oct.–March.

Denver Botanic Gardens (720-865-3500; www.botanicgardens.org), 1005 York St. Open in the summer Wed.–Fri. 9–5 and Sat.–Tues. 9–8; Sept.–Apr. open daily 9–5. A wide walking path makes a winding loop through the numerous horticultural displays at the Botanic Gardens. The individual gardens are thematically organized. The Japanese Garden, for example, uses large ponds, carefully placed rocks, and plants to create a balanced atmosphere. In addition to the more exotic displays, indigenous plants are highlighted in the Plains Garden. Be sure to check out the tropical plants in the Boettcher Memorial Tropical Conservatory. To make a day of your visit, head over to the Monet Garden for lunch at the Monet Deck Cafe. Adult admission $13, seniors $10, youths (4–15) and students $9, and children under 4 free. Rates all cheaper in fall and winter.

Downtown Aquarium–An Underwater Adventure (303-561-4450; www.aquariumrestaurants.com), 700 Water St. Open Sun.–Thurs. 10–10. and Fri. and Sat. 10–11. When Denver's Ocean Journey went belly-up after less than three years, there was fear Denver would soon be without an aquarium. In 2002, however, the site was purchased by Landry's Restaurants, and a full-service seafood restaurant, bar, and ballroom were added. In addition to the million gallons of underwater exhibits that focus on various ecosystems and the importance of conservation, the centerpiece of the restaurant is a 150,000 gallon tank that holds an impressive variety of fish. Adult aquarium admission $13.75, seniors $12.95, children (4–12) $8.25, and children under 4 free.

Butterfly Pavilion and Insect Center (303-469-5441; www.butterflies.org), 6252 W. 104th Ave. Open daily in the winter 9–5; summer, daily 9–6. If you have kids who are crazy about bugs, the Butterfly Pavilion is the perfect place to spend an afternoon. This insect zoo lets visitors get up close to invertebrates from around the world. They have a petting tank, called Water's Edge, where you can see and touch sea stars and other ocean dwellers. Or you can step into the tropical conservatory, a warm and humid greenhouse that is home to over 1,200 butterflies. Adult admission $7.95, seniors $5.95, children (3–12) $4.95, and children under 3 free.

✷ Outdoor Activities

ALPINE SKIING **Loveland Ski Area** (303-569-3203 or 1-800-736-3754; www.skiloveland.com), 3877 US 6, Georgetown. Loveland is right off 1-70 at exit 216, 13 miles west of Georgetown. One of the most accessible ski areas to Denver, Loveland is less than 60 miles away. The ski area is comprised of two sections: Loveland Basin and the gentler Loveland Valley. Since Loveland has never developed a resort, it's seen primarily as a spot for locals to go day skiing. This means fewer amenities, but it also translates into cheaper lift tickets and shorter lines. With 77 trails on 1,385 skiable acres, there is terrain here for everyone.

About 20 percent is rated for beginners, the rest is split between intermediate and advanced skiers. For freeskiers and snowboarders, there is a terrain park with some nice features.

BICYCLING There are hundreds of miles of bike paths, trails, and bike lanes throughout Denver. The city's 200-plus parks are all connected by bike routes. One of the most popular is the Cherry Creek Path, which runs about 15 miles from the Cherry Creek Reservoir in Aurora to downtown Denver, following Cherry Creek until it meets the South Platte River. This paved path is wide enough that even on the busiest days, there's plenty of room for everyone.

Cherry Creek Bike Rack (303-388-1630; www.cherrycreekbikerack.com), 171 Detroit St. Open Mon.–Fri. 7–7, Sat. 10–5, and Sun. 10–5. This organization strives to assist bike commuters in metro Denver. They have rental bikes and provide free bike parking at various locations around town.

Golden Bike Shop (303-278-6545; www.goldenbikeshop.com), 722 Washington Ave., Golden. Open Sun.–Fri. 10–7. Outside of Denver proper, the Golden Bike Shop has road bikes, mountain bikes, and cruisers for rent. A 24-hour rental runs $24–60.

GOLF There are over 70 golf courses in the greater Denver area. While a number of these are private, there are, nonetheless, enough public courses to keep you playing fresh greens for a long time.

Arrowhead (303-973-9614; www.arrowheadcolorado.com), 10850 W. Sundown Tr., Littleton. Located in the foothills, Arrowhead features rolling terrain with stunning geological features. Greens fees $75–139.

City Park (303-295-2096; www.denvergov.org/golf), 2500 York St. This fine public course, owned by the city, is located right in town across from the zoo and the Museum of Nature & Science. Greens fees $23–27.

The Ridge at Castle Pines North (303-688-4301; www.theridgecpn.com), 1414 Castle Pines Pkwy., Castle Rock. The rolling greens have been carved out of the region's natural covering of scrub oak and pine. The courses two loops were designed to allow wildlife to pass through an untouched natural corridor. Greens fees $60–140.

Riverdale Golf Courses (303-659-6700; www.riverdalegolf.com), 13300 Riverdale Rd., Brighton. The courses at Riverdale, the Dunes and the Knolls, have been longtime favorites of Front Range golfers. The Dunes is a great beginners' course, whereas the Knolls provides more challenging play. Greens fees for Dunes are $29–41 for 18 holes; Knolls $20–25.

HIKING There are a number of great places in the Denver area for hiking. Chatfield Lake State Park has a number of trails and hooks up with Waterton Canyon. Waterton Canyon is the eastern terminus of the Colorado Trail, which climbs up and through Colorado, ending near Durango. Closer to the mountains, there are trails at Red Rocks Park, and south of town there's the 2-mile loop at Roxborough State Park. (See Green Space for more details on the parks.)

HORSEBACK RIDING There are trails to ride and horses to rent at **Cherry Creek State Park** and **Chatfield Lake State Park**. The stables at both parks can be found at the same place online, www.painthorsestables.net. Check out the Web site for a list of guided rides and lessons.

PADDLING **Confluence Kayaks** (303-433-3676; www.confluencekayaks.com), 1615 Platte St. Open Mon.– Thurs. and Sat. 10–6., Fri. 10–7, and Sun. noon–5. This paddling outfit offers kayak lessons at Chatfield Lake State Park and on the South Platte River. They rent everything you need for a day on the water, from wetsuits to kayaks. If you are new to the area, be sure to ask about guided tours. They also rent bikes.

Geo Tours (303-756-6070 or 1-800-660-7238; www.georafting.com), 229 CO 8, Morrison. The closest white-water rafting to Denver is on Clear Creek near Idaho Springs. Geo Tours offers tours for rafters of all levels on Clear Creek. They also do trips on the upper Colorado and Arkansas rivers. Day trips and multiday trips available.

GREEN SPACE **City Park,** located east of downtown between York St. and Colorado Blvd., north of Colfax. City Park is home to some of Denver's busiest attractions, the Denver Zoo and the Museum of Nature & Science. The 330-acre park goes back to the 19th century when the state gave Denver acreage to create parks throughout the city. City Park was (and still is) the biggest in Denver. It was designed in a classic style, reminiscent of Central Park in New York City. Considering how many people flock to the park's museum and zoo, it is surprising to find the park rarely crowded. So there is always plenty of room to toss the Frisbee, host a picnic, or simply roll out a blanket and take a nap. There are two lakes in City Park, and you can rent a paddleboat and toodle around to your heart's content.

Confluence Park is located downtown, across the river from REI and at the confluence of the Platte River and Cherry Creek. When settlers first arrived to the area, the South Platte River ran much wider and shallower than it does today. At one point, this section of the waterway was so polluted that it was avoided with a vengence. Today the water here flows so clean that you will often see swimmers venturing in for a dip.

Chatfield Lake State Recreation Area (303-791-7275; www.parks.state.co.us/parks/chatfield), 11500 N. Roxborough Park Rd., Littleton. Open daily 5–10. The main entrance to the park is right off CO 470, just 1 mile south on Wadsworth. This is the most popular park in the Denver area. The centerpiece of the park is the Chatfield Reservoir, a beautiful lake for boating, fishing, or swimming. For boaters, the lake has two boat ramps and the full-service **Chatfield Marina** (303-791-5555), where you can rent boats and boat slips. On the west side of the lake, the park maintains a swim beach with rest rooms—open all summer, Memorial Day–Labor Day. Over 10 miles of trails (paved and unpaved) are open to hiking, biking, and horseback riding. You can rent horses and ponies at the **Chatfield Stables** (303-933-3636; www.painthorsestables.net). They have a number of scheduled trail rides and lessons—details on their Web site. Campground details can be found under Lodging. Daily park passes $5.

Cherry Creek State Park (303-690-1166; www.parks.state.co.us/parks/cherry creek), 4201 S. Parker Rd., Aurora. Located 1 mile south of I-225 on Parker. Open daily 5–10 in the summer. Over 1.5 million people visit Cherry Creek every year. The 840-acre reservoir is chock full of trout, walleye, and pike (just to mention a few of the species sought here). You can rent a boat or boat slip at the **Cherry Creek Marina** (303-779-6144). A swim beach on the east side of the lake stays pretty busy in the summer. A system of trails runs throughout the 4,300-acre park. Horseback riding can be arranged through **Paint Horse Stables** (303-690-8235; www.painthorsestables.net). Their Web site has a complete list of lessons and trail rides available. You can also use the paved paths for bike riding and rollerblading. Campground details can be found under Lodging. Daily park pass $7 (except from Labor Day till the end of Sept. when it is $8).

Roxborough State Park (303-973-3959; www.parks.state.co.us/parks/roxborough), 4751 North Roxborough Dr., Littleton. Open 7–8. Take Carpenter Peak Trail up to the top for fantastic views. The trail is 6.4 miles and takes you to an elevation of 7,160 feet. For a less strenuous hike, try the Fountain Valley Trail. This 2-mile trek winds through the rock formations that really make the park unique and worth visiting.

Waterton Canyon, located on W. Waterton Rd., Littleton. Located on the south end of Chatfield Lake State Recreation Area, the Waterton Canyon trail follows the S. Platte River 6.5 miles up to the Strontia Springs Dam. The canyon is home to bighorn sheep that climb the steep walls. The trail can be used for hiking, biking, and horseback riding. Dogs are not allowed due to the bighorn sheep. It is one of the most popular day hikes in the Denver area. It is also the eastern terminus of the Colorado Trail, which continues on to Durango (see Durango for more information).

Castlewood Canyon State Park (303-688-5242; www.parks.state.co.us/parks/castlewoodcanyon), 2989 South CO 83, Franktown. Open daily 8–9. This day park offers plenty of opportunities to explore Castlewood Canyon. A paved trail along the canyon rim, the Canyon View Nature Trail, is perfect for walkers of all abilities. For more of a challenge try Rimrock Trail, an unpaved 2-mile hike. Creek Bottom Trail, a 1.7-mile hike, takes you to the canyon bottom.

✷ Lodging

HOTELS "ı" ♿ **Adam's Mark Hotel** (303-893-3333 or 1-800-444-2326; www.adamsmark.com/denver), 1550 Court Pl. The Adam's Mark is the largest hotel in Denver. Its 1,225 rooms, 92 suites, and 133,000 square feet of meeting space make it a popular place for conventions. This is a full-service hotel with all the expected amenities, from free wireless Internet in the lobby (not in the rooms) to self-service guest laundry to 24-hour room service. The hotel has several options for dining and drinking, including the Bravo! Ristorante, which is known for its singing serving staff. Rooms $127–339.

"ı" ♿ **Brown Palace Hotel** (303-297-3111 or 1-800-321-2599; www.brownpalace.com), 321 17th St. It says something about the Brown Palace that they have a hotel historian and archivist on staff. The hotel opened in 1892, during the days when men got rich mining in the mountains, and came to Denver to settle into "society." In the years since, it has hosted many of the rich, powerful, and famous, including a number of U.S. presidents. Teddy Roosevelt was the first in 1905. Historical tours are offered on Wed. and Sat. at 2. For private tours outside these two times, there is charge. Not just a place to tour, however, the Brown Palace has 241 rooms, 33 executive staterooms, and three presidential suites. They offer 24-hour room service, twice daily maid service, and a full-time concierge. The service is impeccable, worthy of the hotel's near-legendary status in Denver. Rooms $235–315 and suites $315–985.

"I" ♿ **Hotel Teatro** (303-228-1100 or 1-888-727-1200; www.hotelteatro.com), 1100 14th St. The hotel has 110 rooms, each with 12-foot ceilings and luxurious furnishings. The building was built in 1911, and originally housed the Denver Tramway Company. For guests who come to town to enjoy the theatre, the hotel is directly across from the Denver Center for the Performing Arts. Rooms $189–1,400.

"I" ♿ **The Magnolia Hotel Denver** (303-607-9000 or 1-888-915-1110; www.magnoliahoteldenver.com), 818 17th St. The Magnolia in Denver opened in 1983 in the American National Bank Building, which was built in 1910. The hotel has 246 rooms. In the evenings, fresh chocolate chip cookies and milk are available in the Club Room. One of the nicer features of the hotel, the Club Room has plenty of comfortable seating and a beautiful fountain. Rooms $150–280.

"I" ♿ **Oxford Hotel** (303-628-5400 or 1-866-654-6376; www.theoxfordhotel.com), 1600 17th St. The Oxford Hotel has been taking care of guests in this grand style in Denver since 1891. The hotel's spacious accommodations are decorated with European antiques and fine linens, and amenities include a full-service spa and babysitting services. Unique among hotels of its time, the Oxford has an atrium that allows daylight to fill the lobby and guest rooms. Rooms and suites $149–389.

BED & BREAKFASTS Both the Gregory Inn and the Queen Anne Bed & Breakfast Inn offer room service through **Room Service by Jeeves** (303-534-8646; www.roomserviceselect.com). This service allows you to order off the menus of nearly forty local restaurants and have the food delivered directly to your room.

"I" **Adagio Bed & Breakfast** (303-370-6911 or 1-800-533-4640; www.adagiobb.com), 1430 Race St. Located just south of Colfax in the Wyman Historic District, the Adagio has five guest rooms and one guest suite, all decorated in bright colors and named after composers. In addition to breakfast, guests also have the option of dinner—on Friday they have a barbeque. Close to City Park and downtown. Rooms $105–155 and suite $199; dinner $40 and barbeque $14.95.

"I" **The Capitol Hill Mansion** (1-800-839-9329; www.capitolhillmansion.com), 1207 Pennsylvania St. A few blocks from the Colorado State Capitol, the Mansion has five guest rooms and three two-room suites. From the moment you walk in the door, you will appreciate the simple elegance of this bed & breakfast. Most of the rooms are modestly decorated. The Snowlover Balcony Room, however, stands out with a bold, 28-foot mural depicting an alpine forest in winter. Amenities include cable TV, wireless Internet, and private baths. You can ask for a room with a whirlpool bath or a fireplace if that suits your mood. Rooms $114–194. Children 2 and up are an extra $25.

Castle Marne (303-331-0621 or 1-800-926-2763; www.castlemarne.com), 1572 Race St. The Castle Marne is decorated in high Victorian fashion. The dining room, with its cherry panelling and beautifully hand-painted ceiling, is a thing to behold. Three of the nine rooms have their own private hot tubs. The Presidential Suite has a whirlpool for two and a sitting room in the castle tower. They serve a gourmet breakfast, and dinner is also available if you call ahead. Rooms $105–270 for double occupancy; dinner $77.

The Gregory Inn (303-295-6570 or 1-800-925-6570; www.gregoryinn.com), 2500 Arapahoe St. I may be a bit biased toward the Gregory Inn, for this is where my wife and I stayed after our wedding before flying out on our honeymoon. Simply one of the best bed & breakfasts in Denver, the Gregory Inn has eight rooms and the Carriage House. Rooms have a variety of amenities. All of the rooms have a refrigerator, CD player, and large-screen LCD cable TV. Fireplaces are also part of the each room's charm. Many have whirlpool baths (for two), and one even has its own porch and porch swing. The Carriage House is meant for longer stays. It has a full kitchen, living room, and dining area. Rooms $119–199; Carriage House $249–259.

The Holiday Chalet (303-437-8245 or 1-800-626-4497; www.holidaychalet.net), 1820 E. Colfax Ave. Centrally located in the city's historic Wyman District, this restored Victorian brownstone is within easy reach of many of Denver's more popular attractions. The Museum of Nature & Science is just up the street, as is the Denver Zoo. LoDo is just a short drive or bus ride away. They have 10 rooms. You have several options when it comes to breakfast, like French crepes or cowboy pancakes. Unlike many B&Bs in Denver, they are very family friendly. They have cribs and offer babysitting for $10/hour. Rooms $94–145.

Queen Anne Bed & Breakfast Inn (303-296-6666; www.queenannebnb.com), 2147-51 Tremont Pl. Ten rooms and four suites all decorated with their own themes, the most unusual of which is the Aspen Room with a wraparound mural depicting an aspen grove. (The furniture is also made out of aspen wood.) Old wood floors throughout have a reassuring creak. In addition to breakfast, they serve Colorado wines in the evening. Amenities include a phone, but not cable TV. Several rooms have special bath tubs, and the Rooftop Room has private deck with hot tub. Rooms $95–195 and suites $165–195.

CAMPGROUNDS **Chatfield Lake State Recreation Area** (303-791-7275; www.parks.state.co.us/parks/chatfield), 11500 N. Roxborough Park Rd., Littleton. Natural grassland surrounds the four camping areas at Chatfield. There are a total of 197 sites divided in four sections, loops A–D. The majority of sites have full hook-ups, but 77 sites in loops B and C have only electrical. Rest rooms and showers are centrally located, and each loop has its own laundry facility as well. If you are traveling with horses, campers can overnight their animals in the Chatfield Stables. Sites with full hook-ups $22; with just electrical $18.

Cherry Creek State Park (303-690-1166; www.parks.state.co.us/parks/cherrycreek), 4201 S. Parker Rd., Aurora. Cherry Creek has 125 sites, from basic tent sites to those with full hook-ups. Showers and laundry facilities are located conveniently throughout the campground. Sites with full hook-ups $22 and tent sites $14.

Denver East/Strasburg KOA (303-622-9274 or 1-800-562-6538; www.koa.com/where/co/06124), 1312 Monroe St., Strasburg. Located about 40 miles east of downtown Denver, the Strasburg KOA has an outdoor swimming pool and hot tub for campground guests. There are facilities for all sorts of campers—you can park your RV, pitch your tent, or rent one of their Kamping Kabins. Plenty of trees make for comfortable camping. Rates begin at $20 for a basic tent site, and go up to $36 for a site with full hook-ups.

✴ Where to Eat

Denver is second only to San Francisco in the number of restaurants per capita, and you will find restaurants everywhere in the greater Denver-Aurora metro area. All these restaurants competing for a piece of the pie, so to speak, has resulted in top-notch dining. It seems every strip mall and shopping center has unique offerings for breakfast, lunch, and dinner.

DINING OUT ♿ **Bistro Vendôme** (303-825-3232; www.bistrovendome.com), 1424-H Larimer Square. Dinner Tues.–Thurs. 5–10; Fri. and Sat. 5–11; Sun. 5–9. Brunch Sat. and Sun. 10–2. If you are longing for a taste of the Old World, look no further than Larimer Square's Bistro Vendôme. The European feel of this French bistro begins with its location. Tucked away from the busy streets and bustling crowds, to get there you walk through the Kettle Arcade to the Sussex breezeway. White table linens and intimate dining spaces complete the feel. The menu features traditional French bistro fare, with appetizers like steak tartar, escargot, and French onion soup. For a main course, the steak frites comes highly recommended. And for the perfect complement to your meal, the bar has over 60 different French wines. Dinner entrées $15–23.

♿ **Buckhorn Exchange** (303-534-9505; www.buckhorn.com), 1000 Osage St. Open for lunch Mon.–Fri. 11–2; dinner (or as they say, "supper") Mon.–Thurs. 5:30–9, Fri. and Sat. 5–10, and Sun. 5–9. First opened in 1893 by Henry "Shorty Scout" Zietz, one of Buffalo Bill Cody's frontiersmen, the Buckhorn Exchange is truly a living piece of Colorado history. It is a history you feel when you walk in the front door, with mounted animal heads and walls covered with historic memorabilia. Be sure to check out the liquor license on the wall—it was the first the state issued back in 1949. The house specialty is steak, but there's plenty of variety for the adventurous diner. From rattlesnake and Rocky Mountain oysters to buffalo prime rib and elk, game is a centerpiece of their menu. Entrées average $28–30.

♿ **The Capital Grille** (303-539-

2500; www.thecapitalgrille.com), 1450 Larimer St. Lunch Mon.–Fri. 11:30–2:30 and dinner Mon.–Thu. 5–10, Fri and Sat. 5–11, and Sun. 4–9. In a town known for great steak places, the Capital Grille has quite a reputation. Not too stuffy, but entirely classy. Dinner $22–42.

Y ♿ **Elway's** (303-399-5353; www.elways.com), 2500 E. 1st Ave. Lunch Mon.–Sun. 11–2; dinner Mon.–Thurs. 5–10, Fri. and Sat. 5–11, and Sun. 5–9; and brunch Sat. and Sun. 11–2. Part steakhouse, part classy sports bar, Elway's has become a popular place for dining in the Cherry Creek area. Cofounder and local hero, John Elway (former quarterback for the Denver Broncos, for those who don't keep up with sports) has been known to visit the bar and sign autographs from time to time. Though their specialty is steak, which is always well commented on, they have great burgers too—try the smash burger if you get a chance. Dinner entrées under $30.

Y **Mizuna** (303-832-4778; www.mizunadenver.com), 225 East 7th Ave. The menu changes monthly, but fine food is a constant at Mizuna. Dishes represent a mixture of culinary traditions—Italian, French, American—and diners are never disappointed. Dinner around $30.

Y ♿ **Panzano** (303-296-3525; www.panzano-denver.com), 909 17th St. Breakfast Mon.–Fri. 7–10; lunch Mon.–Fri. 11–2:30; and dinner Mon.–Thurs. 5–10, Fri. and Sat. 5–11, and Sun. 4:30–9:30. Italian, excellent pizza, and salads. Dinner entrées $14–30.

Y ♿ **Strings** (303-831-7310; www.stringsrestaurant.com), 1700 Humboldt St. Open Mon.–Fri. 11–10, Sat. 5–10, Sun. 5–9. Located between downtown Denver and City Park, Strings has been a popular Denver staple for nearly 20 years. The menu features New American cuisine, and diners rave about their pasta dishes. Surprising for such an upscale restaurant, kids are more than welcome—they even have their own section of the menu. Lunch $9–25 and dinner $15–35.

Y ♿ **Tamayo** (720-946-1433; www.modernmexican.com/tamayo), 1400 Larimer St. Lunch Mon.–Fri. 11:30–2; dinner Sun. and Mon. 5–10, Tues.–Thurs. 5–10:30, and Fri. and Sat. 5–11. People rave about their margaritas. Dinner entrées $17–27.

Y ♿ **Vesta Dipping Grill** (303-296-1970; www.vestagrill.com), 1822 Blake St. Open for dinner Sun.–Thurs. 5–10 and Fri. and Sat. 5–11. Beneath every entrée on the Vesta Dipping Grill menu you will find a list of suggested sauces for dipping—or you can choose from any of the 30 sauces they offer. It is a fun concept that might get tired if the food weren't so darn good. This is considered required dining for people who enjoy food and can make it to Denver's Lower Downtown. Dinner entrées $18–32.

Y ♿ **The Fort Restaurant** (303-697-4771; www.thefort.com), 19192 Hwy. 8, Morrison. Open Mon.–Fri. 5:30–10, Sat. 5–10, and Sun. 5–9. Walking into the replica of Bent's Fort feels like a step back into the early 1800s. In keeping with the décor, the menu strives to replicate the diet of the early mountain men, trappers, and pioneers who made their way to the original Bent's Fort on the Santa Fe Trail to buy and sell goods. Buffalo is their specialty (they serve more than 50,000 buffalo dinners every year), but the entire menu gets rave revues—a menu that includes beef and seafood, game, pork, and poultry. Some of the items are rather unique, like roast bison marrow bones as an appetizer and rosemary infused panna cotta with huckleberries for dessert. Dinner $30–50.

EATING OUT ♿ **Brother's BBQ** (720-570-4227; www.brothers-bbq.com), 568 N. Washington St. Open every day 10–10 (later if they have a crowd). Founded in 1998 by two brothers from England, Brother's BBQ is considered by many to be Denver's best barbeque. Their menu combines various barbeque traditions from around the country, so there's something here for every barbeque fanatic. Most entrées $6–12.

♿ **Casa Bonita** (303-232-5115; www.casabonitadenver.com), 6715 W. Colfax Ave. Open Sun.–Thurs. 11–9:30 and Fri. and Sat. 11–10. There is an online joke that says something like, "You know you're from Colorado when you take your out-of-town guests to Casa Bonita even though you would never go there otherwise." There's some truth to this. Though the restaurant has seen better days, it's still worth a trip. With seating for 1,100 people, it has been said to be the largest restaurant in North America. The food isn't bad, but what people come for is the experience. Inside, Casa Bonita resembles a Mexican village at night. The over-the-top dining entertainment features a large pool with cliff divers, an old-time cowboy shootout (with the villain inevitably falling off a cliff into the pool), caves to explore, and an arcade. Kids love this place. Sopaipillas come with every meal. Entrées $11–20.

CityGrille (303-861-0276; www.citygrille.com), 321 E. Colfax Ave. Open Mon.–Thurs. 11–11, Fri. and Sat. 11–midnight, and Sun. 2–11. The CityGrille is known for the best burgers in Denver. The menu offers three takes on the traditional hamburger—the steakburger, the buffaloburger, and the crowd-pleasing CitiGrille burger. Or you can go Mexican with chile rellenos, smothered in their award-winning green chili. Dishes $8–10.

♿ **Parisi** (303-561-0234; www.parisidenver.com), 4401 Tennyson St. Open Mon.–Sat. 11–9. The dining experience at Parisi is casual—you order at the counter and either find a table in their dining room or take your food to go. Even though it's laid back, they serve up some of the best Italian in Denver. You have to try one of their wood-oven baked pizzas. Entrées $6–15 (higher end is for the pizza, which you can share).

♿ **Pete's Kitchen** (303-321-3139; www.petesrestaurantstoo.com/petesKitchen.html), 1962 E. Colfax Ave. Open 24 hours a day, every day. Since 1942, diners have been coming to Pete's Kitchen on Colfax. If you need a late-night bite, there is no place better in town. They serve a traditional "Greek diner" menu of gyros and hamburgers, kabob sandwiches, and chicken-fried steak. The green chili is outstanding. Their breakfast burrito is constantly winning "best in Denver" awards, and like the rest of the breakfast menu it is served all day—and all night for that matter. Entrées $7–10, sandwiches and breakfast $5–8.

♿ **Rocky Mountain Diner** (303-293-8383; www.rockymountaindiner.com), 800 18th St. Open Mon.–Thurs. 11–10, Fri.–Sat. 11–11, and

Sun. 11–9. Located right across from the federal courthouse in downtown Denver, the Rocky Mountain Diner has a mixed menu of good ol' southern comfort food (like country-fried steak and oven-roasted beef brisket) and something they call "Mountain Mex" (roast duck enchilladas and the Santa Fe burger). Most entrées around $12.

♿ **Spicy Pickle Sub Shop** (303-860-0730; www.spicypickle.com), 988 Lincoln St. Open Mon.–Thurs. 10:30–7, Fri. 10:30–6, and Sat. and Sun. 11–6. Though you can now find Spicy Pickles in 14 states, this is the original pickle. "Spicy" is the optimal word to describe the eats—not hot, but spicy. Everything on the menu, from panini to salad, has a particular zing that makes it a standout place for lunch. Their chicken caesar salad may be the best I have ever had. Panini, subs, and large salads around $7.

♿ **WaterCourse Foods** (303-832-7313), 837 E. 17th Ave. Open Mon.–Fri. 6:30–10 and Sat. and Sun. 8–10. The vegetarian menu at WaterCourse Foods is extensive—relying heavily on mushrooms, seitan, and tofu—making it a favorite spot for local herbivores. The po' boy sandwich is highly praised, as is the tempeh burger. All dishes can be served vegan. Dishes $8–10.

♿ **White Fence Farm** (303-935-5945; www.whitefencefarm.com), 6263 W. Jewell Ave. Open Tues.–Sat. 4:30–8:30 and Sun. 11:30–8. Southwest of downtown, this is the perfect place for a family dinner—especially if you have a large group. The menu has plenty of options like steak and seafood, but nearly everyone orders the family-style farm chicken. The chicken comes with a mess of sides like coleslaw, cottage cheese, corn fritters, and farm-made gravy (especially nice on the mashed potatoes), all served family-style. Most nights they have live country and bluegrass playing in the American Barn. Reservations are a good idea. Dinners run $7.95–21.95 and Family-Style Farm Chicken is $12.95 per person—they sometimes have coupons online.

BAKERIES & COFFEE SHOPS ♿ **Hooked on Colfax** (303-398-2665; www.myspace.com/hookedoncolfax), 3215 E. Colfax Ave. Open "every freakin' day" 7–10. In addition to their great coffee, Hooked on Colfax gets kudos for "going green" with corn cups and straws. They also sell books. Great place to kick back and read. The basement is finished up nice and can be reserved for meeting or study groups.

♿ **Lube and Latte** (303-274-0713; www.lubeandlatte.com), 2595 Kipling St. Open Mon.–Fri. 6–6 and Sat. 7–5. People who are waiting for work on their cars don't want to sit in dirty, industrial waiting rooms, drinking two-day-old coffee and reading two-year-old magazines. So Eilis and Dustin McNamara-Olde came up with the idea of a coffee shop that is also an auto service station. Brilliant! And you don't even need to have anything wrong with your car to stop by and enjoy mocha or their very own 10w-20 (coffee with a couple shots of espresso).

BARS, TAVERNS & BREW PUBS ♿ **Wynkoop Brewing Company** (303-297-2700; www.wynkoop.com), 1634 18th St. Open every day 11 AM–2 AM. When the city was beginning to breathe new life into Denver's lower downtown, the Wynkoop brew pub was one of the first places to set up shop. Sandwiches $8 and dinner entrées around $20.

✷ Entertainment

PROFESSIONAL SPORTS Denver is a great town for sports fans. Within a few square miles there are teams playing in the NFL, NBA, NHL, and Major League baseball. Denver is also home to professional soccer, lacrosse, and arena football teams.

The **Denver Broncos** (720-258-3333; www.denverbroncos.com) have been all the way twice, winning the Superbowl in 1998 and 1999. They play downtown at INVESCO Field at Mile High. The open-air stadium makes for some tough games when the weather turns cold in late fall—but that doesn't seem to be an issue for the hardcore fans filling the seats at every game. The regular season runs September through December.

For major league baseball fans, the **Colorado Rockies** (303-762-5437 or 1-800-388-7625; www.coloradorockies.com) play at Coors Field just north of LoDo in Denver. The thin air tends to straighten a pitcher's curve ball, and hitters swear the ball always carries a little farther in Colorado. The regular season starts in April and runs through September.

The **Denver Nuggets** (303-405-1100; www.nba.com/nuggets) play in the National Basketball Association at the Pepsi Center in Denver. The regular season runs October through April.

The **Colorado Avalanche** (303-405-1111; www.coloradoavalanche.com), play National League Hockey at the Pepsi Center. Always a team to take seriously, in 1996 and 2001, they brought the Stanley Cup home to Denver. The regular season runs September through March.

The **Colorado Rapids** (303-825-4625; www.coloradorapids.com), plays professional soccer, part of Major League Soccer, at the Pepsi Center. The regular season runs April through October.

In 2003, the **Colorado Crush** (720-258-3400; www.coloradocrush.com) came to play football in the Arena Football League as an expansion team. They play at the Pepsi Center—the small size of the field makes for interesting and exciting football. The regular season runs March through July.

Since 2003, the **Colorado Mammoth** (303-405-1101; www.coloradomammoth.com) have been playing in the National Lacrosse League at the Pepsi Center. The regular season runs December through April.

THEATERS ♿ **Red Rocks Amphitheatre** (720-865-2474; www.redrocksonline.com), 18300 W. Alameda Pkwy., Morrison. Everyone who's anyone has performed at Red Rocks. Bono waving a large white flag during U2's legendary concert in 1983 is just one of many iconic images that have secured the place of Red Rocks in rock-and-roll history. The park's natural ampitheatre, formed by two 300-foot monoliths creates perfect acoustics, and performers have been coming to the site since the early 1900s take advantage of its unique qualities.

♿ **Denver Center for the Performing Arts** (303-893-4100 or 1-800-641-1222, box office; www.denvercenter.org), 1101 13th St. Specializing in live theatre, the DCPA is often a key stop for touring Broadway productions. All the big shows are here, so check out their site to see what's on the schedule while you are in town.

MUSIC 🍸 **Grizzly Rose Saloon & Dance Emporium** (303-295-2353; www.grizzlyrose.com), 5450 N. Valley Hwy. This is the area's best-known country music nightclub. A lot of stars have played the stage here—Willie Nelson, LeAnn Rimes, and John Michael Montgomery, to name a few. Weekly dance lessons teach everything from line dancing to cowboy cha-cha.

Opera Colorado (303-357-2787; www.operacolorado.org), 695 S. Colorado Blvd., Ste. 20. The opera company puts on performances at the Ellie Caulkins Opera House, which is part of the Denver Center for the Performing Arts.

✷ Selective Shopping

REI–Flagship (303-756-3100; www.rei.com/stores/denverflagship), 1416 Platte St. Open Mon.–Fri. 10–9, Sat. 10–7, and Sun. 10–6. Occupying the old Denver Tramway Power Company Building, REI's flagship store sits right on the South Platter River across from Confluence Park. Before you even walk through the door, you get a sense of REI's outdoor spirit. The landscaping, with a thick grove of aspen and a boulder for climbing, captures the natural feel of Colorado. There's even a singletrack bike loop for customers looking to test the new

THE AMPHITHEATRE AT RED ROCKS

mountain bikes. Over 5 million bricks were used when the building was originally built. Three stories tall, half of the space indoors was left open, leaving room for a massive climbing wall. Everything you could want for any outdoor adventure is here. So if you can't find what you're looking for, be sure to ask.

Rockmount Ranch Wear (303-629-7777 or 1-800-776-2566; www.rockmount.com), 1626 Wazee St. Open Mon.–Fri. 7–5 and Sat. and Sun. 11–4. Rockmount is the home of western fashion. The store was founded in 1946 by Jack Weil, who now at the age of 106 still gets into work every day. It was Jack who revolutionized the cowboy uniform, introducing the distinctive slim-fitting western shirt with snaps instead of buttons. Rockmount clothing is still predominantly made in America. Be sure to check out their store to get a glimpse of living history as they continue to thrive in downtown Denver.

Savory Spice Shop (303-477-3322 or 1-888-677-3322; www.savoryspiceshop.com), 1537 Platte St. Open Mon.–Fri. 10–6, Sat. 10–5, and Sun. 11–4. Located just north of the Platte River off 15th Street, this store is a real delight for aspiring cooks. They carry a large assortment of spices that they grind right there in the shop. The selection is amazing—they have at least a dozen different kinds of peppercorns alone. There are also spice mixes of their own creation. A personal favorite is the Mt. Massive steak seasoning. Shopping for your kitchen can feel a little strange if you are on vacation, but everything is available on their Web site when you get home.

Tewksbury & Co (303-825-1805; www.tewksburycompany.com), 1512 Larimer St., R-14. Open Mon.–Fri. 10–7, Sat. 11–6, and Sun. noon–5. This tobacconist shop on Larimer carries a fine selection of cigars and pipe tobacco, as well as other tobacciana. They also have a wide selection of wines from a number of Colorado's wineries. Every day, 1:30–5, they host a wine tasting. This is a great opportunity to sample a number of area wines if you can't make the trek to each individual winery.

✷ Special Events

May: **Downtown Denver Arts Festival** (303-330-8237; www.downtowndenverartsfestival.com), Denver Pavilions (16th Street Mall & Glenarm Street). Over 125 Colorado artists come to participate in this fine art and fine craft exhibition.

September: **Taste of Colorado** (303-295-6330; www.atasteofcolorado.com), Civic Center Park. Held every year over Labor Day Weekend, the festival brings together the great food by local eateries, an art fair, and a full weekend of musical performances.

BOULDER

Part university town and part upwardly mobile hippy enclave, Boulder has a character all its own. The city touts cultural resources found nowhere else in the state—this is the only town I know of that has its own pottery studio. The residents of Boulder as whole are passionate about the outdoors and outdoor recreation. This in turn translates into a passion for the environment and healthy living. Boulder residents lead North America in organic food consumption. A quick look at a list of corporations that call Boulder home reveals many familiar names—Celestial Seasonings, Wild Oats Market, and Horizon Organic Dairy—all companies known for their promotion of natural goodness.

On a warm day, the city's parks, bike paths, and sidewalks are full of people jogging, inline-skating, and riding their bikes. A stroll through Boulder's Pearl Street Mall on a spring afternoon finds buskers making their music wherever they can—audience or no. During my last trip, it was a cold day and there were still four guitarists, two percussionists, and a guy wailing on the sax, all adding their signature sounds to the laid-back atmosphere of downtown.

Part of Boulder's vibrancy comes from the University of Colorado at Boulder. Not only is the university one of the largest employers in Boulder County, the annual influx of nearly 30,000 students means the population, to some extent, is always changing—and Boulder seems to be a town that is not at all afraid of change.

Boulder's history goes back to the 19th century. In 1858, prospectors looking for gold settled near the mouth of Boulder Canyon. Soon the town of Boulder City was established. The town came to be a trading post of sorts, supplying the many miners heading into the mountains with gear and equipment. With the growth of retail, saloons and houses of ill repute were established to cater to miners and their vices. Rail service came in 1873, and in 1874, Boulder became home to the new University of Colorado.

In the 20th century, Boulder continued to grow and change. Tourism, which had been an industry in Boulder from early on, was greatly boosted by the building of the Hotel Boulderado in 1909. Several decades later at the end of World War II, the university's enrollment swelled with folks taking advantage of the GI Bill.

In recent decades, numerous tech companies have come to make Boulder

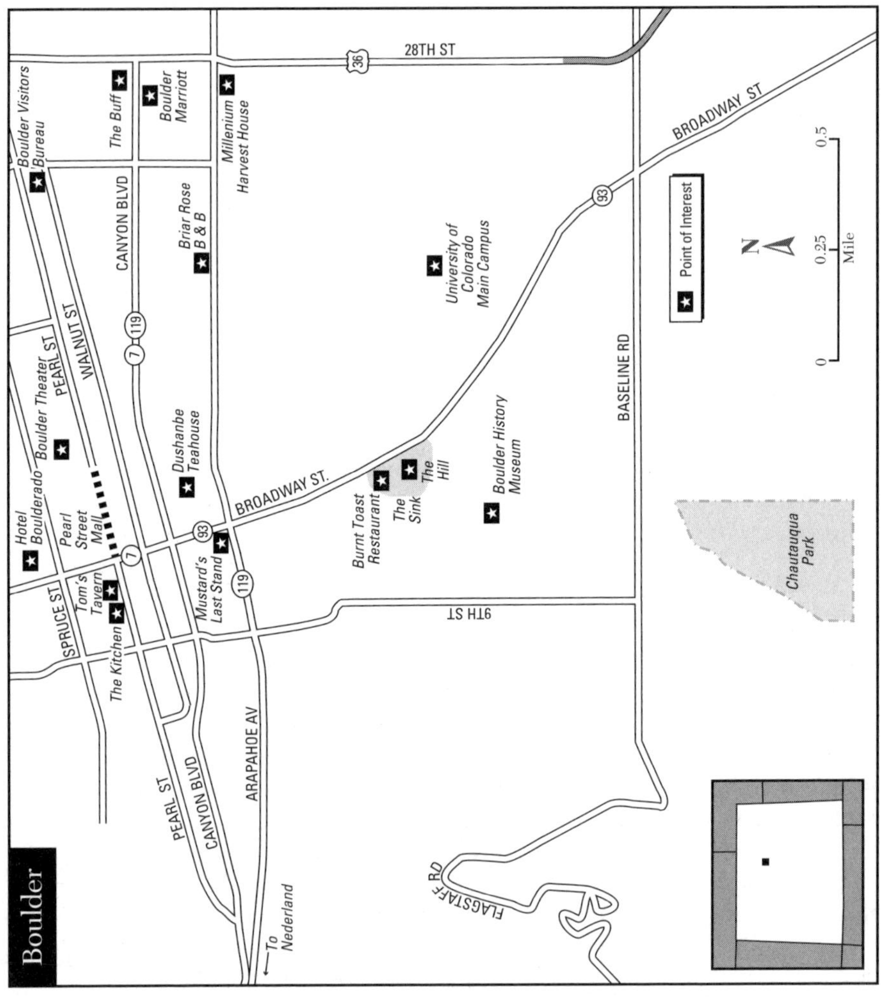

their home. Sun Microsystems and IBM are two of the county's largest employers. Not only does the city provide the kinds of cultural, recreational, and entertainment activities that help attract the best employees, the nearby university is constantly bringing the brightest and best students and faculty to study and do research.

Shopping and business districts like the Hill and the Pearl Street Mall, and recreational opportunities in the nearby mountains and Boulder Canyon, mean visitors can mountain bike in the morning, enjoy a bowl of soup at the Kitchen before hiking into the Flatirons, and be back for fine dining at the Dushanbe Teahouse for dinner.

GUIDANCE **Boulder Convention & Visitors Bureau** (303-442-2911 or 1-800-444-0447; www.bouldercoloradousa.com), 2440 Pearl St. In addition to their main office on Pearl St., the Visitors Bureau maintains two visitor kiosks in Boulder. One is located right downtown on the Pearl Street Mall, in front of the courthouse. The other is several miles southeast of town on US 36.

More Web sites:

www.getboulder.com

www.boulderdowntown.com

www.bouldercolorado.gov

www.totalboulder.com

GETTING THERE *By car:* From Denver, take I-25 north to the Denver–Boulder Turnpike (US 36), which takes you right into the city. From the north, take exit 240 off I-25 onto CO 119. That will take you west to the Diagonal Highway (still CO 119), which leads directly into Boulder.

By air: The **Denver International Airport** (303-342-2000 or 1-800-AIR2DEN; www.flydenver.com) is about a 45-minute drive from Boulder. **SuperShuttle** (303-444-0808; www.supershuttle.com) takes passengers from DIA to Boulder. And the DIA operates **skyRide** (303-299-6000; www.rtd-denver.com/skyRide), which also offers affordable transportation to and from the airport.

By train: **AMTRAK** (1-800-USA-RAIL; www.amtrak.com) does not have direct service to Boulder, but does operate their Throughway bus service, which stops at the Greyhound stop at the gas station at the corner of 30th and the Diagonal Highway.

By bus: **Greyhound** (1-800-231-2222; www.greyhound.com) has a regular stop in Boulder at the gas station at the corner of 30th and the Diagonal Highway. Tickets are not available at this stop and must be bought in advance.

GETTING AROUND *By car:* Getting around by car is no problem in Boulder. There is plenty of parking downtown, including a number of parking structures.

By bus: The Denver RTD operates the bus system in Boulder. The routes are named for easy identification—Hop, Skip, Jump, Bound, Stampede, Dash, and Bolt. Hop makes a regular tour down Pearl Street. Real-time arrival of buses can be found on NextBus (www.nextbus.com), which tracks individual buses with GPS. You can even watch the bus icons move around on a map.

MEDICAL EMERGENCIES The **Boulder Community Hospital** (303-440-2273; www.bch.org), 1100 Balsam Ave., operates two emergency rooms in Boulder. One is at the main campus at the corner of Balsam and N. Broadway. The other is at another campus at the corner of 48th Street and Arapahoe. This east campus is called **Boulder Community Foothills Hospital** (720-854-7000), 4747 Arapahoe Ave.

✷ To See & Do

HISTORIC SITES ♿ **Chautauqua National Historic Landmark** (303-442-3282; www.chautauqua.com), 900 Baseline Rd. In the late 19th century, there

CHAUTAUQUA AUDITORIUM

was a movement in the U.S. to promote adult education. The movement began in upstate New York at Chautauqua Lake with a meeting of Sunday school teachers. At first, the intention was to improve teacher education, but soon the mandate was to bring a "college outlook" to the working masses and the middle class. In 1898, the Colorado Chautauqua opened in Boulder as a retreat for educators. Today, Chautauqua continues to entertain and educate thousands through countless concerts, lectures, art exhibits, and other programs. The park offers free tours of historic Chautauqua. In addition to the Auditorium and the Dining Hall (both built in 1898), the site has numerous historic buildings, including 98 cottages. Tour times vary, so check the Web site for current details. Admission is free.

Mapleton Historic District. The Mapleton neighborhood dates back to the late 19th century and the houses are really quite stunning. **Historic Boulder** (303-444-5192), 1123 Spruce St., is an organization that works to preserve historic sites in Boulder. At their office on Spruce Street you can get self-guided walking tour brochures for this neighborhood. They also have brochures that will guide you through Columbia Cemetery, the University of Colorado, the Whittier Neighborhood, Chautauqua, Historic Downtown Boulder, and the University Hill neighborhood.

MUSEUMS ☂ ♿ **Boulder History Museum** (303-449-3464; www.boulderhistorymuseum.org), 1206 Euclid Ave. Open Tues.–Fri. 10–5, and Sat. and Sun. noon–4. In the 60-odd years since the museum's creation, more than 35,000 objects, all with significance to the story of Boulder, have been donated by local families. To keep the museum fresh, displays are changed several times a year.

Adult admission $5, seniors $3, children and students $2, and children under 5 free.

☂ ♿ **Boulder Museum of Contemporary Art** (303-443-2122; www.bmoca.org), 1750 13th St. Open Tues.–Fri. 11–5 (Wed. night until 8), Sat. 9–4, and Sun. noon–3. Back in 1972, local artists created the Boulder Arts Center to support and promote the visual arts. Over the years, the mission of the Center broadened, and the name changed to the Boulder Museum of Contemporary Art. Today, the BMoCA includes art from all over the world and has become a venue for performance art as well. See Web site for current shows and exhibitions. Admission $5; seniors and students $4.

♿ **Leanin' Tree Western Art Museum** (303-530-1442, ext. 5; www.leanintreemuseum.com), 6055 Longbow Dr. Open Mon.–Fri. 8–5 and Sat. and Sun. 10–5. First and foremost, Leanin' Tree is a manufacturer of greeting cards. They began back in 1949 with four Western-themed Christmas cards, and today have over 3,000 different cards for sale at numerous independent outlets around the country. The company maintains a fantastic Western Art Museum with numerous paintings and sculptures. Outside they have a sculpture garden to display large-scale works. A quick walk around will not take a lot of time, and it's a great stop to make before or after taking the tour at Celestial Seasonings. Admission free.

NATURAL ATTRACTIONS **Boulder Falls.** Driving west up CO 119 to Nederland, there are signs along the road for Boulder Falls. It's about 11 miles west of town. Parking is on the south side of the road and the falls are on the north. This 5-acre park holds a real gem of a waterfall, just a short walk from the highway. Often referred to as the "Yosemite of Boulder Canyon," water cascades down 70 feet to the canyon floor. The park is open dawn to dusk.

BOULDER FALLS

Flatirons. Located to the southwest of town, there is no geological feature more synonymous with Boulder than the Flatirons. They are conglomerate sandstone that has been heaved up at an angle, and subsequently exposed by erosion. Geologists estimate they were heaved up to their current position 35 to 80 million years ago. The largest have been numbered north to south, one to five. For a view of the Flatirons, try driving south on CO 93 south of town. Or try the Flatirons Vista Trail (see Outdoor Activities, Hiking).

SCENIC DRIVES **Boulder Canyon.** The drive up to Nederland on CO 119 (aka Boulder Canyon Dr.) follows Boulder Creek up to the Barker Reservoir. There are a number of places to pull over and take in the scenery.

Peak-to-Peak Scenic and Historic Byway. This 55-mile drive through the mountains begins in Black Hawk/Central City and makes its way north to Estes Park. The byway is easy to get to from points all along the Front Range and offers views of the Continental Divide.

TOURS ✐ ☂ ♿ **Celestial Seasonings** (1-800-434-4246 or 303-581-1202; www.celestialseasonings.com), 4600 Sleepytime Dr. Visitors to Boulder should make an effort to tour the Celestial Seasonings factory. The facility cranks out enough tea to make 1.2 billion cups a year, making it the largest herb tea manufacturer in North America. Factory tours take about 45 minutes and include a short informative video. Visitors get see tea in many of its incarnations, from the dried leaves that arrive in crates to the sifted form that makes it into the tea bags. A highlight of the tour is the stop in the mint room, where peppermint and spearmint clear your sinuses. Tours begin on the hour at 10, with the last at 3. On Sunday, the first tour is at 11. Space is limited and openings are doled out on a first-come, first-served basis. After the tour, take a look around in the tea shop or grab lunch in the café.

✐ ☂ ♿ **National Center for Atmospheric Research** (303-497-1147; www.ucar.edu/ucar/visitucar.html), 1850 Table Mesa Dr. Open Mon.–Fri. 8–5 and Sat. and Sun. (and holidays) 9–4. Primarily a scientific research facility, scientists at the NCAR study such things as the world's changing climate, the science of hurricanes, and how to come up with better models for predicting floods and tornados. For the public, NCAR offers guided and self-guided tours of the Mesa Lab. The visitor center has a number of exhibits that teach about the sun, weather and climate, and instrumentation and technology. The Walter Orr Roberts Weather Trail is also a popular hike. The trail is paved and wheelchair accessible. Admission is free.

WINERIES & BREWERIES ♿ **Augustina's Winery** (303-545-2047; www.winechick.biz), 4715 N. Broadway, B-3. This small winery north of Boulder has a tasting room. Tasting hours vary, so call ahead. For your convenience, the wines at Augustina's have been nicely paired with some down-to-earth foods and activities. The Boulder Backpacking Wine, for example, is the perfect complement to an evening campfire after a day of hiking, and the WineChick Pinot Noir "goes well with activities involving peanut butter." If things aren't too rushed, someone would be happy to give you a tour of the facilities.

MORK & MINDY

In 1978, a young Robin Williams made a cameo on the sitcom, *Happy Days,* as the alien Mork. Later that year, the spinoff, *Mork & Mindy,* debuted on ABC. The show took place in Boulder. Presumably, the idea was that an alien wearing rainbow-striped suspenders, who drank with his finger, and slept upside down, would not stand out among the other crazies in Boulder. Though the show was shot on a set, the outdoor shots of the house they lived in were from Boulder. The house is still there of course—two blocks off Pearl on Pine Street, near the corner of 16th and Pine. Remember that this is someone's residence, so please don't go knocking on the door asking for a tour of Mork's loft.

MORK & MINDY'S PLACE

♿ **BookCliff Vineyards** (303-449-9463; www.bookcliffvineyards.com), 1468 Pearl St. Tasting room open Mon., Wed., and Thurs. 3–7; Fri.–Sat. 1–9; and Sun. 1–7. Locals John Garlich and Ulla Merz grow grapes on the weekends out in Palisade. Most of their grapes go to other wineries, but they keep a third for their own winery here in Boulder. As their reputation grows, so does their wine production. The tasting room is open everyday but Tuesday. Friday evenings in the summer they often have live music until 9:30.

Boulder Creek Winery (303-516-9031; www.bouldercreekwine.com), 6440 Odell Pl. Tasting room open Jan.–May, Fri.–Sun. 1–5; Memorial Day–Labor Day, Thurs.–Sun. 1–5:30; and Oct.–Dec., Fri.–Sun. 1–5. Try any of the award-winning wines in their tasting room, and take a self-guided tour of the winery to see how it all comes together.

Ciatano Winery (303-823-5011; www.ciatanowinery.com), 16858 N. St. Vrain Dr., Lyons. Open daily 10–6. Located in the mountains north of Lyons, Ciatano is in a great location. After wine tasting, take advantage of the winery's spacious grounds: Fill one of the available picnic baskets with meats and cheeses from the deli and enjoy a nice picnic lunch.

Redstone Meadery (720-406-1215; www.redstonemeadery.com), 4700 Pearl St. #2A. Tasting room open Mon.–Fri. noon–6:30 with tours at 1 and 3; Sat. noon–5 with a tour at 12:30. The brewing of mead, or honey wine, goes back at least to 1100 B.C. Aristotle wrote of mead, and warriors in the epic of Beowulf sang songs and told their tales in the mead-hall. And yet there are few places in the world where mead is still brewed today. Luckily, one of those places is in Boulder. At Redstone Meadery you can taste the fruit of the bee and get a tour of their facilities.

✷ Outdoor Activities

One of the reasons people give for moving to Boulder is the accessibility of the great outdoors. Runners, hikers, rock climbers, and cyclists have a seemingly endless number of trails, paths, and climbs for their recreational pursuits, many of which are close to town. If there is nothing here that strikes your fancy, the staff at most of the hotels and inns in Boulder can direct you to local trailheads, or stop by one of the outfitters or shops listed below. These folks live the outdoors and are happy to share their local knowledge.

ALPINE SKIING & SNOWSHOEING **Eldora Mountain Resort** (303-440-8700; www.eldora.com), P.O. Box 1697 Nederland, CO 80466. Take CO 119 up to Nederland, follow CO 119 to the south for 1 mile and then turn right on CO 130. Lifts run Mon.–Fri. 9–4; weekends and holidays 8:30–4. The elevation at the top of Eldora is 10,800 feet, making it 1,600 feet above the base of the resort. There are 680 skiable acres, which includes 55 trails, 12 lifts, and a Terrain Park. With 300 inches of snow falling annually, the resort relies little on snowmaking. The RTD out of Boulder operates regular bus service to and from Eldora during ski season. Adult lift ticket $56 and children 15 and under $36.

ELDORA SKI AREA OUTSIDE NEDERLAND

BICYCLING The city of Boulder has 38 miles of trails open to off-road cyclists. In addition, the 7-mile **Boulder Creek Path,** which runs from Boulder Canyon out to Arapahoe Road near the Valmont Reservoir, is a cyclist's dream, allowing bikes to access the heart of Boulder without having to drive in the street.

Community Ditch Trail. Starting at the Doudy Trail trailhead, located west of CO 93 on Eldora Springs Dr., the Community Ditch Trail runs east to the Marshall Reservoir. The 4-mile route is a combination of trail and dirt roads. There are not many trees along this route, so it's best ridden in the morning or evening when there is some respite from the sun. The views of the Flatirons are impressive. At its eastern terminus, the trail connects with the **Greenbelt Plateau Trail,** which offers another 1.6 miles of riding through open grasslands.

Switzerland Trail. The trail is built on the old railroad bed of the Switzerland Trail Railway, and as such, it's popular with the four-wheeling crowd. To get there, take CO 119 west out of Boulder. In about 3 miles turn right on Fourmile Canyon Road (CO 118). Continue 10 miles to Sunset. Turning right in town will put you on the Switzerland Trail. Riding south takes you to Bald and Sugarloaf mountains. Or you can start at Sugarloaf Mountain Road trailhead and go north to Gold Hill.

The Bikesmith (303-443-1132; www.boulderbikesmith.com), 2432 Arapahoe Ave. Located at Arapahoe and Folsom. Open daily 9–6. The Bikesmith rents full- and front-suspension mountain bikes, cruisers, road bikes, and even recumbent bikes. The shop also offers service if you need a repair or just a tune-up. Rentals for 24 hours run $27–47.

University Cycles (303-444-4196 or 1-800-451-3950; www.ubikes.com), 839 Pearl St. Open Mon.–Fri. 10–7, Sat. 10–6, and Sun. 10–5. University Cycles rents town cruisers, mountain bikes, and some really nice road bikes. The shop also has all the service and parts support a cyclist could need. Rentals for 24 hours run $20–75.

FISHING Several area lakes are popular with anglers. Boulder Reservoir (303-441-3461; www.ci.boulder.co.us), 5565 51st St., is north of town off the Diagonal Highway. Barker Reservoir is just east of Nederland at the top of Boulder Canyon. Public access to the lake on the west and north shores provides opportunities for bank fishing. Brainerd Lake is found in the Roosevelt National Forest and is the centerpiece of the Brainerd Lake Recreation Area. High in the mountains, the scenery around Brainerd is simply beautiful. The recreation area also has a number of trails for hiking. Walden Ponds Wildlife Habitat (east of town at 75th and Valmont streets) was built up on the site of old gravel pits. Five ponds were created, and great effort went into making the area a fitting wetland for local wildlife. The ponds are stocked with several species including large and smallmouth bass, bluegill, and channel catfish. Bass are catch-and-release only. One pond, Wally Toevs Pond, is set aside for seniors and the handicapped and requires a special $5 pass.

Kinsley Outfitters (303-442-6204 or 1-800-442-7420; www.kinsleyoutfitters.com), 2070 Broadway. Open Mon.–Sat. 9–6 and Sun. noon–5. The Orvis-endorsed guides and instructors at Kinsley Outfitters offer a number of guided fly-fishing trips, seminars, and classes. The store is stocked with Orvis as well as other brands. A full-day guided fishing trip for one person costs $250.

Rocky Mountain Anglers (303-447-2400; www.rockymtanglers.com), 1904 Arapahoe Ave. Open Mon.–Sat. 9:30–6 and Sun. 10–5. The folks at Rocky Mountain Anglers offer everything from gear to fully guided fishing trips. They also report on the conditions they find on the waters they fish on their Web site. A fully guided day trip for one person runs $245.

GOLF **Flatirons** (303-442-7851; www.flatironsgolf.com), 5706 Arapahoe Ave. The Flatirons first opened in 1993. This is the closest golfing to Boulder. Golfers enjoy mountain views and a course lined with old-growth trees. Greens fees $26–31 for 18 holes.

Indian Peaks (303-666-4706), 2300 Indian Peaks Tr., Lafayette. This course, designed by Hale Irwin, features 1,200 trees, 87 bunkers, 6 lakes, and a couple of streams. While working around these obstacles, golfers enjoy beautiful views of the nearby Indian Peaks. Greens fees $37–45 for 18 holes.

HIKING There are so many trails and paths in and around Boulder—and up in the mountains—that is it nearly impossible to keep track of them all. The **City of Boulder Open Space & Mountain Parks** (303-441-3440; www.osmp.org) maintains miles of paved paths and trails throughout Boulder and the surrounding area. There are 33 trailheads—nearly half of these permit bicycles, and less than half permit horseback riding. Complete information, including an interactive map, can be found on the Web site.

Boulder Creek Path (303-413-7200) runs from the Boulder Canyon in the west to Arapahoe Road near Cherryvale. The 7-mile path is mostly paved but turns to dirt and gravel in the canyon. Following Boulder Creek, the path connects a number of city parks and runs through the heart of Boulder. It is open to pedestrians and cyclists. Speed limit signs are posted along the way.

Chautauqua Park. A network of trails connect Chautauqua Park with Flagstaff Mountain, Saddle Rock, and Green Mountain. One loop is particularly enjoyable, and pretty easy-going—the **McClintock–Enchanted Mesa Loop**. Start behind the Chautauqua Auditorium at the McClintock trailhead. Take the trail out about a mile, and come back via the Enchanted Mesa Trail. This 2.1-mile hike has views of the Flatirons and Bear Peak. Another hike, one of the more difficult you will find in Boulder, is the **Royal Arch Trail**. This trail begins at the Bluebell picnic shelter, about a half-mile up Bluebell Road from the Ranger Cottage at Chautauqua. From there the trail climbs into Bluebell Canyon on its way to the Royal Arch, a unique geological feature in the mountains. In all, the trail climbs 1,200 feet in 3 miles. There are plenty of steep sections, but the views are incredible.

Flagstaff Mountain. Located west of Boulder, take Baseline Avenue west. Just before it ends, veer left on Flagstaff Road and begin climbing. From the summit of Flagstaff Mountain, overlooking Boulder, there are a several trails of varying difficulty. Trailheads at Realization Point (at the turnoff for Flagstaff Summit Road) and one at the summit offer several short hiking options. The **Boy Scout–May's Point Loop** is a 1.2-mile circuit that most hikers find relatively

THE UNIVERSITY OF COLORADO AT BOULDER

easy to handle. The trailhead is off Flagstaff Summit Road about a half-mile from Realization Point. A little more difficult is the 1.1-mile **Ute–Range View Loop.** The trailhead for this easy-to-moderate route is at Realization Point. Both hikes offer views of the Indian Peaks. A daily parking permit on Flagstaff Mountain is $3. There are six self-serve stations on the way up the mountain. No biking on these trails.

Flatirons Vista and **Doudy Trails.** The Flatirons area is popular with hikers, and with over 650 climbing routes, it is not unusual to find rock climbers making their arduous way up the Flatirons themselves. For a nice trail, try the Doudy Draw Trail, which is south of town on CO 93, just south of the intersection with CO 128. It's a moderate trail, and the loop around is just over 3 miles.

PADDLING As all paddlers know, the best conditions for rafting or kayaking are found when the winter snows melt and rivers swell with spring runoff. Boulder Creek is very popular with area kayakers. Near the mouth of Boulder Canyon, the city maintains a kayak course on the creek with 20 slalom gates. The put-in is at the west end of Arapahoe Avenue where it meets Canyon Boulevard. The city of Lyons also has a white-water park on the North St. Vrain River. It is located in Meadow Park across from Lyons Town Hall. The park is about 400 yards long and features eight drops and a rodeo hole.

Boulder Outdoor Center (303-444-8420 or 1-800-364-9376; www.boc123.com), 2707 Spruce St. The BOC has everything a paddler needs from gear and boat rentals to solid information on local conditions. The center offers indoor kayaking instruction and organizes paddling trips around the state. You can get connected with other paddlers on the BOC Web site—buy and sell used gear or read about trips others are planning.

Whitewater Tubing (303-319-5763; www.whitewatertubing.com), 204 Canyon Blvd. (the Watershed School). Tubes can be rented June–Labor Day, daily 10–6. It's not technically paddling, but tubing is a great way to enjoy the water and keep cool. Tube rental $6, or you can buy a tube for $11–20.

GREEN SPACE **Boulder County Open Space & Mountain Parks** (303-678-6200; www.co.boulder.co.us/openspace), 5201 St. Vrain Rd., Longmont. The county of Boulder is committed to maintaining green spaces for the public's enjoyment. There are numerous parks, trails, and scenic areas throughout the county. The Web site has a map of all the open space in the county.

City of Boulder Open Space & Mountain Parks (303-441-3440; www.osmp.org) P.O. Box 791 Boulder, CO 80306. The Open Space & Mountain Parks Web site has information on all the city's parks and trails. It also includes information on trail and park usage—regulations for dogs on city property, where bikes and horses are allowed, etc. The city also hosts a number of free nature hikes, and the site has the current schedule.

Eldorado Canyon State Park (303-494-3943; www.parks.state.co.us/parks/eldoradocanyon), 9 Kneale Rd., Eldorado Springs. Open sunrise to sunset. Kayakers come to Eldorado to ride the rapids in South Boulder Creek. Anglers come to fish those same waters. One of the biggest draws to Eldorado Canyon are the nearly 500 rock climbing routes up the canyon walls. There are also some great trails here for day-hikers, including the impressive Eldorado Canyon Trail, which connects the Inner Canyon section of the park with Crescent Meadows to the west. This 3.5-mile hike gains 1,000 feet in elevation, and sections of the trail are considered difficult hiking. Just south of Boulder, Eldorado makes a great day trip, whether you go for the activities or just to picnic in this beautiful park. Day pass Oct.–Apr. $6 and May–Sept. $7; walk-in pass $3.

* Lodging

HOTELS ♿ **Boulder Marriott** (303-440-8877; www.marriott.com), 2660 Canyon Blvd. The Marriott is located in the heart of Boulder. Most of the hotel's 157 rooms offer mountain views. Guests will appreciate the indoor pool and fitness area. They also provide numerous amenities for business travelers. Rooms $159–249.

The Bradley Boulder Inn (303-545-5200 or 1-800-858-5811; www.thebradleyboulder.com), 2040 16th St. This cozy boutique hotel is located right in town, just a block from the Pearl Street Mall. The Great Room, with its large stone fireplace, decorated in original art donated by local galleries, sets the tone. The inn's 12 rooms are all tastefully decorated and extremely comfortable. Everything is included in your room rate, from the parking to breakfast and wireless Internet. Rooms $175–245.

♿ **Hotel Boulderado** (303-442-4344 or 1-800-433-4344; www.boulderado.com), 2115 13th St. Borrowing design sensibilities from the Palace Hotel in San Francisco and the Brown Palace in Denver, the Hotel Boulderado opened its doors on New Year's Day, 1909. The original investors hoped that bringing first-class accommodations to Boulder would stimulate growth and establish Boulder's future. Keeping with the grand tradition of opulent Victorian hotels, the Boulderado features a stained-glass canopy ceiling and a stunning cantilevered cherrywood staircase that reaches from the basement to the fifth floor. Each of the hotel's 160 rooms is individually decorated. Amenities include cable TV, wireless Internet, and air-conditioning. Rooms $154–294 and suites $264–389.

🐾 ♿ **Millenium Harvest House** (303-443-3850 or 1-800-545-6285; www.millenniumhotels.com/boulder), 1345 28th St. In keeping with the desire to offer guests Western hospitality, beds at the hotel are decorated in "a unique pioneer look." The beds are dressed in patchwork quilts and the photos on the walls are often of local scenes. None of this is overwhelming, however, and the furniture and décor is all classy. No knotty pine dressers here. The hotel offers several getaway packages that highlight activities in Boulder, like the Take a Hike package, which includes lodging, a picnic lunch, trail maps, and transportation to and from the trailhead. There are even backpacks you can use. Rooms $80–239.

♿ **St. Julien Hotel & Spa** (720-406-9696 or 1-877-303-0900; www.stjulien.com), 900 Walnut St. Located across from Boulder's Central Park, the St. Julien Hotel is a relative newcomer to Boulder. The hotel opened in early 2005, and brought 200 rooms and 11,000 square feet of meeting space to the heart of the city. The hotel also holds a spa and fitness center. Everything about St. Julien is high-end, from the elegant and comfortable guest rooms to the tiled pool area. The hotel caters to business travelers and tourists alike. Rooms $239–469.

Boulder Outlook Hotel & Suites (303-443-3322 or 1-800-542-0304; www.boulderoutlook.com), 800 28th St. The Boulder Outlook began years ago as a Holiday Inn. New owners bought the place in 2002 and have tried to create a hotel experience that is representative of the Boulder "outlook." The Outlook staff is helpful when it comes to planning outdoor activities or using the hotel's indoor bouldering rocks, and they contribute to community projects and organizations. You will recognize the usual hotel layout when it comes to rooms, but the décor is bright and colorful. Rooms $69–179 and suites $109–189.

Niwot Inn (303-652-8452; www.niwotinn.com), 342 2nd Ave., Niwot. This small hotel, located halfway between Boulder and Longmont right off Diagonal Highway (CO 119), has the feel of a B&B. The 14 rooms are named after famous Colorado 14-ers. Wireless Internet is available throughout the inn, including the 740 square feet of meeting space. Many rooms have jetted tubs and fireplaces. For a romantic stay, consider the Crestone Suite. Rooms $139–169.

BED & BREAKFASTS **The Alps Boulder Canyon Inn** (303-444-5445 or 1-800-414-2577; www.alpsinn.com), 38619 Boulder Canyon Dr. This inn has a long history, going back before 1870, when it was a stage stop for people traveling in and out of the mountains. Today, it is one of the better B&Bs in Colorado, recently voted the best in Boulder. The inn is found a short drive west of town, a couple miles into Boulder Canyon. The property has fishing in Boulder Creek. All 12 rooms at the Alps Inn have private baths, fireplaces, satellite TV with DVD players, and both wireless and Ethernet Internet connections. Most rooms have two-person whirlpool tubs. In addition to an outstanding breakfast, guests are served dessert nightly, and the inn's famous cowboy cookies are served throughout the day. The breakfasts are outstanding. Rooms $99–274.

The Briar Rose (303-442-3007 or 1-888-786-8440; www.briarrosebb.com), 2151 Arapahoe Ave. From the outside, the Briar Rose looks like a quiet country cottage, and happily, that sensibility is carried throughout the house. What is unexpected is that such a secluded and peaceful retreat can be found right in the middle of town, just several blocks from the Pearl Street Mall. Guests can relax in the parlor or out in the beautiful gardens. Amenities include fireplaces, TV, and air-conditioning. Rooms $129–179.

CAMPGROUNDS Roosevelt National Forest has numerous campgrounds in the mountains. Those listed here have rest rooms and drinking water, but none have showers. All sites can be reserved online at www.reserveusa.com or by calling 1-877-444-6777. Below are listed a few of those closest to Boulder.

Camp Dick Campground (Boulder Ranger District office, 303-541-2500). From Lyons, head 12 miles west on CO 7, and then south on CO 72 for 4 miles. At an elevation of 8,600 feet Camp Dick offers 41 sites for both tents and RVs near the Middle St. Vrain Creek. This is a wheelchair-accessible campground, including accessible facilities and fishing. Sites run $13 for a single, $16 for large sites.

Cold Springs Campground (Clear Creek Ranger District office, 303-567-3000), located in the mountains, 9 miles south of Georgetown on CR 381. Cold Springs sits at a lofty 9,200 feet. There are 38 sites, a playground, and plenty of trails for mountain biking and hiking. Sites are $12/night.

Kelly Dahl Campground (Boulder Ranger District office, 303-541-2500), 3 miles south of Nederland on CO 119. The 46 campsites are right on the Peak to Peak Scenic Byway. There are trails for hiking and horseback riding. Sites $12/night.

Peaceful Valley Campground (Boulder Ranger District office, 303-541-2500). From Lyons, head 12 miles west on CO 7, and then south on CO 72 for 3.5 miles. Located near Camp Dick, Peaceful Valley is a smaller campground with only 17 sites. Campers can enjoy mountain biking, hiking, fishing, and other outdoor activities. Sites run $13 for a single, $16 for large sites.

CABINS & COTTAGES **Colorado Chautauqua Association** (303-442-3282; www.chautauqua.com), 900 Baseline Rd. Sixty of Chautauqua's historic turn-of-the-century cottages are available for rent. There are even several cottages that have been designated Heritage Cottages, meaning they have been well preserved or well restored, and each has a unique story to tell. (For more on Chautauqua, see To See & Do, Historic Sites.) Cottages rent for $99–242.

✷ Where to Eat

DINING OUT ♿ **The Boulder Dushanbe Teahouse** (303-442-4993; www.boulderteahouse.com), 1770 13th St. Open Sun.–Thurs. 8–9 and Fri.–Sat. 8–10. Tea time daily 3–5. The teahouse was a gift from Boulder's sister city, Dushanbe, in Tajikistan—over 40 Tajikistani artisans worked on the teahouse, which was then shipped to Boulder and assembled. From the carved cedar columns to the Fountain of the Seven Beauties to the remarkably detailed ceiling, the teahouse is simply stunning. The menu is a potpourri of international influences, including Indian, Cuban, Italian, and Asian dishes. Lunch $10–12 and dinner $10–16.

🍸 ♿ **The Flagstaff House Restaurant** (303-442-4640; www.flagstaffhouse.com), 1138 Flagstaff Rd. Open for dinner Sun.–Fri. 6–10 and Sat. 5–10. If you are looking for an excellent dining experience with fabulous views, be sure to make reservations at the Flagstaff House Restaurant, which stands 1,500 feet above Boulder with a view of the city. When asking about fine dining in Boulder, the Flagstaff always gets first mention. This elegant restaurant has been around since 1951 and has a reputation for excellence in regards to menu, service, and ambiance. Dishes include seafood, steak, and chicken, as well as buffalo, venison, and quail. The dress code is business casual. First course around $20; main course $20–69. The restaurant also has the

"Chef's Nine Course Tasting Menu," which is ordered for the whole table, $68/person ($129/person with wine).

🍸 ♿ **The Kitchen** (303-544-5973; www.thekitchencafe.com), 1039 Pearl St. Open Mon.–Fri. 8–close, Sat. and Sun. brunch 9–2, and dinner 5:30–close. The Kitchen uses locally grown organic produce whenever possible; as a result, the menu changes daily based on the seasonal availability of various ingredients. Recent items included such dishes as Monroe Farm Summer Squash Salad and House Made Gnocchi. The tomato soup is always a favorite with customers. Recipes for many of their menu items are posted on their Web site. So if you have a great meal and can't get back to Boulder soon enough, you can try to make it at home. Dishes $20–30.

🍸 ♿ **Laudisio** (303-442-1300; www.laudisio.com), 1710 29th St. Open Mon.–Thurs. 11:30–9, Fri. 11:30–10, Sat. 3–10, and Sun. 3–9. Recently relocated to the Twenty-Ninth Street Mall, the jury is still out on whether Laudisio's, now with a larger dining room, will be able to maintain the intimate dining experience that was previously celebrated at the Iris Avenue location. The open kitchen and wood-burning oven will certainly help, and all told, the restaurant continues to be one of the classier Italian spots in town. Dinner $16–35.

🍸 ♿ **The Mediterranean** (303-444-5335; www.themedboulder.com), 1002 Walnut St. Open Sun.–Wed. 11–10 and Thurs.–Sat. 11–11. They also have a Tapa Hour Mon.–Fri. 3–6:30. Since it opened in 1993, the Mediterranean has been impressing patrons with its extensive menu, which offers everything from tapas to pizza to paella. It seems the entire Mediterranean region, from Greece to Morocco, is represented here. The décor is bright and inviting and seems alive with geraniums. Tapas $3–6, pizzas $7–10, and main dishes $10–28. These are dinner prices; lunch is cheaper. During the Tapa Hour, snacks are very affordable.

🍸 ♿ **Sunflower** (303-440-0220; www.sunflowerrestaurant.net), 1701 Pearl St. Open for dinner Tues.–Sat. 5–10 and Sun. 5–9; lunch, Tues.–Fri. 11–2:30; brunch Sat. and Sun. 10–3. This is one of the best health-conscious restaurants in Colorado. Chef and owner Jon Pell creates fine cuisine using natural foods, like cage-free poultry and free-range beef. The menu has everything from organic brown rice to grilled ahi tuna. Main entrées $20–30.

La Chaumière (303-823-6521; www.lachaumiere-restaurant.com), 12311 N. Saint Vrain Dr., Lyons. Open for dinner Tues.–Sat. 5:30–10 and Sun. 5:30–9. North of Boulder to Lyons and then a little farther north to Pinewood Springs, there is a restaurant with an outstanding menu and a relaxed French country feel. La Chaumière began in 1970 when a French cook bought a diner in Pinewood Springs called the Stagecoach Inn. It was transformed into a French eatery and remains so today, though under different management. The menu includes French classics like cassoulet, a traditional casserole that they make with wild game and pork, and filet mignon. Reservations are recommended.

🍸 ♿ **Gold Hill Inn** (303-443-6461; www.goldhillinn.com), 401 Main St., Gold Hill. *Gourmet* magazine wrote in 2004 that the Gold Hill Inn "must be one of the best restaurant values in America." That in itself should be enough to inspire diners, but add to that live music and a richly historic setting, and this restaurant is a must if you are in the mountains outside Boulder. The dining hall was built in 1924 to match the neighboring 19th-century log hotel, so the feel is rustic and elegant. Dishes include such highfalutin fare as roast lamb venison and coquilles Saint-Jaques. The atmosphere, however, is warm and inviting. A six-course meal is $31.

EATING OUT ♿ **The Buff** (303-442-9150; www.buffrestaurant.com), 1725 28th St. Open for breakfast and lunch Mon.–Fri. 6:30–2 and Sat. and Sun. 7–2. The Buff is a great place for breakfast. They have the usual bacon and eggs, but also offer interesting diversions like salmon and eggs or banana bread French toast. You can even get a breakfast panini. Dishes around $8.

Burnt Toast Restaurant (303-440-5200; www.burnttoastrestaurant.com), 1235 Pennsylvania Ave. Breakfast and lunch Mon.–Fri. 7–3; dinner, Tues.–Sat. 6–9 and Sat. and Sun. brunch 9–3. The Burnt Toast is located just off Broadway, east of campus on the Hill. The food is pretty good, but the service has a reputation for being a bit slow. But people don't come here for snappy service, they come to take it easy and relax. Students often study here during the school year. Breakfast dishes, like omelets and *huevos rancheros,* are around $8. Brunch around $9 and dinner $10–16.50.

♿ **Café Gondolier** (303-443-5015; www.cafegondolier.com), 1738 Pearl St. Open Mon 11:30–9, Tues.–Fri. 11:30–10, Sat. 4:30–10, and Sun. 4:30–9. The oldest family-owned restaurant in Boulder, Café Gondolier has been serving fine home-style Italian since 1960. Hand-cut pasta, fresh-made sauces, and a fantastic thin-crust pizza have kept them thriving for over 45 years. Patrons rave about the food and the service. Tuesday and Wed. are "all-you-can-eat spaghetti" nights. Be sure to check out the 100-year-old espresso machine in the main dining room. Recently retired, it had been serving espresso in Boulder since the late 1940s. Dinner entrées run $12–20.

Jalino's Pizza (303-443-6300; www.jalinospizza.com), 1647 Arapahoe Ave. Open Sun.–Thurs. 10:30–12 and Fri. and Sat. 10:30–2 AM. Like a lot of things in life, people either love or hate the pizza at Jalino's. Those who love it, however, praise the quality of ingredients, the delicious sauce, and the variety of toppings, like artichoke hearts and chorizo. They also go on about the pasta and desserts. There is no dining room. Call ahead for carry-out and delivery. Pizzas $11–28.

♿ **Mustard's Last Stand** (303-444-5841), 1719 Broadway St. Open Mon.–Fri. 10:30–9 and Sat. and Sun. 11–9. Every university town worthy of the name has at least one great hot dog joint. Boulder is no exception. Mustard's Last Stand, across from the amphitheater, is just such a place. In addition to Chicago-style hot dogs, they serve a nice charred burger. And you certainly will appreciate their hand-made fries. With a row of stools facing the street, it's also a great place to people watch. Hot dogs and hamburgers with fries go for around $6.

🍸 ♿ **The Sink** (303-444-7465; www.thesink.com), 1165 13th St. The restaurant is open 11–10, and the bar 11 AM–2 AM. The Sink has been around in one form or another since 1923. It began as a European-style restaurant, served as a bar for a time, and even became sort of an artist showroom with their off-the-wall gallery. In 1955 they secured permanent status as a top-notch burger joint with the creation of the Sink Burger, and since have solidified their place in the hearts of Boulderites with their pizzas and their famous Buddah Basil Pie. Burgers around $8 and pizzas $15–28.

Y ♿ **Wild Mountain Smokehouse & Brewery** (303-258-9453; www.wildmountainsb.com), 70 E. First St., Nederland. Up Boulder Canyon to Nederland, there is a new spot for good eats. The Wild Mountain Smokehouse & Brewery serves up a full menu of pulled pork, prime rib, ribs, and game sausage. The brewery cranks out several different beers, like Mountain Siren Cherry Wheat and Otis Pale Ale. All go great with an appetizer like the large soft pretzel served with whole-grain beer mustard. Dinner entrées $13–20 and sandwiches around $8.

BAKERIES & COFFEE SHOPS ♿

Breadworks (303-444-5667; www.breadworks.net), 2644 N. Broadway. Open Mon.–Sat. 7–7 and Sun. 7–6. For many locals, this is the best spot in town for great artisan breads.

Laughing Goat Coffeehouse (303-440-4628; www.thelaughinggoat.com), 1709 Pearl St. Open daily 7–11. The folks at the Laughing Goat serve up a great cup of coffee. They also keep the grand coffeehouse tradition alive with weekly open poetry readings and live music. See their Web site for a schedule of events.

Moe's Broadway Bagel (303-444-3252; www.moesbagel.com), 2650 Broadway. Open daily 7– 4. The ambience at Moe's is true to Boulder—from bright colors inside to "flower power" bumper stickers—but the bagels are all New York. It's the bagels, cooked fresh every morning, that bring in the regulars.

BARS, TAVERNS & BREW PUBS Y ♿

Dark Horse Bar (303-442-8162; www.darkhorsebar.com), 2922 Baseline Rd. Open daily 11–2. The Dark Horse has been serving Boulder's drinking public since 1975. Locals like to gather on game day and watch the Buffs with friends. On different nights the bar has dancing, karaoke, DJs, and live music.

Y ♿ **Tom's Tavern** (303-443-3893), 1047 Pearl St. Open Mon.–Thurs. 10–10, Fri. and Sat. 10–11, and Sun. 11–8:30. Just west of the Pearl Street Mall, Tom's has been serving Boulderites burgers and beer since the 1960s. CU alumni have plenty of fond memories grabbing a bite at Tom's, and it's just that kind of place. In many ways it feels like a 1960s diner, but the number of microbrews they have on hand keeps the tavern idea front and center.

✷ Entertainment

♿ **Boulder's Dinner Theatre** (303-449-6000; www.theatreinboulder.com), 5501 Arapahoe Ave, at the corner of 55th St. and Arapahoe. Dinner begins Tues. and Wed. at 5:30 and Thurs.–Sat. at 6:15. The Sun. matinee starts at 12:15, dinner at 6:15. The show starts 90 minutes after seating for dinner. Since 1977, the good folks at Boulder's Dinner Theatre have been mixing fine dining and Broadway-style entertainment. In the true dinner theater tradition, the performers are also the wait staff. Tickets $34–53, which includes meal.

♿ **Boulder Chamber Orchestra** (1-888-397-6952; www.boulderchamberorchestra.org), 4641 10th St. One of the things that defines Boulder is an intense appreciation for the arts. This has been illustrated by the quick success of the Boulder Chamber Orchestra, which has only been in existence since 2004. Season runs Oct.–Apr. All concerts are held at First Baptist Church, 1237 Pine St., in Boulder. See Web site for schedule of performances.

Boulder Philharmonic Orchestra (303-449-1343; www.boulderphil.org), 2995 Wilderness Pl. In the summer they perform a series of outdoor concerts that are free to the public.

Chautauqua Auditorium (303-442-3282; www.chautauqua.com), 900 Baseline Rd. Several years ago, we saw one of our favorite performers at Chautauqua. This is a fantastic venue. The inside has a rustic homey feel. During the day, you can see sunlight peaking between the boards that make up the auditorium walls. Musicians and fans alike have commented on the building's acoustics—because of its wooden construction, there are few places where music carries so well. Though it can seat more than 500 people, there's not a bad seat in the place. This, of course, makes it the perfect location for the Colorado Music Festival (see Special Events). Check out the Web site to find a current schedule of performances.

e-town Radio Show (303-443-8696; www.etown.org). Music fans across the country listen to e-town every week on National Public Radio. Hosted by Nick and Helen Forster, the show features musical guests from across the musical spectrum—they are always great. Usually recorded locally at the Boulder Theater (303-786-7030; www.bouldertheater.com), 2032 14th St., be sure to check the schedule as they sometimes take the show on the road.

✷ Selective Shopping

The Hill (www.thehillboulder.com), located just west of the CU Boulder campus, the Hill business district is centered along 13th Street south of Broadway. The Hill claims to be a virtual extension of the CU campus, and it is. Surrounded by sorority and fraternity houses and off-campus housing, the Hill is right in the thick of student life. Plenty of shopping and restaurants, but parking can be tough.

Pearl Street Mall and Downtown Boulder (303-449-3774; www.boulderdowntown.com). Downtown Boulder has numerous shops, art galleries, and restaurants. The centerpiece of the city is the Pearl Street Mall. Several blocks of Pearl Street were closed to cars and laid with brick for foot traffic. On any given afternoon or evening a stroll down this tree-lined street will reveal couples walking hand in hand, families window shopping, and the sound of buskers playing on the corners.

Boulder Arts & Crafts Cooperative (1-866-656-2667; www.boulderartsandcrafts.com), 1421 Pearl St. In 1976 a group of artists rented space to display and sell their work on the recently constructed Pearl Street Mall. Today, 42 local artists own and operate this co-op, and an even greater number of artists sell their wares here.

Boulder Book Store & Café (303-447-2074; www.boulderbookstore.com), 1107 Pearl St. Open Mon.–Fri. 10–10, Sat. 9–10, and Sun. 10–8. This four-story bookstore on Pearl Street is a bit of a surprise. It honestly doesn't look all that big from the outside. But 20,000 square feet of retail space offers a lot of selection. Next door, and connected to the bookstore, is the café—itself a great place to read with a nice cup of coffee.

Boulder Map Gallery (303-444-1406; www.bouldermapgallery.com), 1708 13th St. This place has maps, lots of them—everything from wall maps and posters to globes and reproduction antique maps. Especially of interest to people traveling around Colorado, they have trail maps from all over the state.

Hangouts (303-442-2533; www.hangouts.com), 1328 Pearl St. It seems almost a cliché, but only in Boulder are you going to find an entire store dedicated to hammocks. Right on the Pearl Street Mall, Hangouts specializes in Mayan and Brazilian design hammocks.

BREDO MORSTØL

Up in the mountains in Nederland, there's a frozen dead guy in a Tuff Shed. His name is Bredo Morstøl. When Morstøl died in 1989, his grandson, Trygve Bauge, had him cryogenically frozen in the hope that someday medical science will be advanced enough to reanimate his body and fix whatever it was that caused him to have his fatal heart attack in the first place.

In 1993, Bauge brought his grandfather to Nederland where he stored the body in a shack behind the house of his mother, Aud (Morstøl's daughter). No one knew there was a frozen dead guy up there, but then Bauge was deported back to Norway for overstaying his visa. Then Aud was evicted from her unfinished home because it's illegal to live in a house without electricity or water. Suddenly there was a crisis—who would keep Morstøl from thawing out? Aud, who has since been deported herself, let the authorities know about the body and suddenly it was the town's problem.

After passing some laws to make it illegal to store a frozen body in your backyard, the town still had to decide what to do about Morstøl, who was grandfathered in under the new ordinance (no pun intended). Over time, volunteers stepped up and began helping out. Tuff Shed donated a new shelter for the old man, replacing the deteriorating shack that had been his home for some years. Others gave, and continue to give, their time, regularly loading the shed with dry ice.

In 2002, Nederland decided to celebrate their most distinguished citizen, and the idea of **Frozen Dead Guy Days** (www.nederlandchamber.org/FrozenDeadGuyDays) was born. A bit irreverent, the festival is quite a party and worth the trip.

Into the Wind (303-449-5356; www.intothewind.com), 1408 Pearl St. Open Mon.–Fri. 9–6. Into the Wind sells more than just kites; there are all sorts of wind-up toys and novelties here. That said, the store is one of the biggest mail-order kite sellers in the country—if you have any kite questions, this is the place to go.

Mountain Furniture Arts (303-443-2030), 4 E. First St., Nederland. Open Mon.–Sat. 10–6 and Sun. noon–5. Lew Collins at Mountain Furniture Arts makes some of the finest furniture on the Front Range. His showroom is right downtown in Nederland. The pieces in his showroom represent several styles—Mission, Shaker, and many have a Southwest feel. He also does a lot of custom work if you like what you see, but don't see what you like.

* Special Events

May: **BolderBOULDER** (303-444-7223; www.bolderboulder.com), 4571 Broadway St. As 10K races go, this is a big one. In 2007, nearly 50,000 runners joined the fray, making it the third largest road race in the U.S. and fifth in the world. In fact, when the runners gather at Folsom Stadium for a tribute to veterans at the end of the race, it's the largest Memorial Day gathering in the country.

May: **Kinetic Conveyance Race** (303-444-5600; www.kbcoradio.com). Every year out at Boulder Reservoir, a crowd gathers to watch a collection of goofy human-powered vehicles race across mud, land, and water. Competitors let their creativity go wild in building their various conveyances—and it's a kick to watch all that crazy hard work sink like a rock when it hits the water.

June–August: **Colorado Music Festival** (303-449-1397; www.coloradomusicfest.org), 900 Baseline Rd., Cottage 100. The six-week music festival features regular concerts at Chautauqua Auditorium. The performances showcase everything from children's choirs to klezmer quartets to chamber orchestras.

June–August: **Colorado Shakespeare Festival** (303-492-0554; www.coloradoshakes.org), 277 University of Colorado in Boulder. For 50 years, Boulder has been keeping the work of Shakespeare alive with this fantastic festival. Forty-five minutes before each show, there's a prologue where a member of the CSF company comes out and tells the audience a little about the play they are about to see. For outdoor performances, you can bring a picnic or purchase a gourmet picnic supper from Falstaff's Fare.

FORT COLLINS

In 2006, *Money* magazine listed Fort Collins as the number one place to live in the United States. A great job market, lots of outdoor activities, plenty of culture, and that fresh mountain air all set Fort Collins apart. At its heart, Fort Collins is a college town, the home of Colorado State University. The university goes back to 1879, when it was called the Colorado Agricultural & Mining College (the name changed in 1957). The university remains the largest employer in Fort Collins.

The town goes back to the 19th century as well. In 1862, the 9th Kansas Volunteer Cavalry built a post along the Cache la Poudre (pronounced *poo-der*) River called Camp Collins in the present-day town of Laporte. They were there to protect the nearby Cherokee Trail and the Overland Stage Line. In 1864, a terrific flood swept away the entire encampment. No lives were lost, but the troops were faced with finding another place to rebuild. A couple months later, Fort Collins was established along the river, in the area of today's Willow St. The military left the fort in 1866, but farmers and ranchers who had settled nearby remained. Since 1860, farmers had been pulling water out of the Cache la Poudre via a growing system of irrigation ditches. In 1877, the railroad came to Fort Collins, in a way assuring the town's future.

The original town streets ran parallel to the river. The new part of town is aligned with the points of the compass. A good part of the old town has been preserved as a historic district, and Old Town Square at the corner of College and Mountain avenues is booming. Restaurants and shops, not to mention a thriving art community, continue to bring vitality to the local economy. Annual festivals and events bring in over a half million people to the city each year. Fort Collins also enjoys a temperate climate, perfect for enjoying nearby Horsetooth Mountain and Reservoir or any of the town's 40 parks and 23 miles of trails for biking and walking.

GUIDANCE **Fort Collins Convention & Visitors Bureau** (970-232-3840 or 1-800-274-3678; www.ftcollins.com), 19 Old Town Square, Suite 137. Open Mon.–Fri. 8:30–5. The Visitors Information Center is located right in Old Town Square—you can't miss it.

Colorado Welcome Center at Fort Collins (970-491-3583), 3745 E. Prospect Rd. (exit 268 off I-25). Open daily in the summer 8–6. In addition to the plethora of brochures, maps, and visitor guides, the Welcome Center in Fort Collins

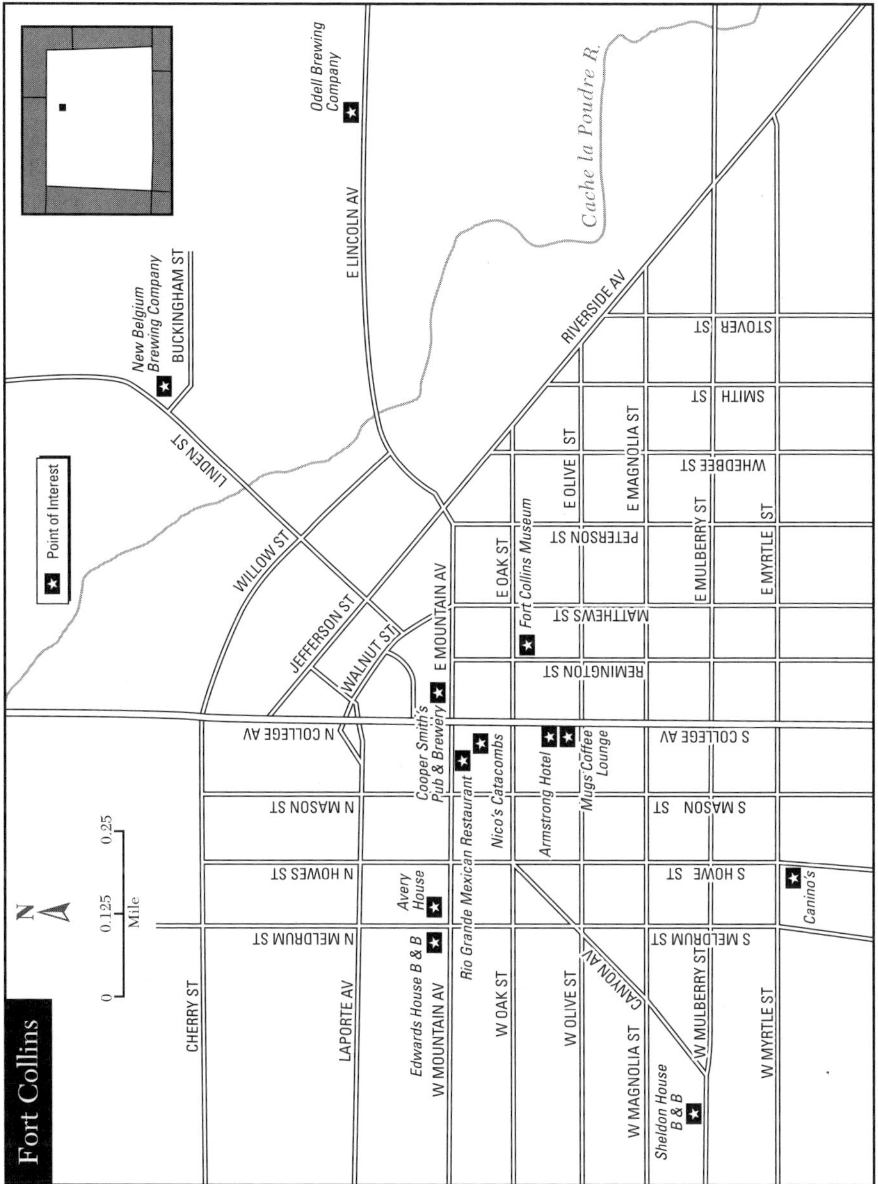

is home to the Rocky Mountain Nature Association bookstore. There's also a couple hundred acres of nature preserve around the center, complete with trails.

More Web sites:

www.fcgov.com

www.downtownfortcollins.com

www.artsalivefc.org (to keep up with the Fort Collins art scene)

GETTING THERE *By car:* Fort Collins is 60 miles north of Denver on I-25. It's the last big town before Wyoming.

By air: The **Denver International Airport** (303-342-2000 or 1-800-AIR2DEN; www.flydenver.com) is about an hour drive from Fort Collins.

By train: **AMTRAK** (1-800-872-7245; www.amtrak.com) does not have direct service to Fort Collins, but does operate their Throughway bus service, which stops at the Greyhound Station at 250 N. Mason St.

By bus: **Greyhound** operates regular service to and from Fort Collins from the **Fort Collins Greyhound Station** (970-221-1327 or 1-800-231-2222; www.greyhound.com), 250 N. Mason St.

GETTING AROUND *By car:* The town is fairly car friendly with plenty of on-street parking as well as a parking structure a couple blocks west of the Old Town Square off Mountain Avenue.

By bus: The city operates a bus system, **Transfort** (970-221-6620; www.ci.fort-collins.co.us/transfort), which offers numerous routes connecting the whole town.

MEDICAL EMERGENCIES **Harmony Urgent Care Center** (970-495-7000 or 970-297-6250; www.pvhs.org), 2127 E. Harmony Rd. #140. Open daily 9–9, the center is set up to handle minor emergencies—sprains, minor fractures, strep throat, flu, etc.

Poudre Valley Hospital (970-495-7000 or 1-800-252-5784; www.pvhs.org), 1024 S. Lemay Ave. The hospital offers 24-hour emergency care.

✷ To See & Do

BREWERIES ☂ ♿ **Anheuser-Busch Brewery** (970-490-4691; www.budweisertours.com), 2351 Busch Dr. Tours given Oct.–May Thurs.–Mon. 10–4; June–Aug. daily 9:30–4:30; and Sept. daily 10–4. This is the big daddy of breweries in Fort Collins. No microbrew here—it's all macrobrew. To see the famous Budweiser Clydesdales, come on the first Saturday of every month for Clydesdale Camera Day.

☂ ♿ **Fort Collins Brewery** (970-472-1499; www.fortcollinsbrewery.com), 1900 E. Lincoln Ave., B. Tasting room open Mon.–Sat. noon–6. Tasting until 5:30, pints until 5:45, and beer to go until 6. Though they don't have official tours, there's often a brewer happy to talk about the process, and you can see most of the operation through windows in the hallway.

☂ ♿ **New Belgium Brewing Company, Inc.** (970-221-0524 or 1-888-622-4044; www.newbelgium.com), 500 Linden St. Guided tours Mon.–Fri. 1–4 and Sat. 11–4. Closed at 3 on every third Wed. of the month. Self-guided tours can be had whenever the brewery is open. New Belgium is the brewer of Fat Tire, a beer known and loved by mountain bikers and beer drinkers the world over. It is also the greenest brewery in Fort Collins. In 1998, the employees at New Belgium agreed to use money from their bonus pool to convert the brewery to wind power, ending the operation's reliance on the local power plant (a big source of CO_2 emissions). The plant reuses water and is outfitted with many green innovations to cut waste and maximize resources.

Odell Brewing Company (970-498-9070; www.odellbrewing.com), 800 E. Lincoln Ave. Tasting room open Mon.–Sat. 11–6. Tours Mon.–Sat. at 1, 2, and 3. When Doug Odell started brewing commercially in 1989, the Odell Brewing Company was only the second microbrewery in Colorado. The company started with 90 Schilling, a fantastically light Scottish ale. The beers on tap in the tasting room change from week to week. There is live music on Wed. evenings.

OTHER ATTRACTIONS **Avery House** (970-221-0533; www.poudrelandmarks.com), 328 W. Mountain Ave. Open for tours Sun. and Wed. 1–3. As one of the town's early residents, Franklin Avery wore many hats. He surveyed Fort Collins in 1873, founded the First National Bank, and worked to develop water projects that benefited area farmers. His house, built in 1879 out of local sandstone, still stands at the corner of Mountain Avenue and Meldrum Street.

Farm at Lee Martinez Park (970-221-6665), 600 N. Sherwood St. There is a lot for kids to enjoy at the Farm—including plenty of animals, from turkeys and geese to horses and goats. There are pony rides and hayrides and opportunities to feed the animals. Picnic spots and playgrounds make this a nice place to bring lunch. And if it rains, there's always the farming museum and Silo Store. Admission $4.

Fort Collins Museum (970-221-6738; www.fcgov.com/museum), 200 Mathews St. Open Tues.–Sat. 10–5 and Sun. noon–5. Since 1941, the museum has been educating the public on the history of Fort Collins and the Cache la Poudre River valley from prehistoric times to the present. There is an extensive

HISTORIC AVERY HOUSE

collection of artifacts, including a courtyard and four historic buildings from the 19th century. Admission is a suggested donation of $2.

☂ ♿ **Fort Collins Museum of Contemporary Art** (970-482-2787; www.fcmoca.org), 201 S. College Ave. Open Tues.–Fri. 10–6 and Sat. noon–5. The museum, which resides in the old Fort Collins Post Office, began in 1990 as the Once West Contemporary Art Center. The museum presents new works in an ever-changing series of exhibitions. Adult admission $2, seniors and students free.

✐ ♿ **Swetsville Zoo** (970-484-9509), 4801 E. Harmony Rd. Open daily, dawn to dusk. What started as one man's hobby, fabricating unique animals and such out of metal, has become a full-fledged attraction. In the beginning, Bill Swet would make something and put it out in the yard. People driving by would stop to see his newest creation. Now they go out of their way to tour his sculpture garden, with more than 150 whimsical creatures. Admission free, donations appreciated.

✷ Outdoor Activities

FISHING The Cache la Poudre River offers some nice holes for fishing, as do the North Platte and Laramie rivers. Horsetooth Reservoir has several boat ramps and is regularly stocked with fish.

St. Peter's Fly Shop (970-498-8968; www.stpetes.com), 202 Remington St. St. Pete's has a great reputation with anglers. Everyone who works at the shop is intimately knowledgeable about the nuances of fly-fishing in northern Colorado and southern Wyoming. They lead guided fly-fishing trips and offer instruction for beginners.

GOLF **Collindale Golf Course** (970-221-6651; www.fcgov.com/golf/collindale.php), 1441 E. Horsetooth Rd. Collindale is a municipal course close to town. There is a new clubhouse with a full-service grill. Greens fees $26–29 for 18 holes.

SWETSVILLE ZOO

HIKING & BIKING **Horsetooth Mountain Park** (970-679-4570; www.larimer.org/parks/htmp.htm) has 29 miles of trails for hiking and biking. Parking and the trailhead are 6.5 miles west of Taft Hill Road on Harmony (aka CO 38E). The hike to Horsetooth Falls is an easy 2.5-mile round-trip that takes you into the foothills. Mountain bikers might enjoy a lengthier ride—there's a nice 5-mile loop that follows Soderberg Trail up and around via Wathen Trail. See the Web site for an excellent trail map.

Lory State Park (970-493-1623; www.parks.state.co.us/parks/lory) 708 Lodgepole Dr., Bellvue. Parking at the Timber Group Picnic Area, mountain bikers can start at the Timber Trail trailhead and take the trail up to the ridge just beneath Arthur Rock. The trail is moderately difficult and makes for a nice 7-mile trip. Hikers might enjoy the 3.4-mile round-trip up to Arthur Rock, with its fantastic views of the Front Range. Start at the southernmost parking area, and follow the Arthur Rock Trail to the top. It's not an easy trail, but the view is worth the huffing and puffing. Lory State Park also has an impressive Mountain Bike Park with all sorts of tracks and jumps.

Devil's Backbone Open Space. Larimer County maintains a number of parks and open spaces. The Devil's Backbone Open Space, 3 miles west of Lake Loveland on CO 34 in Loveland, has some distinct features—most notable is the sharp spine of rocks that juts up for about a mile to the northwest. There are a number of trails at the site. More adventurous hikers and mountain bikers can connect up with the Blue Sky Trail. It's a 9.6-mile hike from Devil's Backbone to the Soderberg trailhead, which is in Horsetooth Mountain Park; it's the trail following the Inlet Bay of Horsetooth Reservoir. You will climb nearly 500 feet on the Blue Sky Trail, so know your limitations.

Recycled Cycles (970-223-1969; www.recycled-cycles.com), 4031 S. Mason St. If you need to rent a bike while you are in town, this shop sells and rents used bikes at affordable rates—they usually have everything from mountain bikes to cruisers. Day rental about $25.

PADDLING The Cache la Poudre River that runs through Fort Collins is known for its white-water. A few outfitters in town offer guided rafting trips.

A-1 Wildwater Rafting (970-224-3379 or 1-800-369-4165; www.a1wildwater.com), 2801 N. Shields St. A-1 takes people rafting down the Poudre River. Depending on the section of river the company is riding, you can see class II to IV rapids. For some fun on the water on your own, they also rent kayaks and duckies.

Mountain Whitewater Descents (970-419-0917 or 1-888-855-8874; www.mountainwhitewaterdescents.com), 13289 N. CO 287. The guides here will take you down the Poudre River on full or half-day trips. Paddlers can encounter rapids from class II to IV.

GREEN SPACE **Boyd Lake State Park** (970-669-1739; www.parks.state.co.us/parks/boydlake), 3720 N. CR 11-C, Loveland. Open daily 5–10. This is a busy park down in Loveland, with plenty of swimming, boating, and other water sports. The park sponsors a series of outdoor concerts every summer. Daily pass $6.

Colorado State Forest State Park (970-723-8366; www.parks.state.co.us/parks/stateforest), 56750 CO 14, Walden. So far west of Fort Collins on CO 14, the Colorado State Forest State Park might rightly belong in the Northwest Colorado section of this book. But the access from Fort Collins is the easiest route even though it is 76 miles away. The state forest has 71,000 acres of rugged mountain wilderness. It's a prime destination for backcountry hikers and skiers. The park maintains nine yurts and huts and six cabins. These shelters can accommodate larger groups, some up to eight people. Two cabins hold 15 and 21 lodgers. The yurts are managed by the **Never Summer Nordic Yurt System** (970-723-4070; www.neversummernordic.com), 247 CR 41, Walden.

In addition to numerous trails and roads, the park keeps things lively with geocaching. Eight geocaches have been set up around the park for participants to find with their GPS devices (available for rent at the Moose Visitor Center). The visitor center, which is an excellent introduction to the park, is also a place you might see moose. It is located near Gould on CO 14. Daily park pass $5.

Horsetooth Reservoir (970-679-4570; www.larimer.org/parks/horsetooth.htm), located due west of Fort Collins. Both CO 42C and CO 38E head up to the reservoir. Centennial Drive runs along the east shore of the reservoir. This 1,900-acre lake is bordered by 2,000 acres of public land. There is swimming, boating, camping, hiking, biking, and rock climbing throughout the area. Daily auto pass $6 (except in the summer when it's $7 on Fri., Sat., Sun., and holidays). Same for boat passes.

HORSETOOTH RESERVOIR

Lory State Park (970-493-1623; www.parks.state.co.us/parks/lory), 708 Lodgepole Dr., Bellvue. Open daily 6–10. Mountain bike trails, dirt bike jumps, and the Corral Center Mountain Bike Park make Lory a great excursion for mountain bikers. Boaters can access Horsetooth Reservoir, which borders the park on the east. (See Outdoor Activities, Hiking & Biking.) Daily pass $6/car or $3/individual.

✷ Lodging

HOTELS **Armstrong Hotel** (970-484-3883; www.thearmstronghotel.com), 259 S. College Ave. Built in 1923, this hip hotel is located a few blocks from Old Town Square, right in the heart of things. The 37 rooms have been decorated in a mix of vintage and modern styles. Rooms $89–130.

BED & BREAKFASTS **Edwards House Bed & Breakfast** (970-493-9191 or 1-800-281-9190; www.edwardshouse.com), 402 W. Mountain Ave. This B&B was built in 1904 and is decorated throughout with antique furnishings. The full breakfast includes a selection of fresh fruit and baked goods. The eight rooms are all quite spacious and comfortable. Rooms $99–170.

Sheldon House Bed & Breakfast (970-221-1917 or 1-877-221-1918; www.thesheldonhouse.com), 616 West Mulberry St. Jack and Maryann Blackerby at the Sheldon House are wonderful hosts who will make you feel right at home. The house, built around the turn of the century, was moved to its present location in the 1950s. They provide an excellent breakfast daily. There are four rooms, each with a private bath. Rooms $90–125.

CAMPGROUNDS **Fort Collins Lakeside KOA** (970-484-9880 or 1-800-562-9168; www.fclakesidecg.com), 1910 N. Taft Hill Rd. The campground has a swimming pool for summer use, sauna and hot tub, and a beautiful gazebo overlooking the lake. Not a lot of trees, but the campground is clean and orderly. Tent sites $30, RVs $37–50, and Kamping Kabins $10–110.

Fort Collins Poudre Canyon KOA (970-493-9758 or 1-800-562-2648; www.koa.com/where/co/06114), 6670 N. US 287. The Poudre Canyon KOA has a swimming pool for use in the summer, cabins for rent, and an outside covered kitchen area for campers. The campground has some trees for shade. Rates $27–95 (tent sites on the low end, Kamping Lodge on the high).

Riverview RV Park and Campground (970-667-9910 or 1-800-447-9910 for reservations; www.riverviewrv.com), 7806 W. US 34, Loveland. Located alongside the Big Thompson River west of Loveland, the campground has plenty of sites, many next to the river, for RVs (pull-through and back-in) as well as tent sites. They also maintain several cabins that sleep four (double bed and a bunk bed)—remember to bring your own bedding. RV and tent sites $16–33. Rates depend on hook-ups, on the river or off-river, number of people and vehicles in your party, etc. Cabins are $37.

RANCHES **Sylvan Dale Guest Ranch** (1-877-667-3999; www.sylvan

dale.com), 2939 N. CR 31D, Loveland. The Sylvan Dale Guest Ranch is west of Loveland, just north of US 34, along the banks of the Big Thompson. During the summer, the ranch offers six-night vacation packages—giving guests a chance to get the whole dude ranch experience. Activities include horseback riding, white-water rafting, fishing, overnight pack trips to cow camp, and a ranch party. Throughout the rest of the year, the ranch is available for folks looking for more of a B&B experience. Adult six-day rate $1,475–1,835. Bed & breakfast room rates $72–295.

✷ Where to Eat

DINING OUT ♿ **Canino's** (970-493-7205; www.caninositalianrestaurant.com), 613 S. College Ave. In 1976, Clyde Canino opened his Italian restaurant in Fort Collins. The onetime residence that houses the restaurant is a historic landmark, built in 1903, and contributes to the cozy atmosphere. For Italian in Fort Collins, there are few places better. Dinner entrées and pizza $10–20.

Nico's Catacombs (970-484-6029; www.nicoscatacombs.com), 115 S. College Ave. Open for dinner Mon.–Thurs. 5–9:30 and Fri. and Sat. 5–10. At the top of almost every list of where to eat in Fort Collins, you will find Nico's Catacombs. A flight of stairs from College Avenue leads down to the restaurant, with its cozy subterranean charm. Nico's has been serving Continental cuisine since 1979, and the wine list is extensive. Entrées $25–35.

EATING OUT ♿ **Austin's American Grille** (970-224-9691; www.austinsamericangrill.com), 100 W. Mountain Ave. Open Sun.–Thurs. 11–9 and Fri. and Sat. 11–10 (open an hour later all week in the summer). Located right at the corner of Mountain and College, Austin's is in the thick of things. The menu is good old American fare with appetizers like coconut shrimp and iron skillet cornbread and dinner entrées like St. Louis ribs and buffalo meatloaf. People get excited about the ribs. Entrées $12–20.

♿ **Cafe Bluebird** (970-484-7755; www.cafebluebird.com), 524 W. Laurel St. This is one of the best places for breakfast in Fort Collins. It may seem your typical restaurant, but the menu is full of unique twists on traditional dishes. You can play it safe with a couple of eggs and grilled homemade wheat toast, or try something different like their Corgie Street Benedict (poached eggs with grilled smoke salmon, tomatoes, and fresh spinach). The restaurant also serves lunch. Breakfast and lunch dishes $7–8.

♿ **Enzio's** (970-484-8466; www.enzios.com), 126 W. Mountain Ave. Among the throng of Italian eateries in Fort Collins, Enzio's stands out for having some of the best food. It's also one of the more affordable. They're just a block west of the Old Town Square. Dinner entrées $10–20.

♿ **Rio Grande Mexican Restaurant** (970-224-5428; www.riograndemexican.com), 143 W. Mountain Ave. Open Sun.–Wed. 11–10 and Thurs.–Sat. 11–10:30. For summer dining, the Rio Grande has a shaded patio and a pleasant fountain. The menu is Tex-Mex, and diners will go on and on about the fresh chips and salsa, the green chili, and the Rio's famous margaritas. Dinner entrées $10–15.

♿ **Silver Grill Cafe** (970-484-4656; www.silvergrill.com), 218 Walnut St.

Open for breakfast and lunch daily 6:30–2. The Silver Grill Cafe has been serving breakfast and lunch since 1933. The cafe has an extensive espresso menu. Always save room for one of their giant cinnamon rolls. Breakfast and lunch dishes $7–8.

♿ **Suehiro Japanese Restaurant** (970-482-3734), 223 Linden St. Open for lunch Mon.–Fri. 11:30–2 and dinner Mon.–Sat. 5–9. Suehiro has been voted the best sushi in Fort Collins. Carry-out is available. Be sure to make reservations during the school year because the place packs out with college students. Entrées $8–12.

BAKERIES & COFFEE SHOPS "1" ♿ **Mugs Coffee Lounge** (970-472-6847; www.mugscoffeelounge.com), 261 S. College Ave. Open daily 6 AM–1 AM. Coffee, tea, and "blendies" are the key to the menu at Mugs. They also have a huge food menu, including breakfast and lunch eats. The pizza-on-a-pita is pretty good.

BARS, TAVERNS & BREW PUBS ♿ **CooperSmith's Pub & Brewery** (970-498-0483; www.coopersmithpub.com), 5 Old Town Square. This place is hopping all weekend long. They brew all the beer served right on the premises. They have nearly 20 brews on tap, including hard cider and a raspberry mead. They have different menus for the pub and the billiard room. Both serve CooperSmith's wood-fired stove pizzas. The pub side has excellent pub grub—bangers and mash and an interesting take on shepherd's pie called Highland Cottage Pie. Sandwiches $8 and dinner entrées $20.

♿ **Sundance Steakhouse & Saloon** (970-484-1600; www.sundancesteakhouse.com), 2716 E. Mulberry St. The Sundance Saloon could be listed under Entertainment—it may be the most popular place in northern Colorado to hear, and dance to, country music. On Wednesday, there are dance lessons earlier in the evening. Instructors teach line dancing and couples dancing (only $5/person if you take both lessons). Live music is a regular feature of Sundance. The steakhouse serves up a nice steak as well as burgers and such. Dishes $8–25.

* Entertainment

♿ **Avogadro's Number** (970-493-5555; www.avogadros.com), 605 S. Mason St. Open Mon.–Thurs. 7–10, Fri. 7–11, and Sat.–Sun. 8–10. Though named after a "constant" only chemists would readily recognize, Avogadro's Number is all about music. Local bands play here regularly, as do some big names in folk, jazz, and bluegrass. They also serve a rather ordinary menu for breakfast, lunch, and dinner—standouts would be the tempeh burgers and falafel.

Mishawaka Amphitheatre (970-482-4420; www.mishawakaconcerts.com), 13714 Poudre Canyon Hwy., Bellvue. The Mish has a regular schedule of live outdoor performances throughout the summer. The remainder of the year, concerts are held inside with a smaller audience. The Kitchen at Mishawaka has indoor and outdoor seating, and a fine menu to make your evening more of a "dinner and a show" kind of event. Sandwiches and such run $6–10. Parking is tight, so the theater prefers that you buy tickets in advance instead of at the box office, as the latter just makes things more congested.

✱ Selective Shopping

Old Town Square (www.downtown fortcollins.com) is the restored shopping district in the heart of old Fort Collins. It's located at the northeast corner of Mountain and College avenues. There are plenty of restaurants and art galleries and other shops for a pleasant afternoon of shopping. The Web site lists all the festivals and events planned for the area.

First Friday Gallery Walk (970-482-2232; www.artsalivefc.org), downtown Fort Collins. The first Fri. of the month, from 6–9 in the evening, the downtown art galleries stay open later for a gallery walk. Refreshments are served at the galleries as you take a self-guided tour to see their new exhibits. Maps available at almost all the galleries in town and the visitors center in Old Town Square.

Illustrated Light (970-493-4673; www.illustratedlight.com), #1 Old Town Square, Ste. 103. Open daily 11–9. This gallery specializes in photographic arts. Contemporary as well as vintage photographs are on display, and the images are simply stunning.

Trimble Court Artisans (970-221-0051; www.trimblecourt.com), 118 Trimble Ct. This artist co-op features all local artists, with a great selection of pottery, watercolors, etc. All the artists take turns watching the store, so you will find them very knowledgeable and passionate about the art on display.

✱ Special Events

June: **Colorado Brewer's Festival** (970-484-6500; www.downtownfort collins.com), downtown Fort Collins. In a town that celebrates beer, this annual festival is a big event. Beer sampling and live music are the main attractions. Participating breweries are all from Colorado.

June/July: **Greeley Stampede** (970-356-2855 or 1-800-982-2855; www .greeleystampede.org). Touted as "the world's largest Fourth of July rodeo and western celebration," the Stampede is one of Colorado's biggest annual events. Located just east of Loveland in Greeley, home of the University of Northern Colorado, the event runs over the weekends leading up to July 4, and brings some of country music's biggest names for a series of concerts.

August: **Bohemian Nights at NewWestFest** (970-484-6500; www .newwestfest.com and www.bohemian -nights.org), downtown Fort Collins. This annual festival brings more than 50 musical acts to Fort Collins to perform on five stages over three days. Recent headliners included Los Lobos and Bruce Hornsby. Other entertainment includes belly dancing, ballet, Mexican folk dance, and other acts. For the kids, there are puppet shows and magic shows.

ESTES PARK

In some ways, Estes Park is a town with a bit of a split personality. You can spend a ritzy weekend at the Stanley, play a round of golf on a world-class course, and enjoy fine dining at a number of high-end eateries. Or you can buzz into town with a passel of kids in tow, park your RV (or rent a cabin) at the local KOA, spend your days at the tourist shops in town, and splurge on pizza for dinner. Or simply stop in town for supplies and to arrange plans with an outfitter before heading into Rocky Mountain National Park for a bare-bones backcountry camping trip. Whatever your idea of a great mountain vacation, Estes Park can fit the bill.

The beautiful Estes Valley has attracted people for centuries. Nearly 12,000 year ago, the first people to arrive on this continent used the valley as a hunting ground. Later, the Ute and Arapaho set up camp here in the summers. And from early in the 19th century, mountain men trapped on area rivers and hunted game throughout this region. They were followed by the miners who were drawn to Colorado by the discovery of gold in the Denver area. Soon the mountains were swarming with miners hoping to find an elusive gold vein of their own.

It was in 1859 that one man, Joel Estes, who had made a fortune of his own mining in California, stumbled upon the valley. So taken was he with this lush meadow, he moved there with his wife and 13 children. They brought with them a herd of cattle and stayed for six years. By the late 1860s, Estes had found cattle ranching to be impractical. The Early of Dunhaven came to buy the entire valley in order to create a hunting preserve and resort.

His plans were shot down by the valley's other residents, but the tourism potential of what was now called Estes Park had been recognized. Soon the Elkhorn Lodge was catering to guests looking for a mountain retreat. By 1909, F. O. Stanley had built the landmark Stanley Hotel, which brought big-city luxury lodging to town. And in 1915, Rocky Mountain National Park was established.

Stanley proved to be a real asset to the burgeoning tourist industry in the valley. He made the first auto road to Estes Park and operated an early shuttle service bringing guests into the mountains via the Big Thompson Canyon.

Within the past 30 years, two floods have devastated the area. In 1976, a sudden storm inundated the Big Thompson River. As a wall of water swept down the canyon toward Loveland, 145 people lost their lives. Four hundred homes were destroyed, as were many businesses. Just six years later, in 1982, there was the Lawn Lake Flood. The natural dam that held Lawn Lake in the mountains broke. Unlike the Big Thompson flood, which caused almost all its damage downriver of town, the flood of 1982 devastated downtown Estes Park.

Today Estes Park has been rebuilt, and the town is a thriving tourist destination. Seen as the gateway to Rocky Mountain National Park, there are hundreds of hotels, motels, campgrounds, cabins, lodges, and resorts catering to thousands of annual visitors.

GUIDANCE **Estes Park Visitors Center** (970-577-9900 or 1-800-443-7837; www.estesparkcvb.com), 500 Big Thompson Ave. Right near the intersection if Big Thompson and St. Vrain avenues, the visitor center can be your first stop whether you are coming from Loveland or Lyons. Helpful staff, plenty of brochures, and clean rest rooms make for a good start in town.

More Web sites:

www.estesparkresort.com

www.estes-park.com

www.estespark-colorado.com

www.estespark.us

GETTING THERE *By car:* From Loveland in the east and Grand Lake in the west, US 34 is the main route to and through town (in town it's called Big Thompson Avenue). Coming up from the south, take I-25 to exit 243 and head

ENTERING ESTES PARK

west on CO 66. In Lyons, stay to the right on US 36 and arrive in Estes Park from the south on St. Vrain Avenue.

By air: The **Denver International Airport** (303-342-2000 or 1-800-AIR2DEN; www.flydenver.com) is a 1.5-hour drive from Estes Park.

By shuttle: **Estes Park Shuttle and Mountain Tours** (970-586-5151; www.estesparktransportation.com) offers shuttle service to and from the Denver International Airport, as well as several locations in Boulder, Lyons, and Longmont.

GETTING AROUND *By car:* Downtown Estes Park is entirely walkable once you get there. There is plenty of parking behind the shops on the south side of Elkhorn Avenue. If you get to town early enough in the day to pick your spot, park east of Moraine Avenue, near the Riverside Plaza, where trees keep the lot shady.

By shuttle: The **Estes Park Shopper Shuttle** (970-577-9900) operates a free shuttle that makes stops all around the Estes Park area, even out to Rocky Mountain National Park. All routes begin at the visitor center on Big Thompson Avenue.

MEDICAL EMERGENCIES The **Estes Park Medical Center** (970-586-2317; www.epmedcenter.com), 555 Prospect Ave., offers 24-hour emergency service. If an injury requires the care of a larger facility, transportation is possible by ambulance or the Air Life Helicopter Transport service.

✷ To See & Do

Enos Mills Cabin Museum & Nature Trail (970-586-4706; www.home.earthlink.net/~enosmillscbn), 8 miles south of Estes Park on CO 7. Open all year. Summer hours Wed.–Fri. 10–3. Call ahead for hours in winter. Enos Mills is called the father of Rocky Mountain National Park for his efforts in convincing Congress to protect and preserve this section of the Rockies. At 14, Mills left his family in Kansas and came to stay in Estes Park with relatives. He was resourceful, and the museum resides in the log cabin he built in 1885, when he was 15 years old. A friend of John Muir, an avid outdoorsman, and passionate conservationist, the story of Enos Mills is woven into the history of Estes Park. The museum has many exhibits that illustrate his life and impact. Adult admission $5 and children (6–12) $2.50.

⛱ ♿ **Estes Park Museum** (970-586-6256; www.estesnet.com/museum), 200 Fourth St. Open May–Oct., Mon.–Sat. 10–5 and Sun. 1–5; Nov.–April, Fri.–Sat. 10–5 and Sun. 1–5. Located just east of town off St. Vrain, the museum tells the story of Estes Park, from the Native Americans who settled here in the summers to reap the park's rich resourced to the American settlers who created the Estes Park that exists today. Exhibits include several historic buildings and a Stanley Steamer. Free admission.

Estes Park Aerial Tramway (970-586-3675; www.estestram.com), 420 E. Riverside Dr. Open summers, daily 9–6:30. The tramway takes you right up to the top of Prospect Mountain. It has a great view of Estes Park and panaramic views of the surrounding peaks. There are some trails for hiking and a deli for lunch. Adults $9, seniors $8, children (6–11) $4, and children under 6 free.

ꝏ **Get Married.** Weddings are a big deal in Estes Park. Three to four thousand couples get married here every year. The first thing you need is a marriage license, which you can get from the **Larimer County Clerks Office** (970-577-2025), 1601 Brodie Ave., for $10. They are open Mon.–Fri. 7:30–4:30. There is no waiting period, you just need your ID, and if you've been married before, you will need to tell them who issued the divorce or death certificate. Everything else you could possibly need for the wedding—from a live band and a champagne fountain to a ring and a preacher—can be found through the businesses listed on the **Estes Park Wedding Association** Web site, www.estesparkweddings.com.

Historic Fall River Hydro Plant (970-577-7683; www.estesnet.com/hydro plant), Fish Hatchery Rd. Take US 34 northwest toward RMNP, and then turn left on Fish Hatchery Road, which dead-ends at the Hydro Plant. In the summer (Memorial Day–Labor Day), the plant is open Tue.–Sun. 1–4. Call for an appointment in the winter. This historic facility was built by F. O. Stanley to power the Stanley Hotel, making it the first fully electric hotel in the country. Free admission.

MacGregor Ranch (970-586-3749; www.macgregorranch.org), 180 MacGregor Ln. Open summers, Tues.–Fri. 10–4. The MacGregor Ranch has 42 buildings, 28 of which are listed on the National Register of Historic Places. As the last working ranch in Estes Park, visitors can experience MacGregor Ranch as a true piece of living history. A museum puts the ranch in historic context, and guests can take self-guided tours of the blacksmith shop, milkhouse, and other buildings and exhibits. Free admission, but donations keep them running.

♿ **Stanley Hotel** (970-586-3371 or 1-800-976-1377; www.stanleyhotel.com), 333 E. Wonder View Ave. The Stanley Hotel has a long-standing reputation for being haunted. Stephen King's stay in room 217 was the inspiration for his novel, *The Shining*. The ABC mini-series was filmed here. As the story goes, most of the ghosts reside on the fourth floor. The hotel gives one-hour ghost tours for $10 from 10–5 (no one under 5). Call 970-577-4110 for reservations.

♿ **Stanley Museum** (970-577-1903; www.stanleymuseum.org), Lower Stanley Village. Open in the summer, daily 10–5; rest of the year 10–3. The Stanley Museum tells the story of F. O. Stanley, the Stanley Steamer, and the historic Stanley Hotel. The museum also manages historic tours of the hotel.

* Outdoor Activities

FISHING For fly-fishing, Fall River and the Big Thompson River stretch for miles and have plenty of secluded spots for the avid angler. Lake Estes and Marys Lake are popular as well. There are several fishing outfitters in town with guides who have extensive local knowledge.

Estes Angler (970-586-2110 or 1-800-586-2110; www.estesangler.com), 338 W. Riverside Dr. In addition to guided fishing trips with access to private water, Estes Angler also posts up-to-date fishing reports on their Web site. One-person trips $125 and $225 for half- and full-day outings.

HISTORIC STANLEY HOUSE

Rocky Mountain Adventures (970-586-6191 or 1-800-858-6808; www.shop rma.com), 358 E. Elkhorn Ave. These folks offer guided fly-fishing trips on the Big Thompson River, Rocky Mountain National Park, the Cache la Poudre River, and other spots. One-person trips $125 and $210 for half- and full-day outings.

Wild Basin Outfitters (303-525-7373; www.wildbasinoutfitters.com), 12976 Peak to Peak Hwy., Allenspark. The guides at Wild Basin take guests on a range of fly-fishing trips. They primarily fish in Rocky Mountain National Park, Roosevelt National Forest, and the Indian Peaks Wilderness. Offerings include half-day to multiple-day trips, with backcountry hiking and horseback riding trips as well. One person trips $165 and $250 for half- and full-day outings.

FOUR-WHEEL TOURS **American Wilderness Tours** (970-586-1626; www .awtep.com), 875 Moraine Ave. (summer address). AWT offers a unique way to experience Rocky Mountain National Park. One of their four-wheel, off-road vehicles will take you far into the park, to places most people have to hike to see. They also have evening tours that include dinner. Adult day tour $30, children (4–11) $15, and children under 4 free.

GOLF **Estes Park Golf Course** (970-586-8146 or 1-866-586-8146; www .golfestes.com), 1080 S. St. Vrain. Located south of town, this 18-hole course offers fantastic views of the surrounding mountains. It is considered one of the most beautiful courses in the country. Don't be surprised to find deer and elk wandering the course. Greens fees $33 for residents, $41 for nonresidents.

AN ALLUVIAL FAN IN ROCKY MOUNTAIN NATIONAL PARK

ROCKY MOUNTAIN NATIONAL PARK

Rocky Mountain National Park (970-586-1206 from 8–4:30 or 970-586-1333 for a recorded message 24 hours a day; www.nps.gov/romo), 1000 US 36. The park is open 24 hours a day, every day. There are six visitor centers; most are open daily in the summer. Check Web site for seasonal hours.

Rocky Mountain National Park (RMNP) was established by an act of Congress in 1915. The original intention of the park was to set aside a portion of the Rocky Mountains so that its scenic and naturally beauty could be enjoyed for future generations. The park is truly majestic and includes canyons, meadows, and soaring peaks. Over the years, many cultural assets have been discovered and preserved, including ancient trails that hint at the park's deep past and old cattle ranches that look back a century or two.

For a quick overview of the park, Trail Ridge Road (US 34) runs west of

Lake Estes 9 Hole Executive Course (970-586-8176; www.golfestes.com), 690 Big Thompson Ave. Summer season runs mid-April–Oct. This nine-hole course is close to town on the western tip of Lake Estes. Greens fees $13 for residents, $116 for nonresidents. Nov.–Mar. you can play all day for $7.

HIKING & SNOWSHOEING Rocky Mountain National Park offers some of the most spectacular trails and scenery for hiking, and in the winter, cross-country

Estes Park, through the park, and over the Continental Divide, and then descends on the other side to Grand Lake, terminating in Granby. (In the east, US 34 terminates in Berwyn, Illinois.) It is the highest continuous paved road in the U.S.—12,183 feet at it highest point—with 11 miles of road above tree line. The views are phenomenal.

For a nice trip without going all the way to Grand Lake, drive up to the Alpine Visitors Center. At 11,796 feet, the air here is awfully thin, especially for people who have only been as high as Estes Park for a day (watch for signs of altitude sickness—shortness of breath, dizziness—and head back down the mountain if you need to). The road is closed from winter into early spring—they start plowing in April with a goal of having it all cleared for the opening on Memorial Day.

For more scenery, head up to Bear Lake. If you park at Glacier Basin, a shuttle will take you up Bear Lake Road.

To really experience the park, however, you have to get out of your car. The Lawn Lake Flood of 1982 devastated Estes Park and created a unique alluvial fan in Horseshoe Park. When the water came bellowing down the mountain, it brought with it tons of debris. When it hit the wide Horseshoe Park, the flood dropped the thousands of boulders it had been carrying. What remains now is a river that cascades down a slope of rocks. This is especially worth a visit in the spring and early summer when the water levels are higher.

If you have time for more than a quick stop, RMNP has over 355 miles of hiking trails. There are four campgrounds within the park. These are pretty bare-bones, with just water and toilets. There are no water, sewer, or electric hook-ups at any of the sites. Backcountry camping is allowed, but you must purchase a permit in advance.

The park operates a shuttle service, the **Rocky Mountain National Park Shuttle** (970-586-1206; www.nps.gov/romo/planyourvisit/gettingaround.htm), which takes visitors to stops along the main road at campgrounds, trailheads, and scenic stops.

A pass is required to enter the park. The seven-day vehicle pass is $20. Hikers are charged $10.

skiing and snowshoeing. Up in the mountains, the season for winter sports lasts well into the spring. The snow cover on the east side of the park is better suited for snowshoeing, and the park offers free ranger-guided walks. Gear and other guide services can easily be found in Estes Park through various shops and outfitters. (See Rocky Mountain National Park sidebar below for more information.)

Estes Park Mountain Shop (970-586-6548 or 1-866-303-6548; www.estespark

LOCAL WILDLIFE

mountainshop.com), 2050 Big Thompson Ave. The Mountain Shop rents everything for outdoor adventure in Estes Park. For winter they have cross-country skis and snowshoes. For summer trips that have everything from mountain bikes and trailers to backpacks and tents. The shop also has rock climbing lessons and fly-fishing lessons.

Outdoor World (970-586-2114; www.rmconnection.com), 156 E. Elkhorn Ave. Open daily 9–8. The shop rents equipment for hiking, camping, and snowshoeing. The staff is very knowledgeable about area conditions and the proper use of equipment.

The Warming House (970-586-2995; www.warminghouse.com),790 Moraine Ave. Close to RMNP on Estes Park's west side, this outfitter rents equipment for hiking, snowshoeing, and camping. They also lead guided trips in winter and summer.

HORSEBACK RIDING **Sombrero Ranch–Estes Park Stable** (970-586-4577; www.sombrero.com), 1895 US 34. East of Estes Park on Big Thompson Ave., right across from Lake Estes, Sombrero Ranch's Estes Stables have one- and two-hour trail rides, as well as four- and eight-hour rides, on their private 1,000-acre ranch. Trips also take guests into the nearby national forest. For added interest, they also have breakfast rides and steak-fry rides, sleigh rides, and wagon rides. Prices range from $30 for the one-hour ride to $150 for the complete overnight camping package. Sombrero also maintains two stables within Rocky Mountain National Park—**Moraine Park Riding Stables** and **Glacier Creek Stables**. See the Web site for more information on rides right in RMNP.

Wild Basin Livery (303-747-2222; www.wildbasinlivery.com), 12976 CO 7,

Allenspark. About 14 miles south of Estes Park on CO 7 in Allenspark, Wild Basin Livery offers great trail rides through Wild Basin. The 4-hour ride takes you by three spectacular waterfalls. Prices range from $49 for the two-hour ride to $149 for the eight-hour Longs Peak ride.

MOUNTAIN BIKING **Colorado Bicycling Adventures** (970-586-4241 or 1-888-586-4129; www.coloradobicycling.com), 184 E. Elkhorn Ave. To really get an insider's look at what the area has to offer mountain bikers, take one of the off-road or downhill tours offered by Colorado Bicycling Adventures. To tour on your own, stop by, rent a bike, and get advice on where to ride. Mountain bikes run $23 for a full-day rental and up to $53 for three days.

PADDLING & BOATING **Lake Estes Marina** (970-586-2011; www.estesvalley recreation.com/marina.html), 1770 Big Thompson Ave. Located at the east end of Lake Estes, the marina has a ton of boats for rent—motor boats, large and small pontoon boats, paddleboats, kayaks, and canoes. The large pontoon boats can hold up to nine people for a party on the lake. They also rent bikes.

Rapid Transit Rafting (1-800-367-8523; www.rapidtransitrafting.com), 161 Virginia Dr. Rapid Transit takes guests on rafting trips on both sides of the Continental Divide. In the west, they ride the Colorado River with class II and III rapids. Closer to town, the Cache la Poudre running toward Fort Collins has class II–IV rapids. Full-day trip on the Colorado $85, and half-day trip on the Cache la Poudre $51.

SEGWAYING **Segway of Northern Colorado** (970-577-1729; www.segwayof ncolorado.com), 431-A Elkhorn Ave. For something new, you might want to take a tour of town on a Segway Human Transporter. Though it's a bit pricey, they offer different tours, like wildlife tours and shopping tours. You can also rent a Segway and make your own plans. This is a unique way to get around Estes Park and the surrounding area.

✷ Lodging

HOTELS **Estes Park Center–YMCA of the Rockies** (970-586-3341; www.ymcarockies.org), 2515 Tunnel Rd. (See Northwest Colorado for the Winter Park portion of YMCA of the Rockies, Snow Mountain Ranch.) The Estes Park Center offers visitors lodge rooms, cabins, and vacation homes. The Jackson Stables (www.jacksonstables.com), are also on site. Rooms $69–129 and cabins $89–334.

Fawn Valley Inn (970-586-2388 or 1-800-525-2961; www.fawn valleyinn.com), 2760 Fall River Rd. Frontage on Fall River for fishing. Cable TV and DVD player, heated pool and hot tub. A huge DVD library of over 1,000 movies. With such a wide selection of accommodations—condos, suites, and cabins, all with different amenities—rates also range widely: $80–255.

Stanley Hotel (970-586-3371 or 1-800-976-1377; www.stanley hotel.com), 333 E. Wonder View Ave. In 1903, F. O. Stanley, maker of the famous Stanley Steamer, moved west

THE VIEW FROM YMCA OF THE ROCKIES

for his health. He arrived in Estes Park, and by 1907 had decided to build a hotel. The Stanley Hotel was completed in 1909, and many of the original buildings are still in use. The hotel stands as an iconic landmark of Estes Park. Rooms $109–259.

"1" ♿ **Taharaa Mountain Lodge** (970-577-0098 or 1-800-597-0098; www.taharaa.com), 3110 S. St. Vrain Ave. This lodge/B&B has nine rooms and nine suites. Each room has a fireplace and a fantastic view. Every morning, guests enjoy a full gourmet breakfast. Rooms $150–180 and suites $180–330.

"1" **Boulder Brook on Fall River** (970-586-0910 or 1-800-238-0910; www.boulderbrook.com), 1900 Fall River Rd. Two standard suites and three theme suites. Open year-round right on Fall River. Each suite has a private riverfront deck, and there are jetted tubs, fireplaces, cable TV, and DVD players. Suites $109–209.

BED & BREAKFASTS "1" **Anniversary Inn** (970-586-6200; www.estesinn.com), 1060 Mary's Lake Rd. This 100-year-old log inn has three rooms and one Sweetheart's Cottage. The cottage and two of the rooms have Jacuzzi tubs. Full breakfast is served on the enclosed porch every morning. Less than 2 miles from downtown Estes Park. Rooms $100–145, cottage $175.

"1" ♿ **Baldpate Inn** (970-586-6151; www.baldpateinn.com), 4900 S. CO 7. Built in 1917, the inn has always been an inn—12 rooms in the main lodge and four cabins. Located 7 miles south of Estes Park, the inn sits on Twin Sisters Mountain. Rooms all have double or twin beds and have shared or private baths. The cabins all have private baths. The inn boasts of having the world's largest key collection—there is an interesting story about how this collection came about, so be sure to ask about it when you visit. Rooms $100–115 and cabins $185.

Mountain Valley Home (970-586-3100 or 1-800-987-2765; www.amountainvalleyhome.com), 1420 Axminster Ln. This is a newer home (2002) with five suites. Enjoy wine and appetizers in their Tuscan Wine Room. There is a kitchen for guest use, and a gourmet breakfast is served. Hosts Lynn and Paul know Estes Park, and they can offer help finding places to eat and things to do. Rooms $149–239.

Romantic RiverSong (970-586-4666; www.romanticriversong.com), 1765 Lower Broadview Rd. Ten guest rooms, named after wildflowers, on 27 wooded acres. Fireside candlelight dinners. Rooms $150–295.

Sonnenhof Bed & Breakfast (970-577-7528; www.sonnenhofestespark.com), 650 Lakewood Ct. Three suites, all with Jacuzzi, fireplace, and private patio or deck. Rooms $150–180.

Allenspark Lodge Bed & Breakfast (303-747-2552; www.allensparklodge.com), 184 Main, CO 7, Allenspark. Built in 1933, this rustic three-story lodge has hand-peeled pine logs and lots of character. The lodge has 12 rooms, seven of which have private baths. There is also an apartment with full kitchen and bath. The most popular room is the Hideaway Room. Tucked into the back end of the third floor, this room has views on three sides and a clawfoot tub. Rooms $75–120.

CAMPGROUNDS **Estes Park Campground** (970-586-4188 or 1-888-815-2029; www.estesparkcampground.com), 3420 Tunnel Rd. Open May–Sept. Close enough to RMNP that you can hike into it from your campsite. Rustic sites $25–28, partial hook-ups $29–33, and full hook-ups $36–40.

Estes Park KOA (1-800-562-1887; www.estesparkkoa.com), 2051 Big Thompson Ave. Just east of downtown Estes Park, the KOA is a great spot for parking your RV or renting Kamping Kabins (there are a ton of cabins here). There is also a tent site, if you don't mind camping on the main thoroughfare through Estes Park. Sites $20–48 and Kabins $47–140.

Marys Lake Campground & RV Park (970-586-4411 or 1-800-445-6279; www.maryslakecampground.com), 2120 Marys Lake Rd. There are 90 RV sites here that accommodate double slide-outs and have a full selection of hook-ups, including cable TV. Tent campers have spacious sites, and there are pop-up campers for rent. People fish right there in Marys Lake—the camp store has everything you need from licenses to gear. A swimming pool, game room, and convenience store are just some of the extras at the campground. RV sites $26–40 and tent sites $26.

CABINS & COTTAGES **Cascade Cottages** (970-586-4748), 4140 Fall River Rd. Open Memorial Day–Labor Day. As the only commercial lodging left within RMNP, Cascade Cottages has a lot going for it before you even get there. And they must be doing something right because they are booked a year in advance without doing any advertising. The cabins are bare-bones, with bathrooms and kitchen facilities. They are heated for chilly mountain nights. The location is perfect, and a stay here is peaceful and relaxed. In the winter, the owners can be contacted at 316-687-6126.

"1" **Glacier Lodge** (970-586-4401 or 1-800-523-3920; www.glacierlodge.com), 2166 CO 66. Glacier Lodge offers more than just their 28 cabins. They have a list of activities that rival area dude ranches. There are a number of lodging options from one-bedroom units ($100–153) to full homestyle units that can have up to eight bedrooms ($250–950). Rates vary dramatically by size and season. Four-night minimum stay in summer.

"1" **Streamside on Fall River** (970-586-6464 or 1-800-321-3303; www.streamsideonfallriver.com), 1260 Fall River Rd. (CO 34). One mile west of Estes Park, Streamside has cabins that creep right to the edge of Fall River. Cabin decks overlook the river, and they all have fireplaces for cool evenings. Close to town and RMNP. Rates $99–295.

✷ Where to Eat

DINING OUT ♿ **Twin Owls Steakhouse** (970-586-9344; www.twinowls.net), 800 MacGregor Ave., at the Black Canyon Inn. Open daily for dinner at 5. Rustic mountain lodge, rough hewn logs, moss rock fireplace, etc. They offer great steak from beef that has only been fed organically grown grass. Reservations are recommended. Entrées $20–30.

Fawn Brook Inn (303-747-2556), CO 7, Business Loop 357, Allenspark. For years, people have been making the trip to the Fawn Brook Inn for the elegant Continental dining experience. The restaurant has been described glowingly as a classic German inn. The menu features classic dishes like beef Wellington. Dinner entrées $25–30.

EATING OUT ♿ **Dunraven Inn** (970-586-6409; www.dunraveninn.com), 2470 CO 66. The more than 13,000 one-dollar bills wallpapering the bar are autographed tips for owner Dale Hatcher left by grateful diners. (As he runs out of space, the money goes to local charities.) The inn has a definite local feel, and the Italian menu is suplimented with seafood and steak. Try the chicken Parmesan; it nearly overflows with cheesy goodness. Reservations recommended. Pasta dishes $10–12, pricier entrées $20–35.

♿ **Ed's Cantina & Grill** (970-586-2919; www.estesparkcoffee.com/eds), 390 E. Elkhorn Ave. Open daily 7–9 (10 in the bar). Ed's serves burgers and burritos, and this is a great place for a quick bite to eat. When weather permits, there's patio seating by the river. Breakfast under $6 and lunch and dinner under $10.

♿ **Mama Rose's** (970-586-3330 or 1-877-586-3330; www.mamarosesrestaurant.com), 338 E. Elkhorn Ave. Located in Barlow Plaza along the Riverwalk. Open daily in the summer for dinner 4–9; winter, daily 4–8. Closed in Jan. and the first week of Feb. Diners come to Mama Rose's for the service, the outdoor seating along the river, and, of course, for great Italian. Reasonably priced, the restaurant is busy in the summer, but lines move quickly. Perfect for eating out with the whole family. Dishes $8–21.

♿ **Penelope's World Famous Hamburger and Fries** (970-586-2277), 229 W. Elkhorn Ave. Open daily at 11, they close when there are no more customers. Right downtown, Penelope's was recently voted best hamburger in Estes Park—and the handmade fries aren't too bad either. Lunch is under $10.

Wapiti Bar & Grill (970-586-5056; www.wapitipub.com), 247 W. Elkhorn Ave. Open year-round, daily 8–9. Wapiti is named for the Shawnee word for elk. People return to the restaurant year after year for the food and kid-friendly environment. There is seating indoors and out. For variety, you can order a burger made of beef, elk, buffalo, or veggies. Dishes run from $8 for burgers or the fantastic fish and chips to $22 for their signature entrées.

BAKERIES & COFFEE SHOPS ♿ **Notchtop Bakery & Cafe** (970-586-0272), 459 E. Wonderview Dr., #4. More than just a coffee shop and bakery, Notchtop serves breakfast, lunch, and dinner as well. Healthy ingredients, great bread, and coffee. Breakfast is highly rated.

BARS, TAVERNS & BREW PUBS ♿ **Estes Park Brewery** (970-586-5421; www.epbrewery.com), 470 Prospect Dr. After a long day of hiking in RMNP, the Estes Park Brewery is a great place to relax, get a little food, and enjoy some great beer.

SNACKS ♿ **14'ers Café** (970-586-8300), 116 E. Elkhorn. There are plenty of places along Elkhorn to get the tourist's requisite fudge, taffy, and gourmet popcorn. This café goes a little above and beyond the usual with homemade ice cream and sandwiches.

✷ Entertainment

Estes Park Music Festival (970-577-9900 or 1-800-443-7837; www.estesparkmusicfestival.org), Stanley Hotel. Winter concerts are held on Sunday afternoons at 2, Nov.–April, at the Stanley Hotel. The summer series of concerts is held at various locations throughout Estes Park. See Web site for schedule.

✷ Selective Shopping

Earthwood Artisans (970-586-2151; www.earthwoodartisans.com), 145 E. Elkhorn Ave., and **Earthwood Collections** (970-577-8100), 109 W. Elkhorn Ave. Open year-round. Summer hours 10–9. These two galleries represent more than 230 local and regional artists. They carry a huge collection of oil paintings, watercolors, ceramics, and sculpture—much of it celebrating Colorado and the Rocky Mountains.

Wynbrier Ltd. Wildlife Gallery (1-800-921-4161; www.wynbrier.com), 120 E. Elkhorn Ave. There are plenty of shops in Colorado selling wildlife art. The Wynbrier Gallery is the oldest such shop in Estes Park, and it has a huge selection—everything from obsidian knives to art prints.

MacDonald Bookshop (970-586-3450), 152 E. Elkhorn Ave. Open daily in the summer 8–9:30; winter, 8–6. This bookstore has been in business for over 78 years and has an excellent local-interest section covering Estes Park and a great selection of books on Colorado history.

✷ Special Events

March: **Cowboy Poetry & Music Roundup** (970-586-3341 ext. 1010;

www.estesparkcvb.com), Estes Park Center–YMCA of the Rockies. Fiddle playing, poetry readings, and a whole lot of cowboy fun.

May: **Estes Park Jazz Fest and Art Walk** (www.estesnet.com/Events/jazzfestartwalk.htm). Just like the name suggests, this festival brings together a series of jazz performances and an art walk for two days in May.

July: **Rooftop Rodeo** (970-586-6104; www.rooftoprodeo.com), Stanley Park Fairgounds. The rodeo comes to Estes Park for six days in July every year.

September: **Longs Peak Scottish Irish Festival** (970-586-6308; www.scotfest.com), Stanley Park Baseball Fields & Rodeo Grounds. Always held the weekend after Labor Day, the festival is the largest of its kind. The festival features a heavy armor jousting competition, Irish and Highland dancing, and medieval games competitions.

Northwest Colorado

2

BRECKENRIDGE & SUMMIT COUNTY

Breckenridge (aka "Breck") is one of the most popular ski destinations in the state. With nearly 9,000 permanent residents, Breckenridge hotels, lodges, and B&Bs can accommodate 25,000 during peak seasons. Just driving through town, it's hard to imagine that there are over 100 restaurants and dozens of bars and saloons. One of the most charming aspects of Breckenridge is that so much of the town's history remains intact. With nearly 250 structures, the town is the largest historical district in Colorado. These structures have been restored and preserved to tell the story of the town's past.

Like most Colorado mountain towns, the story of Breckenridge began with the promise of gold. In 1859, gold was discovered near the Blue River. The mining camp that sprang up in the valley was officially established later that year. It was named in honor of President James Buchanan's vice president, John Cabell Breckinridge. During the Civil War, however, John Breckinridge sided with the South, and the town that bore his name quietly altered the spelling to Breckenridge.

By 1861, Breckenridge was a thriving little community. There were soon a few stores, hotels, and saloons. The U.S. post office came to town, and it was the county seat of Summit County. By the 1880s, the railroad had come to town, and the population was nearly 2,000. Breckenridge became a trading center, supplying area miners and everyone else trying to make a living in Summit County. The town's growth, however, was primarily tied to the discoveries of gold, then silver, then zinc and lead. As these resources were discovered and subsequently mined out, the local economy rose and fell.

During these early years, Father John L. Dyer, a Methodist minister, lived in Breckenridge. Dyer came to town in 1862 to take over the Blue River Mission in Summit County. His circuit grew to include towns as far away as Leadville and Fairplay. At 50 years old, he took to his calling with a passion. Strapping a pair of "Norwegian snowshoes" (i.e., skis) to his feet, he trudged the mountains, hiking regularly over 13,188-foot Mosquito Pass, to care for his flock. His devotion earned him the nickname the Snowshoe Itinerant, and in 1977 he was inducted into the Colorado Ski and Snowboard Hall of Fame.

By the turn of the century, hard-rock and placer mining had all but died out, and local companies were literally scraping by, using dredging boats to scour the

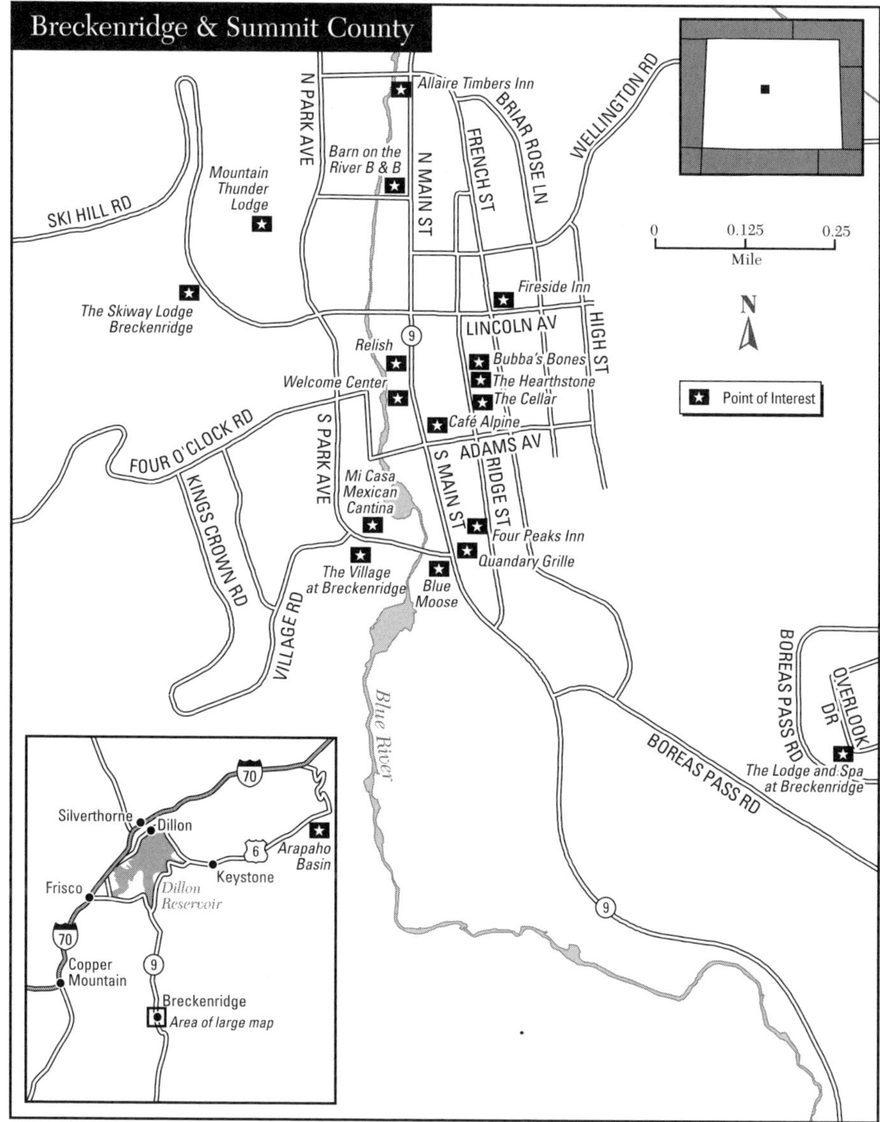

area river bottoms for gold and other metals. In the years leading up to World War II, the town would be so desperate to keep people employed that they allowed the dredge boats down the Blue River through town, destroying most of the town's original buildings on the west side of the river.

When the Country Boy Mine was flooded and subsequently closed in 1945, it meant the end of mining in Breckenridge. As people moved on to find work, the town's population plummeted below 400. For 15 years, people struggled to stay on. Then in 1961, the Rounds and Porter Lumber Company out of Wichita got a permit to build a ski area. And beginning with one lift up Peak 8, Breckenridge's fortunes turned.

Today 1.5 million visitors come through every year. They come to ski not only the Breckenridge ski area, but Keystone, Copper Mountain, and Arapaho Basin as well. In the summers, people come to hike and bike and to celebrate during any one of the town's great summer festivals. While you're in the area, be sure to visit the neighbors: Frisco and Dillon have great recreational facilities—and a lake in the mountains is a great place to spend a hot day.

Most of the attractions, lodgings, and restaurants listed below are open year-round. Many, however, reduce hours significantly for about six weeks in the spring and fall. Be sure to call ahead during these two off-seasons. Unless otherwise indicated, all addresses are in Breckenridge.

GUIDANCE The **Breckenridge Welcome Center** (1-877-864-0868), 203 S. Main St., is operated by the Breckenridge Resort Chamber (970-453-2913 or 1-800-221-1091; www.gobreck.com). The center is open daily 9–5. It is located in the Blue River Plaza. The building that houses the welcome center includes a 19th-century log cabin that was discovered when construction crews were working on the property. The cabin was left intact and is now the center's interpretive museum.

Summit County Chamber of Commerce (970-668-2051 or 1-888-786-6482; www.experiencethesummit.com). The chamber operates two information centers off I-70. One is in Frisco at exit 203. The other is in Silverton off CO 9 N. Information centers open daily 9–5.

GETTING THERE *By car:* Breckenridge is very accessible from I-70. Take either exit 201 or 203 into Frisco and follow CO 9 south 9 miles to Breckenridge. If you are heading to Copper Mountain, the ski area is right off the interstate at exit 195. For Keystone, take exit 205 at US 6 and follow that east about 8 miles to the ski area.

By air: The closest airport is the **Denver International Airport** (1-800-AIR2DEN; www.flydenver.com), which is about 100 miles east of Breckenridge. **Colorado Mountain Express** (970-926-9800 or 1-800-525-6363; www.cmex.com) runs a shuttle between the DIA and Breckenridge. They will also bring you to nearby Keystone and Copper Mountain.

By train: **AMTRAK** (1-800-USA-RAIL; www.amtrak.com) offers their Throughway bus service in Frisco, meeting passengers at the Frisco Transfer Center (1010 Meadow Dr.).

By bus: **Greyhound** (1-800-231-2222; www.greyhound.com) picks up and drops off passengers at Frisco Transfer Center (1010 Meadow Dr.). Tickets must be bought beforehand, online or by calling the number above.

GETTING AROUND *By bus:* **Summit Stage** (970-668-0999; www.summitstage.com); **Breckenridge Free Ride** (970-547-3140); and **Shuttle at Keystone Resort** (970-496-4200).

MEDICAL EMERGENCIES **St. Anthony Summit Medical Center** (970-668-3300; www.stanthonyhosp.org), CO 9 at School Rd., Frisco. The center has a 24-hour emergency department.

✷ To See & Do

HISTORICAL SITES & MUSEUMS The **Summit Historical Society** (www.summithistorical.org) has an extensive list of historical sites in Summit County, including old mining projects, log cabins, Victorian homes, barns, etc. Hours for the following sites change from season to season. It would be good to call before making plans. Aside from the Country Boy Mine, all these sites are free—donations are appreciated.

Breckenridge Historic District (1-800-980-1859; www.breckheritage.com), 115 S. Main St. With 249 structures, Breckenridge has the largest historical district in Colorado. Walking tours leave from the welcome center (203 S. Main St.) in the summer Tue.–Sat. 10 and 2, and Sun. at 10.

Barney Ford House Museum (1-800-980-1859; www.breckheritage.com), 111 E. Washington Ave. Open daily 11–4. Barney Ford was born into slavery in 1822. He escaped and headed west, eventually settling in Colorado, where he made and lost several fortunes in various entrepreneurial enterprises. Barney Ford and his wife Julia were considered prominent citizens in both Breckenridge and Denver. His house in Breckenridge is open to the public.

Edwin Carter Museum (1-800-980-1859; www.breckheritage.com), 111 N. Ridge St. Open daily 11–4. Edwin Carter came to Breckenridge in 1860 as a prospector but was dismayed by the impact mining was having on the environment and wildlife in the region. He set about collecting specimens of Rocky Mountain mammals and raptors so there would be a record of the creatures for future generations.

Dillon Schoolhouse Museum (970-468-2207; www.townofdillon.com), 403 LaBonte St., Dillon. Open Tues.–Sat. 1–4. From 1883 to 1910, this building was a one-room schoolhouse. It later served as a church. It's been restored to the way it would have looked at the turn of the century.

Frisco Historic Park (970-668-3428; www.townoffrisco.com), 120 Main St., Frisco. Open in the summer Tues.–Sat. 9–5 and Sun. 9–3; winter, Tues.–Sat. 10–4 and Sun. 10–2. What began with a schoolhouse in 1983 has grown to include nine more historic structures—including an old jail, a ranch house, and a log chapel—all of which are used as exhibit space to share the history of Frisco with guests.

MINES **Lomax Placer Gulch** (1-800-980-1859; www.breckheritage.com), 301 Ski Hill Rd. Summer tours Tue.–Sat. 10 and 2 and Sun. at 10. A unique look at mining history, the Lomax Placer Mine was a hydraulic mine, using water at high pressure to push loose earth into the mine's ore recovery equipment.

Washington Gold and Silver Mine (1-800-980-1859; www.breckheritage.com), in Illinois Gulch south of Breckenridge off Boreas Pass Rd. Summer tours Tue.–Sat. 10 and 2 and Sun. at 10. At one time this was one of the largest hard-rock mining operations in the area. The tour lets you explore a shaft house and mining cabin.

✐ **Country Boy Mine** (970-453-4405; www.countryboymine.com), 0542 French Gulch Rd. Open daily in the summer. See site for hours and winter schedule. The privately owned Country Boy Mine was once one of the region's biggest gold and silver producers. Today, guests can tour the mine and see what it was like 100 years ago. The tour is 45 minutes long and takes you 1,000 feet underground. Afterwards, visitors pan for gold or take a ride down the 55-foot ore chute. Adult admission $17.95, children (4–12) $12.95, and children under 4 free; gold-panning $9.95.

SCENIC DRIVES **Hoosier Pass.** The road south out of Breckenridge, CO 9, takes you over Hoosier Pass (elevation 11,539 feet) and through Alma, the highest incorporated town in the U.S., on its way to Fairplay. Fantastic scenery in both directions.

✷ Outdoor Activities

ALPINE SKIING & SNOWBOARDING **Arapahoe Basin Ski Area** (970-468-0718 or 1-888-272-7246; www.arapahoebasin.com), 28194 US 6, Keystone. The ski area is open daily 9–4. The summit of Arapahoe Basin (known lovingly as A-Basin) is 13,050 feet above sea level. With a vertical drop of 2,257 feet to the base, this is the highest ski area in the country. Most of the runs start above timberline, and even without snowmaking equipment, the ski season at Arapahoe lasts into June (and sometimes July). Most of the trails at Arapahoe are appropriate for intermediate and advanced skiers. In the summer of 2007, the ski area added a quad lift that opened access to Montezuma Bowl, increasing the terrain by 80 percent to 900 skiable acres. The ski area also has two terrain parks, one for beginners and the other for more advanced snowboarders. There are few amenities at Arapahoe Basin, but there is a lot of fun. In March, the ski area's Early Riser parking lot becomes "the Beach." Imagine a skier's tailgate party, and you won't be far off. Adult full-day lift ticket $54, semi-seniors (60–69) $46, youths (15–19) $45, children (6–14) $24, children under 5 free, and 70-plus-year-old seniors $10.

Breckenridge Ski Resort (970-453-5000 or 1-800-789-7669; www.breckenridge.com), P.O. Box 1058, Breckenridge, CO 80424. The ski area is open daily 8:30–4. Skiing in Breckenridge is found on four mountains along the Ten Mile Range: Peaks 7, 8, 9, and 10. Twenty-nine lifts service the ski area's 2,358 acres. The highest chairlift in North America ascends Peak 8, bringing skiers up to 12,840 feet. With such a variety of terrain, there are runs here for everyone. Most of the beginner runs are on the lower sections of Peaks 8 and 9. Intermediate skiing is mostly found on Peaks 7 and 9. Black-diamond runs are concentrated on Peaks 8 and 10. Overall, more than half of the trails are rated for advanced and expert skiers and a third for intermediate. A classic descent for intermediate skiers is to take the Four O'Clock Trail 3.5 miles from the Vista Haus warming hut into town. Full-day lift ticket around $81 for adults.

Copper Mountain (1-866-841-2481; www.coppercolorado.com), 209 Ten Mile Cir., Copper Mountain. Open daily 9–4 (and as early as 8:30 on weekends). With 2,433 acres of skiable terrain, including high alpine bowls and the Catalyst Terrain Park, Copper Mountain has something for everyone. There are plenty of long beginner and intermediate runs. For advanced skiers, there's free snowcat access to the Tucker Mountain. Snowboarders come for the Superpipe and the

Catalyst Terrain Park—for younger beginners, there's the Kidz Terrain Park. Adult full-day lift ticket $72, seniors $58, and children (6–13) $34.

Keystone (970-496-2316 or 1-877-625-1556; www.keystone.com), P.O. Box 38, Keystone, CO 80435. Lifts run 9–4 (later for night skiing). Three mountains—Keystone Mountain, North Peak, and the Outback—make up the Keystone Ski Area. This is a great spot for beginner and intermediate skiers (though half of the ski area is advanced/expert terrain). The longest trail, the 3.5-mile Schoolmarm, is an easy run that's great for getting a feel for the mountain. Keystone has one of the state's biggest night-skiing operations. On certain nights, the beginner slope, Dercum Mountain, and the A51 Terrain Park are kept lighted until 9 PM. Full-day lift ticket around $81 for adults.

BICYCLING The name of the Ten Mile Recreation Pathway is a bit misleading. Named after the Ten Mile Range, the pathway offers over 50 miles of paved path connecting Breckenridge to Frisco, Dillon, Copper Mountain, and Keystone. Several loops are possible for a variety of bike rides. Stop by any visitor or welcome center for a map. (See below for Mountain Biking.)

CROSS-COUNTRY SKIING & SNOWSHOEING **Breckenridge Nordic Center** (970-453-6855; www.breckenridgenordic.com), 1200 Ski Hill Rd. The Nordic ski area at Breckenridge maintains over 32 kilometers of groomed trails for cross-country skiers, and another 16 for snowshoeing. The ski area was recently expanded in the White River National Forest. Adult day pass $15, seniors and youths (7–17) $10, and children under 7 free.

Frisco Nordic Center (970-668-0866; www.frisconordic.com), 18484 CO 9, Frisco. Located in the Peninsula Recreation Area in Frisco, the Frisco Nordic Center offers nearly 40 kilometers of cross-country and snowshoeing trails, as well as lessons and equipment rental. Adult day pass $15, seniors and youths (7–17) $10, and children under 7 free.

Gold Run Nordic Center (970-547-7889), 200 Clubhouse Dr. Based at the Breckenridge Golf Club, the Nordic Center has 20 kilometers of groomed

FRISCO HISTORIC PARK & MUSEUM

cross-country skiing, over 7 miles of snowshoe trails, and access to the backcountry. Adult day pass $15, seniors and youths (7–17) $10, and children under 7 free.

The **Summit Huts Association** (970-453-8583; www.summithuts.org), 524 Wellington Rd., manages backcountry huts in Summit County. To reserve cabins, or see a map of cabins on a network of trails, contact the 10th Mountain Division Hut Association (970-925-5775; www.huts.org).

DOGSLEDDING **Good Times Adventures** (970-453-7604 or 1-800-477-0144; www.goodtimesadventures.com), 6061 Tiger Rd. This is a great opportunity to really experience dogsledding. This outfitter takes guests out on a 6-mile relay, where they alternate between mushing and riding as passengers on the sled. The tour takes about an hour. Adult price $65 and children (4–8) $35. This activity is not recommended for kids under 4.

GOLF **Breckenridge Golf Club** (970-453-9104; www.breckenridgegolfclub.com), 200 Clubhouse Dr. The Elk, the Beaver, and the Bear are the three nine-hole courses that make up this 27-hole golf course designed by Jack Nicklaus. The Elk/Beaver combination is rated the second most challenging course in the state. Greens fees $99.

Copper Creek Golf Club (970-968-3333; www.coppercolorado.com/golf/copper_creek), 104 Wheeler Pl., Copper Mountain. Set against the Ten Mile Range, the front nine at Copper Creek wind through alpine terrain with towering trees, lakes, and streams. The back nine cuts through the forest and the remains of an old mining town. Greens fees $55–89.

Raven Golf Club at Three Peaks (970-262-3636; www.intrawestgolf.com/raven_threepeaks.com), 2929 N. Golden Eagle Rd., Silverthorne. Raven Golf Clubs, wherever they are found around the country, strive to offer the best golfing experience possible. Three Peaks is no exception. The always "tournament ready" course takes full advantage of the quintessentially Colorado setting, winding its way through tall pine and aspen groves, surrounded by snowy mountain peaks. Greens fees $59–149.

HIKING There are over 50 hiking trails in Summit County. One of the most popular is the 5-mile trek to Willow Falls, which takes you through meadows that are full of wildflowers in the summer. Along the way, hikers climb nearly 1,000 feet in elevation.

HORSEBACK RIDING **Breckenridge Stables** (970-453-4438; www.breckstables.com), Village Rd. The stables can be found off Village Road. From the Beaver Run Resort parking area, continue to the opposite end of the parking lot, turn right, and follow the dirt road up the mountain. Just follow the signs for Ten Mile Station until you see Breckenridge Stables. The stables offer 90-minute trail rides in the Ten Mile Range above Breckenridge. They also have breakfast and dinner rides. Trail rides $50; children under 40 lbs. who ride with an adult $25.

MOUNTAIN BIKING The Peaks Trail is a great mountain bike ride. Park your car in Frisco and take the bus to Breckenridge. The trailhead is just past the ski area on Ski Hill Rd. The route takes you on a rolling singletrack path, over mountain streams and through thick forest. The final descent into Frisco is a knee-burner.

Lone Star Sports (970-453-2003; www.skilonestar.com), 200 W. Washington St. In the winter they rent skis; in the summer they rent full-suspension and hard-tail mountain bikes, as well as town cruisers. Full-day, full-suspension rental $27, path bike $19.

PLAYING IN THE BLUE RIVER

RAFTING & PADDLING **Breckenridge Whitewater Park** (970-453-1734), 880 Airport Rd. Behind the Recreation Center on the Blue River, the white-water park is 1,800 feet long, making it the longest in Colorado. Free to use, the park has 15 features to challenge kayakers with varying degrees of experience.

Good Times Rafting Company (970-453-5559 or 1-800-808-0357; www.goodtimesrafting.com), 620 Main St., Ste.11, Frisco. This outfitter leads rafting trips down Breck's Blue River. The half-day trip is $48 for adults.

GREEN SPACE Lake Dillon (aka the Dillon Reservoir) is a great place to get outside to relax or play. Located between Dillon and Frisco, the lake is surrounded by four parks: the Peninsula, Swan Mountain, Dillon Reservoir, and Lowry Air Force Recreation areas. There are plenty of paths and trails, Frisbee-golf courses, and picnic areas. To get out on the water, consider renting a boat at the **Lake Dillon Marina** (970-468-5100; www.dillonmarina.com), 150 Marina Dr., Dillon.

✷ Lodging

HOTELS **The Lodge and Spa at Breckenridge** (970-453-9300 or 1-800-736-1607; www.thelodgeatbreck.com), 112 Overlook Dr. Sitting high above Breckenridge, the lodge offers guests great views of town with the ski mountain as a backdrop. Most rooms have large picture windows to facilitate the appreciation of the fantastic scenery. The décor is western, and amenities include the onsite spa and athletic club. Rooms $79–508.

Mountain Thunder Lodge (970-547-5650 or 1-888-268-8376; www.mountainthunderlodge.com), 50 Mountain Thunder Dr. The stone-and-timber exterior of the Mountain Thunder Lodge is reflected in the hotel's mountain-lodge décor. The rooms are luxuriously appointed, with every unit having a rock fireplace, a slate floor in the bathroom, and granite countertops. Guests enjoy the heated outdoor pool, deck, and hot tubs. Close to the Skiway Skyway, the lodge offers ski-in/gondola-out accommodations. Rooms $130–780.

The Village at Breckenridge (970-547-5725 or 1-800-379-6517; www.villageatbreckenridge.com), 535 S. Park Ave. Located at the base of the mountain, just steps away from downtown Breck, the Village is a sprawling hotel that offers true ski-in, ski-out accommodations. The nearby pedestrian plaza has shopping and dining. Amenities include onsite bar and dining, indoor and outdoor pools and hot tubs, and heated underground parking. Rates run $209–500 during ski season.

Hotel Frisco (970-668-5009 or 1-800-262-1002; www.hotelfrisco.com), 308 Main St., Frisco. For more affordable lodgings outside Breckenridge, consider staying in Frisco. The hotel is close to the free regional shuttle, so it's just a quick shot to the slopes. The rooms have all the amenities you would expect from a hotel, but they have the feel of a homey inn. Rooms $59–299 (in peak ski season, $139 is the cheapest).

BED & BREAKFASTS **Allaire Timbers Inn** (970-453-7530 or 1-800-624-4904; www.allairetimbers.com), 9511 CO 9. The inn has 10 guest rooms, each with a private bath and a deck with a view. Rooms are decorated with log furniture and each has a different mountain pass theme. The suite has a water-filled spa and fireplace. Located on the free shuttle run, the inn is within easy reach of the slopes. Breakfast is served daily, on the deck when weather permits. Rooms $165–400.

Barn on the River Bed & Breakfast (970-453-2975 or 1-800-795-2975; www.breckenridge-inn.com), 303B N. Main St. This B&B is housed in a timber-framed barn built in 1998. Located close to downtown and the gondola in Breckenridge, rooms overlook the Blue River, which adds a calming soundtrack to any stay. This cozy inn is tastefully decorated with antiques. The rooms all have private baths and private decks or balconies for enjoying the mountain scenery. A full breakfast is served daily—but when the powder is fresh you get cereal so you can get out to the slopes quicker. Rooms $149–289.

Fireside Inn (970-453-6456; www.firesideinn.com), 114 N. French St. The Fireside Inn is a B&B *and* hostel. The original house was built in 1879, and a number of additions give it plenty of character. The inn has suites, private rooms with bath, and dormitory-style accommodations with shared bathrooms. The rooms are decorated with antiques, and beds are covered in quilts. A full breakfast is available to all guests for an extra charge. Rooms $63–177; dormitory $27–40/person.

Four Peaks Inn (970-453-3813; www.fourpeaksinn.com), 407 S. Ridge St. One of the nicest B&Bs in town, the Four Peaks Inn is close to downtown and the ski resort. The original home was built in 1880 and is full of period furnishings and historic charm. The hosts prepare a fanstastic breakfast every morning, and they can prepare dinner on request. Spa services are available, as is in-room reflexology massage. Rooms $79–209.

Skiway Lodge (970-453-7573 or 1-800-472-1430; www.skiwaylodge.com), 275 Ski Hill Rd. The Skiway Lodge (previously known as the Hunt Placer Inn) has been consistently recommended as a great spot for a romantic getaway. The inn has four guest rooms and five mini-suites. They all have private baths, king-sized beds, and 37-inch TVs. Most have private balconies. The mini-suites have gas fireplaces, and guests have use of the inn's outdoor hot tub. A continental breakfast is available daily. Rooms $199–365.

✷ Where to Eat

DINING OUT 🍸 ♿ **Café Alpine** (970-453-8218; www.cafealpine.com), 106 E. Adams Ave. Open daily for dinner at 5 (last seating at 9). Check for hours in the off-season. The menu at the Café Alpine changes completely four times a year, and nightly depending on the seasonal availability of ingredients. A full menu is complemented by the full tapas bar on the second floor. This cozy restaurant is the perfect setting to enjoy such entrées as phyllo-wrapped wild mushroom and goat feta or pan-seared halibut. Afterward, be sure to try one of the pastry chef's exquisite desserts. Entrées $25–40.

🍸 ♿ **The Cellar** (970-453-4777; www.thecellarwine.com), 200 S. Ridge St. Dinner served Wed.–Sun. 5–10. The Cellar offers a small-plate menu influenced by the cuisines of France and the Mediterranean. Small plates give diners a chance to sample a number of dishes, and even share among themselves. The Chef's Tasting Menu is highly recommended—each course is paired with wine by the restaurant's sommelier. Small plates $7–15.

♿ **Hearthstone Restaurant** (970-453-1148; www.hearthstonerestaurant.biz), 130 S. Ridge St. Open for dinner daily at 5:30. Housed in a 120-year-old Victorian with fantastic views of the mountains, the menu at Hearthstone features hand-cut steaks, seafood, and wild game. Entrées include such dishes as ginger sea scallops and blackberry elk. The wine list has consistently received the *Wine Spectator* "Award of Excellence." Entrées $17–34.

🍸 ♿ **Relish** (970-453-0989; www.relishbreckenridge.com), 137 S. Main St. Open Tues.–Sun. 5:30–9:30; closed during the spring and fall lull. Chef/owner Matt Fackler opened Relish in 2006 in what was formerly Pierre's Riverwalk Café. The new restaurant boasts Colorado-inspired cuisine with a menu that includes entrées like free-range veal meat loaf with Tillamook cheddar mac & cheese and balsamic grilled buffalo tenderloin. The second-floor dining room is spacious but feels very intimate. Entrées $17–31.

EATING OUT ♿ **Blue Moose** (970-453-4859), 540 S. Main St. Open daily for breakfast 7–1 (closes at noon in the slow season). The often lengthy wait for breakfast is a sign of just how good this place is. Nothing terribly fancy here, just traditional breakfast fare like steak and eggs, buttermilk pancakes, and omelets. Breakfast under $10.

HEARTHSTONE RESTAURANT

🍸 **Bubba's Bones** (970-547-9942), 110 S. Ridge St. Open daily 11–close. The lunch menu at Bubba's is stocked with barbeque sandwiches. They have beef brisket and pork on a bun, as well as turkey, which soaks up barbeque flavor like a sponge. For dinner try the ribs or the hot links. They also have a full-service bar. Lunch $7.50 and dinner $15–19.

♿ **Giampietro Pasta & Pizzeria** (970-453-3838), 100 N. Main St. Open daily 11–10. Over and over, this cozy Italian eatery wins awards for its outstanding pizza. Giampietro serves both New York–style thin crust and Sicilian deep-dish pizza. The antipasti plate is a great appetizer. Classic pasta dishes and a nice wine list balance out the menu. Be sure to order an espresso or cappuccino with dessert. Pizzas $12–24 and other entrées $7–13.

♿ **Mi Casa Mexican Cantina** (970-453-2071; www.micasamexicanrestaurant.com), 600 S. Park Ave. Open daily 11:30–close. Often recommended as the best Mexican restaurant in town, Mi Casa serves an exciting menu with daring dishes like shrimp diablo (shrimp sautéed in a spicy guajillo chile sauce) and mango duck quesadillas. Window seats offer a great dining experience with a view of the Blue River. Dishes $10–16.

♿ **Quandary Grille** (970-547-5969), 505 S. Main St. Open daily 11–close. Located at the Main Street Station, guests have a great view of the mountain. In the summer there is patio seating. The Quandary serves a classic burgers-and-burritos menu. Dinner entrées like steaks, fish tacos, and ribs make for great eating. The proximity to the ski area has made the bar a popular spot with the après-ski crowd. Dinner entrées $13–26.

♿ **Log Cabin Café** (970-668-3947), 121 Main St., Frisco. Open for breakfast and lunch Mon.–Fri. 6–2 and Sat. and Sun. 7–2. Located on the main drag in Frisco in a building that's not entirely unlike a log cabin, this humble restaurant is perhaps one of the best breakfast spots around. The portions are huge, even if you don't order the pork chop breakfast. The menu has both American and Mexican dishes. If you like *huevos rancheros,* be sure to try them here. Breakfast dishes $6–8.

EATING & DINING IN The **Gourmet Cabby** (970-453-7788; www.gourmet-cabby.com) delivers meals from the area's best restaurants right to your door—whether you're at a hotel, campground, or condo. They deliver daily in the summer 9–11, and in winter 8–midnight. They serve Breckenridge and Blue River. See the Web site for menus.

BAKERIES & COFFEE SHOPS ♿ **Cool River Coffeehouse and Bakery** (970-453-1716), 325 S. Main St. Open daily 7–5. Cool River has a great menu, affordable prices, and patio seating. Their breakfast wraps and bagel sandwiches are popular, as are their gourmet lunch sandwiches. The espresso bar has a full drink menu with espressos, lattes, mochas, and smoothies. Breakfast $5 and lunch $5–6.

BARS, TAVERNS & BREW PUBS 🍸 ♿ **Breckenridge Brewery & Pub** (970-453-1550; www.breckenridgebrewery.com), 600 S. Main St. Open daily 11–close. Breckenridge Brewery first opened its doors in 1990 and is the only brewpub in town. The brewery serves its own microbrews like Avalanche Ale and Oatmeal Stout, and for especially discerning drinkers they have small-batch brews on hand. They also serve some great pub food.

Y ♿ **Downstairs at Eric's** (970-453-1401; www.downstairsaterics.com), 111 S. Main St. Open daily 11–midnight. The quintessential hangout, Downstairs at Eric's has an arcade, 18 televisions, and over 120 different beers. The perfect spot to watch the game. The kitchen serves from the menu until close.

SNACKS **Crêpes á la Cart** (970-453-4022), 307 S. Main St. This semi-permanent food cart near the Kenosha Steakhouse serves crepes both savory and sweet. The Philly cheese steak crepe is excellent, and the s'mores crepe deserves its status as the most popular crepe on the menu.

✷ Entertainment

Backstage Theatre (970-453-0199; www.backstagetheatre.org), 121 S. Ridge St. The Backstage Theatre has been bringing live performances to Breckenridge since 1974. Adult admission around $18, children $10.

✷ Selective Shopping

Hamlet's Bookshoppe (970-453-8033; www.hamletsbooks.com), 306 S. Main St. This bookstore is located in a creaky-floored Victorian, which just drips with character—the kind of place booklovers love to visit.

✷ Special Events

January: **International Snow Sculpture Championships.** The best snow artist teams in the world compete in this annual event. Spectators can watch them create art from 12-foot-tall, 20-ton blocks of snow. Contact the Breckenridge Resort Chamber (970-453-2913 or 1-800-221-1091; www.gobreck.com) for more information.

April: **Spring Massive Festival** (www.breckenridge.snow.com/springmassive.asp). This four-week festival kicks off on April Fool's Day with the crowning of the Town Fool. What follows is a series of family activities, live music, competitions, and some sub-festivals, like the Breckenridge Beer Fest. Check the Web site for a complete list of activities and entertainment.

August: **Dillon Open** (www.dillonopen.com), Dillon. The sailing event of the year, the Dillon Open is the highlight of the Dillon Yacht Club's regatta season.

August: **Genuine Jazz & Wine** (1-888-525-0555 or 1-877-225-1187; www.genuinejazz.com). Throughout the festival, jazz of all kinds is performed on two stages in town, including the floating stage on Maggie's Pond, and at various nightclubs. Saturday afternoon of this long weekend features wine tasting.

CRÊPES Á LA CART

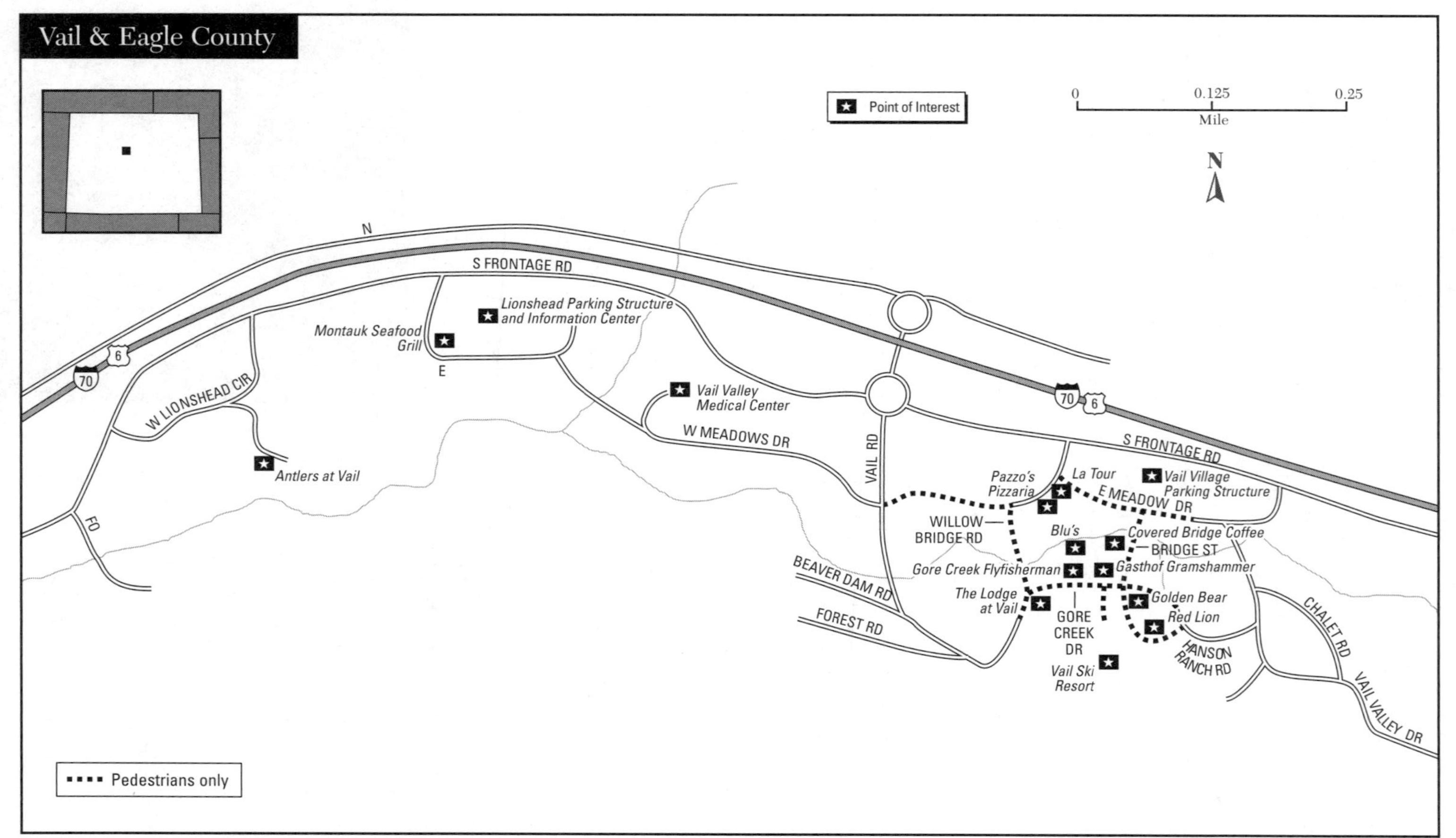
Vail & Eagle County
Point of Interest
0
0.125
0.25
Mile
N
S FRONTAGE RD
Lionshead Parking Structure and Information Center
Montauk Seafood Grill
E
70
6
W LIONSHEAD CIR
Vail Valley Medical Center
W MEADOWS DR
VAIL RD
Antlers at Vail
FO
Pazzo's Pizzaria
La Tour
Vail Village Parking Structure
E MEADOW DR
WILLOW BRIDGE RD
Blu's
Covered Bridge Coffee
BRIDGE ST
Gore Creek Flyfisherman
Gasthof Gramshammer
The Lodge at Vail
GORE CREEK DR
Golden Bear
Red Lion
HANSON RANCH RD
Vail Ski Resort
BEAVER DAM RD
FOREST RD
CHALET RD
VAIL VALLEY DR
Pedestrians only

VAIL & EAGLE COUNTY

Vail is unique among Colorado's ski towns. Skiing isn't something the town added later—the town came because there was skiing. Fifty years ago, if you were driving along I-70 through the Vail Valley, nothing in particular would have grabbed your attention. During World War II, the U.S. Army's 10th Mountain Division trained at nearby Camp Hale. The camp was south of the Vail Valley, and was comprised of a large swath of mountain terrain—its boundary included portions of five counties. Pete Seibert was one of the men who trained and subsequently fought with that original group of men. When he returned from World War II, he had a dream of coming to Colorado to start a ski area. Together with some partners, he did just that.

In 1962, work began on Vail Mountain. Over the years, the ski area grew, and today it is the largest ski area in the country. Not only are there over 5,000 acres for skiing, but the mountain tallies up more than a million "skier days" each year. The town itself began humbly enough—a couple hotels near the base of the mountain that tried to look like they could be found in a quaint Bavarian village. Over the years, the town grew exponentially, expanding north and south along I-70. Today it is divided into unofficial villages—there's West and East Vail, Vail Village, and Lionshead. Farther west is Avon and Edwards and the Beaver Creek ski area.

Because the town wasn't restricted by existing infrastructure, it could grow as it saw fit. Instead of being centered on a formal 19th-century downtown, with retail outlets split by the traditional Main Street, the heart of Vail is Vail Village, an outdoor pedestrian mall with winding stone streets and bridges over nearby Gore Creek. The village is right at the base of the mountain with immediate access to the two major lifts.

The success of Vail as a ski resort and town was not guaranteed. One of the town's greatest promoters was the late President Gerald Ford. When he was still just a lowly congressman from Michigan, Ford bought property here. Later, when he became vice president and then suddenly president, the media began to take notice. During his presidency, he was photographed skiing Vail, and that gave the ski area a certain amount of prestige. Even after his presidency, Ford and his wife remained devoted cheerleaders for the town, lending their names to the city's auditorium and the botanic gardens.

Because the town doesn't have dozens of historic properties to restore or a mining culture to preserve, the focus remains on skiing. And Vail has some of the best skiing around. From the road, the mountain may not look that impressive. There are some nice technical runs, but nothing to make it stand out among the state's other ski areas. Behind the Front Side, however, you find the coveted Back Bowls—these seven huge bowls stretch across 6 miles of terrain. And beyond that is the Blue Sky Basin with its backcountry mystique.

In any season, the town is a great place for roaming around, shopping, and dining. In the summer, you can take advantage of the somewhat cheaper rates for lodging and dining and come up for a vacation of fishing, hiking, or mountain biking.

GUIDANCE **The Vail Valley Chamber & Tourism Bureau** (970-476-1000 or 1-800-525-3875; www.visitvailvalley.com). In the summer, the Vail Village Information Center (970-476-4790), next to the Village parking structure, is open daily 9–2. The Lionshead Information Center (970-476-4941), next to the Lionshead parking structure, is open noon–5. In the winter, both are open daily 9–5.

More Web sites:

www.primavail.com

www.vail.net

GETTING THERE *By car:* Located right on I-70, Vail is 96 miles west of Denver (little more than a 90-minute drive). Travelers from the south may want to cut over on US 50 in Pueblo and follow the Arkansas Valley north (US 285 to US 24) to I-70. Though more scenic, this route is only 7 miles shorter than taking I-25 north to I-70 west.

By air: From the **Eagle County Airport** (970-524-9490; www.eaglecounty.us/airport) in Hayden, American, Delta, Northwest, United, and US Airways operate daily flights connecting the Vail Valley with Denver and several other cities around the country. If you are flying into the **Denver International Airport** (1-800-AIR2DEN; www.flydenver.com), it is about 120 miles east of Vail. The **Colorado Mountain Express** (970-926-9800 or 1-800-525-6363; www.cmex.com) will bring you from the DIA to Vail and Beaver Creek.

By bus: **Greyhound** operates regular service to and from Vail from the Vail Greyhound Transportation Center (970-476-5137 or 1-800-231-2222; www.greyhound.com), 241 S. Frontage Rd. E.

GETTING AROUND *By bus:* **The Vail Transportation Center** (970-479-2178) operates a free bus connecting all of Vail. **Eagle County Regional Transportation,** or ECO, offers bus service connecting Vail with other communities in the Vail Valley and Leadville. Check their Web site for route info (www.eaglecounty.us/eco_transit).

MEDICAL EMERGENCIES The following two medical centers offer 24-hour emergency care.

THE MOUNTAINS AROUND VAIL

Vail Valley Medical Center (970-476-2452; www.vvmc.com), 181 W. Meadow Dr.

Beaver Creek Village Medical Center (970-949-0800), 1280 Village Rd., Beaver Creek.

✷ To See & Do

Betty Ford Alpine Gardens (970-476-0103; www.bettyfordalpinegardens.org), 183 Gore Creek Dr. (Ford Park, east of Vail). Open in the summer from snowmelt to snowfall, daily dawn to dusk. At 8,200 feet, this is the world's highest botanical garden. These beautifully landscaped gardens feature high-altitude plants. This is the perfect spot for a summer stroll. There are over 2,000 varieties of plants here, all native to the Rocky Mountains. Free admission.

☂ ♿ **Colorado Ski Museum–Ski & Snowboard Hall of Fame** (970-476-1876; www.skimuseum.net), Vail Transportation Center, level 3. Open Tues.–Sat. 10–5; closed May and Oct. This fine museum might be of special interest to anyone involved in winter sports. It traces the history of skiing in Colorado for well over a century. Exhibits include the first primitive skis used by miners and a display that tells the story of snowboarding. For 10th Mountain Division buffs, there's an entire room here telling the story of the men trained here in the Rockies in ski warfare. Free admission.

✷ Outdoor Activities

ALPINE SKIING & SNOWBOARDING **Vail Mountain** (www.vail.com). Far and away, Vail is the largest and busiest ski area in the country. The resort has 5,289 acres of skiable terrain, comprised of seven bowls and four terrain parks, serviced by 34 lifts. Every year the mountain sees more than a million "skier days." Vail is comprised of three main sections—the Front Side, the Back Bowls, and Blue Sky Basin. The Front Side is what you see from the village. This is where you find all the beginner runs and terrain parks (though there are slopes here for all level of skiers). Behind the Front Side are seven huge bowls. The Back Bowls span 6 miles and offer terrain for intermediate and expert skiers. Dr. Ruth Westheimer, who skis Vail regularly, loves the China Bowl. Even farther back is the Blue Sky Basin, with backcountry-style terrain serviced by four high-speed quad lifts. Belle's Camp atop the basin offers food concessions and an outdoor grilling area for those who bring their own grub. For freeskiers and snowboarders, Vail has four terrain parks, two pipes, and a superpipe with 18-foot walls. For folks looking for a change of pace, there's a mountain playground of sorts called **Adventure Ridge at Eagle's Nest** (970-476-9090). This section of the ski area is set aside for ski biking, tubing, snowmobiling for the kids, ice skating, and all sorts of other activities. Adventure Ridge is lighted and open 2–9. A full-day lift ticket for Vail Mountain was $85 for adults in 2006–2007. You can expect to pay a little more in 2008 and beyond.

Beaver Creek (www.beavercreek.com). Folks looking for an experience that is more intimate than Vail often head a little farther down the road to Beaver Creek. This ski area has a reasonable 1,805 acres of skiable terrain, and an

THE 10TH MOUNTAIN DIVISION

In 1939, Finnish troops on cross-country skis were able to repel an invading Soviet army of superior size and firepower. As the U.S. was confronted with entering World War II, they considered the success of the Finnish troops and questioned their own military preparedness for winter warfare. So in 1940, the American Alpine Club began working with the War Department to determine what kind of training and equipment would be necessary. They were soon joined in this endeavor by the chair of the National Ski Patrol Association of the National Ski Association. Together they determined that a special unit of alpine soldiers needed to be formed.

In 1942, Camp Hale was established in the Rocky Mountains, north of Leadville. Comprised of volunteers who had previous experience in mountaineering and skiing, the division trained in the mountains throughout the winter of 1943–1944. They were deployed to Italy toward the end of the war in 1945. Their efforts there routed the Germans from seemingly impenetrable strongholds in the Alps. During the Italian campaign, the 10th Mountain Division suffered 4,888 casualties, and 978 men lost their lives in action.

Many of the men who trained here, returned to the Rocky Mountains. Their contribution to the war effort is memorialized by monuments at Camp Hale and at the summit of Tennessee Pass.

impressive 4,040 vertical drop. With 148 trails for skiing, and three terrain parks and a half pipe for snowboarding, visitors can spend a week here without feeling a need to venture out to other mountains. The Birds of Prey Downhill Course at Beaver Creek is the site of an annual World Cup competition. As such, it's a popular run for those out to test their skills on a classic double-black-diamond trail. For beginners, the Cinch Trail, which begins high up on the slope, offers a long easy glide to the bottom of the mountain. A full-day lift ticket for Beaver Creek in 2006–2007 was $85 for adults.

BICYCLING **Vail Bike Tech** (970-476-5995; www.vailbiketech.com), 555 E. Lionshead Cir. This biking outfitter has a shuttle to take riders up to Vail Pass for a thrilling ride back into Lionshead. This tour costs $35 ($45 with a guide). They can also hook you up for the ride to Frisco or Glenwood Springs. (See below for Mountain Biking.)

CROSS-COUNTRY SKIING & SNOWSHOEING **Vail Nordic Center** (970-476-8366; www.vailnordiccenter.com), 1778 Vail Valley Dr. In the winter in Colorado, many golf courses open their property up for cross-country skiers. This Nordic center operates at the Vail Golf Course. There are 17 kilometers of ski trails and 10 kilometers set aside for snowshoeing. The center offers equipment rental and lessons. A daily pass is only $5.

Beaver Creek's Nordic Sports Center & McCoy Park (970-754-5313; www.beavercreek.snow.com), Beaver Creek. Located at the top of the Strawberry Park lift at Beaver Creek, the Nordic Sports Center maintains over 30 kilometers of groomed and rustic trails for cross-country skiing and snowshoeing in McCoy Park. The center offers group lessons, private instruction, and a nature tour.

10th Mountain Division Hut Association (970-925-5775; www.huts.org). For backcountry skiing, huts make it possible for skiers to make multiday trips in the wilderness with the promise of comfortable, reliable shelter and a warm bed at night. The 10th Mountain Division Hut System is comprised of 29 backcountry huts connected by a network of trails (350 miles of suggested routes). Check the Web site for route information, hut availability, and rates.

DOGSLEDDING **Mountain Musher** (970-653-7877; www.mountainmusher.com), 16973 CO 131, Bond. The two dogsled tours Mountain Musher leads every day are on a private trail on the 10,000-acre Diamond Star Ranch. Twelve huskies pull the sled along a route that goes up and down the mountain. Guests can even drive the team themselves for part of the trip. For $160 guests get transportation to and from their hotel and everything they need for a comfortable tour (wool blankets, pillows, and a snack).

FISHING Gore Creek runs right through the middle of Vail and empties into the Eagle River west of town near Minturn. These are the two main waters for anglers in the Vail Valley. (The Colorado River is within easy driving distance if you are so motivated.) Nottingham Lake in Avon is also a good spot. It is stocked by the Colorado Division of Wildlife.

Fly Fishing Outfitters (970-476-3474; www.flyfishingoutfitters.net), US 6, Westgate Bldg., Avon. This outfitter offers Orvis-endorsed guide services. Most of the outfitter's wade and float trips take anglers out on the Eagle, Colorado, and Roaring Fork rivers. A half-day wade trip for one person is $250 (two people $325). A half-day float trip for one person is $300 (two people $350).

Gore Creek Flyfisherman (970-476-3296; www.gorecreekflyfisherman.com), 193 E. Gore Creek Dr. This outfitter has been guiding anglers in Vail Valley for over 20 years. Their guides will take you out on Eagle River, Gore Creek, and the Colorado. If the Vail location is not convenient, they have shops in Beaver Creek Village (970-754-5418; 111 Beaver Creek Plaza) and at the Ritz-Carlton at Bachelor Gulch (970-748-6880; 0130 Daybreak Ridge)—both in Avon. A half-day wade trip for one person $225 (two people $300). Float trips charged per boat—each accommodates one or two guests.

GOLF The Vail Valley is home to more than 18 golf courses. Theoretically, because of the altitude, the ball should sail farther here. Most of these courses have a dress code of some sort—stay away from denim, make sure there's a collar on your shirt, and check with each course beforehand to see their own particulars.

Vail Golf Club (970-479-2260; www.vailgolfclub.net), 1778 Vail Valley Dr. This 18-hole public course is just minutes from the Village. Greens fees $45–99.

Eagle Ranch Golf Club (970-328-2882; www.eagleranchgolf.com), 50 Lime Park Dr., Eagle. Located in the gently rolling Eagle Valley, this course is an Arnold Palmer Signature Design.

Greens fees $69–99.

HIKING There are numerous places for day hiking and backpacking in and around Eagle County. One of the most popular hikes in Vail is the 3,100-foot ascent to Booth Lake. Beginning at the end of Booth Falls Rd. (exit 180 on I-70), the 6-mile hike takes you by Booth Creek Falls and then above treeline to the pristine alpine lake. For an easier hike, turn around at the falls, which are about 2 miles in.

Vail Mountain (www.vail.com). Vail is so huge, there are plenty of trails for summer hiking. One of the benefits of hiking a ski mountain is that you can knock out some heavy climbing early on with the chairlifts. Eagle's loop offers an easygoing 1-mile trek with views of Holy Cross Mountain. A summer lift ticket (without bike haul) runs $18.

Beaver Creek Hiking Center (970-845-5373; www.beavercreek.snow.com), located at the Beaver Creek ticket office. In the summer the ski resort offers several guided hikes. The Nordic Walking trip is a 90-minute hike that uses Leki hiking poles for more of an upper body workout. Other hikes include interpretive nature walks and standard trips. Nordic Walking costs $16.

Paragon Guides (970-926-5299 or 1-877-926-5299; www.paragonguides.com), P.O. Box 130, Vail, CO 81618. For a hiking trip where you don't have to bust your hump carrying gear, consider llama trekking. Paragon Guides leads half-day trips, full-day trips, and peak ascents all summer. They also offer multiday backpacking trips throughout the central Rockies.

HORSEBACK RIDING **Beaver Creek Stable** (970-845-7770; www.vailhorses.com), 45 W. Thomas Pl., Beaver Creek. Operating on the Beaver Creek ski mountain, the stable has one- and two-hour trail rides that take you into the mountains, through aspen groves and meadows full with wildflowers. To make the ride more of an event, consider the picnic ride—the same route as the two-hour trip, but you are treated to a catered deli lunch in a mountain meadow midway.

MOUNTAIN BIKING **Vail Mountain** (www.vail.com). For an afternoon of downhill mountain biking, Vail has four trails on the Front Side. The Old Nine Line is plenty steep and technical—downhill gear (helmets and pads) are necessary. For $23, riders get a one-day lift ticket and bike haul.

Beaver Creek Hiking Center (970-845-5373; www.beavercreek.snow.com), located at the Beaver Creek ticket office, operates three-hour, guided mountain bike tours on the mountain. The $85 fee includes lift ticket and bike haul pass. Bikes can be rented for the trips at discounted rates.

To tackle the mountain on your own, bike rental is offered at **Beaver Creek Sports** (970-845-6221; www.beavercreeksports.com). Unlimited rides on the chairlift with bike haul is $23 for adults, $11 for children.

TrailWise Guides (970-827-5363 or 1-800-261-5364; www.trailwiseguides.com). The guides at TrailWise lead both instructional mountain biking tours for beginners and all-out adventure rides for the already initiated. Realizing that visitors to Vail may only have a couple opportunities to ride, they make it their business to ensure that guests get the best ride possible—taking into consideration the expectations and experience level of all riders. They provide everything you need except the clothes on your back.

GREEN SPACE The **Eagles Nest Wilderness** east of Vail is part of the White River and Arapahoe National Forests. With over 180 miles of trails contructed throughout the wilderness, there are seemingly endless opportunities to enjoy the park.

✱ Lodging

HOTELS "1" ♿ **Gasthof Gramshammer** (970-476-5626 or 1-800-610-7374; www.pepis.com), 231 E. Gore Creek Dr. Right in the heart of Vail Village sits the distinctive safety-yellow Bavarian-styled chalet that is the Hotel Gasthof Gramshammer. Owned and operated by Pepi Gramshammer, former international ski racer, and his wife Sheika, the hotel was one of the first in the valley after the ski resort opened. This European-style guest house offers tastefully decorated spacious rooms at affordable rates. Rooms, suites, and apartments $215–780 (winter rates).

"1" ♿ **The Lodge at Vail** (970-476-5011 or 1-800-367-7625; www.lodgeatvail.rockresorts.com), 174 E. Gore

GASTHOF GRAMSHAMMER

Creek Dr. This luxurious award-winning hotel has earned a reputation for rustic elegance and attentive personal service. Located at the base of Vail Mountain, the hotel has four hot tubs, a sauna, and a heated outdoor pool. The lodge offers complimentary ski waxing. Rooms $135–1,100.

Vail Cascade Resort & Spa (970-476-7111 or 1-800-420-2424; www.vailcascade.com), 1300 Westhaven Dr. Located at the base of Vail Mountain, with Chair 20 right outside, the Vail Cascade Resort offers luxury accommodations with ski-in/ski-out access to the slopes. The onsite spa offers a complete menu of services, and the health club has facilities for racquetball and basketball. Rooms $129–1,300.

Minturn Inn (970-827-9647 or 1-800-646-8876; www.minturninn.com), 442 Main St., Minturn. With the intimate atmosphere of a B&B and the attention to customer care of a boutique hotel, this log home from 1915 has been entirely refurbished and now offers luxury accommodations. It's the perfect alternative to the "hustle and bustle" of Vail Village. Some rooms have Jacuzzis for two. A full breakfast with hot entrée is served daily. Rooms $99–319.

Ritz-Carlton Bachelor Gulch on Beaver Creek Mountain (1-800-241-3333 or 970-748-6200; www.ritzcarlton.com/en/Properties/BachelorGulch), 130 Daybreak Ridge, Avon. With heavy western accents, the Ritz-Carlton Bachelor Gulch epitomizes the ski-town mountain lodge. Catering to almost every need imaginable, the hotel even has a resident yellow lab, Bachelor, to take with you on hikes in the mountains. Want to take a bath? Call the bath butler to draw you the perfect, fragrant steeping tub for your weary bones. The amenities here are really quite beyond all expectations. The rooms are luxuriously appointed with mountain and valley views and Frette linens on the beds. Rooms $150–6,000.

BED & BREAKFASTS **Intermountain** (970-476-4935; www.vailbb.com), 2754 Basingdale Blvd. For a truly authentic B&B experience, Intermountain has two rooms, both with a private bath. The Aubergine Room has a king bed that can be made into two twins. This cozy and intimate inn is run by Kay and Sepp Cheney, who have worked hard to create a welcoming environment. Every morning a full breakfast is served with homemade pastries and fresh orange juice. Rooms $150–180.

CONDOS "1" ♿ **Antlers at Vail** (970-476-2471 or 1-800-843-8245; www.antlersvail.com), 680 W. Lionshead Pl. Close to the gondola and the Lionshead Mall, Antlers rents condos—from studios with one bath to full-on condos with four bedrooms and four baths. Condos feature full kitchens, balconies, wide-screen TVs, and gas fireplaces. Pets are allowed in some rooms. Condos $185–2,375.

✻ Where to Eat

DINING OUT Be sure to call and make reservations for the restaurants below, especially during ski season.

♿ **Chap's Grill & Chophouse** (970-479-7014; www.vailcascade.com), 1300 Westhaven Dr. Open for breakfast, lunch, and dinner daily 7–10 (seating for dinner begins at 5:30). This upscale mountain-town eatery prides itself on serving great steaks and masterfully prepared regional game. Favorites include pepper-crusted double elk chop and the Blackfoot buffalo rib eye. The western influence menu is complemented by the dark woods of the dining room and wrought iron accents. Dinner entrées $26–38.

♿ **Montauk Seafood Grill** (970-476-2601; www.montaukseafoodgrill.com), 549 E. Lionshead Cir. Open nightly 5–9:30. For seafood, there really is no better restaurant than Montauk in the valley. Fresh fish is flown in daily. Their signature dish is the Hawaiian ahi, seared rare. Like many restaurants in Vail, Montauk offers huge discounts in the off-season. Entrées $18–28.

♿ **La Tour** (970-476-4403; www.latour-vail.com), 122 E. Meadow Dr. Open nightly for dinner at 5:30. Chef-owner Paul Ferzacca has a motto of sorts: "Simplicity is the mother of beauty." This helps define the menu

ANTLERS AT VAIL

at La Tour, which features contemporary French cuisine. Dishes are rich and flavorful, but not so much that they confuse the palate. The dining room is warm and unpretentious. Entrées $24–46.

Beano's Cabin (970-949-9090), Larkspur Bowl, Beaver Creek. Open nightly in the winter (Nov.–April) 5–10. The only way to get to Beano's Cabin on Beaver Creek Mountain is by sleigh or on horseback. Reservations required. Colorado cuisine is the theme of this innovative menu, which features such dishes as "Duck Trap River," smoked salmon quesadilla, and the gingerbread-encrusted Colorado rack of lamb. Chef Steven Topple's reputation goes beyond Colorado. He was recently invited to prepare a five-course dinner at the James Beard House in New York. Prix fixe starts around $90.

♿ **Mirabelle** (970-949-7728; www.mirabelle1.com), 55 Village Rd., Avon. Open nightly for dinner at 6 (closed Sunday). Located at the entrance of Beaver Creek, the restaurant has made itself at home in a restored Victorian that once was a family farmhouse. Warm colors and white linens create a comfortable environment in which to enjoy Chef Daniel Joly's menu of French-influenced European cuisine. Entrées $25–49.

EATING OUT Aside from a few fast-food joints, there are really no chain restaurants in Vail. This is bad news for those who rely on Applebee's for a sense of continuity on the road. For everyone else, however, it means taking a chance on local grub—a scary prospect for some, but there's enough good food to make the risk worthwhile.

♿ **Blu's** (970-476-3113; www.blusrestaurant.com), 193 E. Gore Creek Dr. Open daily 9–11. Although it has a "something for everyone" menu, Blu's is best known for its outstanding breakfasts. Eyebrows are raised at the green eggs and ham, but don't miss out on the awesome breakfast burritos. For a truly hearty start to the day, consider the steak and eggs. Breakfast and lunch dishes $8–10; dinner $15–30.

Pazzo's Pizzeria (970-476-9026), 122 E. Meadow Dr. A classic pizza joint, you will find that Pazzo's is conveniently located across from the Village parking structure. Decent pizza and a host of other Italian dishes on the menu (calzones, lasagna, spaghetti . . . nothing too fancy) make this a safe bet for family dining. Pizzas $11–25, sandwiches and entrées $7–13.

♿ **Minturn Saloon** (970-827-5954; www.minturnsaloon.com), 146 Main St., Minturn. Dining room opens nightly at 5 (bar at 3:30). From the outside, this joint looks like an Old West saloon—in part because it is. Built in 1901, the saloon's bar comes from Missouri and was built in 1830. While the atmosphere is western, the food is all Mexican (with some surpisingly classy dishes like the quail and enchilada). To get here from the slopes, take the Minturn Mile off Vail Mountain and ski the 3.5 miles of backcountry right up to the saloon. Dishes $8–29.

♿ **The Gashouse** (970-926-3613), 34185 US 6, Edwards. For some, the dining room's numerous mounted animal heads might be a bit distracting. For others, it's all part and parcel of this quirky restaurant's fun atmosphere. The menu offers classic comfort food, like fried chicken and ribs, as well as some upscale entrées, like

BRIDGE STREET

the quail or the elk tenderloin. Housed in a rustic log cabin that once served as a gas station, the ambiance is rounded out with license plate accents. Entrées $10–36.

BAKERIES & COFFEE SHOPS **Covered Bridge Coffee** (970-479-2883), 227 Bridge St. Open daily at 7:30. Next to a covered bridge in Vail, this coffeehouse serves more than a great cup of joe—they have some fantastic smoothies and unique dessert lattes.

♿ **Loaded Joe's Coffeehouse Lounge** (970-748-1480; www.loadedjoes.com), in the Benchmark Shopping Center. Open every morning at 7. Loaded Joe's is a gourmet coffeehouse with a split personality. When the sun goes down, it morphs into a hip lounge that screens independent movies and hosts dance night with a DJ and cheap beer.

BARS, TAVERNS & BREW PUBS **The Red Lion** (970-476-7676; www.theredlion.com), 304 Bridge St. The Red Lion is a favorite après-ski hangout. Nearly every night, Phil Long, one of Vail's most popular entertainers, puts on his live show. Some folks say it's too crowded, and if you are looking for an intimate getaway, you might want to try somewhere else.

Samana Lounge (970-476-3433; www.samanalounge.com), 228 Bridge St. This is the swankest club in town. For a chic, urbane martini lounge, you will want to check out the scene here first.

✷ Entertainment

The Vail Valley Foundation (www.vvf.org) works to promote athletic, cultural, and educational endeavors in the Vail Valley. As such, it is a great resource for finding cultural events in the area. Check the calendar for a list of concerts, performances, and talks throughout the valley.

The Bravo! Vail Valley Music Festival (1-877-812-5700; www.vailmusicfestival.org) runs concerts in Vail for about six weeks every summer. They also have a short series of concerts in the winter, so check the site for current happenings.

✱ Selective Shopping

The Golden Bear (970-476-4082; www.thegoldenbear.com), 953 S. Frontage Rd. W., Ste. 302. Martha's Vineyard has the Black Dog Tavern T-shirts and Vail has the Golden Bear pendants. Now, you can't throw it on to go play a game of one-on-one with the boys, but it's still a nice reminder of your trip—and it tells people "hey, I went to Vail."

Kemo Sabe (970-479-7474; www.kemosabe.com), 230 Bridge St. There are two of these "cowboy stores" in Colorado—one in Aspen, and the other here in Vail. For western wear, it's the only place to shop. You won't find a lot of cowboys shopping here, but Kemo Sabe works with you to bring out your own "inner cowboy." With Stetson hats, classic boots, and personal shoppers, there's no other western retailer like it.

✱ Special Events

April: **Spring Back to Vail** (www.springbacktovail.com). The most recent headliner at Spring Back to Vail was Kid Rock. For two weeks, bars all over town help celebrate the end of the season with après-ski parties, and the town gathers together for the annual World Pond-Skimming Championships (how far will momentum carry you across a pool of water?).

April: **Taste of Vail** (www.tasteofvail.com). Like the Taste of Colorado in Denver, this festival celebrates the culinary achievements of area restaurants and wineries. Plenty of concessions for the most discriminating foodie.

July: **Rocky Mountain Antique Festival** (www.rmafest.com), Beaver Creek. Antiques dealers from all over the West (and a few easterners) gather in Beaver Creek in July for this annual hawking of wares. Collectors of European and American antiques will be impressed by the quality and variety of items on display. There are also food vendors and street entertainment to round out the weekend.

KEMO SABE FOOTWEAR

WINTER PARK & GRAND COUNTY

Anyone who has taken the Ski Train to Winter Park knows something of the Moffat Tunnel. For 6.2 miles, any train heading west out of Denver enters the mountains by going under the Continental Divide, right through James Peak. For about 12 minutes, passengers only see dark tunnel walls from their train windows. When daylight shines again, they are in Winter Park.

Before 1927, the only "direct" way to the Fraser Valley was to climb a treacherous road over Berthoud Pass in the south or take a six-hour train ride over Rollins Pass that may or may not be delayed by avalanches and rockslides. The train opened the Fraser Valley to logging operations; it also had an effect on the small local communities. In 1940, Denver installed a ski tow at its 90-acre mountain park and opened a ski area with three runs and two jumps. Thus, Winter Park was born. The nearby communities of Old Town and Hideaway Park eventually became "Winter Park" when the town was formally established in 1978.

Today, the Winter Park ski area is really two or three interconnected ski areas (depending on who you talk to). Winter Park and Mary Jane both have their own base areas, and there's also Vasquez Ridge. There are plenty of trails, from easy runs to backcountry steeps to the moguls on Mary Jane, which have a great reputation for shaking your teeth loose. Because Denverites often see Winter Park as their own personal ski park, the mountain gets lots of traffic—over a million "skier days" each year.

For many years Winter Park was primarily used for day-skiing. The Ski Train drops you off in the morning and takes you back to Denver at night. As such, the sprawl of resorts and restaurants you find in other ski towns are surprisingly absent. Within the last five or six years, however, the city of Denver has brokered a deal with a ski-resort developer. The plan is to pump a ton of money into Winter Park, upgrade the facilities, and see if it can't be made into a more traditional resort town. The jury is out on whether or not the plan is working.

But skiing isn't all there is to Grand County. The Fraser River winds its way north through Fraser, Tabernash, and Granby to empty into the Colorado, which continues on to Hot Sulfur Springs and Kremmling. This region of the state is a paradise for hunting and fishing. In the winter, it's popular with snowmobilers.

The county also has several impressive lakes. In the northeast, there's a chain of lakes—Grand Lake, Shadow Mountain Lake, and Lake Granby. Nestled in

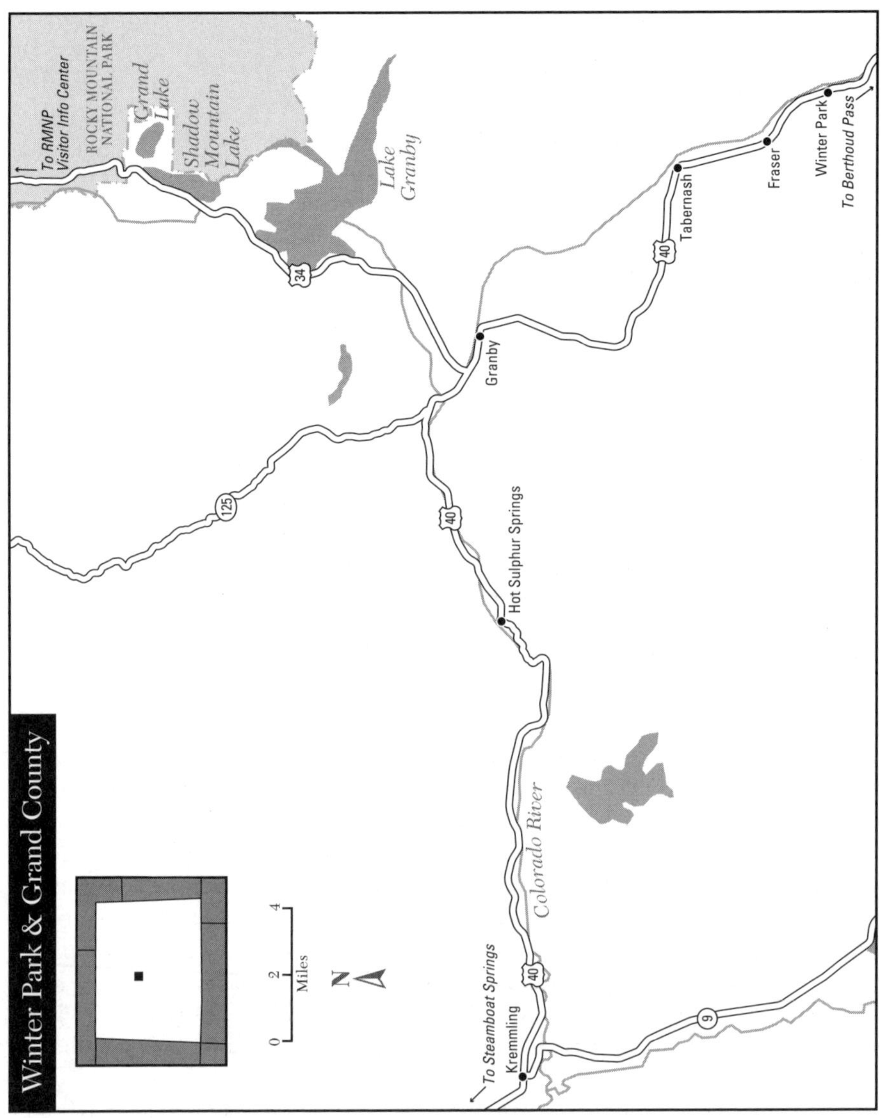

the pines along the north shore of Grand Lake is a town of the same name. Grand Lake can be a bit touristy. It seems to fancy itself an Old West saloon town—a wide main street, wooden sidewalks, and western facades complete the effect. But beyond the cheesy trappings, Grand Lake offers unique opportunities to experience Colorado's natural beauty. Nearby marinas rent boats for getting out on the water, and the western portal of Rocky Mountain National Park is just a mile or so from town.

Most of the attractions, lodgings, and restaurants listed below are open year-round. Many, however, reduce hours significantly for about six weeks in the spring and fall. Be sure to call ahead during these two off-seasons. Unless otherwise indicated, all addresses are in Winter Park.

GUIDANCE **Winter Park–Fraser Valley Chamber of Commerce** (970-726-4118 or 1-800-903-7275; www.winterpark-info.com or www.playwinterpark.com). Open daily 8–5, the chamber's visitor center is located east of town on US 40.

Grand Lake Area Chamber of Commerce (970-627-3402 or 1-800-531-1019; www.grandlakechamber.com). The chamber's visitor information center is located on US 34, right as you turn to head into town. Open daily in the summer 9–5.

Granby Chamber of Commerce (970-887-2311; www.granbychamber.com), 365 E. Agate Ave., Ste. B. The visitors can get tourist information in Granby Mon.–Fri. 9–5.

Kremmling Area Chamber of Commerce (1-877-573-6654; www.kremmling chamber.com), 203 Park Ave. Visitor center is open Mon. 11:30–5:30, Tues.–Fri. 8:30–5:30 (closes at 3 on Wed.), and Sat. 10–4. The new visitor center in Kremmling has clean rest rooms and plenty of information on area activities.

GETTING THERE *By car:* To get to Winter Park and Grand County from Denver, head west on I-70 to exit 232, then drive north on US 40. The twisty route takes you up switchbacks and over Berthoud Pass (elevation 11,314 feet). Though only about 70 miles from Denver, the route can take over an hour and a half in the winter.

By air: The closest airport is the **Denver International Airport** (1-800-AIR-2DEN; www.flydenver.com), which is about 68 miles east of Winter Park. **Home James Transportation Services** (970-726-4730 or 1-800-359-7503; www.home jamestransportation.com) runs a shuttle between the DIA and Winter Park—over 20 runs a day. They also have chartered jet service to Winter Park out of DIA.

By train: One of the most convenient ways to get to Winter Park is via the **Winter Park Ski Train** (303-296-4754; www.skitrain.com). The train leaves Denver's Union Station and arrives at the very base of the Winter Park ski area. Set up as a way for skiers to spend the day on the mountain, round-trip tickets are good for one day. **AMTRAK** (1-800-872-7245) offers train service from their station in Fraser at 205 Fraser Ave. All trains heading into Grand County pass through the Moffat Train Tunnel—a 6.2-mile stretch of track that runs through the mountain under the Continental Divide.

GETTING AROUND *By bus:* The resort operates a free shuttle service, the **Lift** (970-726-4163), which makes the rounds between Fraser and the Winter Park ski area. It runs in the summer and during the ski season.

MEDICAL EMERGENCIES **Seven Mile Medical Clinic** (970-726-8066), 145 Parsens Rd. Not a 24-hour facility.

✷ To See & Do

☂ ♿ **Cozen Ranch House Museum** (970-725-3939; www.grandcountymuseum .com/cozensranch.htm), east side of US 40 between Winter Park and Fraser.

Open Thurs.–Sat. 10–4. Visitors can tour one of the oldest homesteads in the Fraser Valley. In the main house, some interesting items, like the original wallpaper, are still visible. There are also some historical photos of the Cozen family and early life in Fraser. Adult admission $4, seniors $3, students $2, and kids under 6 free.

☂ **Kaufmann House Museum** (970-627-9644; www.kauffmanhouse.org), Pitkin and Lake Ave., Grand Lake. Built in 1892, this small lodge was run as a hotel until Ezra Kaufmann died in 1920. The museum tells the story of the business of tourism and life in Grand Lake around the turn of the century. Open daily in the summer 11–5. Admission is free.

☂ ♿ **Pioneer Village** (970-725-3939; www.grandcountymuseum.com/county museum.htm), east end of Hot Sulphur Springs on US 40. Open in the summer Wed.–Sat. 10–4; winter, Tues.–Sat. 10–5 and Sun. 1–5. Housed in the historic Hot Sulfur Springs school, the museum tells the story of Grand County. Included is an exhibit on early skiing in Colorado. Adult admission $4, seniors $3, students $2, and kids under 6 free.

✴ Outdoor Activities

ALPINE SKIING & SNOWBOARDING **Winter Park's several ski areas** (970-726-5514 or 303-892-0961; www.skiwinterpark.com), 239 Winter Park Dr. This ski area began as one of Denver's mountain parks. In 1940, when the first ski tow was installed, there were only three formal trails. Today Winter Park is known for incredible moguls, long, easy runs, and great terrain parks. The ski area is really two interconnected ski areas—Winter Park and Mary Jane, both of which have their own base area. Winter Park remains the most accessible for beginners and intermediate skiers. For more technically advanced skiing, Mary Jane has advanced and expert runs. The ski area's Vasquez Cirque is home to the

KAUFFMAN HOUSE MUSEUM IN GRAND LAKE

park's extreme skiing areas. Overall, Winter Park has a 3,060-foot vertical drop and 2,886 acres of skiable terrain, and receives an incredible 370 inches of snow annually. Adult two-day lift ticket $106–158 and children (6–12) $56–70.

West Portal Boots & Boards (970-726-1665; www.skiwinterpark.com). Located at the base of Winter Park ski area, the shop rents and sells gear for both skiers and snowboarders. Services include equipment repair and tune-ups.

SolVista Basin (970-887-3384 or 1-888-283-7458; www.solvista.com), 1000 Village Rd., Granby. The smaller SolVista ski area has 287 skiable acres on two interconnected mountains. The East Mountain is best suited for beginner and intermediate skiers. The West Mountain has little for beginners but plenty of trails for intermediate and advanced skiers. The ski area has a terrain park and halfpipe. There's also a separate learn-to-ski park. Adult full-day lift ticket $46, seniors $31, kids (6–12) $21, and children under 5 free.

ALPINE SLIDE **Alpine Slide** (1-800-979-0332; www.skiwinterpark.com). Accessed from the Arrow chairlift, the alpine slide at Winter Park is the state's longest. It runs 3,030 feet and has 26 turns. Riders control their speed. There are two parallel tracks—for slower and faster riders. Adult pass $14 and children (6–13) $10.

BOATING **Beacon Landing** (970-627-3671; www.beaconlanding.us), 1026 CR 64, Granby. Located on the largest of the county's lakes, Lake Granby, the Beacon Landing Marina rents pontoon boats and fishing gear—everything you need for a day on the water.

Trail Ridge Marina (970-627-3586; www.trailridgemarina.com), 12634 US 34, Grand Lake. Located on Shadow Mountain Lake, the marina has fishing boats, pleasure boats, and pontoon boats for rent. If you've brought along your own vessel, they have slip and dock rentals.

TRAIL RIDGE MARINA ON SHADOW MOUNTAIN LAKE

CROSS-COUNTRY SKIING & SNOWSHOEING **Devil's Thumb Cross-Country Center** (970-726-8231; www.devilsthumbranch.com), 3530 CR 83, Tabernash. With 125 kilometers of groomed trails on 4,000 acres, this is one the best spots for cross-country skiing and snowshoeing in the Fraser Valley. Eight kilometers of trails are reserved for skijoring (a sport where skiers are pulled by a dog), and they have some lighted trails for night skiing. Skis and snowshoes are available for rent, and the ranch offers lessons and tours. Full-day ski and snowshoe pass for adults $15, children under 12 and seniors $6.

YMCA Nordic Center at Snow Mountain Ranch (970-887-2152; www.ymcarockies.org), US 40 between Winter Park and Grand Lake. With 100 kilometers of groomed trails, the Nordic center has routes for skiers and snowshoers of all abilities. The ranch offers equipment rental and instruction packages. In addition to ski facilities, there's ice skating, sleigh rides, and tubing down a great sledding hill. Full-day ski and snowshoe pass for adults $15, children under 12 $8.

Winter Park Tour Center (1-800-729-7907; www.winterparkresort.com). The resort offers snowshoe tours that depart from the base of the mountain. Call for more information.

DOGSLEDDING **Dog Sled Rides of Winter Park** (970-726-8326; www.dogsledrides.com/winterpark), Kings Crossing Rd. A 45-minute dogsled tour through the forests of Winter Park covers 4–5 miles. Once guests are comfortable with the experience, they can try their hand at mushing. Reservations by phone are required.

FLY-FISHING ON THE COLORADO

FISHING **Mo Henry's Trout Shop** (970-726-9754; www.mohenrys.com), 540 Zerex St., Fraser. Since 2004, these two brothers have been sharing their passion for fly-fishing with everyone who walks through the door of their shop. For fishing information only locals know, be sure to check out Mo Henry's first.

Grand County Fishing Company (970-531-9988; www.grandflyfishing.com), 234 CR 803, Fraser. For fishing on the Fraser River, this outfitter has access to 4 miles of private water. They also take guests out on the Colorado, Green, and upper South Platte rivers. A half-day wade trip will set you back $185—but the per person rate decreases for each person you add to the party (up to four).

GOLF **Grand Elk Ranch & Club** (970-887-9122 or 1-877-389-9333; www.grandelk.com), 1300 Ten Mile Dr., Granby. This nice 18-hole course blends into the surrounding Fraser Valley. With plenty of wild grass, this is more of a target-oriented course than others in the area. Greens fees $49–99.

Pole Creek Golf Club (970-887-9195; www.polecreekgolf.com), 6827 CR 51, Tabernash. Three nine-hole courses—Meadow, Ranch, and Ridge—make up Pole Creek. The beautifully wooded mountain surroundings make a pleasant backdrop to this links-style course. Greens fees $69–89.

HORSEBACK RIDING **Sombrero Ranch** (970-627-3514; www.sombrero.com), 1471 CR 491, Grand Lake. Located in Grand Lake, with access to nearby Rocky Mountain National Park, Sombrero Ranch offers trail rides to fit any schedule. They have breakfast rides and steak-fry rides as well. The two-hour ride runs $45 (kids under 11 are just $35).

MOUNTAIN BIKING **Winter Park Resort** (970-726-5514 or 303-892-0961; www.skiwinterpark.com). In the summer, the Winter Park ski area opens its trails for mountain bike use. Fifty miles of trails connect with 600 miles of trails in Fraser Valley. The ski area has plans to add 10 new trails for cyclists of varying ability over the next year or so. A one-trip lift ticket costs $18, or you can purchase unlimited rides for the day for around $39. Your best bet might be to start with the one-trip ticket and then upgrade to unlimited if you need more downhill fun. Bikes are available for rent at the base of the ski area at **West Portal Bike Rentals** (970-726-1665).

SNOWMOBILING **Trailblazer Snowmobile Tours** (970-726-8452 or 1-800-669-0134; www.trailblazersnowmobile.com), CR 50. Snowmobiling is a big activity in Grand County, from Kremmling over to Grand Lake. In the Winter Park area, this outfitter leads guided rides into the Arapahoe National Forest. They have half- and full-day rides and can accommodate the entire family.

GREEN SPACE Rocky Mountain National Park is truly one of Colorado's great natural treasures. Grand Lake is the park's western portal. On US 34, heading east, visitors first come upon the **Kawuneeche Visitor Center** (970-627-3471; www.nps.gov/romo), the best place to get started exploring. (See Estes Park for more information.)

✷ Lodging

HOTELS **Iron Horse Resort** (970-726-8851 or 1-800-621-8190; www.ironhorse-resort.com), 101 Iron Horse Way. One of Winter Park's first ski-in/ski-out lodges; from the resort you can ski right to a lift line. The resort rents condo units, from deluxe studios to lodging with two bedrooms and three baths. Condos in the summer run $95–289; winter, $109–839.

The Vintage Hotel (970-726-8801 or 1-800-472-7017; www.vintagehotel.com), 100 Winter Park Dr. Just seconds from the Mary Jane base area, the hotel offers both traditional hotel rooms as well as suites with kitchenettes, fireplaces, and whirlpool tubs. Most of the accommodations at the Vintage Hotel enjoy fabulous views of the surrounding mountains. There are ski lockers and gear rental on-site. Rooms and suites $60–550.

Zephyr Mountain Lodge (1-800-729-5813; www.zephyrmountainlodge.com), 201 Zephyr Way. Within the Winter Park Resort, this is the only true ski-in/ski-out lodge. It's at the base of the mountain, and rooms come with excellent views. The spacious condo-style rooms have full kitchens and gas fireplaces. There are four outdoor hot tubs, and the hotel has a free shuttle to ferry guests into town. While many of the hotels and lodges in the area have dated décor, the Zephyr Mountain Lodge has a contemporary, hip western feel. Rooms $156–983.

Beaver Village Lodge (970-726-5741 or 1-800-666-0281; www.beavervillage.com), 79303 US 40 (south end of town). The Beaver opened back in 1940. It was the first lodging in town and has been here since the ski area opened. Convenient to the resort and close to downtown, the lodge is on the free shuttle route. The wood-paneled hallways and rooms are considered dark by some, but cozy by others. There's a hot tub, sauna, and game room on-site. During ski season, they offer a breakfast and dinner buffet that is included in

BEAVER VILLAGE LODGE

the lodging rate. In the winter rooms run $35–170 per person.

Snow Mountain Ranch–YMCA of the Rockies (1-800-777-9622; www.ymcarockies.org), 1101 CR 53, Granby. (See Front Range for the Estes Park portion of YMCA of the Rockies.) The ranch offers a wide variety of programs for families and groups. In addition to a swimming pool, ropes course, and horseback riding, there are opportunities for mountain biking in the summer and Nordic skiing in the winter. Snow Mountain Ranch offers visitors lodge rooms, cabins, and campsites. Lodge rooms $74–119, cabins $149–389, and campsites $25–35.

BED & BREAKFASTS **Outpost Bed & Breakfast** (970-726-5346 or 1-800-430-4538; www.winterpark-inn.com), 687 CR 517, Fraser. Offering views of the Indian Peaks, the Outpost B&B has a large back deck and a spacious yard—perfect for enjoying a summer day or evening in the mountains. The inn's seven rooms all have private baths and are decorated with antiques and both Victorian and southwestern accents. The full gourmet breakfast is served by candlelight. Rooms $95–145.

Wild Horse Inn (970-726-0456; www.wildhorseinn.com), 1536 CR 83, Fraser. From *Travel & Leisure* magazine to the inn's many guests, everyone agrees this is the best B&B in the valley. The inn's main building, a log and stone structure reminiscent of a classic mountain lodge, is tucked back in the woods, just off the road that leads to Devil's Thumb Ranch. The inn offers seven rooms and three log cabins—the Mariposa, the Meadowcreek, and the Saddleblanket. Each cabin has a kitchenette, fireplace, and a tub for two. The décor throughout the inn could be called rustically elegant—nothing overblown, every detail tasteful. A full gourmet breakfast is served every morning. On-site massage is available (arrange in advance). Rooms $135–235 and cabins $195–260.

The Snowberry Bed & Breakfast (970-726-5974; www.thesnowberry.com), 1001 CR 83, Fraser. Chris and John Cribari, who own the Wild Horse Inn, recently opened another B&B up the street. The Snowberry has a distinctly European feel—French country perhaps—with all the old-world charm that implies. The B&B has five rooms, each with a private bath. The back deck has views of the Indian Peaks. And, of course, a full breakfast is served every morning. Rooms $155–225.

CAMPGROUNDS **Elk Creek Campground** (970-627-8502 or 1-800-355-2733; www.elkcreekcamp.com), 143 CR 48, Grand Lake. Open April–Oct. Just outside Grand Lake, near Rocky Mountain National Park, the Elk Creek Campground has wooded sites and many opportunities to view wildlife. It's not uncommon to catch sight of elk and moose. Tent sites $22–24 and RV sites (depending on hook-ups) $30–38.

CABINS & COTTAGES **Shadow Mountain Guest Ranch** (970-887-9524 or 1-800-647-4236; www.colorado-directory.com/shadowmtnranch), 5043 CO 125, Granby. Northwest of Granby, the Shadow Mountain Guest Ranch has five log cabins, each with plenty of character. A big ranch-cooked breakfast comes with all cabin rentals. Cabins $145–325.

✻ Where to Eat

DINING OUT 🍸 **Lodge at Sunspot** (970-726-1446 or 1-800-510-8025; www.skiwinterpark.com), Winter Park Resort. For a special mountain dining experience, take the Zephyr Express Lift for seven minutes to 10,700 feet. There you will find the Lodge at Sunspot, a large stone and log structure that offers panoramic views of the mountains. Inside, there are two dining options: the Provisioner (a classy food court) and the Dining Room (the more formal eatery, serving five-course meals and the like). The Dining Room is open for lunch and dinner during ski season. Reservations required for special dinners, and highly recommended otherwise. Prix-fixe dinner $39–59.

🍸 ♿ **Ranch House Restaurant at Devil's Thumb Ranch** (970-726-5632 or 1-800-933-4339; www.devilsthumbranch.com), 3530 CR 83, Tabernash. Hours vary by season—please call for current hours and to make reservations (highly recommended). Located on the Devil's Thumb Ranch, the Ranch House offers a fine menu prepared with organically grown, local produce and meats. Though the menu changes regularly, you can expect to find dishes like elk, antelope, and bison as well as steak and seafood. The intimate dining room has exposed beams and fits easily in the ranch environment. Dinner entrées $17–37.

🍸 ♿ **Back Street Steakhouse** (970-627-8144; www.davenhavenlodge.com), 604 Marina Dr., Grand Lake, at the Daven Haven Lodge. Open daily in the summer 11–9. Call for winter hours. Featured in *Bon Appétit,* this steakhouse has a reputation for fine dining. In keeping with the surroundings, there is nothing pretentious about the restaurant; just great food in a casual atmosphere. As you might suspect, the restaurant serves fantastic steaks, from prime rib to premium-cut Angus beef. The Jack Daniel's pork chops are a house specialty. Lunch up to $10 and dinner entrées $7–28.

EATING OUT 🍸 ♿ **Deno's Mountain Bistro** (970-726-5332; www.denosmountainbistro.com), 78911 US 40. Open for lunch and dinner at 11:30 and 5, respectively. The building that Deno's calls home has been in Winter Park for decades. At one time it housed a pharmacy and barbershop. As the Village Inn, there was a restaurant, bar, gas station, and stables. Today the bistro serves lunch and dinner. The lunch menu is full of sandwiches and burgers, as well as some unexpected items, like the baked goat cheese fondue and penne pomodoro. For dinner the menu is a bit more upscale with steak, seafood, and chicken. They also have a great wine list. Dinner $18–30 and lunch $7–10.

♿ **Hernando's Pizza Pub** (970-726-5409; www.hernandospizzapub.com), 78199 US 40. Open for dinner 4–10 during ski season; open fewer hours in the off-season. Since 1967, Hernando's has been dishing out pizza pies in Winter Park. The dining room is especially comfortable with stained-glass windows and a number of fireplaces. There are other items on the menu besides pizza, like pasta and Italian sandwiches, but don't do yourself a disservice—try the pizza. Pizzas $7.75–17.55 and pasta $7.

♿ **Sagebrush BBQ & Grill** (970-627-1404 or 1-866-900-1404; www.sagebrushbbq.com), 1101 Grand Ave., Grand Lake. Open daily 7–10. Located at the corner of Grand Avenue and Pitkin Street, the Sagebrush is an oddity in a tourist town—this is exceptional family dining. Known especially for outstanding barbeque, Sagebrush also serves up one of the best bean burritos in Colorado. The breakfast menu isn't too shabby either. Lunch and dinner entrées $8–18 (more for crab and steaks and the barbeque combo platter).

BAKERIES & COFFEE SHOPS

♿ **Rocky Mountain Roastery** (970-726-4400; www.rockymountainroastery.com), 543 Zerex, Fraser. Open daily 7–8. Boasting their "high mountain roasting process," this coffee shop offers a number of signature blends at two locations. The Original Roastery in Fraser has been in town sine 1993. Out at the Winter Park ski resort be sure to check out RMR Too (970-726-6838).

BARS, TAVERNS & BREW PUBS

♿ **Buckets Saloon and Laundry** (970-726-3026; www.bucketssaloon.com), 78415 US 40. The laundry opens daily at 9 and the bar is open nightly 4–2. Everyone knows what a drag it can be to take time out from your vacation to do laundry. This combination saloon/laundry might just be the answer. The bar has an arcade and pool tables and often has live music. Ski bums with no TVs come to watch their favorite programs, and there are always people with enough alcohol in them to try karaoke.

✷ Selective Shopping

Trail Ridge Art Company (970-726-4959; www.trailridgeart.com), Copper Creek Sq. Open Mon.–Sat. 10–9 and Sun. 10–6. This gallery sells the work of over 60 Colorado artists, many of them local. The gallery also has a paint-your-own-pottery studio for the kids.

✷ Special Events

July: **Grand Lake Regatta and Lipton Cup Races** (970-627-3377). This annual race brings sailors into the mountains—fantastic photo ops with full sails set against the Rocky Mountains.

STEAMBOAT SPRINGS & THE YAMPA VALLEY

Steamboat Springs is known for its unique western character. Images of Steamboat always include one of cowboys skiing. Much of that is due to the town's most famous ski personality, Billy Kidd, who won the silver medal in the slalom in 1964. He's the director of skiing at Steamboat, and he can often be seen coming down the mountain in his signature cowboy hat. He also invited rodeo stars to town back in 1975 to compete in what has become an annual ski competition.

It's this western, blue-collar vibe that gives Steamboat its personality. This is not a town of pampered lifties "doing Steamboat." It's a town of hard-working farmers and ranch hands who happen to live in a town with ski bums (and some pampered lifties). As such, there's no shortage of affordable dining and lodging, because this is a place where people live. Driving in from the south, the entrance into downtown is marked by the giant neon sign in front of the Rabbit Ears Motel. This historic landmark has been greeting drivers for over 50 years.

The town of Steamboat Springs has been around since the late 19th century. In 1865, three French trappers heard an unexpected sound as they worked the Yampa Valley. It was a chugging noise that they at first mistook for the sound of a steam-powered paddleboat coming down the Yampa River. It turned out to be the bubbling of the region's hot springs. This is how the town got its name. Several years later, in 1874, James Harvey Crawford came upon the Yampa Valley and staked a claim.

Unlike most ski towns in Colorado, Steamboat did not spring to life as a mining town. Instead, it began as, and to some extent remains, a town rooted in ranching and farming. It did not explode onto the scene like Aspen or Breckenridge, but instead grew slowly over the years.

In 1912, a Norwegian skier moved into town. Carl Howelsen was passionate about skiing—mainly cross-country and jumping—and his passion was contagious. By 1913, Steamboat had a ski jump, and Howelsen was teaching local youths how to compete in this new sport. Howelsen is credited with kicking off skiing as a sport in Colorado. Considering the impact skiing has had across the state, that's no an insignificant contribution. During the 1930s, alpine skiing

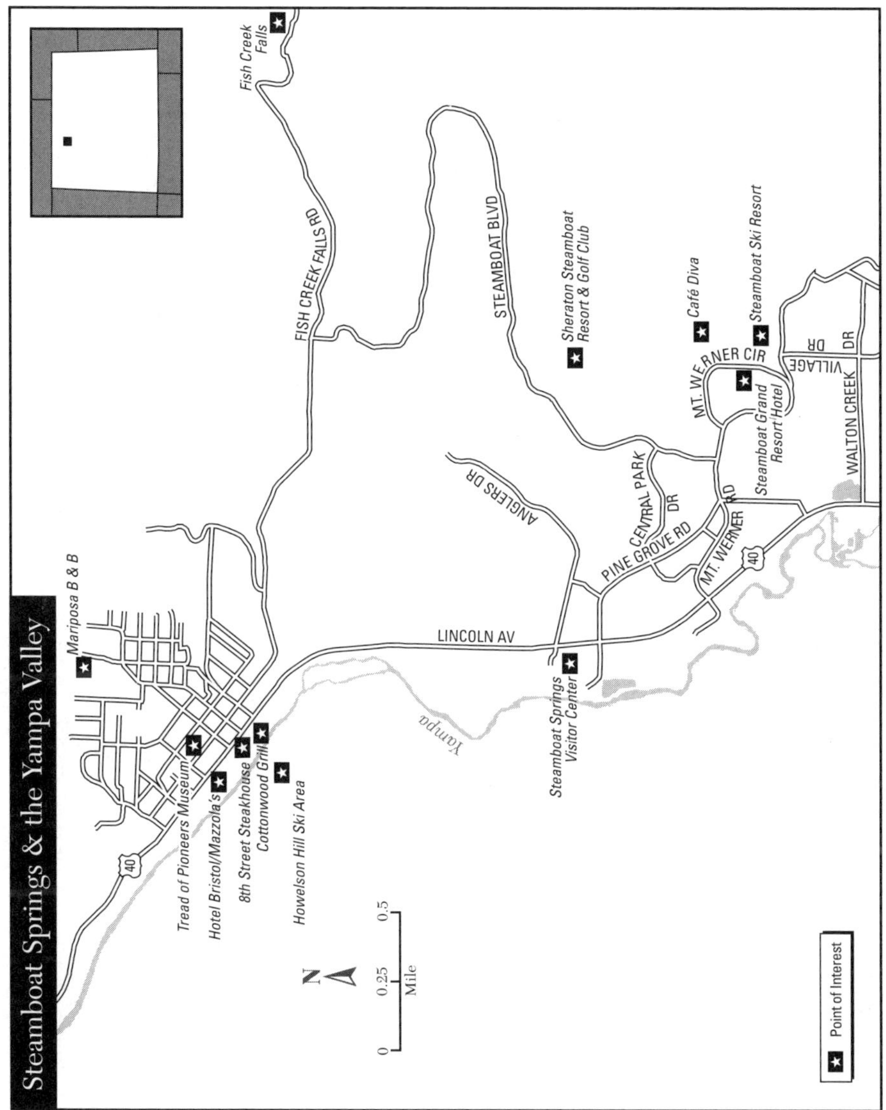

started to become popular all over, and it soon replaced ski-jumping in Steamboat. In 1961, the Steamboat ski area opened. Soon there were several lifts, and the resort took off from there.

Over the years, Steamboat has sent more athletes to the Winter Olympics than any other town in the country, earning it the nickname Ski Town, USA. The town gets 331 inches of snow annually. Called Champagne Powder, the snow is the fluffiest and driest snow you can find anywhere, and when there's fresh powder, skiers are followed down the mountain by arcing plumes of the stuff. Many skiers dismiss Steamboat Springs, because they say it lacks the extreme steeps found at other ski areas. Steamboat, however, has a great reputation for its easygoing long glides and stunningly beautiful wooded runs.

GUIDANCE The **Steamboat Springs Chamber Resort Association** (970-879-0880; www.steamboatchamber.com or www.steamboatsummer.com), 1255 S. Lincoln Ave. The association operates the Steamboat Springs Visitor Center, which is open year-round Mon.–Fri. 8–5. In the winter they add hours on Sat. 10–4.

GETTING THERE *By car:* Steamboat is a bit off the beaten track—about 155 miles from Denver (three hours driving). The best route is I-70 west to Silverthorne, then CO 9 north to Kremmling. Then turn left on US 40 and follow the road northwest over Rabbit Ears Pass (elevation 9,426) and into Steamboat Springs; US 40 continues west into Utah.

By air: From the **Yampa Valley Airport** (970-276-5001) in Hayden, Delta and United operate daily flights connecting Steamboat Springs with Salt Lake City and Denver. If you are flying into the **Denver International Airport** (1-800-AIR2DEN; www.flydenver.com), it is about 180 miles east of Steamboat. The **Alpine Taxi** (970-879-2800 or 1-800-343-7433; www.alpinetaxi.com) operates a shuttle service that will pick up guests at the DIA or the Yampa Valley Airport and bring them to Steamboat.

GETTING AROUND *By bus:* **Steamboat Springs Transit** (970-879-3717) is a "free to user" bus system that provides service between downtown and the ski resort base area. It operates year-round.

By taxi: **Alpine Taxi** (970-879-8294 or 970-879-2800; www.alpinetaxi.com) operates a local taxi service.

MEDICAL EMERGENCIES The **Yampa Valley Medical Center** (970-879-1322; www.yvmc.org), 1024 Central Park Dr., offers round-the-clock emergency medical service.

✱ To See & Do

Tread of Pioneers Museum (970-879-2214), Eighth and Oak Sts. Open Tues.–Sat. 11–5. Housed in a 1908 Queen Anne–style Victorian, the museum tells the story of pioneer life in Routt County. There are exhibits on Native American life, and the museum has an impressive firearms collection. Of interest to many coming to Steamboat is the exhibit on the history of skiing. Adult admission $5, seniors $4, and children under 12 $1.

✓ **Fish Creek Falls.** A short hike takes you to an overlook with a view of the 283-foot Fish Creek Falls. Another tad-more-difficult trail leads down to the creek itself. During the summer, families put on their bathing suits and suntan lotion and play on the rocks by and in the creek. The parking lots for the short hike to the falls are at the end of Fish Creek Rd. (CR 32). To get there from town, take Third Street one block north and turn right, and then follow this road 4.5 miles to the parking area. There are two lots—head for the second unless it's already full. There's a $3 fee for parking.

Strawberry Park Natural Hot Springs (970-879-0342; www.strawberryhotsprings.com), Strawberry Park Rd. Open Sun–Thu. 10–10:30 and Fri. and Sat. 10–midnight. The hot springs water hits the mountain air at around 150 degrees and cools as it flows into the successive stone pools. While you soak, enjoy views of the steep canyon walls and nearby creek. Tent sites, cabins, and other lodgings are available for a longer stay. Clothing is optional after dark. Adult soak $10, teens (13–17) $5, and children (3–12) $3.

FISH CREEK FALLS

* Outdoor Activities

ALPINE SKIING & SNOWBOARDING

Steamboat Ski Resort (970-879-0740 or 1-877-237-2628; www.steamboat.com), 2305 Mt. Werner Cir. Steamboat is really an entire mountain range, adding up to 165 trails on 2,965 skiable acres. From summit to base, skiers enjoy an overall 3,668-foot vertical drop. The regulars who ski these slopes every year come back for the ski area's easy-going descents; more than half of the terrain is for intermediate skiers. They also come for the phenomenal snow. Steamboat gets 331 inches of the stuff annually—not just any snow, but the area's trademarked Champagne Powder, purportedly the fluffiest and driest snow you can find anywhere. For freeskiers and snowboarders, Steamboat has four terrain parks and the much touted Mavericks Superpipe. Adult lift tickets (three of four days) $68–85/day, seniors $58, teens $50, and children $39.

Howelsen Hill Ski Area (970-879-8499), 137 10th St. In 1912, the Norwegian skier Carl Howelsen brought the sport of skiing to Steamboat and soon was organizing the Steamboat Springs Winter Sports Club, training youth to compete in cross-country skiing and ski jumping. The hill that bears his name was used primarily for ski jumping until the popular rise of alpine skiing in the early 1930s. Today, the ski area is on the Colorado Register of Historic Places, and stands as the oldest ski area still open in Colorado. The hill has a vertical drop of only 440 feet, and only 15 trails, but there are runs for every ability. There is also a small terrain park and trails for Nordic skiing. Adult lift ticket $15, seniors and youth (7–18) $10, and kids (under 7) $5.

Ski Haus (970-879-0385; www.skihaussteamboat.com), 1457 Pine Grove Rd. Open daily 9–6. For affordable rental gear, the Ski Haus has all the skis and snowboards you need.

Steamboat Powder Cats (970-879-5188 or 1-800-288-0543; www.steamboatpowdercats.com), 1724 Mount Werner Cir. This snowcat outfit takes skiers up to Buffalo Pass. On a good snow day, you can expect to make 10–16 runs. A full day of skiing runs $299–400.

BOATING **Steamboat Lake Marina** (970-879-7019; www.steamboatlakemarina.com), 61450 CR 62, Clark. To get out onto the water at Steamboat Lake State Park, check out the marina, where you can rent pontoon boats, fishing boats, canoes, paddleboats, and kayaks.

CROSS-COUNTRY SKIING & SNOWSHOEING **Steamboat Ski Touring Center** (970-879-8180; www.nordicski.net), P.O. Box 775401, Steamboat, CO 80477. With 30 kilometers of trails groomed for both classic and skate skiing, the Ski Touring Center is the most extensive and convenient cross-country location to the Steamboat ski area. An additional 10 kilometers have been set aside for snowshoeing. The center also rents equipment, offers instruction, and leads ski tours. Adult day pass $16 and seniors and children (12 and under) $10.

The Nordic Center at Vista Verde Guest Ranch (970-879-3858 or 1-800-526-7433), P.O. Box 465, Steamboat, CO 80477. There are 30 kilometers of groomed ski trails on this 500-acre ranch. Lessons, guided tours, and equipment rental are available. Your trail pass also comes with lunch. Adult trail pass with Nordic lunch $20 (with ranch lunch $40) and children under 12 $10 ($20).

THE VIEW OF STEAMBOAT SKI AREA FROM TOWN

Ski Haus (970-879-0385; www.skihaussteamboat.com), 1457 Pine Grove Rd. Open daily 9–6. For affordable rental gear, the Ski Haus has equipment for all winter sports—alpine skis and snowboards, as well as a full selection of touring, Nordic, and telemark packages. They even have snowshoes.

DOGSLEDDING **Red Runner Dog Sled Tours** (970-879-3647), 33567 US 40. After a thrilling 8-mile tour through the Steamboat Springs backcountry pulled by Alaskan and Siberian huskies, guests pile into a tipi for hot chocolate and snacks. Owner Carol Bloodworth does an exceptional job of allowing guests to participate in the activity. Call for more information and to make reservations.

FISHING **Steamboat Flyfisher** (970-879-6552 or 1-866-268-9295; www.steamboatflyfisher.com), 507 Lincoln Ave. Open daily 7:30–7:30. With so many options for fishing around Steamboat, a guided fishing outing might be the best way to get the lay of the land (so to speak). The guides at Steamboat Flyfisher customize trips to meet each angler's expectations. Multiday trips give you a chance to experience more of what the Yampa Valley has to offer.

GOLF **Haymaker Golf Course** (970-870-1846; www.haymakergolf.com), 34855 US 40 E. With the tagline "Golf as it was intended to be," the Haymaker Golf Course promotes itself as a course for golfers. There is no residential development crowding the course's 233 acres, just beautiful views of nearby Mt. Werner and 18 holes of golf. Greens fees $81–93 in the summer.

Sheraton Steamboat Resort and Golf Club (970-879-1391; www.sheratonsteamboatgolf.com), 2200 Village Inn Ct. This mountain course takes advantage of its natural surroundings, incorporating rollicking streams and elevation changes. From the course you can see the ski area above the trees. Greens fees $80–140.

HIKING With Medicine Bow/Routt National Forest (www.fs.fed.us/r2/mbr), the Flat Tops Wilderness, and four state parks, the mountains around Steamboat are full of trails for hiking. One exhilirating trail in the Flat Tops Wilderness takes hikers across the Devils Causeway, a narrow rocky spine that splits two valleys. At times the trail is only 3 feet wide and drops hundreds of feet on either side.

HORSEBACK RIDING **Del's Triangle 3 Ranch** (970-879-3495; www.steamboathorses.com), 55675 CR 62, Clark. The ranch runs summer and winter trail rides. In the winter, guests can meet the ranch shuttle at the gondola. Winter rides last two hours and cost $65. This is a fantastic way to see the mountains.

MOUNTAIN BIKING There are some great mountain bike trails around Steamboat. For example, over 25 miles of singletrack can be accessed from Rabbit Ears Pass in the Routt National Forest.

Steamboat Ski Resort (970-879-0740 or 1-877-237-2628; www.steamboat.com), 2305 Mt. Werner Cir. For mountain biking in a ski town, start with the ski mountain. With an $8 lift ticket, you can take your bike up the mountain and enjoy 50 miles of trails with a lot of exciting descents.

Ski Haus (970-879-0385; www.skihaussteamboat.com), 1457 Pine Grove Rd. Open daily 9–6. In the summer, this purveyor of ski equipment rents mountain bikes. A full-suspension ride runs $48/day.

RAFTING **Bucking Rainbow Outfitters** (970-879-8747 or 1-888-810-8747; www.buckingrainbow.com), 730 Lincoln Ave. The Yampa River runs right through Steamboat Springs. The rapids here are gentle class II and III, but a rafting trip down the Yampa is a nice way to spend a warm summer afternoon. Bucking Rainbow also leads trips on other rivers farther afield, like the Colorado, Elk, and Eagle. For hardcore white-water fans, the full-day Cross Mountain Canyon trip is all class IV and V. Trips down the Yampa, however, are $45 for adults, $35 for kids.

SNOWMOBILING **Steamboat Snowmobile Tours** (970-879-6500 or 1-877-879-6500; www.steamboatsnowmobile.com), located between mile markers 151 and 152 on US 40 east of Steamboat. Open daily 8–10. Fly across the snow on Rabbit Ears Pass, driving your own snowmobile. These folks lead several snowmobile tours, from a short two-hour affair to a full day. They also have lunch tours and the Rocky Mountain Sunset Dinner tour. Drivers $115–255 (a bit cheaper for passengers).

GREEN SPACE **Steamboat Lake State Park** (970-879-3922; www.parks.state.co.us/parks/steamboatlake), north on CO 129 to Hahns Peak Village. Overlooking the park are Sand Mountain and the impressive Hahns Peak. The Steamboat Lake reservoir is perfect for boating and fishing. There's a swim beach at the Dutch Hill area, but even in late summer, the water does not get warmer than the low 70s. In the winter there's cross-country skiing and snowshoeing. Daily park pass $6.

✔ **Yampa River State Park** (970-276-2061; www.parks.state.co.us/parks/yampariver), 6185 US 40, Hayden. This unique state park encloses a 134-mile stretch of the river that reaches from Hayden to Dinosaur National Monument. The main park headquarters is in Hayden and has a campground and visitor center. Daily park pass $6.

✷ Lodging

HOTELS ♈ ♿ **Steamboat Grand Resort Hotel** (1-877-269-2628; www.steamboatgrand.com), 2300 Mt. Werner Cir. The hotel's 327 rooms and suites are located near the base of the ski area, walking distance to the gondola. Rooms are clean and tastefully decorated, if a little small. The deluxe king room comes with a Jacuzzi for two. The hotel also has studios, condos, and penthouses available for larger parties. Accommodations $117–2,300.

♈ **Hotel Bristol** (970-879-3083 or 1-800-851-0872; www.steamboathotelbristol.com), 917 Lincoln Ave. Built in 1948, the Hotel Bristol has become a landmark in downtown Steamboat Springs. For years it served as a B&B, but reopened in 1997 as a 24-room hotel. The rooms are tastefully decorated with a subdued western theme, blending the historic charm of the building with modern comforts. Downstairs is Mazzola's, one of the best restaurants in town. Rooms $99–209.

BED & BREAKFASTS **Mariposa** (970-879-1467 or 1-800-578-1467; www.steamboatmariposa.com), 855 N. Grand St. The décor at Mariposa (Spanish for "butterfly") could be described as southwestern. There's more than a hint of Santa Fe, from the lodgepole furnishings, stucco walls, and exposed-beam ceilings. The rooms are comfortable with handmade quilts on each bed. The sunroom overlooks the nearby Soda Creek. The innkeepers, Bob and Cindy Maddox, live next door, which allows guests to avoid the feeling that they are intruding (if they want to stretch out on a couch for a nap for example). In the morning, guests are taken care of with a full breakfast. Rooms $129–169.

CAMPGROUNDS **Yampa River State Park** (970-276-2061; www.parks.state.co.us/parks/yampariver), 6185 US 40, Hayden. Campground open in the summer only. The state park's Headquarters Campground has 50 sites. Thirty-five have electricity; the rest are walk-in tent sites. The campground has shower and laundry facilities. Tent sites $14, RV $38, and tipi $25.

CABINS & COTTAGES 🐾 ♿ **Columbine Cabins** (970-879-5522; www.cabinsatcolumbine.com), P.O. Box 716, Clark, CO 80428. Located 29 miles north of Steamboat Springs on CO 129, Columbine Cabins is nestled under aspens and evergreens. Fifteen cabins are available with one to two bedrooms. Log walls, exposed beams, and wood stoves all add to the rustic charm of these lodgings. All have kitchens, and all but one have running water. The Caron House, the largest cabin, is the only one with a full bath. Bathrooms and shower facilities are located in the modern lodge. The lodge also offers laundry and a rec room with pool table and couches. Outside there's a wood-fired steam sauna. Cabins $75–160.

CONDOS **Torian Plum** (970-879-8811 or 1-866-599-9019; www.torianplum.com), 1855 Ski Time Square Dr. Operated by ResortQuest, the Torian Plum offers condos with ski-in and ski-out access to Steamboat. The accommodations range from 700-square-foot units with one bedroom and one bath to five-bed, six-bath apartments with 3,200 square feet of living space. Torian Plum has two sections: Plaza Tower and the newer Creekside. Units have full kitchens, fireplaces, and Jacuzzi tubs. Depending on the season and size, condos rent anywhere from $179–2,129.

✱ Where to Eat

DINING OUT During ski season, be sure to make reservations at any of the fine-dining restaurants you hope to visit.

🍸 **Café Diva** (970-871-0508), 1855 Ski Time Square Dr. Open nightly at 5:30. The menu changes seasonally at Café Diva, which is located in the Torian Plum Plaza, at the ski area base. Chef Kate Rench, who trained at the French Culinary Institute in New York, blends the classic flavors of world cuisine to create an innovative and highly praised menu. Entrées $20–30.

🍸 ♿ **Cottonwood Grill** (970-879-2229; www.cottonwoodgrill.com), 701 Yampa St. Open daily for dinner at 5:30 (hours vary in spring and fall). Located in downtown Steamboat Springs on the Yampa River, Cottonwood Grill serves cuisine from the Pacific Rim, blending American and Asian flavors to produce a unique menu. Recent entrées included sake Chilean sea bass and pink pepper–crusted NY strip steak. Warm natural woods and the soft colors in the dining room create a relaxing environment for dinner. In the summer, eat riverside with white linen tablecloths and the grass beneath your feet. Entrées $25–33.

🍸 **La Montaña** (970-879-5800; www.la-montana.com), 2500 Village Dr. A meal at La Montaña is truly a fine-dining experience. Though the kitchen serves southwestern and Mexican food, it is a far cry from the usual burritos and fajitas you will find elsewhere. Signature southwestern dishes include the exceptional *camarones de La Montaña,* which is shrimp stuffed with crab meat, jack cheese, and *pico de gallo,* and then wrapped in bacon. The dining room is festive and completes the experience. Entrées $14–32.

EATING OUT Steamboat Springs has plenty of options for eating out, including small regional chains like Beau Jo's and the Egg & I. Because the town has nearly 10,000 year-round residents, and locals have to eat, Steamboat isn't heavy on fancy restaurants like other ski towns.

🍸 **8th Street Steakhouse** (970-879-3131; www.8thstreetsteakhouse.com), 50 Eighth St. Open daily for dinner 5–close. This classic western steakhouse in downtown Steamboat has great food and is the kind of place you can take the whole family. For the kids, they have authentic saddle seats, and there are free s'mores for dessert. None of the handcrafted steaks here will disappoint. Dinner entrées $12–24, but with dishes like Kobe steak, porterhouse, and lobster tail, the menu tops out at $40.

♿ **Mazzola's Majestic Italian Diner** (970-879-2405; www.mazzolas.com), 917 Lincoln Ave. Open nightly 5–10. Pizza served until midnight, slices until they close. Mazzola's has been through several hands since the Mazzola family first opened the joint back in 1970. Today, the restaurant continues the tradition of serving a classic, made-from-scratch Italian menu. The restaurant prides itself on its family-dining affordability and offers 20 great wines for under $20. From the red-and-white checkered tablecloths to the incredible food, Mazzola's is not to be missed. Entrées $9–24 and pizzas $11–17.

🍸 ♿ **Rex's American Grill & Bar** (970-870-0438; www.rexsgrill.com), 3190 S. Lincoln Ave. Open daily for breakfast, lunch, and dinner 6:30–11. Recently opened by the folks who own Mazzola's downtown, this new eatery has been impressing locals with it affordable, classic American menu. It's where you go if you are looking for delicious half-pound burgers and great comfort food, like buttermilk fried chicken and mac & cheese. There are some creative upscale items on the menu as well—the shrimp and elk sausage, for example, is a great take on the traditional surf and turf. Dinner entrées $12–24 and lunch sandwiches $8–10.

🍸 ♿ **Tap House Sports Grill** (970-879-2431; www.thetaphouse.com), 729 Lincoln Ave. Open daily 11:30–2

AM. This sports bar has a large nonsmoking dining room that serves a traditional bar menu that won't empty your wallet. Excellent burgers and fries, plates of onion rings, and nachos piled high keep bringing people back. The Tap House has a small video arcade and 40 televisions, including some seriously wide screens. With the satellite connection, they're showing every game you can imagine. To get in on some of the local action, come on Tuesday for Wing Day—33-cent wings all day. Dishes $6–16.

♿ **Backcountry Provisions** (970-879-3617; www.backcountryprovisions.com), 635 Lincoln Ave. Open daily 7–5. Catering to Steamboat's recreational adventuring types, Backcountry Provisions provides hearty sandwiches made from the finest deli meats and cheeses. Eat in, or take it with you for the trail.

BAKERIES & COFFEE SHOPS ♿ **Gondola Joe's Café** (970-871-5150), Gondola Square. Open daily in the winter 7–5. There's always time to grab a cup of coffee and a bagel sandwich in the morning, especially at Gondola Joe's, right next to the gondola at the Steamboat Springs base area. While you're there, you can buy a boxed lunch for later in the day.

BARS, TAVERNS & BREW PUBS 🍸 ♿ **Slopeside Grill** (970-879-2916; www.slopesidegrill.com), 1855 Ski Time Square Dr. Known as much for their pasta dishes and brick-oven pizza as the succulent baby back ribs, the Slopeside Grill is also a great place for an après-ski drink. The Second Happy Hour, 10–midnight (9–11 in the summer) has $6 pizzas and $2 pints (including Guiness).

🍸 **The Tugboat Grill and Pub** (970-879-7070), 1860 Ski Time Square Dr. Open daily 11–close. Located at the base of the mountain in Ski Time Square, the grill serves lunch and dinner daily, and is known for being pretty family friendly (at least earlier in the day). The pub, however, is the main attraction—everyone seems to agree that the Tugboat rocks. With live music and dancing almost every night, the bar stays busy with tourists and locals and a devoted après-ski drinking crowd.

✱ Entertainment

Strings in the Mountains Music Festival (970-879-5056; www.stringsinthemountains.com), P.O. Box 774627, Steamboat, CO 80477. Over 85 performances are produced every summer in Steamboat Springs. Concerts celebrate many musical traditions, including chamber music, jazz, rock, country, and bluegrass.

✱ Selective Shopping

F. M. Light & Sons (1-800-530-8908; www.fmlight.com), 860 Lincoln Ave., has been serving Steamboat Springs since 1905, beginning as a men's clothier serving area ranchers and farmers. The shop is your best shot for getting authentic western duds, including Stetson hats and cowboy boots. Run by the same family for over 100 years, F. M. Light & Sons is living history.

✱ Special Events

January: **Cowboy Downhill** (970-879-6111; www.steamboat.com). This annual ski rodeo is one of those events that epitomize a town. Steamboat Springs prides itself on its great ski

F. M. LIGHT & SONS CLOTHIERS

hills and western cowboy heritage. Both of these come together when the cowboys take to the slopes—many of them for the first time—to compete on skis. The tradition began in 1975, when the city invited some professional rodeo cowboys competing in Denver to enjoy the state's other sport. They had so much fun they keep coming back.

February: **Steamboat Springs Winter Carnival** (970-879-0880; www.steamboatchamber.com). Since 1914, the folks in Steamboat have been fighting off cabin fever with a celebration of winter. The carnival includes strange seasonal activities that include children being pulled through the streets on skis while being pulled by horses, a donkey jump, and an adult snow shovel race.

July: **Cowboys' Roundup Days** (970-879-0880; www.steamboatchamber.com). Every year the Steamboat Springs Chamber puts on a "salute to the West" festival culminating on the Fourth of July. There are fireworks, tours of local working ranches, and an old-time cattle drive through the middle of town.

September: **Steamboat Brewers' Festival** (www.steamboatbrewersfestival.com). Colorado brewers, beer tasting, plenty of food, and live music make for a festive Saturday in September.

ASPEN & SNOWMASS

Aspen has an international reputation as a glamorous retreat for the nation's rich and famous, with expensive restaurants, dozens of art galleries, and boutiques that sell $300 jeans. This is the side of Aspen that most people hear about—the celebrity stories that make headlines and sell newspapers. But Aspen is much more than a ritzy getaway.

As a ski town, it offers what many consider the best and most varied terrain in Colorado. Recreational activities are available year-round. Thousands come in the summer for mountain biking, hiking around the Maroon Bells, and fishing the area's rivers and mountain streams. Surrounding the town of Aspen are nearly 2 million acres of the White River National Forest. The Roaring Fork River barrels through Aspen and the valley that bears its name, on its way north to meet up with the Colorado. Encircling peaks reach above 14,000 feet—mountaintops that remain snowcapped nearly year-round. In 1972, John Denver recorded "Rocky Mountain High," a song that celebrates his passion for these mountains. (The song became one of Colorado's two official state songs in 2007.) It is this aspect of Aspen that continues to draw visitors, even when the town itself may seem too pricey or ostentatious.

Aspen's roots go back to 1879, when miners from Leadville crossed over Independence Pass into the Roaring Fork Valley. These gentlemen found the silver they were looking for, and within a year three mining camps had sprung up and were subsequently organized into the town of Aspen. Several years later, Jerome B. Wheeler (one-time president of Macy's in New York) came to Aspen. He bought some mining claims and began investing in the community.

From the time the railroad came to town in 1887 to the repeal of the Sherman Silver Purchase Act in 1893, Aspen was the richest silver mining region in the country. The town grew to 12,000 people and supported six newspapers, two banks, and a telephone service. Wheeler built the hotel and the opera house that bear his name. The change that came in 1893 was radical. With the government no longer buying silver, the market plummeted overnight, and those who had made their fortune in this metal, like Jerome Wheeler, were left bankrupt. The town began to die, and by 1930, there were only 700 people left.

Little by little, skiing came to Aspen. During the Depression, the WPA built a boat tow on Aspen Mountain. There were thoughts of bringing a full-fledged

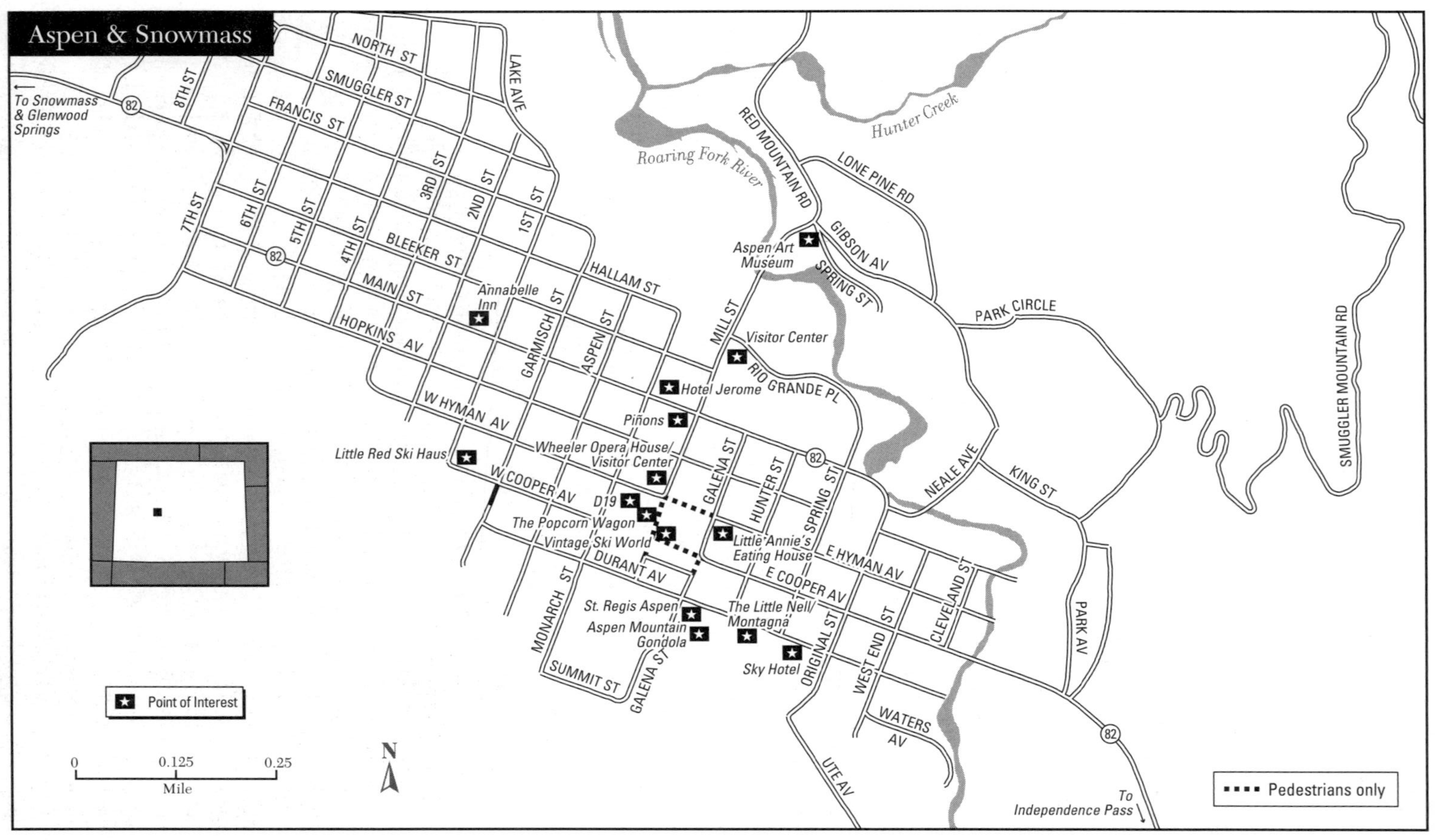

Aspen & Snowmass
To Snowmass & Glenwood Springs
82
8TH ST
7TH ST
6TH ST
5TH ST
4TH ST
3RD ST
2ND ST
1ST ST
NORTH ST
SMUGGLER ST
FRANCIS ST
BLEEKER ST
MAIN ST
HOPKINS AV
HALLAM ST
LAKE AVE
GARMISCH ST
ASPEN ST
W HYMAN AV
W COOPER AV
DURANT AV
MONARCH ST
SUMMIT ST
GALENA ST
MILL ST
HUNTER ST
SPRING ST
ORIGINAL ST
WEST END ST
CLEVELAND ST
E HYMAN AV
E COOPER AV
WATERS AV
UTE AV
PARK AV
NEALE AVE
KING ST
PARK CIRCLE
RIO GRANDE PL
SPRING ST
GIBSON AV
LONE PINE RD
RED MOUNTAIN RD
SMUGGLER MOUNTAIN RD
Roaring Fork River
Hunter Creek
Aspen Art Museum
Visitor Center
Hotel Jerome
Piñons
Annabelle Inn
Little Red Ski Haus
Wheeler Opera House/ Visitor Center
D19
The Popcorn Wagon
Vintage Ski World
Little Annie's Eating House
St. Regis Aspen
Aspen Mountain Gondola
The Little Nell/ Montagna
Sky Hotel
To Independence Pass
Point of Interest
Pedestrians only
0
0.125
0.25
Mile
N

resort to the area, but World War II stalled any plans that were being considered. However, in 1945, Walter Paepcke and his wife Elizabeth moved to Aspen. Paepcke was an industrialist, and he had a dream of transforming Aspen into a resort community with a world-class ski area.

Paepcke was not just envisioning a pampered retreat for the wealthy—his desire was to create a cultural center, a place where artists and intellectuals could flourish. The town today owes much of its character to the efforts of the Paepckes.

By the 1970s, Aspen's reputation as a ski town had been established. Big names came to ski the town's four ski areas—Aspen Mountain, Aspen Highlands, Buttermilk, and Snowmass. Throughout the 1970s and '80s, the celebrities began to make Aspen their own.

Underneath all the hype, Aspen remains a world-class ski resort. And it continues to be a shame that many skiers, put off by its reputation, will miss out on skiing here.

GUIDANCE The **Aspen Chamber Resort Association** (www.aspenchamber.org), 425 Rio Grande Pl. The main visitor center (970-925-1940) is located at the chamber offices on Rio Grande Pl. It is open Mon.–Fri. 8:30–5. The visitor center at the Wheeler Opera House (970-920-7148) is open Mon.–Sun. 10–6.

More Web sites: www.aspensnowmass.com

GETTING THERE *By car:* Aspen and Snowmass are south of I-70 and Glenwood Springs on CO 82. Snowmass Village is off Brush Creek Rd., about 4.7 miles north of Aspen. From Denver, it's a 3.5-hour drive to Aspen when the weather is good if you take I-70 to CO 82. You can knock almost 50 miles off the odometer

WHEELER OPERA HOUSE

if you take I-70 to CO 91 to Leadville, and then US 24 to CO 82. However, this latter route takes you over Independence Pass, which is closed in the winter.

By air: The **Aspen/Pitkin County Airport** (970-920-5384; www.aspenairport.com), 0233 E. Airport Rd., is located between Aspen and Snowmass on CO 82. United has a regular shuttle route to Denver, and Delta flies between Aspen and Salt Lake City. There's a free shuttle bus that will take you to Rubey Park (430 E. Durant Ave.) in Aspen.

If you are coming into the **Denver International Airport** (1-800-AIR2DEN; www.flydenver.com), which is a four-hour drive from Aspen (about 220 miles), the **Colorado Mountain Express** (970-926-9800 or 1-800-525-6363; www.cmex.com) runs a shuttle between the DIA and Aspen/Snowmass.

GETTING AROUND *By shuttle:* Aspen's **Roaring Fork Transportation Authority** (970-925-8484) has free shuttle service all over town from 6:30 AM to 2:15 AM. The hub is at Rubey Park, 430 E. Durant Ave. They also provide shuttle service to all the ski areas, Maroon Bells, and Glenwood Springs.

By taxi: The Ultimate Taxi (970-925-6361; www.ultimatetaxi.com), driven by Jon Barnes, offers the best ride in town—transportation and a floor show, complete with live music and special effects. A half-hour ride costs $125.

MEDICAL EMERGENCIES **Aspen Valley Hospital** (970-925-1120), 0401 Castle Creek Rd. The hospital has 24-emergency care.

✷ To See & Do

✓ **Maroon Bells.** It is said that the Maroon Bells are North America's most photographed peaks. It's hard to imagine a more perfect alignment of natural features—the two 14,000-foot peaks tower over the lush valley with wildflowers, meadow, and a lake. It's simply breathtaking. A short hike from the parking lot goes out and around the lake. There are other, longer trails if you want to make a day of hiking the Bells. Because the U.S. Forest Service, the caretakers of the Maroon Bells Scenic Area, wants to control the traffic to and from the Bells, visitors must come by bus (or nonmotorized transportation). To catch the bus, park at Aspen Highlands and purchase bus tickets at Pro Mountain Sports inside. The bus picks you up outside. Adult ticket $6, seniors and children (6–16) $3, and children under 7 free.

⚲ ♿ **Aspen Art Museum** (www.aspenartmuseum.org; 970-925-8050), 590 N. Mill St. Open Tues.–Sat. 10–6 (until 7 on Thurs.) and Sun. noon–6. The Aspen Art Museum is a noncollection institution that promotes contemporary art with an everchanging rotation of shows and exhibits. Adult admission $5, seniors and students $3, and children under 12 free.

⚲ **Holden/Marolt Mining and Ranching Museum** (970-925-3721; www.aspenhistory.org/hm.html), 40180 CO 82. Call to schedule a tour. The area's mining and ranching history is preserved at this museum, located on the site of the Holden Lixiviation Mill (1891). Adult tour $6, seniors $5, and children under 12 free. Admission also gets you into Wheeler/Stallard Museum.

Wheeler/Stallard Museum (970-925-3721; www.aspenhistory.org/wsh.html), 620 W. Bleeker St. Open Tues.–Sat. 1–5. The museum resides in a Queen Anne home from 1888. The first floor has been restored to what it would have looked like in the 19th century. The second floor is a gallery with different shows exhibited regularly. Adult tour $6, seniors $5, and children under 12 free. Admission also gets you into Holden/Marolt Museum.

Independence Pass to Twin Lakes. The drive over to Twin Lakes crosses the Continental Divide and takes you over Independence Pass. It's one of the most scenic routes in the area. The pass is the highest paved path in North America at 12,095 feet. The road, CO 82, is closed in the winter.

✷ Outdoor Activities

ALPINE SKIING & SNOWBOARDING Aspen is home to four ski areas, each with its own distinct personality. Aspen and Snowmass see 300 inches of annual snowfall, and all the ski areas have impressive vertical drops.

The town of Aspen sits at the base of **Aspen Mountain.** Littered with black-diamond runs, most of this 673-acre ski area is for advanced skiers; the rest is for intermediate. There are no runs for beginners at Aspen Mountain. The overall vertical drop is 3,267 feet. The gondola in town takes passengers right to the top of the ski area.

THE MAROON BELLS

Aspen Highlands is just out of town on Maroon Creek Rd. The ski area is 1,010 acres with a 3,635-foot vertical drop. Half of the runs are for advanced skiers (they love the 50-degree drop into Highland Bowl), a third for intermediate, and a measley fifth for beginners.

The largest of Aspen's four ski areas, **Snowmass** has 3,128 skiable acres with 4,406 vertical feet of drop. There are plenty of long runs and steep descents. Only 6 percent of the terrain is for beginners. The mountain is accessed by 23 lifts. Snowmass is 10 miles from Aspen and has its own resort village.

Buttermilk is the smallest of Aspen's ski areas at 435 acres, with nine lifts. There's a 2,030-foot vertical drop, and there are an even number of trails for skiers of varying abilities. A great destination for snowboarders, Buttermilk has terrain parks and a superpipe. The Winter X Games are held here annually.

One lift ticket to **Aspen/Snowmass** (www.aspensnowmass.com) buys you access to all four of Aspen's ski areas. Adult lift ticket $87, children (13–17) $78, children (7–12) $58, and children under 7 free. The day rate decreases with multi-day tickets.

Aspen Mountain Powder Tours (970-920-0720 or 1-800-525-6200 ext. 3720; www.stayaspensnowmass.com). For snowcat access to backcountry slopes, consider a Powder Tour. Skiers will experience 10,000 vertical feet of ungroomed descents. The $315 fee includes lunch and snacks.

BICYCLING Maroon Creek Road is one of the area's most scenic bike rides. The paved road steadily climbs a gentle grade for nearly 10 miles from CO 82 to where it ends at the Maroon Bells and the Pacific Peaks. You will have to pay a $5 fee at the ranger station. Independence Pass, on the other hand, has nothing gentle about it. The road climbs 4,000 feet in 17 miles on its way to Twin Lakes. From Aspen to Twin Lakes is about a 37-mile trip, just 21 miles to the pass. Steep and twisty, the route makes you pay for the fantastic panoramic views of the Collegiate Peaks.

CROSS-COUNTRY SKIING & SNOWSHOEING **10th Mountain Division Hut Association** (970-925-5775; www.huts.org). For backcountry skiing, huts make it possible for skiers to make multiday trips in the wilderness with the promise of comfortable, reliable shelter and a warm bed at night. The 10th Mountain Division Hut System is comprised of 29 backcountry huts connected by a network of trails (350 miles of suggested routes). Check Web site for route information, hut availability, and rates.

Aspen/Snowmass Nordic Trail System (970-429-2039; www.aspennordic.com). A network of cross-country ski trails in Aspen and Snowmass are connected by the Owl Creek Trail. Snowshoers are welcome to use the trails—just don't walk on the groomed tracks. See the Web site for complete trail information. The trails are open to the public. There is a recommended $5/person trail fee (kids free)—donation boxes can be found at the trailheads and the ski centers in Aspen and Snowmass.

Ashcroft Ski Touring (970-925-1971; www.pinecreekcookhouse.com/ashcroft

.html), 11 miles up to the end of Castle Creek Rd. at the Cabin Nordic Center. Nearly 22 miles of groomed trails on 600 acres, the Nordic center also rents out ski and snowshoe equipment. Adult day pass $15, seniors $5, and children under 12 $10.

FISHING **Aspen Flyfishing** (970-920-6886; www.aspenflyfishing.com), 601 E. Dean St. For fly-fishing trips, the guides at Aspen Flyfishing take anglers wading on the Roaring Fork and lower Frying Pan Rivers. For float-fishing, they head out to the Roaring Fork or go north to the Colorado. The outfitter also has access to a private lake stocked with trout, and there are trips available just for kids. Half-day wade trip for one $225; three guests $375. Half-day float trip for one or two $350.

Taylor Creek Fly Shops (970-920-1128; www.taylorcreek.com), 183 Basalt Center Cir., Basalt. From gear to guides to fishing reports, Taylor Creek Fly Shops is one of the oldest in Colorado. They have an impressive roster of guides with decades of experience fishing this part of Colorado.

GOLF **Aspen Golf and Tennis** (970-544-1772; www.aspenrecreation.com), 39551 CO 82. As part of the Aspen Recreation Center, the golf course prides itself on offering a great course with reasonable fees. Greens fees for 18 holes $45–95.

River Valley Ranch Golf Club (970-963-3625; www.rvrgolf.com), 303 River Valley Ranch Dr., Carbondale. About 45 minutes away in Carbondale, River Valley Ranch sits at the base of Mt. Sopris, incorporating the valley's Crystal River into the course design. Greens fees $40–90.

Snowmass Club (970-923-9155 or 1-800-525-0710; www.snowmassclub.com), 239 Snowmass Club Cir. This semiprivate course in Snowmass Village charges upwards of $175 for 18 holes, including a cart. Members only until one o'clock.

HIKING There are plenty of hikes in the mountains around Aspen. One of the most popular is the hike from Aspen to Crested Butte via West Maroon Pass (mountain bikers like the longer Pearl Pass route). **Dolly's Mountain Shuttle** (970-349-2620) can drive you back to Aspen for only $50/person.

Aspen Alpine Guides (970-925-6618; www.aspenalpine.com), P.O. Box 659, Aspen, CO 81612. Throughout the summer, hikers take guided trips into the mountains around Aspen, led by the good folks at Aspen Alpine Guides. Tours include day hikes and fitness hikes, as well as rock climbing and backpacking. You can climb area 14er or make the trek to Crested Butte. In the winter, trips include cross-country skiing and snowshoeing.

HORSEBACK RIDING **Aspen Wilderness Outfitters** (970-922-6600; www.aspenwilderness.com), 554 Valley Rd. Guided horseback rides can be taken all over the Aspen region, inluding to the Maroon Bells. Aspen Wilderness Outfitters leads trail rides and pack rides (overnighters). They also run Snowmass Stables, which offers shorter rides around Snowmass and Buttermilk. Reservations required. Two-hour rides $70.

Maroon Bells Lodge and Outfitters (970-920-4679; www.maroonbellsaspen.com), 3125 Maroon Creek Rd. On the ride up to the Maroon Bells you can't miss the Maroon Bells Lodge—it's the large log lodge with the red roof on your right heading toward the Maroon Bells Scenic Area. Located on the T Lazy 7 Ranch, the outfitter offers guided trail rides and pack rides, as well as wagon and sleigh rides. Several ride-and-dine packages are available—all include a gourmet meal. Rides start at $75 and go up to $195 for the all-day ride with gourmet box lunch.

Aspen Carriage and Sleigh (970-925-3394; www.aspencarriage.com), P.O. Box 38, Aspen, CO 81612. It's kind of classy to take the family out on a carriage or sleigh ride. A 20-minute tour through town will set you back $50 (adults $20, kids $10, $50 minimum). In the winter there's an hour-long Christmas Light tour for $150 (adults $60, kids $30, $150 minimum). The carriages can also be reserved to serve as a classy taxi service.

MOUNTAIN BIKING Government Trail is one of Aspen's most classic rides. It begins at the Snowmass Ski Area, and on the way to Aspen follows some of the state's best singletrack—much of the way through aspen groves.

Timberline Bike Tours (970-274-6076; www.timberlinebike.com), 555 E. Durant Ave., located in Ute City Cycles. These folks lead hut-to-hut mountain bike tours, as well as day trips on the area's best singletrack. The Woody Creek trip is a great start for beginners. It is a combination of paved and dirt-trail riding, with a stop at the Woody Creek Tavern for lunch. Day trips $70–110.

Aspen Sports (970-925-6331; www.aspensports.com), 408 E. Cooper Ave. A great selection of rental bikes—mostly the town cruiser types. Since they have a location in Snowmass, you can ride one way and drop the bike off there. They also rent out of the St. Regis Hotel. A 24-hour rental is $24–60.

RAFTING & PADDLING **Blazing Adventures** (970-923-4544 or 1-800-282-7238; www.blazingadventures.com), 48 Upper Village Mall, Snowmass. In addition to biking and Jeep tours, this outfitter leads half-day trips down the upper and lower Roaring Fork and the Colorado rivers. Certain trips include class IV rapids. Half-day trips start at $80.

Aspen Seals (970-618-4569; www.aspenseals.com). For something new, why not try riding the rapids on your stomach. They call it "whitewater sledging," which is essentially riding the river on a glorified kick board. Aspen Seals rides the Roaring Fork and Arkansas rivers. There are a number of trips for people of varying abilities, $90–110.

PARAGLIDING **Aspen Paragliding** (970-925-7625; www.aspenparagliding.com), 426 S. Spring St. For a unique adventure in Aspen, try soaring above the valley on a parachute. No experience is necessary; guests fly tandem with a guide. The take-off is a few running steps down a gentle slope (no freediving off the mountain), and the entire activity takes about two hours. The flight will last about 15 minutes, but if conditions are good it could be longer. Tandem flights $215.

GREEN SPACE **White River National Forest** (www.fs.fed.us/r2/whiteriver). Aspen is surrounded by green space. The White River National Forest has eight wilderness areas. Within the Aspen/Sopris Ranger District, there are eight 14-ers, hundreds of miles of trails for mountain biking and hiking, and eight campgrounds. The Aspen office (970-925-3445) is at 806 W. Hallam St.

✷ Lodging

HOTELS "1" 🐾 ♿ **The Little Nell** (970-920-4600 or 1-888-843-6355; www.littlenell.com), 675 E. Durant Ave. Located right at the base of the Silver Queen Gondola, the Little Nell has 15 rooms and 77 suites. The hotel's outdoor pool is heated for year-round use, allowing guests to sit in the pool (or Jacuzzi) at the base of Aspen Mountain. Internet service is available, and pets are allowed (always on a leash). The hotel prides itself on exceptional customer service, including a ski concierge for slope-side amenities. Rooms and suites $270–4,600.

"1" 🐾 ♿ **St. Regis Aspen** (970-920-3300 or 1-888-454-9005; www.stregisaspen.com), 615 E. Dean St. This five-star hotel is strategically located at the base of Aspen Mountain close to the gondola and two popular ski lifts. The property is exquisitely decorated with bronze sculptures and classic oils. The hotel is known for exceptional concierge service, and the staff caters to every whim of their guests—guests who come with high expectations for being pampered. Rooms and suites $495–2,000.

PARASAILING IN ASPEN

"ı" 🐾 ♿ **Hotel Jerome** (970-920-1000 or 1-800-331-7213; www.hotel jerome.com), 330 E. Main St. In 1889, town founder Jerome Wheeler built the Hotel Jerome, which he hoped would rival elegant lodgings in Europe and New York. The hotel has served Aspen for well over 100 years, offering guests top-of-the-line accommodations in a historic setting. Digital TVs, 24-hour room service, and an efficient concierge desk are just some of the accommodations you can expect. Rooms $265–1,530.

"ı" ♿ **Annabelle Inn** (970-925-3822 or 1-877-266-2466; www.annabelleinn .com), 232 W. Main St. Since 1948, the Annabelle Inn (which went by the moniker "the Christmas Inn" until 2005) has been an Aspen lodging mainstay. The inn's 35 rooms are all uniquely decorated and include flat-panel TVs with cable and Internet access. Premium rooms have a balcony, a mountain view, and a fireplace. Ski movies are shown nightly next to one of the inn's two hot tubs—perfect for soaking after a chilly day on the slopes. A buffet breakfast is served every morning. Rooms $100–399.

"ı" 🐾 ♿ **Sky Hotel** (1-800-882-2582 or 970-925-6760; www.theskyhotel .com), 709 E. Durant Ave. Strategically located at the base of Aspen Mountain, the Sky Hotel is hands down Aspen's swankest hotel. Amenities include a heated outdoor pool and spa and a great lounge, 39 Degrees. Rooms $199–659.

BED & BREAKFASTS "ı" ♿ **The Little Red Ski Haus** (970-925-3333 or 1-866-630-6119; www.littleredskihaus .com), 118 E. Cooper Ave. This 13-room B&B is the most celebrated in Aspen. You will be hard pressed to find an inn as elegant and well-appointed as the Little Red Ski Haus. Built in 1888, the inn has recently undergone an extensive restoration that added a dining room and bar in the cellar. Several of the rooms can be combined to create suites. All have private baths, some with whirlpool tubs. Breakfasts are incredible. Rooms $89–615.

CAMPGROUNDS "ı" **Aspen-Basalt Campground** (970-927-3405 or 1-800-567-2773), 20640 CO 82, Basalt, just south of mile marker 20, between Glenwood Springs and Aspen. The new bikeway to Aspen runs just behind this campground, and the Roaring Fork River flows behind it as well, providing easy fishing access. All of the 75 sites have either electric and water or full hook-ups. Hot showers available year-round. Sites $35–38.

Silver Bar, Silver Bell, and **Silver Queen Campgrounds,** White River National Forest. Located along Maroon Creek Rd., these three campgrounds have potable water and vault toilets. In addition to camping fees, campers have to purchase a $10 vehicle permit to enter the park. Reservations can be made by calling 1-877-444-6777 or visiting the Web site, www.recreation.gov.

CABINS & COTTAGES "ı" 🐾 **Avalanche Ranch** (970-963-2846 or 1-877-963-9339; www.avalanche ranch.com), 12863 CO 133, Carbondale. With Mt. Sopris above and the Crystal River below, Avalanche Ranch is right in the middle of some beautiful scenery. The ranch is an hour from Aspen. There are 14 cabins and a ranch house. Cabins have bathrooms with tubs or showers and kitchens. Cabins $85–189.

Taylor Creek Cabins (970-927-9927; www.rent-cabins-colorado.com), Basalt. The cabins can be found outside of Basalt on Frying Pan Road (call or visit Web site for directions). These cozy cabins are situated across from the Frying Pan River. A quick glance might suggest they are rustic, but inside the accommodations are all modern. Guests enjoy access to this private stretch of the river. A three-night minimum stay is required. Cabins $150.

✷ Where to Eat

DINING OUT Getting a table in Aspen's nicer dining rooms will require reservations—especially during peak months in the summer and winter.

D19 (970-925-6019; www.d19aspen.com), 305 S. Mill St. Open Mon.–Fri. 11:30–10, Sat. 11:30–midnight, and Sun. 9–10. The D19 serves a contemporary Italian menu with a distinctive American twist. The ambiance is clearly Old World, with a focus on simple elegance and quality service. Seating at the bar is available on a first-come basis, and when the weather permits, patrons can dine on the patio. Dishes $25–36.

♿ **Matsuhisa** (970-544-6628; www.nobumatsuhisa.com), 303 E. Main St. Hours change seasonally. In 1998, Nobu Matsuhisa brought his signature style of Japanese cuisine to Aspen. Seafood tops the menu with dishes like Chilean sea bass topped with truffles and baby abalone with light garlic sauce. A sushi bar is available in the lounge. Dishes $12–37 (up to current market price on many entrées).

♿ **Piñons** (970-920-2021), 105 S. Mill St. Open for dinner nightly at 6. Closed in winter. This restaurant remains a local favorite, and reservations are a must here. The western-themed menu features dishes like pan-roasted pork tenderloin and macadamia nut ahi. The chocolate peanut butter pie is a great dessert. Dishes $25–38.

♿ **Pine Creek Cookhouse** (970-925-1044; www.pinecreekcookhouse.com), 11399 Castle Creek Rd. Open daily for lunch noon–2 and dinner 6–8:30. The dining experience at Pine Creek begins with just getting there. In the winter, guests have to cross-country ski, snowshoe, or come by sleigh. The cookhouse itself is the picture of rustic elegance, contributing to an overall memorable evening. Dinner for two, including the sleigh ride, can cost $250. For a more affordable option, ask about their summer hikers' buffet.

♿ **Montagna** (970-920-6330; www.littlenell.com), 675 Durant Ave. Open for breakfast, lunch, and dinner. Located in the Little Nell at the base of the gondola, Montagna might be best known for its extensive wine cellar, featuring 20,000 bottles. The tiered dining area is comfortable, and the food is meticulously prepared. As much as possible, everything at Montagna is created in-house, from cheese to homemade mayo. Classic dishes are reinvented and brought up a notch. Dinner entrées $14–37.

Krabloonik (970-923-3953; www.krabloonik.com), 4250 Divide Rd., Snowmass. Lunch served Mon.–Fri. 11–2. Dinner served daily at 5:30. In the summer there is no lunch seating, and dinner is on weekends only at 5. For another unique dining experience, consider taking a two-hour dogsled dinner tour out to the Krabloonik log restaurant or simply ski down the Dawdler Catwalk through the Snowmass campground parking lot. In the evenings, guests gather around the restaurant's sunken fire pit. The menu features many game dishes, all masterfully prepared. Lunch $14–20, dinner $22–70, and meal with dogsledding $225–295.

EATING OUT ♿ **Little Annie's Eating House** (970-925-1098), 517 E. Hyman Ave. Open daily 11:30–10. Locals love this laid-back restaurant with its red-and-white-checked tablecloths and homestyle eating. Comfort food tops the menu—ribs, burgers, chili, thick soups, and latkes are all favorites. Dishes $13–25.

♿ **Boogie's Diner** (970-925-6610; www.boogiesaspen.com), 534 E. Cooper Ave. Open daily 10:30–9:30 (if there's enough business). This is a classic 1950s diner with a singing wait staff, found upstairs in Boogie's Retail Store, one of the chicest denim retailers in the country. Hamburgers, fries, and shakes are supplemented with vegetarian dishes. Dishes $8–16.

♿ **The Big Wrap** (970-544-1700), 520 E. Durant Ave. Open daily 9–6. Nothing beats a wrap for a quick and possibly healthy lunch. This could be the most affordable meal option in Aspen, and they deliver. Wraps around $6.

The Popcorn Wagon (970-925-2718), 305 S. Mill St. Open daily 11 AM–2 AM. Located on the Mill Street Mall adjacent to Wagner Park, the Popcorn Wagon is an authentic Cretor's Special Model D popcorn wagon from 1913. They serve a whole mess of food from crepes to Polish sausage dogs. It's open really late for the bar-hopping crowd. Dishes $5–8.

♿ **Woody Creek Tavern** (970-923-4585), 0002 Woody Creek Plaza, Woody Creek. Open daily 11:30–11. Great down-home cooking and great

THE FOUNTAIN AT SOUTH MILL STREET MALL

mountain hospitality define this quirky tavern just a few miles out of Aspen. Back in the day, Hunter S. Thompson used to hang out here. Dishes $8–18.

BARS, TAVERNS & BREW PUBS ♿ **Bentley's at the Wheeler** (970-920-2240), 221 S. Mill St. Bar open daily 11 AM–2 AM. Right next to the Wheeler Opera House, Bentley's gets its fair share of tourists and locals alike. The bar has sort of an old-Victorian-saloon feel to it, with an excellent beer selection. The dining is pretty good as well.

♿ **The J-Bar** (970-920-1000; www.hoteljerome.com), 330 E. Main St. Open daily from 11:30 AM–1 AM. Located in the Hotel Jerome, the J-Bar has been serving Aspenites since 1889. For awhile during Prohibition, the bar became a soda fountain. Later it was a soda fountain/bar. It's no wonder then that the J-Bar's signature drink is the Aspen Crud (French vanilla ice cream and bourbon).

✷ Entertainment

Belly Up (970-544-9800; www.bellyupaspen.com), 450 S. Galena St. This all-ages club has a regular schedule of live music. Everybody from G. Love to Lucinda Williams to Method Man and Redman have played here. Check out the Web site for coming performances.

Aspen District Theater (970-925-6098), 199 High School Rd. The theater is home to the Aspen Santa Fe Ballet (970-925-7175; www.aspensantafeballet.com). The ballet performs a regular season of world-class dance.

Crystal Palace (970-925-1455; www.cpalace.net), 300 E. Hyman Ave. Open for a summer and winter season. Dinner seats at 7:30 on show nights. Aspen's dinner theater offers a cabaret-style show. Music and wit satirize topical events and people. Tickets for dinner and show $75; children 12 and under $40.

Wheeler Opera House (970-920-5770; www.wheeleroperahouse.com), 320 E. Hyman Ave. The opera house has been entertaining patrons since 1889. Today both live performances and movies fill the calendar.

✷ Selective Shopping

Elliott Yeary Gallery (970-429-1111; www.elliottyeary.com), 419 E. Hyman Ave. This fine art gallery specializes in exhibiting contemporary work and caters to both collectors and first-time art buyers.

Huntsman Gallery of Fine Art (970-920-1910; www.huntsmangallery.com), 410 E. Hyman Ave. This gallery carries the sculptures of Don Huntsman as well as dozens of others. Artists working in oils seem to dominate the space.

Ute Mountaineer (970-925-2849; www.utemountaineer.com), 308 S. Mill St. From snowshoes to carabiners to GPS units, Ute Mountaineer can supply all your outdoor gear needs.

Vintage Ski World (970-925-9195; www.vintage-aspen.com), 416 E. Cooper Ave. This shop specializes in vintage ski equipment as well as classic and antique ski posters and prints. For those who celebrate ski culture, there's no better shop in town.

✷ Special Events

January: **Winter X Games** (970-925-1220; www.stayaspensnowmass.com). This is the biggest annual event in winter action sports. Athletes from around to world come to compete on snowboards and skis, snowmobiles and motorcycles.

July: **Aspen Ideas Festival** (970-925-7010; www.aifestival.org). The Aspen Ideas Institute sponsors this event annually to bring together leaders from around the world to participate in programs, seminars, and discussions on some of the most relevant and important issues of our time.

September: **Jazz Aspen Snowmass** (970-920-4996; www.jazzaspen.com). The four-day jazz festival over Labor Day weekend concludes a summer full of free and paid concerts, as well as a festival in June.

September: **Aspen Filmfest** (970-925-6882; www.aspenfilm.org). The festival, which has been held annually since 1979, features independent films and documentaries.

October: **John Denver Week** (www.john-denver.org). This week-long festival celebrates the life and music of John Denver.

GLENWOOD SPRINGS ✓

Glenwood Springs sits at the confluence of the Roaring Fork and Colorado Rivers. Situated at the end of the Roaring Fork Valley, many travelers pass through Glenwood Springs on their way south to Aspen. Though not a particularly popular ski destination, the town does have its faithful corps of regular visitors.

Historically, the thing that has brought visitors to Glenwood Springs over the years has been the great hot springs pool. Early on, Utes came to bathe in the pool and rest in the nearby vapor caves. They saw the springs as a gift from Manitou and named the place *Yampah,* meaning "big medicine." In 1860, Capt. Richard Sopris led an expedition into the area and became the first white man to see the massive hot springs pool. In 1879, James Landis settled in the area and became the first owner of the hot springs property. Not long after that, a tent city was born on the site and named Defiance. A few years later, the region's Ute population was moved to reservations in Utah, and the whole western part of the state was opened to settlers. When the town was incorporated in 1885, the name was changed to Glenwood.

In the 1880s, the Glenwood Hot Springs Pool was built and soon was attracting highfalutin guests from around the world. Before skiing was a recreational sport in the U.S., back when Aspen was a mining town, Glenwood Springs was one of the world's premiere travel destinations. The "grand dame," Hotel Colorado, was built in 1893 and hosted such guests as Presidents Taft and Roosevelt, and the "unsinkable" Molly Brown. While filming in the area, the great western screen star Tom Mix even stayed there.

As the resort town grew, attractions were added. In 1897, the Glenwood Caverns and Fairy Caves were opened to the public and were proclaimed in advertisements as the "Eighth Wonder of the World."

Travelers today come for the hot springs, but also to enjoy the region's recreational opportunities. There's rafting on the Colorado River, hiking up to Hanging Lake, and biking through Glenwood Canyon. The Glenwood Caverns and Adventure Park can keep a family entertained all day, and the town has numerous places for both fine dining and gathering the family around the trough.

GUIDANCE **Glenwood Springs Chamber Resort Association** (970-945-6589 or 1-888-4GLENWOOD; www.glenwoodsprings.com) 1102 Grand Ave. The

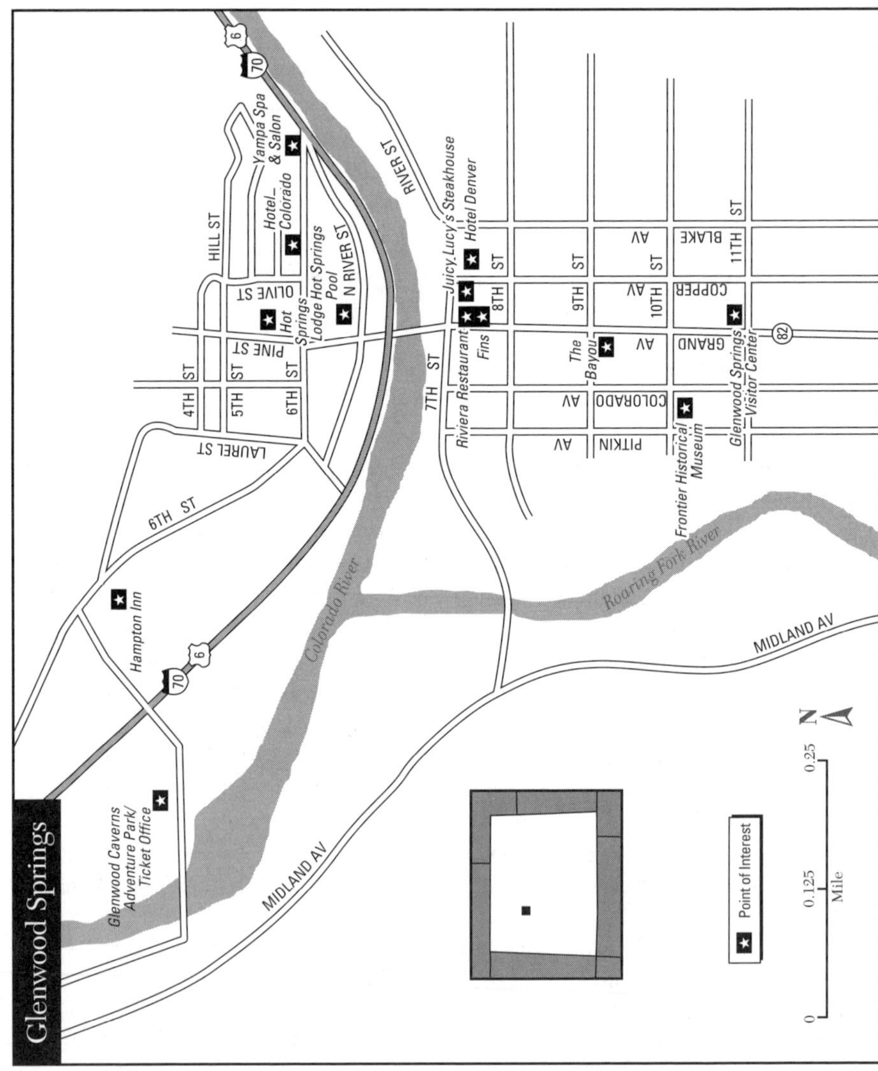

visitor center is open in the summer (Memorial Day to Labor Day) Mon.–Fri. 9–5, and weekends 10–3; winter, Mon.–Fri. 9–5. Outside there's a 24-hour, unmanned information kiosk that has brochures covering lodging, dining, and attractions in Glenwood Springs.

GETTING THERE *By car:* Glenwood Springs is right on I-70 at exits 114 and 116. It's about 180 miles west of Denver (three hours, give or take) and 117 miles east of the Utah border.

By air: The **Aspen/Pitkin County Airport** (970-920-5384; www.aspenairport .com), 0233 E. Airport Rd., is about 37 miles south of Glenwood Springs on CO

82. Both United and Delta fly into this airport. The **Denver International Airport** (1-800-AIR2DEN; www.flydenver.com) is about 180 miles east of Glenwood Springs. It's a three-hour drive, but the **Colorado Mountain Express** (970-926-9800 or 1-800-525-6363; www.cmex.com) does offer a shuttle from the DIA to Glenwood Springs.

By train: **AMTRAK** (1-800-872-7245) offers train service from their station at 413 Seventh St. The station is open daily 9:30–5.

By bus: **Greyhound** (970-945-8501 or 1-800-231-2222; www.greyhound.com) operates regular service to and from Glenwood Springs from their station at the Phillips 66 Station (51171 US 6). Open daily 4 AM–midnight.

GETTING AROUND *By bus:* **Ride Glenwood Springs** (970-384-6400; www.ci.glenwood-springs.co.us/transpo) provides transportation around Glenwood Springs. Also, **Roaring Fork Transportation Authority** (970-925-8484) provides shuttle service to all of Aspen's ski areas, the Maroon Bells, and Glenwood Springs.

MEDICAL EMERGENCIES **Valley View Hospital** (970-945-6535; www.vvh.org), 1906 Blake Ave., has 24-hour emergency service.

✱ To See & Do

♿ **Hot Springs Pool** (970-945-6571 or 1-800-537-7946; www.hotspringspool.com), 401 N. River St. Open daily 7:30–10. A visit to Glenwood Springs must

HOT SPRINGS POOL

include a day, or at least a few hours, of soaking and swimming in the town's legendary Hot Springs Pool. The sandstone lodge and bathing pools were built in the 1880s. The first guests to "take the waters" in Glenwood stayed across the street at the Hotel Colorado. (The Hot Springs Lodge was built in 1986.) The spring expels 3.5 million gallons of mineral-rich springwater every day. This water is channeled into two pools—the smaller hot pool, which stays about 104 degrees, and the large main pool where the water is a more tolerable 90 degrees. In the summer there's a Kiddie Pool with fountains for young children, and there are two waterslides for kids of all ages. Adult pool $13–17.50, and children (3–12) $8.25–10.75. Additional fees for waterslide, mini-golf, and towel and suit rental.

? ♿ **Yampah Spa & Salon** (970-945-0667; www.yampahspa.com), 709 E. Sixth St. Open daily 9–9. Another way to enjoy the region's geothermic qualities is to spend some time in the natural vapor caves at the Yampah Spa & Salon. Hot mineral water flows through the floor of the cave's three main chambers, creating a natural steam bath. Vapor cave pass $12.

Glenwood Caverns Adventure Park (1-800-530-1635; www.glenwoodcaverns.com), 5100 Two Rivers Plaza Rd. Open daily in the summer 9–8. Reduced hours in the fall and spring, and only open Thurs.–Sun. in the winter. Glenwood Caverns began as a cave tour. Thousands have come to explore the caverns and the historic Fairy Caves. Guests today can take the 70-minute walking tour or gear up for a more strenuous exploration of the caverns. The Adventure Tour and Wild Tour offer guests a chance to see parts of the caves not accessible without getting a little dirty. In addition to the caverns, the park has several attractions, like the Tramway, a climbing wall, and horseback riding. There are also rides like the Canyon Flyer. This alpine coaster is like an alpine slide, but its track system allows for more dips, jumps, and hairpin turns. For a zip-line experience, try the Alpine Flyer, which takes you whizzing through the trees as you descend the 650 vertical feet to the end of the ride. Adult park entrance and cave tour $18, seniors $16, and children (3–12) $13. Rides and other activities cost more.

TRAM TO GLENWOOD CAVERNS

? **Frontier Historical Museum** (970-945-4448; www.glenwoodhistory.com), 1001 Colorado Ave. May–Sept., open Mon.–Sat. 11–4; Oct.–April, open Mon. and Thurs.–Sat. 1–4. The museum documents the history of Glenwood Springs and Garfield County, from the first expedition by Captain James Sopris to the establishment and growth of Glenwood as a resort destination. Adult admission $3, seniors $2, and children (3–12) $1.

✓**Doc Holliday's Grave.** In 1887, Doc Holliday came to Glenwood Springs hoping the recoup somewhat from his tuberculosis. He died there on Nov. 8 of that year. Many speculate that the sulfur from the springs did his lungs more harm than good. He was buried in the Linwood Cemetery overlooking the town. The short hike to his grave begins at Bennett Street and E. 12th Street. There is a sign and a bench. It's a moderate climb with a great view of town at the top.

Ruedi Reservoir. For a scenic drive, head south on US 82, turning east in Basalt on Frying Pan Rd. The windy drive up to Ruedi Reservoir is often a bit congested with cyclists. The route takes you along the Frying Pan River. At the end you are rewarded with a stop at the 1,000-acre Ruedi Reservoir.

✷ Outdoor Activities

ALPINE SKIING & SNOWBOARDING **Sunlight Mountain Resort** (970-945-7491 or 1-800-445-7931; www.sunlightmtn.com), 10901 CR 117. Lifts open 9–4. This intimate ski area has 470 skiable acres, with 67 runs and a 2,010-foot vertical drop. The majority of terrain is rated for intermediate skiers, with advanced skiers and beginners splitting the remainder. The terrain park has plenty of new jib park features with jumps, fun boxes, and rails. Adult lift ticket $45, seniors and children (6–12) $35, and kids under 5 and seniors over 70 $10.

GLENWOOD CANYON ✓

The spectacular Glenwood Canyon is the largest canyon on the upper Colorado River. It's a beautiful 13-mile stretch of scenery—the walls rise 2,000 feet above the canyon floor. As far back as the 1880s, pioneers used the canyon as a throughway. The first travelers brought wagons along a rough path beside the river, and by 1902 the Taylor State Road connected Denver and Grand Junction. When the interstate highway system was first conceived, there were no plans to connect Denver with Utah, but by the 1960s it became clear that I-70 would need to be extended west.

The Glenwood Canyon section of the highway became one of the most difficult engineering feats of its day. In order to preserve the canyon's fragile environment, special care was taken to avoid unnecessary blasting. Huge retaining walls, tunnels, and complex bridges had to be created. Construction on the road began in 1964 and was finally completed in 1993.

There are four rest stops accessible from both the highway and the paved path that runs east from Glenwood Springs to Dotsero. A favorite stop for exploring the canyon is the parking lot for the Hanging Lake Trail (see Hiking on next page).

Sunlight Mountain Ski & Bike Shop (970-945-9425; www.sunlightmtn.com), 309 Ninth St. You can rent ski equipment on the mountain or in town at the resort's ski and bike shop. This is also a great place to rent skis for those staying in Glenwood but skiing in Aspen.

BICYCLING **Glenwood Canyon Bike Path.** A 17-mile paved path runs along the Colorado River, through Glenwood Canyon, from Glenwood Springs to Dotsero. There is little elevation gain along the scenic route, making for an enjoyable ride in either direction.

Sunlight Mountain Ski & Bike Shop (970-945-9425; www.sunlightmtn.com), 309 Ninth St. For a nice day trip, the shop offers bike rental and shuttle ride packages. For $25 (kids $20), you get a bike and a drop-off anywhere along the Glenwood Canyon Bike Path.

CROSS-COUNTRY SKIING & SNOWSHOEING **Sunlight's Cross-Country Skiing and Snowshoeing** (970-945-7491 or 1-800-445-7931; www.sunlightmtn.com), 10901 CR 117. The Sunlight Mountain Resort has 18 miles of groomed ski and snowshoe trails. Equipment can be rented at the Sunlight Mountain Ski & Bike Shop in town (309 Ninth St.) or at the mountain. There is no fee for use of the trails.

FISHING **Roaring Fork Anglers** (970-945-0180 or 1-800-781-8120; www.alpineangling.com), 2114 B Grand Ave. This outfitter has been serving anglers for over 25 years. Their guides will take you out on the Roaring Fork, Colorado, Frying Pan, and Crystal rivers. With hundreds of miles of great trout water in the region, these folks can get you to the sweet spots. Half-day wading trip $225 (cheaper per person when you bring friends). Float trip $345.

GOLF **Glenwood Springs Golf Club** (970-945-7086; www.glenwoodgolf.com), 193 Sunny Acres Rd. Since 1952, golfers have been enjoying this nine-hole course in northwest Glenwood Springs. Greens fees $37.

✔ **Rifle Creek Golf Club** (970-625-1093 or 1-888-247-0370; www.golfcolorado.com/riflecreek), 3004 CO 325, Rifle. This course was designed in 1960 to take advantage of the area's natural beauty. Following the terrain led the back nine to be a more target-oriented course than the more traditional front nine. Greens fees $39.

✔ HIKING **Hanging Lake Trail,** just off I-70 in the heart of Glenwood Canyon. To find the trailhead, you must travel east on the interstate. If you're heading west, turn around at the Grizzly Creek rest area. It is several miles west of the Shoshone exit. From the trailhead, it's 1 mile to the lake, but it's a steep mile. At the top, hikers are rewarded with a beautiful mountain lake, fed by several waterfalls cascading from the wooded cliff above. With over 80,000 hikers making the trek up to Hanging Lake every year, it is important that everyone follow the three basic rules that have been put in place to protect the trail and the lake: 1) leave no trace; 2) no dogs on the trail; 3) no swimming in the lake.

HANGING LAKE

PADDLING **Colorado Whitewater Rafting** (970-945-8477 or 1-800-993-7238; www.coloradowhitewaterrafting.com), 2000 Devereaux Rd. This rafting outfitter is a local favorite. They have full- and half-day trips, but the most popular is the three-hour tour through Glenwood Canyon on the Colorado River. Adult half-day trip $47 and youth (under 13) $35.

Rock Gardens Adventures (970-945-6737 or 1-800-958-6737; www.rockgardens.com), 1308 CR 129. The Shoshone Half-Day trip is RGA's most popular. It's a float down the Colorado River through Glenwood Canyon. Adults $47 and youths $35.

✷ Lodging

HOTELS **Hotel Colorado** ✓ (970-945-6511 or 1-800-544-3998; www.hotelcolorado.com), 526 Pine St. The Hotel Colorado was built in 1893 to offer first-class accommodations for wealthy travelers who were making their way to Glenwood Springs to take the waters. Over the years, many presidents have stayed here, including Teddy Roosevelt, who made several visits. He once stayed for three weeks in 1905 while hunting bear. The tradition of elegance continues today at this five-star hotel. The hotel has several eateries, including a fantastic restaurant, Baron's, and a courtyard café in the summer. Rooms $145–450.

Hotel Denver (970-945-6565 or 1-800-826-8820; www.thehoteldenver.com), 402 Seventh St. This historic hotel has all the conveniences modern travelers have come to expect but with the charm and comfort of an intimate lodge. The rooms are tastefully decorated with thick quilts and antiques. Hardwood floors,

HISTORIC HOTEL COLORADO

four-poster and sleigh beds, and great views of the springs are found in many rooms. The hotel's largest suite, the Cupola, has a kitchenette, three televisions, and a private rooftop hot tub. Rooms $124–339.

"1" ♿ **Hot Springs Lodge** (970-945-6571 or 1-800-537-7946; www.hotspringspool.com), 415 E. Sixth St. Located across the street from the springs and next to the Hotel Colorado, one of the best amenities is that guests get free access to the Hot Springs Pool—on the day they check in and the day they check out. Otherwise, the accommodations are pretty standard. Rooms $129–251.

"1" ♿ **Hampton Inn** (970-947-9400 or 1-800-426-7866; www.hamptoninn.com), 401 W. First St. There are a number of chains in Glenwood Springs. The Hampton Inn is one of the nicer of those next to the highway. They have a fine complimentary breakfast, and the staff is excited to share dining recommendations and information about area attractions. Rooms $189–219.

BED & BREAKFASTS "1" **The B&B on Mitchell Creek** (970-945-4002; www.mitchellcreekbb.com), 1686 Mitchell Creek Rd. Overlooking Mitchell Creek, this secluded B&B offers two rooms with king-sized beds and a private entrance. Each room has its own deck and fire pit for campfires along the creek. A full breakfast is served every day. Rooms $125.

Four Mile Creek (970-945-4004; www.fourmilecreek.com), 6471 CR 117. This B&B is part of the Four Mile Ranch, originally homesteaded in 1885. Two rooms are available in the historic log home, and there are two log cabins that sleep up to four guests. A full breakfast is served every morning in the main dining room. Rooms $85 and cabins $135–145.

CAMPGROUNDS ♿ **Glenwood Canyon Resort** (970-945-6737 or 1-800-970-6737; www.glenwoodcanyon resort.com), 1308 CR 129. Open year-round. Located just west of Glenwood Springs, the resort is right off exit 119 (the same as the No Name rest area). There are sites for RVs and tent, and the resort rents out cabins. The campground is well shaded and there are fantastic tent sites right along the Colorado River. Warm showers and coin-operated laundry are available. And the resort has ready access to the Glenwood Canyon Bike Path and fishing on the Colorado River. Tent sites $28–35, RV $44–46, and cabins $55–249.

✱ Where to Eat

DINING OUT 🍸 ♿ **Fins Grille & Raw Bar** (970-945-4771; www.fins grille.com), 710 Grand Ave. Open daily for dinner at 5. For fresh seafood (cooked or otherwise), there's no other place in town. This casually contemporary eatery has a raw bar and full menu of entrées from the grill. There are plenty of steaks on hand for you land-lubbers. For special evenings, they have live music on most Thursdays and Saturdays. Entrées $15–25.

🍸 ♿ **Rivers** (970-928-8813; www .theriversrestaurant.com), 2525 S. Grand Ave. Open daily at 5. Overlooking the Roaring Fork River, the Rivers Restaurant serves innovative American cuisine. The outdoor deck is open when weather permits. Start with an appetizer, like the grilled elk quesadilla, and continue with the fantastic warmed spinach salad with smoked bacon and toasted walnuts. Dinner entrées include steak and fresh seafood as well as duck and game. Entrées $15–25.

🍸 ♿ **Riviera Restaurant** (970-945-7692), 702 Grand Ave. Open daily for dinner at 5. The Riviera Supper Club sign that hangs out front remains because it is a Glenwood Springs landmark. The restaurant inside, however, is a completely new venture. The open dining room, now full of natural light, was transformed with contemporary décor. The eclectic menu features classic dishes like prime rib and porterhouse steak as well as the more daring Riviera duck and seafood risotto. Entrées $18–25.

EATING OUT ♿ **The Bayou** (970-945-1047), 919 Grand Ave. Open for dinner Sat.–Thurs. 4–10 and Fri. and Sat. 4–midnight. Folks may be surprised to find a New Orleans-style restaurant in the mountains of Colorado—even more so when they find out how good it is. Folks come for the Cajun cuisine, like gumbo, shrimp creole, and blackened chicken. And if you like your food spicy hot, they have a hot sauce for every tolerance. Dinner dishes average $15.

Daily Bread (970-945-6253), 729 Grand Ave. Open daily for breakfast and lunch. This café and bakery serves breakfast and lunch. The menu is full of hearty and affordable food. All the baked goods are made on the premises. A regular favorite is the cinnamon roll French toast. Dishes $4–10.

🍸 **Italian Underground** (970-945-6422), 715 Grand Ave. Open daily for dinner 5–10. With red-and-white checkered tablecloths, brick walls, and a dining room filled with antiques, this out-of-the way Italian eatery has tons of charm. It also could very well be the best Italian place in town. They serve everything from pizza to chicken cacciatore, and there's a full bar. Dishes $9–15.

✓ 🍸 ♿ **Juicy Lucy's Steakhouse** (970-945-4619), 308 Seventh St. Open daily 11–10. This family steakhouse serves only prime graded beef that is handcut and aged on the premises. They also serve chicken, fish, lamb, and elk. Just underneath the bridge, with the right seat, you can enjoy the nearby river from the window. Entrées $12–25.

BAKERIES & COFFEE SHOPS ♿
Sacred Grounds (970-928-8804; www.sacredgrounds.biz), 725 Grand Ave. Open Mon.–Thurs. 7–6, Fri. and Sat. 7–8, and Sun. 7–5. In addition to a full coffee menu of espresso, cappuccino, and mocha, Sacred Grounds has deli sandwiches and fantastic baked goods. Be sure to try a brownie if you get a chance.

JUICY LUCY'S STEAKHOUSE

BARS, TAVERNS & BREW PUBS 🍸 ♿
Glenwood Canyon Brewing Company (970-945-1276; www.glenwoodcanyon.com), 402 Seventh St. Open Sun.–Thurs. 11–11 and Fri. and Sat. 11–midnight. Located on the first floor of the Hotel Denver, this brew pub has a full bar and wine menu. They serve lunch and dinner daily. Eight of their handcrafted beers are on tap, and each goes great with a game of pool in the billiard room.

✷ Selective Shopping

Book Grove (970-384-0992 or 1-800-303-7290; www.bookgrove.com), 801 Blake Ave. Open Wed.–Sat. 10–5:30 This bookstore sells used and out-of-print books, including first editions and many autographed books.

✷ Special Events

June: **Strawberry Days** (970-945-6589; www.strawberrydaysfestival.com). The three-day Strawberry Festival kicks off with a parade, led by a vintage car show. There's live entertainment for the whole family, an artisan fair, and free strawberries and ice cream.

GRAND JUNCTION & COLORADO'S WESTERN SLOPE

Colorado's Western Slope is often overlooked as a tourist destination. This is a shame. The region has two of the state's most stunning national monuments—the Colorado National Monument and Dinosaur National Monument. There are also a number of beautiful state parks, one of which features a long stretch of the Colorado River. Towns along the Western Slope run on the small side. As such, they are home to friendly, hard-working people who understand hospitality. Even Grand Junction, the Mesa County seat with 140,000 residents, has a certain small-town charm.

The little tourism there is centers on Grand Junction. In recent years, there has been a surge of interest in the region. Interest in small independent wineries has been growing for well over a decade along Colorado's Front Range. As these wineries seek to educate their customers on Colorado wines, they inevitably point west toward the vineyards that produce their grapes. As an agricultural center, Grand Junction and Palisade have been producing fruit—especially peaches, apricots, and grapes—since the 19th century. As these new wine tourists have learned about the state's wine industry, their curiosity has been peaked, and more and more people are coming out to tour the wineries and vineyards of western Colorado.

There have also been an increasing number of recreational tourists. Fruita (pronounced *froo-ta*) has become known for its mountain biking trails. Miles and miles of technical singletrack and the ever-prized slickrock draw thousands of riders annually.

Grand Junction and the Grand Valley have also become prized for the region's natural beauty. The nearby Grand Mesa rises 10,000 feet above the valley floor, making it the tallest mesa (or flat-topped mountain) in the world. To the north, you see the eastern section of the Book Cliffs, which continue west nearly 200 miles into Utah.

This boom in tourism has allowed Grand Junction to offer more resources for travelers. The town offers everything from hotel chains along the highway to several exceptional B&Bs. More than a dozen restaurants can be found in Grand Junction's downtown area. As the town becomes savvier about catering to visitors, be sure to stop by the area visitor centers to see what's new.

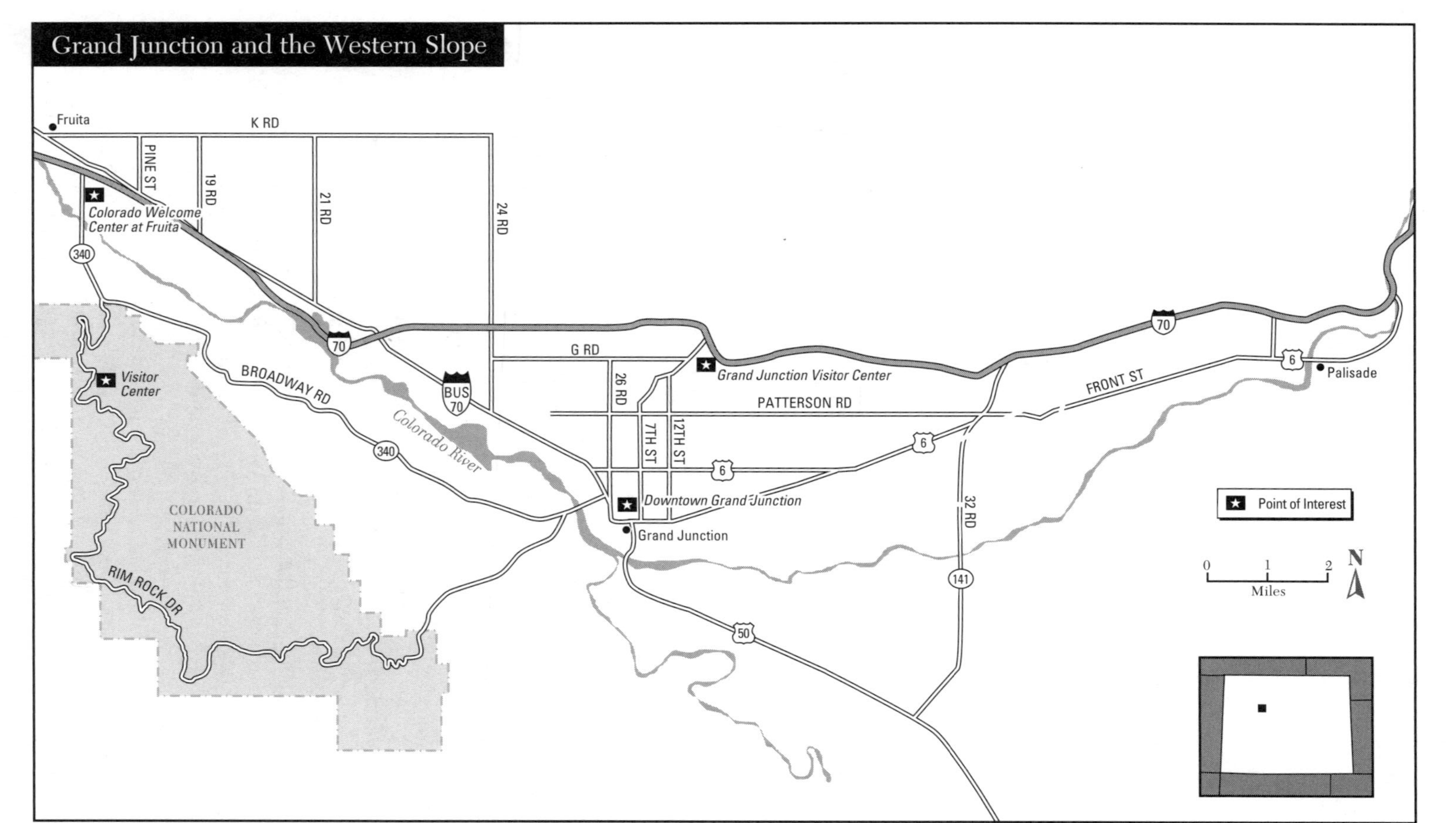
Grand Junction and the Western Slope
Fruita
K RD
PINE ST
19 RD
21 RD
24 RD
Colorado Welcome Center at Fruita
340
70
BUS 70
G RD
26 RD
7TH ST
12TH ST
Grand Junction Visitor Center
PATTERSON RD
FRONT ST
6
Palisade
Visitor Center
BROADWAY RD
Colorado River
COLORADO NATIONAL MONUMENT
RIM ROCK DR
Downtown Grand Junction
Grand Junction
32 RD
141
50
Point of Interest
0
1
2
Miles
N

GUIDANCE **Grand Junction Visitor and Convention Bureau** (970-256-4060; www.visitgrandjunction.com), 740 Horizon Dr., Grand Junction. Open daily in the summer 8:30–8; winter, 8:30–5.

Colorado Welcome Center at Fruita (970-858-9335), 340 CO 340, Fruita (exit 19 on I-70). Open daily in the summer 8–6. Complimentary maps and untold hundreds of brochures covering all of Colorado.

Colorado Welcome Center at Dinosaur (970-374-2205), at the corner of US 40 and CO 64 in Dinosaur. Open daily in the summer 8–6. Closed Nov.–Feb.

More Web sites: www.visitgrandjunction.com

GETTING THERE *By car:* The Western Slope is easily accessed from the east and west by I-70.

By air: The **Grand Junction Regional Airport** (970-244-9100; www.walkerfield.com) is located 1 mile north of I-70 off Horizon Dr. (exit 31). The airport serves airlines like Frontier, Southwest, Delta, and United.

By train: **AMTRAK** (1-800-872-7245) offers train service from their station at 339 S. First St., Grand Junction. The station is open daily 10–6.

By bus: **Greyhound** (970-242-6012 or 1-800-231-2222; www.greyhound.com) operates regular service to and from Grand Junction from their station at 230 S. Fifth St. Station closed daily 4:30 PM–10:30 PM.

MEDICAL EMERGENCIES The following Grand Junction hospitals offer 24-hour emergency care.

Community Hospital (970-242-0920 or 1-800-621-0926; www.gjhosp.org), 2021 N. 12th St.

St. Mary's Hospital (970-244-2273; www.stmarygj.org), 2635 N. Seventh St.

✷ To See & Do

MUSEUMS ☂ ♿ The **Museum of Western Colorado** (www.wcmuseum.org) has several museum and historical sites in the Grand Junction area, each exploring different aspects of the region's history. Admission can be purchased for each attraction or you can purchase a combination ticket that gets you into the three sites mentioned here. Adult combo $12, seniors $10, and children $8.

☂ **Museum of the West** (970-242-0971; www.wcmuseum.org), 462 Ute Ave., Grand Junction. Open Mon.–Sat. 9–5 and Sun. noon–4. This museum tells the story not just of Colorado, but of the American West. Exhibits are designed for interaction—not merely rows of glass displays where you look but can't touch. The museum has one of the finest firearm collections around, as well as an excellent exhibit of Southwest pottery. They even have a full-sized WAAIME uranium mine. Adult admission $5.50, seniors $4.50, children $3, and family groups $16.

☂ **Dinosaur Journey** (970-858-7282; www.dinosaurjourney.org), 550 Jurassic Ct., Fruita. Open Mon.–Sat. 10–4 and Sun. noon–4. Step back in time to the age of dinosaurs. Exhibits include full-sized models that "come to life" and demonstrations that show how it must have looked and felt when dinosaurs roamed the earth. Adult admission $7, seniors $6, children $4, and family groups $20. For another dinosaur activity offered by the Museum of Western Colorado, consider going on a **Dinosaur Dig** (www.dinodigs.org). The museum offers one- to five-day digs in the Morrison Formation in Colorado and Wyoming.

Cross Orchards Historic Site (970-434-9814; www.wcmuseum.org/cross orchards.htm), 3073 F Rd., Grand Junction. Open May–Oct., Tues.–Sat. 9–4. Cross Orchards gives guests a glimpse back into Grand Junction's agricultural history. Costumed guides introduce life as it was in the early part of the 20th century. The orchards' barn and packing shed and the bunkhouse are all on the National Register of Historic Places. Adult admission $4, seniors $3, children $2.50, and family groups $10.

♿ **Gateway Canyons Automobile Museum** (970-931-2895; www.gateway automuseum.com), 43224 CO 141, Gateway. Open daily 10–7. This 30,000-square-foot museum houses 40 classic cars that illustrate the historic development of automobile design and performance over the past 100 years. The prize of the collection is the 1954 Oldsmobile F-88. This concept car was designed by the legendary Harley Earl but never went into production. All the vehicles here have been preserved in or restored to showroom quality. Adult admission $9, seniors $7, youth (6–12) $5, and children under 6 free.

NATIONAL MONUMENTS **Colorado National Monument** (970-858-3617; www.nps.gov/colm). The park can be accessed from Grand Junction and Fruita. The park visitor center is open daily in the summer (Memorial Day to Labor Day) from 8–6. Open the rest of the year 9–5. To get there, take exit 19 on I-70 in Fruita and follow CO 340 south until you see the turn for the park. The visitor center is about 4.5 miles into the park on the left.

COLORADO NATIONAL MONUMENT

In 1906, a man named John Otto came to Grand Junction and was awed by the beauty of the nearby canyons. Most locals believed the canyon lands to be inaccessible, but Otto settled down there and began building trails. He was convinced that the region should be preserved as a national park and set about making that happen. In 1911, President Taft created the Colorado National Monument, and Otto was paid a symbolic $1/month salary to stay as the park's first caretaker (he remained until 1927).

The beauty of the park is undeniable. The Uncompahgre Plateau rises over 2,000 feet above the Grand Valley, south of Grand Junction and Fruita. It is part of the greater Colorado Plateau, which includes such geological wonders as the Grand Canyon and the Arches (of Arches National Park in Utah). Thousands of years of erosion have dug deep canyons in the plateau and have created numerous rock formations. Independence Monument, for example, was once part of a canyon wall, but now stands alone, 450 feet above the canyon floor. Other rock structures like the Coke Ovens and the ever-popular Window Rock draw over a quarter of a million visitors a year.

The best introduction to the Colorado National Monument is to simply drive the length of Rim Rock Dr. from either end of the park, stopping at the overlooks to take in the scenery. Coming from the east, the rock formations get increasingly dramatic. From the west, the visitor center offers a nice orientation to the park. They can give you information on camping and backcountry hikes as well as the geological history of the plateau and canyons.

Once you've driven the main road and gazed over a number of overlooks, consider taking a short hike. The hike from the visitor center out to Window Rock, for example, is a level 1.5-mile round-trip. Another trail on the east end of Rim Rock Dr. is the Serpents Trail, which follows an older section of the main road. This 1.75-mile hike (one way) has over 50 switchbacks as it climbs the plateau. Park admission $7/vehicle and individuals $4; good for 7 days.

Dinosaur National Monument (970-374-3000 or 435-781-7700; www.nps.gov/dino), 4545 E. US 40, Dinosaur. The temporary visitor center near Jensen, Utah, is open daily in the summer (Memorial Day to Labor Day) 8:30–5:30, and the rest of the year 8:30–4:30. The Canyon Area Visitor Center near Dinosaur, Col., is open daily in the summer (Memorial Day to Labor Day) from 8:30–4:30. In the spring and fall, the center is closed on Monday and Tuesday. It's also closed in the winter, Oct. 29–Feb. 29.

The big attraction at the Dinosaur National Monument was the chance to see and touch fossils at the Dinosaur Quarry Visitor Center. The two-story building surrounded a wall of dinosaur fossils, still embedded in the rock, allowing visitors to see them up close in a sheltered and air-conditioned environment. Built in 1957 on expansive soils, the foundation of the Quarry Visitor Center has deteriorated over the years. In the summer of 2006, the building was determined to be a serious hazard and was closed. It's hoped that it will reopen as early as 2009, though possibly as late as 2012.

Not to worry, there is still plenty to see and do at the park. Throughout the summer, ranger-guided tours take visitors on a Fossil Discovery Hike to see fossils in an ancient river bed. There are also two auto tours that explore other aspects of the park—brochures available at all visitor centers. The Tour of the Tilted Rocks takes visitors 11 miles from the Quarry out on Cub Creek Road to the historic Josie Morris Cabin. Along the way they pass a prehistoric petroglyph site and some nature trails. While out at Josie's Cabin, you might want to take a little hike on the Box Canyon Trail, an easy walk with some great shade from the summer heat.

The Journey through Time tour begins at the visitor center near Dinosaur. This 62-mile round trip introduces visitors to the natural aspects of the park—not so much here about dinosaurs. It highlights the park's ecosystems and its geological beauty.

For a river-rafting trip through the park, contact **Adrift Adventures** (435-789-3600 or 1-800-824-0150; www.adrift.com) about one-day and multiday trips down the Yampa River. For multiday trips, you should also consider **Adventure Bound** (1-800-423-4668; www.raft-colorado.com).

Park admission for noncommercial, private vehicles \$10; motorcycles with a single rider \$5 (two riders \$10); individuals hiking or biking into the park \$5; good for 7 days.

WINERIES ♿ **Two Rivers Chateau and Winery** (970-255-1471 or 1-866-312-9463; www.tworiverswinery.com), 2087 Broadway. The tasting room and winery at Two Rivers are surrounded by 15 acres of vineyard. The property is relatively new—before 1999 it was a vacant lot—but the owners have clearly worked hard to create an Old World feel. When you visit the tasting room, be sure to ask about a tour of the winery.

♿ **Carlson Vineyards** (970-464-5554 or 1-888-464-5554; www.carlsonvineyards.com), 461 35 Rd., Palisade. Open daily 10–5:45 for tasting and tours. The Carlson Vineyards Winery has been producing wine since 1988, and it has become a required stop on all regional winery tours. If Parker or Mary Carlson are around

TWO RIVERS CHATEAU AND WINERY

(and they more often than not are), be sure to take a moment to chat about their wines and perhaps ask for a tour of the winery.

♿ **Plum Creek Cellars** (970-464-7586; www.plumcreekwinery.com), 3708 G Rd., Palisade. Tasting room is open daily April–Oct. 9:30–6 and Nov.–Mar. 10–5. Plum Creek holds Colorado winery license #10—no other winery in the state has one that's older. Doug and Sue Phillips began growing grapes in 1980, and opened the winery in 1984 using only Colorado grapes. When visiting the tasting room, ask about getting a tour of the winery (but call ahead if you have a large group).

♿ **Colorado Wine Room** (970-858-6330; www.coloradowineroom.com), 455 Kokopelli Blvd., Unit A, Fruita. Open Tues.–Sat. 10:30–5:30 and Sun. noon–5. The Colorado Wine Room is both a small winery and a promoter of fine Colorado wines. Four times a year, blind taste tests are conducted that decide which Colorado wines they will sell. Over 25 different wines are offered at any given time.

✷ Outdoor Activities

ALPINE SKIING & SNOWBOARDING **Powderhorn Resort** (970-268-5700; www.powderhorn.com), 48338 Powderhorn Rd., Mesa. Lifts run 9–4 in-season. Half of the trails at Powderhorn are designated intermediate and 20 percent are beginner. The ski area has 600 skiable acres and gives skiers an overall 1,650-foot vertical drop. The resort gets 250 inches of snow annually, meaning they don't often have to rely on snowmaking equipment. The two terrain parks, Pepsi Tyro Park and Mt. Dew Junction Park, offer a progressive number of features to tackle as you improve your skills (though there are no pipes, half, super, or otherwise). Adult lift ticket $49, seniors and students (7–18) $39, seniors over 70 $15, and kids under 7 $10.

GOLF **Redlands Mesa Golf Course** (970-263-9270 or 1-866-863-9270; www.redlandsmesa.com), 2299 W. Ridges Blvd. A couple years back *Golf Digest* magazine named this course the "Best New Affordable Golf Course in the U.S." The course blends into the desert landscape, keeping native features intact wherever possible—including many elevation changes. Greens fees $84.

MOUNTAIN BIKING In Fruita, you can find some of the best singletrack in the country. Much of the effort was spearheaded by Troy Rarick at Over the Edge Sports, owner of a local bike shop. To get acquainted with the local trails, check in at Over the Edge and start asking questions. The Kokopelli's Loop Trail System offers a number of rides. You can piece together loops to fill the day with as much riding as you like. Try Mary's Loop for a technical ride with some slickrock. Kokopelli's Trail takes riders from Loma 142 miles to Moab. Campsites along the way are strategically placed for riders making the multiday trip. The trail is a combination of singletrack, dirt roads, and some pavement.

Over the Edge Sports (970-243-BIKE; www.otesports.com), 202 E. Aspen Ave., Fruita. OTE rents a virtual fleet of full-suspension mountain bikes. Day rate $40–55.

GREEN SPACE **James M. Robb–Colorado River State Park** (970-434-3388; www.parks.state.co.us/parks/jamesmrobbcoloradoriver), Clifton, CO. Open daily 5–10 for day use. The park lies on either side of the Colorado River from Fruita in the west to Island Acres east of Palisade. The park has some nice hiking trails and provides access to the Colorado River for boating and fishing. Daily park pass $6.

✷ Lodging

HOTELS **Gateway Canyons Resort** (970-931-2458; www.gatewaycanyons.com), 43200 CO 141, Gateway. The resort has several lodging options. The Outpost Motor Inn features rooms and suites. The rooms are decorated in a subtle Southwest style, complementing the resort's adobe exterior. Canyon Casitas offers condos with full kitchen, two bedrooms, and one bath. They can sleep six, and pets are welcome. Finally, the Kiva Lodge has 38 luxury rooms and suites that open out to the resort's new pool area. Rooms and suites $69–169, condos $179–239, and luxury rooms and suites $148–309.

BED & BREAKFASTS **Los Altos** (970-256-0964 or 1-888-774-0982; www.losaltosgrandjunction.com), 375 Hill View Dr. From its own lofty hilltop, Los Altos offers guests stunning views of Grand Mesa and the Colorado National Monument. The inn has seven rooms, each with a private bath and French doors that open out to the walk-around balcony. Try the top-floor Vista Suite, with its private captain's walk, for the best views in the house. Full gourmet breakfast served every morning. Rooms $115–205.

Castle Creek (970-241-9105; www.castlecreekbandb.com), 638 Horizon Dr. The innkeepers at Castle Creek designed their bed & breakfast from the ground up with the idea that both men and women should feel at home when they stay at a B&B. The four rooms at the inn are large, with huge bathrooms. Amenities include king-sized beds, jetted tubs for two, cable TV, and wireless Internet. All the rooms are tastefully decorated. The large deck off the back offers guests a place to rest overlooking the nearby creek. Full breakfast served on weekends—Continental on the weekends. Rooms $150.

The Gallery (970-243-2501; www.thegallerybb.com), 547 30 Rd. The main house at the Gallery has two bedrooms, each with a private bath. The kitchen has a refrigerator and microwave for guest use, and the living room has a TV and DVD player. A full breakfast is served daily. The inn also offers a small cottage called the Chicken Coop (no, it's not a restored chicken coop; it's just where the coop used to sit). The cottage has two rooms that share a bath. Only one party can rent the cottage at a time, with a choice of one or both rooms. The Chicken Coop has a small kitchen, and a continental breakfast is brought over every morning. Both spaces are tastefully decorated, and all the art displayed throughout the house is available for purchase. Rooms in the main house $80. Chicken Coop $99 for one room, $140 for both.

Willow Pond (970-243-4958 or 1-877-243-4958; www.willowpondbnb.com), 662 26 Rd. This fabulously remodeled 1916 farmhouse on its wooded lot is close to downtown Grand Junction but seems a world away. The hosts are known for their hospitality and the excellent breakfast they serve guests every morning. Rooms $99–150.

CAMPGROUND **James M. Robb–Colorado River State Park** (970-434-3388; www.parks.state.co.us/parks/jamesmrobbcoloradoriver), Clifton. There's camping in the Fruita Section of the Colorado River State Park. Forty-four sites for RV and tent camping sit alongside the Colorado River. The nearby lake has a swimming beach and opportunities for fishing. Though the campground is open year-round, coin-operated laundry and showers are closed in the winter. Tent sites $14 and RV sites $18–22.

✷ Where to Eat

DINING OUT 🍸 ♿ **Dolce Vita** (970-242-8482), 336 Main St. #A101. Open Tues.–Sat. 11:30–10. For fine Italian dining, there's no better place in town. The cozy atmosphere is perfect for a romantic dinner, but casual enough for a family gathering. The menu is complemented by an extensive wine list. Dinner entrées $15–28 and lunch $8–13.

🍸 ♿ **Moulin Rouge** (970-257-1777), 317 Main St. Open for lunch and dinner Tues.–Sat. Once called Rendez Vous, with the addition of a wine bar and subdued jazz piano music, it is now Moulin Rouge. The menu continues to offer outstanding French cuisine. Entrées $18–25.

🍸 ♿ **626 Rood** (970-257-7663), 626 Rood Ave. Open for lunch and dinner Mon.–Thurs. 11–10:30, Fri. and Sat. 11–11, and Sun. 4–10. One of Grand Junction's finest restaurants, this eatery and wine bar serves contemporary American cuisine. Black bean burgers and fish tacos are featured on the lunch menu. Steak and fresh seafood are prepared nightly for dinner. If you get a chance, be sure to try the lobster mac & cheese. Entrées $31–50.

EATING OUT ♿ **Main Street Cafe** (970-242-7225), 504 Main St. Open

MAIN STREET CAFE

for breakfast and lunch Mon.–Sat. 7–4 and Sun. 7–3. This 1950s restaurant on Main Street serves classic diner food. The mashed potatoes are made from scratch, and there's always a blue plate special. This is the perfect place for a hearty yet cheap breakfast. For the full experience, be sure to try a fountain drink. Dishes $4–8 (a little more for the full steak dinner, but not much).

♿ **Nepal** (970-242-2233), 225 N. Fifth St. Open Mon.–Sat. 11–9:30. Downtown Grand Junction has a bit of everything, including great Indian food. In true Indian restaurant style, there's a lunch buffet with tandoori chicken and fresh naan. Dinner $9–15 and lunch buffet $7.95.

BAKERIES & COFFEE SHOPS ♿ **Main Street Bagel** (970-241-2740; www.mainstreetbagels.net), 559 Main St., Grand Junction. Open Mon.–Thurs. 6:30–4, Fri. and Sat. 6:30–5:30, and Sun. 7–2:30. This is where you come for great coffee and fresh bagels. Right outside is a fountain with some patio seating—a nice option when there's live music downtown. Be sure to try their artisan breads.

✷ Special Events

April: **Fruita Fat Tire Festival** (970-858-7220; www.fruitamountainbike.com), Fruita. Celebrate mountain biking with a ride on the best singletrack around—later grab a beer and listen to some live music.

August: **Palisade Peach Festival** (www.palisadepeachfest.com), Palisade. For four decades the people in Palisade have been celebrating their peaches. The festival features live music, lots of great food, and artists hocking their wares. And of course, there are the peaches.

September: **Colorado Mountain Wine Fest** (www.coloradowinefest.com), Palisade. The other agricultural gem of the Western Slope are the grapes, and grapes mean wine. Wine tasting, grape-stomping, and live music make for a festive weekend.

FRUIT STAND IN PALISADE

South-Central Colorado

3

COLORADO SPRINGS

CAÑON CITY & THE GOLD RANGE

UPPER ARKANSAS VALLEY

SAN LUIS VALLEY

COLORADO SPRINGS

A mild climate and stunning scenery, as well as endless recreational opportunities in the nearby mountains, make Colorado Springs a great place to live. It's also a great place to visit, at least judging by the city's 6 million annual visitors. There are over 50 attractions—museums, springs, parks, caves, the zoo, not to mention Pikes Peak.

Colorado Springs started out as a tourist town. In 1871, General William Palmer, builder of the Denver & Rio Grande Railroad, decided to start a resort community and purchased 10,000 acres east of what is now Old Colorado City. Palmer was a masterful town planner. The city he built had wide, tree-lined boulevards. In an attempt to set Colorado Springs apart from its rowdy neighbors in Colorado City and Manitou Springs, the making, selling, and drinking of alcohol was prohibited (not to be repealed until the end of Prohibition in 1933). In 1883 he built the Antlers Hotel. Marketing his new endeavor, Palmer named the town Colorado Springs and latched onto the bubbling waters in nearby Manitou Springs as a central theme in his advertising. He even enlisted the services of a doctor whose job it was to promote "taking of the waters" as a healthy, invigorating activity.

In the 1890s, Spencer Penrose moved to Colorado. He made a fortune when gold was found in Cripple Creek. In turn he invested heavily in Colorado Springs. He built the Broadmoor Hotel, the Cheyenne Mountain Zoo, and the Pikes Peak Highway. He continues to contribute to the well-being of all Coloradoans through El Pomar Foundation—an organization that gives $20 million to nonprofits throughout the state each year.

Today, Colorado Springs has a population of 370,000, and the greater metro area is closing in on 575,000. With Fort Carson, Peterson and Schriever Air Force Bases, the Air Force Academy, and NORAD, the military has a significant presence in the Springs and remains the city's largest employer. In 1991, Focus on the Family, a Christian organization that offers advice on marriage relationships and child-rearing, moved its headquarters from California to Colorado Springs. This significantly bolstered the community's conservative image.

Visitors who come to Colorado Springs have all the conveniences and resources of a major metropolitan are—restaurants, malls and shopping centers, dozens of hotels, museums, and art galleries. The historic towns of Old Colorado City and

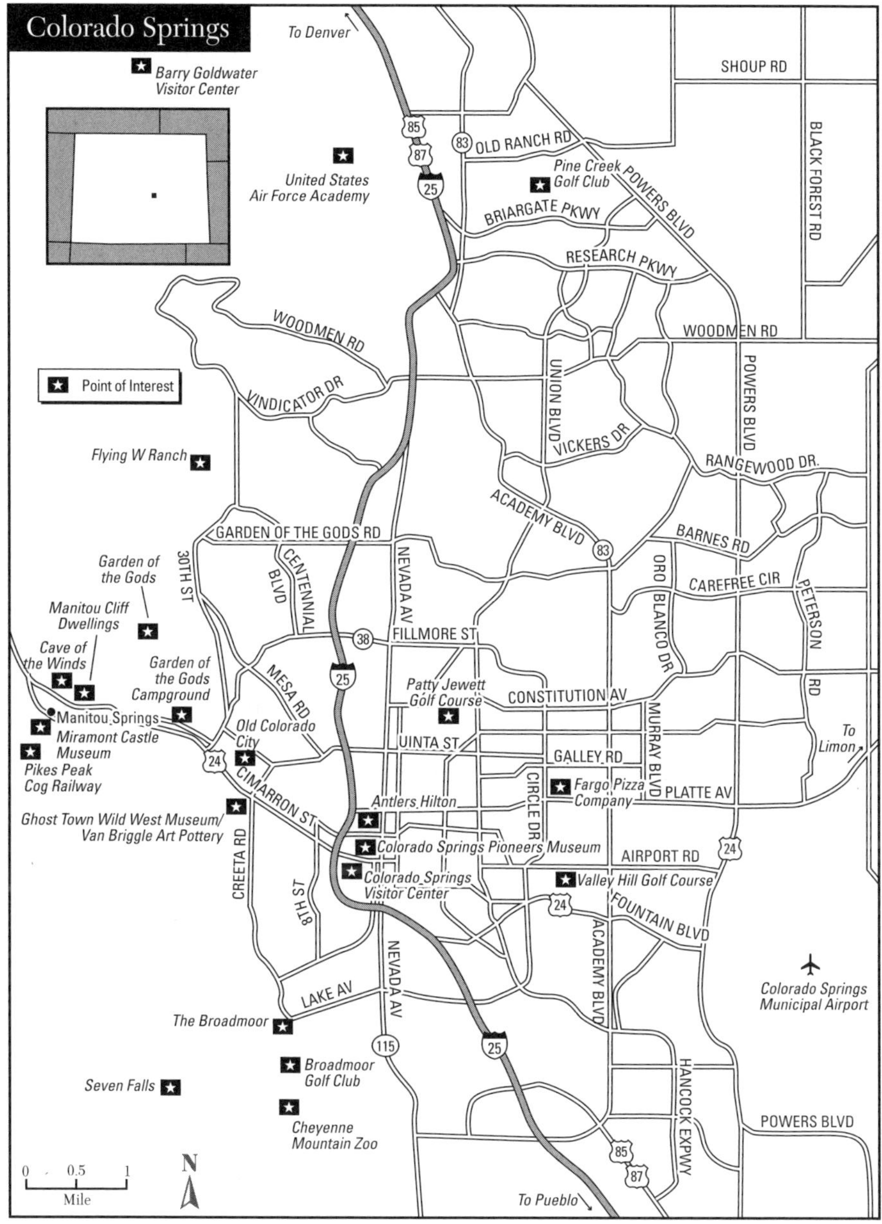

Manitou Springs offer great little shopping districts. Visitors can also take advantage of the great outdoors just beyond their hotel room, as the Garden of the Gods, Cave of the Winds, and, of course, Pikes Peak are just moments away.

GUIDANCE **Colorado Springs Convention and Visitors Bureau** (1-877-745-3773; www.experiencecoloradosprings.com), 515 S. Cascade Ave. The bureau is home to the Pikes Peak Visitors Center. Open Mon.–Fri. 8:30–5; summers daily 8–6; Sept. Mon.–Fri. 8:30–5 and Sat. 9–1. They have information on all area attractions. The staff is well informed and can help guests arrange lodging, find places to eat, and choose fun stuff to do and see.

Manitou Springs Visitors Bureau (719-685-5089 or 1-800-642-2567; www.manitousprings.org), 354 Manitou Ave. Coming into town from Colorado Springs and US 24, the visitor center is located on the right side of the road, just before you hit the main drag. They have maps here that show where all of Manitou's historic springs can be found. They even have cups for those who want to drink from each spring as they go.

More Web sites:

www.pikes-peak.com

www.coloradosprings-travel.com

GETTING THERE *By car:* Interstate 25 runs right through the heart of Colorado Springs and is your main route from the north and south. Coming in from eastern Colorado on I-70, US 24 cuts off in Limon and makes a straight path southwest to Colorado Springs. From the west, the main routes are I-70 and US 50 to I-25.

By air: The most accessible airport is, of course, the **Colorado Springs Airport** (719-550-1972; www.flycos.com). Many cities have direct flights to Colorado Springs. Be sure to also check prices for flights to Denver. The **Denver International Airport** (1-800-AIR2DEN; www.flydenver.com) is about 100 miles north of Colorado Springs, and it's often cheaper to land in Denver and rent a car there.

By train: There is no rail service to Colorado Springs, although **AMTRAK** (1-800-USA-RAIL; www.amtrak.com) has train terminals in Denver to the north, and you can take their Throughway bus service directly to Colorado Springs (see below for bus depot information).

By bus: **Greyhound** operates regular service to and from Colorado Springs from the TNM&O Terminal (719-635-1505 or 1-800-231-2222; www.greyhound.com), 120 S. Weber St.

GETTING AROUND *By car:* Getting around Colorado Springs is a pretty simple proposition. The city stretches out north to west along I-25, and that's the best bet for getting from one side of town to the other. Academy Boulevard is the other north–south corridor, and it meets up with I-25 at both ends of town. It is much slower going. Parking is plentiful in and around town.

By bus: The city operates the Metro, and complete public transportation system of buses. See the city Web site, www.springsgov.com, for a complete schedule. Adult fares $1.25–2.

MEDICAL EMERGENCIES Colorado's two hospital systems have four locations that offer 24-hour emergency and trauma services.

Memorial Hospital (719-365-5000; www.memorialhealthsystem.com), 1400 E. Boulder St.

Memorial Hospital North (719-364-5000; www.memorialhealthsystem.com), 4050 Briargate Pkwy.

Penrose Community Hospital (719-776-5000; www.penrosestfrancis.org), 3205 N. Academy Blvd.

Penrose Hospital (719-776-5000; www.penrosestfrancis.org), 2222 N. Nevada Ave.

✷ To See & Do

Air Force Academy (www.usafa.af.mil). This sprawling 18,000-acre campus receives a million visitors every year. It's no wonder. Located at the base of the Rampart Range, the academy has several hiking trails, a lake for fishing, and picnic areas. The academy itself is an attraction. A self-guided tour begins at the **Barry Goldwater Visitor Center** (719-472-0102), 2346 Academy Dr # 102. Open daily 9–5. Ask for the "Follow the Falcon" brochure, which will take you on a self-guided tour.

Many visitors will want to see the Cadet Chapel up close. The 17-spired chapel makes quite an impression rising above the trees and surrounding buildings. It is open for tours Mon.–Sat. 9–5. The Air Force Academy and chapel tours are all free to the public.

♿ **Cheyenne Mountain Zoo** (719-633-9925; www.cmzoo.org), 4250 Cheyenne Mountain Zoo Rd. Open daily 9–6 from Memorial Day weekend to Labor Day; open daily 9–5 for the rest of the year. Cheyenne Mountain in southwest Colorado Springs is home to the only mountain zoo in the United States. As zoos go, it's pretty small—only 70 acres of the 146-acre site have been developed—but what it lacks in size is made up for with unique animal exhibits and an unparalleled setting. Kids can feed and pet giraffes from a platform in the African Rift Valley or watch gorillas and orangutans in Primate World. In 2008, the zoo will unveil Rocky Mountain Wild, featuring grizzly bears, mountain lions, and moose. Adult admission $12, seniors $10, children (3–11) $6, and children under 3 free. Admission to the zoo allows you free access to the **Will Rogers Shrine of the Sun** (719-578-5367; www.cmzoo.org/shrine.html), 4250 Cheyenne Mountain Zoo Rd. Open daily at 9; closes an hour before the zoo. Built in 1937, the 80-foot observation tower affords views of the entire Colorado Springs area.

♿ **Colorado Springs Fine Arts Center** (719-634-5581; www.csfineartscenter.org), 30 W. Dale St. Open Tues.–Wed. 10–5, Thurs.–Sat. 10–8, and Sun. 10–5. The FAC recently unveiled a 48,000-square-foot, two-story expansion. This is a significant addition for an art museum that is bringing in more visitors every year. The museum has an outstanding collection of Native American and Spanish colonial art. The traveling exhibits are always interesting and worth a visit. Adult admission $7.50; seniors, students with ID, and children (5–17) $6.75; and children under 5 free.

PIKES PEAK

In 1806, Zebulon Pike and his party arrived at the confluence of the Arkansas River and Fountain Creek, near present-day Pueblo, and set up camp. In the distance he saw what he described as a small blue cloud. It was later determined to be the summit of a surprisingly high mountain, and Pike decided to take a side trip and see if he couldn't reach the top. For several days he attempted the summit, but was eventually turned back by waist-deep snow and waning provisions. He boldly predicted that no one would ever be able to conquer this mountain and returned to camp.

Today, over half a million people summit Pikes Peak every year, making it the most visited peak in North America. Rising 14,110 feet above sea level, it is the easternmost of the 14ers. Millions have been inspired by the mountain's grandeur. As a landmark, it was celebrated by the prospectors who came west during the 1859 Gold Rush with the slogan, "Pikes Peak or Bust."

In the summer of 1893, Katharine Lee Bates and fellow teachers from Colorado College climbed Pikes Peak by wagon and mule. So enthralled was she by the view from the summit that she was moved to write the poem, "America the Beautiful."

Summiting Pikes Peak is almost a requirement of tourists making their way to Colorado Springs. You can make your own way to the top by car, train, or by hoofing it.

Pikes Peak Highway (719-385-7325 or 1-800-318-9505; www.pikespeakcolorado.com), P.O. Box 1575-MC060 Colorado Springs, CO 80901. The 19-mile highway is accessed west of town off US 24. It is paved part of the way and stays open year-round (weather permitting). There are 156 curves as the highway ascends to the 14,110-foot summit of Pikes Peak. The views above and below tree line are breathtaking, and there are ample turnouts for motorists to pull off, rest their engines, and take in the mountain. The toll is $35 per car or $10 per adult and $5 per child.

Pikes Peak Cog Railway (719-685-5401; www.cograilway.com), Ruxton Ave. (depot). Open year-round. In the summer the train leaves the station every 80 minutes from 8 to 5:20. Check the schedule on the Web site for other times of the year. The Cog Railway is one of the easiest and most scenic ways to get to the top of Pikes Peak. The unique design of the cog system allows the train to climb very steep terrain, including two 25 percent grades. It is 8.9 miles to the summit from the station, and the round trip takes 3 hours and 10 minutes—giving you 30–40 minutes to grab a bite to eat, use the rest rooms, and take in the panoramic views. Keep in mind that there are no bathrooms on the train, and it's a 75-minute trip to the top. Rates vary by season. Adult tickets $30–32, children (3–12) $16.50–17.50, and children under 3 free (if held on lap).

Barr Trail. The trail was constructed by Fred Barr from 1914–1921 and is the most direct hike up to Pikes Peak. The trailhead is located in Manitou Springs. There is a dedicated trailhead parking area just beyond the Cog Railway parking area on Ruxton Avenue. The trail is 12.6 miles long and climbs 7,300 feet to the summit. Along the way, you walk through three ecological life zones. Drinking water may not be available at the Barr Camp (about halfway), and you will need to treat any water you pull from streams. The weather at the bottom of the trail can be dramatically different from the top (last time I was there it was 75 degrees in Manitou Springs and 32 on the summit), so dress accordingly. A round trip can take experienced hikers 16 hours, so you might want to have someone pick you up at the top.

Crags Trail Hike. *See Outdoor Activities, Hiking.*

For more information, see the Pikes Peak Web site at www.pikespeak colorado.com.

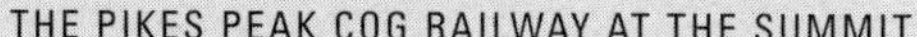

THE PIKES PEAK COG RAILWAY AT THE SUMMIT

↑ ♿ **Colorado Springs Pioneers Museum** (719-385-5990; www.springsgov.com/SectionIndex.asp?SectionID=9), 215 S. Tejon St. Open Tues.–Sat. 10–5. Located in the restored El Paso County Courthouse, the Pioneers Museum celebrates the history of Colorado Springs and the Pikes Peak region. The museum features a restored courtroom circa 1903 and a portion of Helen Hunt's cabin. The museum attracts thousands every year and is a great introduction to the history of the land and the people who have lived here. Admission free.

Garden of the Gods (719-634-6666; www.gardenofthegods.com), 1805 N. 30th St. The park is open daily in the summer 5–11; winter 5–9. Maps are available at the **Garden of the Gods Visitor & Nature Center** (open daily in the summer 8–8; winter 9–5). The Garden of the Gods is an impressive park full of red sandstone formations known as hogbacks, which jut into the sky at an angle. The tallest is 320 feet high. Some of the juniper growing on the rocks are 1,000 years old. Tourists seem to especially enjoy climbing around Balanced Rock. There are 15 miles of trails here, many paved.

Dedicated in 1909, the land that is now the Garden of the Gods was given to the city with the understanding that it would always be open to the public, that no alcohol would be sold there, and that no building would be constructed except those necessary for the public use of the park. These rules still stand and continue to guide the decisions made by park officials. Admission free.

↑ ♿ **Ghost Town Wild West Museum** (719-634-0696; www.ghosttownmuseum.com), 400 S. 21st St. Open summer Mon.–Sat. 9–6 and Sun. 11–6; winter, Mon.–Sat. 10–5 and Sun. 11–5. More tourist trap than museum, Ghost Town tries to re-create an Old West town circa 1880. In addition to the indoor Old Main Street with shooting galleries and old carriages, the museum has a petrified sequoia tree trunk that was discovered in the Florissant fossil beds and a bedroom suite that once belonged to President Chester A. Arthur. There is also a trough to try your hand at gold panning. Adult admission $6.50, children (6–16) $4, and children under 6 free.

↑ **McAllister House Museum** (719-635-7925; www.nscda.org/co/mcallisterhousemuseum.html), 423 N. Cascade Ave. Open summer Wed.–Sat. 10–4 and Sun. 12–4; winter, Thurs.–Sat. 10–4. Built in 1873, the McAllister House preserves the charm and elegance of Colorado Springs in the 19th century. Guided tours offered daily. Adult admission $5, seniors $4, and children (6–12) $3.

↑ **Pro Rodeo Hall of Fame** (719-528-4764; www.prorodeohalloffame.com), 101 ProRodeo Dr. Open daily in the summer 9–5; winter, Wed.–Sun. 9–5. For die-hard rodeo fans, there is no better attraction in town. This is the only museum in the world dedicated to the history and promotion of rodeo. Adult admission $6, seniors $5, military $4, children (6–12) $3, and kids under 6 free.

♿ **Seven Falls** (719-632-0765; www.sevenfalls.com), 2850 S. Cheyenne Canyon Rd. Open year-round, daily 8:30–9:30 (open till 10:30 June–Aug.). Check the Web site for a complete listing of spring, fall, and holiday hours. The South Cheyenne Creek falls majestically 181 feet to the floor of a box canyon. The falls—the creek forms seven of them on its way down—can be viewed from above and below. A steep staircase climbs to the observation deck, but there's also an elevator for those who don't want to hike up the stairs. Along the top of the canyon, two hiking trails offer views of Colorado Springs or another attraction, Midnight Falls. At night, the Seven Falls are lighted for dramatic effect. Adult day admission $8.75, seniors $7.75, children (6–15) $5.50; adult night admission $10.25, seniors $9.25, and children $6.50.

☂ **U.S. Olympic Complex** (719-632-5551; www.olympic-usa.org), 1 Olympic Plaza (1750 E. Boulder St.). Open Mon.–Sat. 9–5. This is where Olympians come to train. Free guided tours of the facility are offered daily. In the summer they run every half hour; every hour in the winter.

☂ **Van Briggle Art Pottery Factory and Showroom** (1-800-847-6341; www.vanbriggle.com), 600 S. 21st St. The Van Briggle Pottery Co. was founded in 1901 and is one of the country's oldest art potteries. The pieces created here have a strong art nouveau sensibility and feature colors common to Chinese ceramics. Today visitors can tour the factory and see how clay is transformed into art. Admission is free.

☂ ♿ **Western Museum of Mining and Industry** (719-488-0880; www.wmmi.org), 225 North Gate Blvd. Open Mon.–Sat. 9–4 (until 5 in summer). The history of mining is the theme of this museum, and the focus is on the technology that has contributed to the history of mining and the people who have been a part of mining in the American West. Guided tours are offered twice daily at 10 and 1. Adult admission $8, seniors and students $6, children (3–12) $4, children under 3 free.

🖍 ☂ **Arcade Amusements** (719-685-9815), 930 Block Manitou Ave., Manitou Springs. Open in the summer 10–10. Located right behind Patsy's, this alley is full of video games, from vintage to modern. World Famous Penny Arcade has classic 1980s favorites and some old classics. The Arcade Derby next door has an old horse racing game. If you like arcades, bring your pennies, dimes, and quarters and prepare to spend a couple hours in heaven.

Beyond Colorado Springs

☂ **Cave of the Winds** (719-685-5444; www.caveofthewinds.com), exit 41 off US 24, Manitou Springs. Open every day but Christmas; 9–9 in summer and 10–5 in winter. The cave was discovered by two boys on a church outing in Williams Canyon near Manitou Springs in the spring of 1880. It soon opened to the public for tours and has been attracting the adventurous for over a century. The popular Discovery Tour takes guests on a 0.75-mile walk through the cave. The 45-minute tour isn't overly strenuous, but you must climb 200 steps as you move through the caverns. The Lantern Tour takes guests underground with only hand-held lanterns to light the path—much like visitors would have experienced the cave a hundred years ago. Discovery Tour: adult admission $18, children (6–11) $9, children under 6 free. Lantern Tour: adult admission $22, children (ages 6–11) $12, not open to kids under 6.

Gold Camp Road. Before the Short Line Railway was dismantled and the rail bed was converted to a road, Theodore Roosevelt took the ride from Colorado Springs to Victor by train and declared that the beauty of the route bankrupted the English language. This 40-mile route is truly spectacular. A collapsed tunnel closed an eastern portion of the road; that section is now a popular hiking and biking trail that can be picked up off N. Cheyenne Boulevard. To get to the rest of Gold Camp Road, take Old Stage Road 5.5 miles to where it hits Gold Camp and then turn right.

Manitou Cliff Dwellings Museum (719-685-5242 or 1-800-354-0071; www.cliffdwellingsmuseum.com), just off US 24 on Cliff Dwellings Rd. in Manitou Springs. Open daily in summer 9–6, winter 10–4, and spring and fall 9–5; closed Thanksgiving and Christmas. Around the turn of the century, material from cliff dwellings in the Mesa Verde area were used to reconstruct these cliff dwellings near Manitou Springs. Tourists benefit by being able to climb inside these dwellings—and the attraction is close to town with plenty of parking. Native dancers perform traditional dances, and there is an extensive gift shop and museum lodged in a 100-year-old pueblo building. Adult admisison $8.50, seniors $7.50, children (7–11) $6.50, and kids under 7 free.

☂ ♿ **Miramont Castle Museum** (719-685-1011; www.miramontcastle.org), 9 Capitol Hill Ave., Manitou Springs. Open Tues.–Sun. 9–5. The Miramont Castle was built in 1895 by the French-born priest Jean Baptiste Francolon. It was later converted into a sanitarium by the Sisters of Mercy. The museum tries to capture Victorian life in Manitou Springs. There is a miniatures museum on the bottom level and a doll collection on the top. The museum also has a Tea Room that serves high tea as well as lunch items. Adult admission $6, seniors $5.50, children (6–15) $2, children under 6 free.

✐ **North Pole: Home of Santa's Workshop** (719-684-9432; www.santas-colo.com), 505 Pikes Peak Hwy., Cascade. Open daily year-round, except in the

MANITOU SPRINGS CLIFF DWELLINGS

MIRAMONT CASTLE MUSEUM

spring; standard hours 10–5, but call for seasonal variations. Kids can ride down the peppermint slide on a potato sack, feed animals, ride a just-their-size Candy Cane Coaster, and get a picture with Santa in his house. Not just for Christmas, the North Pole drums up holiday cheer all year long. Built in 1955, when theme parks were a more local affair, the park still draws crowds of excited children. General admission $16.95 and seniors and children under 2 free.

✷ Outdoor Activities

CROSS-COUNTRY SKIING & SNOWSHOEING **Mueller State Park and the Crags** (719-687-2366; www.parks.state.co.us/parks/mueller), 21045 CO 67 (3.5 miles south of Divide). Around the back of Pikes Peak, this park offers 50 miles of ungroomed trails for cross-country skiing and snowshoeing. Daily pass $6.

Mountain Chalet (719-633-0732 or 1-800-346-7044; www.mtnchalet.com), 226 North Tejon St. This mountaineering store rents and sells snowshoes and Nordic gear. They also have telemark equipment for sale and for rent.

CYCLING **Criterium Bike Shop** (719-599-0149 or 1-888-404-3641; www.criterium-bicycles.com), 6150 Corporate Center Dr. Open Mon.–Sat. 8–8 and Sun. 10–6. A lot of shops will skimp on the bikes they send out as rentals. Criterium, however, has a great mountain bike lineup—Rockhoppers for the more casual rider and full-suspension Stumpjumpers and Epics for more serious riders. They know a bit about the local riding scene too, if you need some inside info to get started. Same-day rentals $30–45.

Challenge Unlimited (719-633-6399 or 1-800-798-5954; www.bikithikit.com), 204 S. 24th St., near Old Colorado City. There are plenty of great spots to ride in Colorado Springs. Two of the most spectacular are the trail down from Pikes Peak and Gold Camp Road. Challenge Unlimited offers tours (guided and not) of these and other routes around the state. They also offer guided bike trips overseas. Depending on your group size, the Pikes Peak tour is $85–105 in the morning; afternoon ride $80–93. The Go for the Gold tour runs $65–75.

Pikes Peak Mountain Bike Tours (719-337-5311 or 1-888-593-3062; www.bikepikespeak.com), 302 S. 25th St. Open May–Oct. If you are the type that gets to the top of Pikes Peak and asks, "I wonder what it would be like to barrel down this mountain on a bike?" then you need to call these guys. The tour begins with a buffet breakfast at the Manitou Pancake and Steak House, after which you ascend to the summit of Pikes Peak via van or cog railway (depending on the tour). The rest is all up to gravity. Tours go on all summer and into Sept. Depending on your group size, the Pikes Peak tour is $85–105 and the Ride-n-Rail $120–125.

FISHING **Eleven Mile Canyon and Reservoir** is located in Eleven Mile State Park (719-748-3401; www.parks.state.co.us/parks/elevenmile), 4229 CR 92, Lake George. Located up in the mountains 32 miles west of Woodland Park and open 24 hours. Trout are the prize catch out at this reservoir—cutthroat, brown, and rainbow. There are northern pike in there are well. The park hosts regular fishing tournaments, and there are plenty of boat ramps. Daily park pass $6.

Manitou Park Lake is north 7.8 miles north of Woodland Park on CO 67. In addition to fishing for the lake's rainbow trout, there are hiking trails, a picnic area, and rest rooms at the lake.

Rampart Reservoir. Boat ramp and parking, open daily 7–7. The Rampart Reservoir Recreation Area is located 4.2 miles east of Woodland Park. The 500-acre reservoir is home to lake, cutthroat, brown, and rainbow trout. It is stocked by the Colorado Division of Wildlife. Day use fee $5.

GOLF **Broadmoor Golf Club** (719-634-7711; www.broadmoor.com), 1 Lake Ave. The three 18-hole courses at the Broadmoor are highly rated. The Mountain Course, for example, has wide fairways and beautiful scenery. The greens fees at Broadmoor are a bit steep at $95–190 (depending on the season), but if golf is your game, these courses will not disappoint.

Patty Jewett Golf Course (719-385-6950; www.springsgov.com), 900 E. Española St. This is the third oldest course west of the Mississippi. The 18-hole golf course has the sense of the classic about it—from the rich wrought-iron gate to the 100-year-old trees that line the drive up to the clubhouse. There is also a separate nine-hole course. Greens fees $26–28.

Pine Creek Golf Club (719-594-9999; www.pinecreek.com), 9850 Divot Trail. Designed by Richard Phelps, this 18-hole course has great views of Pikes Peak and the Colorado Springs skyline. In synch with the surrounding landscape, the course challenges golfers with a 376-foot change in elevation, meandering creek beds, and other natural obstacles. Greens fees $42–52.

Valley Hi Golf Course (719-385-6917; www.springsgov.com), 610 S. Chelton Rd. This newer public course was bought by the city in 1975. The 18-hole course has views of Pikes Peak and Cheyenne Mountain. Their Learn-to-Golf program is a great introduction to the sport for beginners. Greens fees $26–28.

HIKING Hikers in Colorado Springs are just a short drive away from the Pike National Forest, Mueller State Park, and Cheyenne Mountain State Park. All offer exceptional trails for hikers of all levels. Garden of the Gods has paved trails that are great for walking, running, and biking. Below are some trails that deserve special mention.

Colorado Front Range Trail is a moderate, 5-mile, out-and-back hike with little elevation gain. The Front Range Trail is a work in progress. The final product will be a 900-mile trail that stretches from Wyoming into New Mexico, connecting the communities along the eastern edge of the Rocky Mountains. Throughout the state, many sections have been completed. In Colorado Springs, there's a trailhead, about 0.25 mile west of I-25 on Woodmen Road. Parking is on the north side of the road. The trail heads north along Monument Creek and passes through the Air Force Academy. About 2.5 miles in, there's a little lake and a picnic area. It has great views of the mountains.

Crags Trail Hike is a moderate hike that begins on the other side of Pikes Peak. The trailhead is just south of Mueller State Park on CO 67 south of Divide. The 4-mile round-trip gains about 640 feet in elevation. The "crags" are a geological feature of the area and provide interesting scenery for hiking. For a more challenging hike from the same trailhead, hikers can connect with a trail that will take them to the Pikes Peak summit. The trail to the summit begins about 200 feet down the Crags Trail, on the right. This hike is a nearly 12-mile round-trip and is a bit more grueling (though less so than Barr Trail).

Columbine Trail in **North Cheyenne Cañon Park** begins at the **Starsmore Discovery Center** (719-578-6146), 2120 S. Cheyenne Cañon Rd. It follows the North Cheyenne Creek for some time on its way to Helen Hunt Falls and the falls visitor center. Over the 4-mile route you gain nearly 1,000 feet in elevation.

HORSEBACK RIDING **Academy Riding Stables** (719-633-5667 or 1-888-700-0410; www.arsriding.com), 4 El Paso Blvd. This stable offers guests a chance to ride horseback through the Garden of the Gods. As you meander the trails, a guide will point out interesting features of the park. One-hour ride $38, two-hour $55.

Riding Stables at the Broadmoor (719-448-0371 or 1-866-448-0371; www.comtnadventure.com), Old Stage Rd. To get to the stables, get off I-25 at exit 138 and take Lake Avenue west. Once you reach the Broadmoor Hotel, follow signs around to the Cheyenne Mountain Zoo. Before you get to the zoo, turn right on Old Stage Road and go 5.8 miles to the stables. Guides will take you on one- or two-hour horseback rides through the mountains. They have pony rides for younger kids and plenty of animals for petting. Chuckwagon meals available at the kiva. One-hour ride $33, two-hour $53, and pony rides $18.

✷ Lodging

HOTELS **The Broadmoor** (719-577-5775 or 1-800-634-7711; www.broadmoor.com), 1 Lake Ave. More than just a hotel, the Broadmoor is a luxury resort with three golf courses, a tennis club, a spa, and several excellent restaurants. The resort sits at the base of Cheyenne Mountain on 3,000 acres. The first hotel on the property was built in 1918 by Spencer Penrose. Even if you are not staying at the Broadmoor, it's worth a visit. The public can tour the fabulously landscaped grounds, grab a bite to eat at any number of cafés, do some shopping, and even tour the resort's carriage museum. Rooms $280–530 and suites $420–875.

Antlers Hilton Colorado Springs (719-473-5600 or 1-866-299-4602; www.antlers.com), 4 S. Cascade Ave. The Antlers was built by General William Palmer shortly after he founded the city of Colorado Springs. The hotel was the centerpiece of what he hoped would be a resort community. The first Antlers Hotel was opened in 1883. The hotel is on its third incarnation—it's a much more modern facility with all the amenities of high-end lodging. The hotel has 285 rooms and seven suites. Rooms $99–149.

Cheyenne Mountain Resort (719-538-4000; www.cheyennemountain.com), 3225 Broadmoor Valley Rd. Found a few short miles from the Broadmoor, the Cheyenne Mountain Resort has 316 rooms and sits on 218 acres at the base of Cheyenne Mountain. The resort is home to the Country Club of Colorado—the club golf course wraps around a 35-acre recreational lake that is used for sailing and fishing. There are four swimming pools and indoor and outdoor tennis courts. Near the Pro Shop, guests can dine at the Pineview Dining Room and Pub. Each room at the resort has its own private balcony with views of the mountains or the Country Club. Of special interest to business travelers, study areas in the rooms have two desks set up to be used as computer work stations. Rooms $99–199.

The Cliff House (719-685-3000 or 1-888-212-7000; www.thecliffhouse.com), 306 Cañon Ave., Manitou Springs. Located in the heart of Manitou Springs, the Cliff House was built in 1873. The site was originally a stagecoach stop on the route to Leadville. The hotel now boasts 55 guest rooms and suites, each decorated in the style of the late 1800s but with a modern flare. Rooms $145–199 and suites $199–475.

SpringHill Suites Colorado Springs South (719-637-0800 or 1-888-287-9400; www.marriott.com), 1570 N. Newport Rd. Southeast of town, near the airport, the SpringHill Suites have clean, comfortable rooms. The hotel is rather new, with flat-screen televisions, wi-fi, and a definitely contemporary feel. Though a bit on the outskirts of town, guests can quickly get to areas like Old Colorado City and Manitou Springs. Rooms $89–299.

BED & BREAKFASTS **Cheyenne Cañon Inn** (1-800-633-0625; www.cheyennecanoninn.com), 2030 W. Cheyenne Blvd. This historic inn began as a resort house and at one point was a bordello and gaming house. One of the inn's guest rooms has a tower that was once used as a lookout for police raids. The inn now has nine rooms and one cottage. It is close to some of the area's best mountain biking trails. They can hook you up with trail maps, bikes, and helmets. They even offer a helmet cam video package. Pets are welcome in the Petite Maison, the inn's separate cottage (once the madam's house). Gourmet breakfast is served in the dining room or on the veranda if weather permits. Rooms $105–205 and the cottage $225–235.

♿ **Old Town Guest House** (719-632-9194 or 1-888-375-4210; www.oldtown-guesthouse.com), 115 S. 26th St. The Old Town Guest House was built in 1997 as a bed & breakfast. Just a block from Old Colorado City, the inn has eight rooms—each named after a flower. Rooms have TVs and DVD players as well as refrigerators and coffee machines. The amenities are great for business travelers. All the inn's floors can be reached by elevator. Recently voted the best bed & breakfast in Colorado Springs. Rooms $99–215.

Two Sisters Inn (719-685-9684 or 1-800-274-7466; www.twosisinn.com), 10 Otoe Pl., Manitou Springs. The inn has four rooms and a garden cottage with fireplace. Two rooms share a bath; the other two have private baths. Every morning guests are treated to a three-course breakfast featuring fresh Colorado ingredients. Close to downtown Manitou Springs. Rooms $84–125 and cottage $145.

Victoria's Keep (719-685-5354 or 1-800-905-5337; www.victoriaskeep.com), 202 Ruxton Ave., Manitou Springs. Victoria's Keep sits right at the corner of Ruxton Ave. and Capitol Hill Ave. (the road that leads to the Miramont Castle)—walking distance to downtown Manitou Springs. The wooded lot is fronted by a fast-moving creek. The bed & breakfast has six rooms, each with a tub for two, fireplace, and private bath. The house has a wraparound porch where you can sit and listen to the creek. A full gourmet breakfast is served daily. Rooms $90–190.

Eastholme in the Rockies (719-684-9901 or 1-800-487-6420; www.eastholme.com), 4445 Hagerman Ave., Cascade. The inn has four rooms, two suites, and two cabins. The cabins each have a fireplace and a large Jacuzzi or whirlpool tub. Two of the rooms and both suites have a private bath; several have Jacuzzi tubs. A three-course gourmet breakfast is served every morning, and the inn offers an optional dinner for two. Rooms $75–135 and cabins $120–150.

Pikes Peak Paradise (719-687-6656 or 1-800-728-8282; www.pikespeakparadise.com), 236 Pinecrest Rd., Woodland Park. Two suites, two deluxe suites, and two rooms. Amenities include in-room hot tubs, fireplaces, and private decks. Rooms have HD flat-screen TVs and DVD players. Decorated in a contemporary style, the beds have luxurious linens and the baths feature Egyptian cotton towels. Guests enjoy spectacular views of Pikes Peak and the Front Range. Every morning, the inn serves a gourmet breakfast. Rooms and suites $150–230.

CAMPGROUNDS **Garden of the Gods Campground** (719-475-9450 or 1-800-248-9451; www.coloradocampground.com), 3704 W. Colorado Ave. Open April 15–Oct 15. This campground has several accommodation options. There are sites for tent camping and RV sites with a variety of hook-up configurations. Cabins are rustic with a bunk bed and double bed (bring your own linens). The bunkhouses are like the cabins, but they have indoor plumbing. The deluxe bunkhouse even has a kitchenette. Pets are welcome at tent and RV sites. The campground has two heated pools, a game room, and plenty of shower and laundry facilities. Tent sites $33, RV sites $38–47, cabins $45–50, and bunkhouse $60–110. In the off-season, only tent and RV site available (at a cheaper rate).

The Pike National Forest has a number of campgrounds in the Pikes Peak region. Reservations can be made online at www.recreation.gov, where you can also get a complete list of available sites at all federally run campgrounds. **South Meadows** (719-636-1602) is located 5 miles north of Woodland Park on CO 67. This rustic campground has 64 sites, a limited potable water supply, and pit toilets. There are also miles of nearby hiking and biking trails. **Thunder Ridge** (719-687-7818) is east of Woodland Park about 4 miles from the Rampart Reservoir entrance on Rampart Range Rd. The campground has 24 sites. It is shady, and amenities include pit toilets, firewood, and a dumpster. There are trails for hiking and biking, and boaters can push off onto the nearby reservoir.

✱ Where to Eat

DINING OUT 🍸 ♿ **The Broadmoor** (719-577-5733 or 1-800-634-7711; www.broadmoor.com/colorado-springs-dining-restaurants.php), 1 Lake Ave., has several restaurants of outstanding quality. **Charles Court** is a classic Colorado restaurant, serving American fare with local ingredients. Dishes $22–44. The **Penrose Room** is open for dinner Mon.–Sat. The restaurant prides itself on providing classic fine dining in an elegant atmosphere. Live music and dancing complete the experience. Three- and four-course meals cost $62 and $72, respectively. The **Tavern** is open for lunch and dinner, serving steak and seafood. There is a live orchestra with live music and dancing in the evening, Wed.–Sun. Dinner $16–58. Check the Web site for dress code requirements at each.

🍸 ♿ **La Petite Maison** (719-632-4887; www.lapetitemaisoncs.com), 1015 W. Colorado Ave. Open for dinner Tues.–Sat. 5–10 and Sun. 5–9. A charming 19th-century cottage is home to La Petite Maison, which serves contemporary French cuisine. Guests can eat in the dining room or on the patio when the weather permits. Entrées in the $20–30 range.

♿ **MacKenzie's Chop House Downtown** (719-635-3536; www.mackenzieschophouse.com), 128 S. Tejon St. Open for lunch Mon.–Fri. 11–3 and dinner Mon.–Thurs. 5–10, Fri.–Sat. 5–11, and Sun. 5–close. There are a number of great steakhouses in Colorado Springs, and MacKenzie's may be the best. It serves a menu of classic steak, like porterhouse, New York strip, and filet mignon, and there are a host of elegant favorites like Alaskan king crab and almond-encrusted salmon. They have patio dining and allow cigar smoking in the lounge. Dinner entrées $20–30.

🍸 ♿ **Plate World Cuisine** (719-475-8000; www.platecolorado.com), 9420 Briar Village Pt. Open daily 11–closing. Brunch is served Sun. 10–2. The Plate serves an ever-changing menu of international cuisine—meals organized thematically or by region on the menu. A relative newcomer to the Springs dining scene, the Plate has been impressing critics with both the menu and the atmosphere. The dining room has a contemporary style with a definite Asian influence. Entrées $18–25.

🍸 ♿ **Steaksmith** (719-596-9300 or 1-800-201-2736; www.steaksmith.com), 3902 Maizeland Rd. Open for lunch Mon.–Fri. 11–2. Another serious contender for best steak place in the Springs, Steaksmith opened in 1900 and has been satisfying diners with a great selection of steaks (they age the beef themselves) and seafood. For lunch, try one of their burgers, made from filet mignon and top sirloin. Dinner $18–35 and lunch entrées $8–9.50.

EATING OUT ♿ **Amanda's Fonda** (719-227-1975), 3625 W. Colorado Ave. Open Mon.–Sat. 11:30–9 and Sun. noon–9. The product of a family that has spent generations in the restaurant business, many of the dishes at Amanda's come from the late owner's mother and grandmother—and from recipes she developed while living in Guadalajara. It is often cited as the best Mexican food in town. They are known for excellent *arroz con pollo* and an outstanding *molé.* Patio seating by the creek is a favorite with the margarita crowd.

♿ **Bird Dog BBQ** (719-596-4900; www.birddogbbq.com), 5984 Stetson Hills Blvd. Open Mon.–Sat. 11–9 and Sun 11–8. There are several barbeque joints in the Springs, but Bird Dog stands out from the pack. Slow cooked and oak smoked, the meat here drips with flavor. They have the best prime rib brisket in town. All their dishes can be ordered on a bun for an easy lunch. Combo plates offer a sampling of meats—try the turkey for something different. Plates $10–13 and sandwiches $4–6.

♿ **Edelweiss** (719-633-2220; www.edelweissrest.com), 34 E. Ramona Ave. Open daily 11:30–9 and until 9:30 on Fri. and Sat. This German restaurant first opened in 1967. The restaurant's 100-year-old building was first used as a schoolhouse. Edelweiss is authentically Bavarian with hearty dishes like bratwurst and sauerkraut. There's a *biergarten* in the summer, and live music on the weekends. Dinners $15–25.

🖍 ♿ **Fargo's Pizza Company** (719-473-5540; www.fargospizza.com), 2910 E. Platte Ave. Open Sun.–Thurs. 11–9 and Fri.–Sat. 11–11. A bit of a dining novelty, Fargo's is a Victorian pizza parlor. Laid out like an old-timey gambling hall, the women dress in long dresses and the men wear garters on their arms. There is a wraparound balcony, and two mannequins sit at one end in full period dress. Guests order and pay for pizza at the window (then order and pay for drinks at the bar), find a seat, and wait until their number is called up on one of the mirrors around the restaurant. The pizza is pretty good, as is the salad bar. After eating, kids can head to the arcade to play video games. Bring cash—they don't take checks or cards. Large pizza $10–15.

♿ **Giuseppe's Old Depot Restaurant** (719-635-3111; www.giuseppes-depot.com), 10 S. Sierra Madre. Open Sun.–Thurs. 11–9 and Fri. and Sat. 11–10. Before it was an Italian restaurant, the depot served the Denver and Rio Grande Railroad. Built in

1871, a walk through the restaurant still resonates with history. The depot is stretched out along the railroad tracks, and when trains go by, they pass just several feet beyond the windows—surprisingly with little noise and no rattling of dishes. Giuseppe's is the second-largest restaurant in Colorado. The menu includes Italian dishes from stone-baked pizzas to chicken parmesano and lasagna. It also offers some variety with Cajun blackened trout and prime rib. For lunch, try one of the deli sandwiches. Main entrées $10–20, pizzas $10–20, and most sandwiches around $8.

King's Chef Diner (719-634-9135; www.kingschefdiner.com), 110 E. Costilla Ave. Open for breakfast and lunch Mon.–Fri. 7–2 and Sat.–Sun. 8–3. The distinctive clown-castle look of King's Chef may put off some people, but this little diner has quite a loyal following. Big breakfast dishes like the Grump (a heaping stack of hash browns, meat, eggs, cheese, and country gravy), have kept them coming in since 1956. They may be best known for the green chili that smothers everything from breakfast burritos to cheese burgers. Breakfast and lunch dishes $5–10.

♿ **Panino's Restaurant** (719-635-7452; www.paninos.com), 604 N. Tejon St. Open Mon.–Thurs. 11–9 and Fri. and Sat. 11–10. A panino is traditionally a toasted sandwich made from a small loaf of bread. At Panino's in Colorado Springs, the sandwich is rolled in a flat bread, not unlike a thin, toppingless pizza crust. They have paninos for all sorts of appetites, like the Spaghetti Pie with noodles, meat, and cheese smothered in marinara and the classic Rueben with corned beef and sauerkraut. Paninos run $6–8. There is another location at 1721 S. Eighth St. (719-635-1188).

Stagecoach Inn (719-685-9400; www.stagecoachinn.com), 702 Manitou Ave., Manitou Springs. A red stagecoach sits prominently in the front lawn of the Stagecoach Inn, located right on the main street in downtown Manitou Springs. The story goes that there was a stage stop here, and the main dining area was once an electric company that used a large water wheel in Fountain Creek to bring electricity to Manitou Springs. Today, the restaurant serves classic American fare with renowned western hospitality. The restaurant has seating on two decks that overlook the creek. Dinner entrées $12–20, lunch $8–10.

BAKERIES & COFFEE SHOPS ♿

Pikes Perk Coffee & Tea House (719-522-1432; www.pikesperk.com), 5965 N. Academy Blvd. #203. There are Pikes Perk locations all over the Springs, but Academy Boulevard was the first. Playing on the shop name, their tagline is "Coffee with an Altitude." Fresh ground coffee and gourmet-quality ingredients make for a great coffeehouse. They also sell 101 flavors of milk shakes.

BARS, TAVERNS & BREW PUBS ♿

The Golden Bee (at the Broadmoor), (719-577-5733 or 1-800-634-7711; www.broadmoor.com/golden-bee.php), 1 Lake Ave. This pub at the Broadmoor Hotel is really cool. Completely authentic, the entire pub was brought from London. They have a piano player who leads the bar in singing.

♿ **Jack Quinn's Irish Ale House and Pub** (719-385-0766; www.jackquinnspub.com), 21 S. Tejon St. Open

Mon.–Fri. 11–2 AM and Sat. and Sun. noon–2 AM. A classic Irish pub with live music nearly every night.

♿ **Phantom Canyon Brewing Company** (719-635-2800; www.phantomcanyon.com), 2 E. Pikes Peak Ave. Open Mon.–Thurs. 11–1:30 AM, Fri. and Sat. 11–2 AM, and Sun. 9–1:30 A.M. This brewery/restaurant serves fresh ale, unfiltered and unpasteurized. There's also a full lunch and dinner menu of classic pub food. Lunch $7–9 and dinner $10–20.

SNACKS ♿ **Josh & John's** (719-632-0299; www.joshandjohns.com), 111 E. Pikes Peak Ave. A lot of folks agree that this is the best ice-cream place in town. All the ice cream at Josh & John's is made right there in the shop using Colorado dairy goods. Starting with a wide selection of flavors, banana splits, sundaes, and floats round out the menu. They have two locations in the Springs—the other is at 5152 N. Academy Blvd. (719-593-1220).

♿ **Patsy's** (719-633-7215 or 1-866-372-8797; www.patsyscandies.com), 1540 S. 21st St. This exceptional local candy factory is open Mon.–Fri. 9–5:30 and Sun. 10–5. The shop has a great variety of chocolate treats. They also offer factory tour in the summer, Mon.–Fri. at 11 and 2.

✱ Entertainment

Cedars Jazz Club (719-578-5744; www.cedarsjazzclub.com), 3125 Sinton Rd. Open Thu.–Sat. 6–midnight. Cedars features live music by local jazz artists. Rock and ethnic musicians also take the stage on a regular basis.

♿ **Flying W Ranch** (719-598-4000 or 1-800-232-3599; www.flyingw.com), 3330 Chuckwagon Rd. Chuckwagon suppers are served from Memorial Day into late Sept; dinner at 7:30 with show at 8:30 daily. In Sept., it's Fri.–Sat. at 6:45. In the winter, ask about their Winter Steakhouse. Folks come in droves for a night of western cooking and good old cowboy music by the

FLYING W RANCH

Flying W Wranglers. The Wranglers are an exceptional bunch of musicians. From guitar and upright bass to fiddle and mandolin, this group is a favorite among music lovers. Before guests gather for the chuckwagon supper and concert, they usually roam around the ranch's Western Village. There's a mine ride, gift shops, and several historic buildings. General admission $19.50 and children (3–8) $9.50.

Loonees Comedy Corner (719-591-0707; www.loonees.com), 1305 N. Academy Blvd. Open nightly Wed.–Sun. Loonees keeps a good flow of comics coming through the Springs. See their Web site for a list of upcoming headliners. Admission is $6 on Wed. and Thurs., $8 Fri. and Sat. There's a two-item minimum.

The Iron Springs Melodrama Dinner Theater (719-685-5104 or 719-685-5572), 44 Ruxton Ave., Manitou Springs. Shows performed year-round, with a limited schedule fall to spring. For a night of full-on entertainment, consider taking the family to dinner and a show. At the Melodrama Dinner Theater, the audience is encouraged to participate in the performance with boos and hisses for the villain and cheers for the hero. Shows are usually engaging and highly comical. Couple that with a family-style dinner of oven-fried chicken and barbeque beef, and you have a night of fun. The evening concludes with an old-time vaudeville olio—a miscellaneous collection of songs, jokes, and sing-alongs. Adult dinner-and-show ticket $28.50, seniors $27, and children (under 12) $15.50. You can also get tickets for just the show or just the dinner.

✷ Selective Shopping

Old Colorado City (www.shopoldcoloradocity.com or www.old-colorado-city.com), centers on W. Colorado Ave. between S. 21st and 30th streets. This is the raucous town that inspired General William Palmer to start a more chaste city of his own, Colorado Springs, down the road. For a time it was the territorial headquarters. In the park you can visit the log cabin where the territorial legislature convened for business. Today the town is a quaint section of storefronts with an abundance of shops and restaurants. The **Book Sleuth** (719-632-2727; www.booksleuthmysteries.com), 2501 W. Colorado Ave., is a unique bookstore that is solely dedicated to mysteries. Down the street a little is the **Barbeque Mercantile** (719-578-0305; www.bbqmercantile.com), 2619 W. Colorado Ave. In addition to selling grills, smokers, and barbeque accessories, they also have a huge selection of rubs, marinades, and hot sauces.

Manitou Springs (www.manitousprings.org) is located west of Colorado Springs just off US 24. The historic part of town is a fantastic place for a walk. There are numerous art galleries and antiques shops. **Commonwheel Artists Co-Op** (719-685-1008; www.commonwheel.com), 102 Cañon Ave., is one of them. It may be the town's best gallery. There are a lot of pieces here by amazingly talented local artists.

Garden of the Gods Trading Post (719-685-9045 or 1-800-874-4515; www.co-trading-post.com) is located just past the Balanced Rock as you enter the park from the south. Open daily in the summer 8–8 and winter 9–5:30. If you simply must have a Gar-

DOWNTOWN MANITOU SPRINGS

den of the Gods T-shirt, a plastic bow and arrow set, and a couple of souvenir shot glasses, do not miss the Trading Post. No other tourist shop in the Springs has this much of inventory.

✷ Special Events

July: Every year, drivers compete in the **Pikes Peak International Hill Climb** (719-685-4400 ext. 3; www.ppihc.com), a race to the top of Pikes Peak.

July: **Pikes Peak or Bust Rodeo** (www.coloradospringsrodeo.com). Sanctioned by the Professional Rodeo Cowboys Association, this rodeo showcases competitors on their way to the yearly championships.

August: **Pikes Peak Ascent and Marathon** (www.pikespeakmarathon.org). On the first day of the race, the Ascent, runners race to the top of Pikes Peak. The next, they race to the top and back again.

September: During the **Colorado Springs Balloon Classic** (www.balloonclassic.com) the sky above Colorado Springs is filled with nearly a hundred hot air balloons. Great photo opportunities.

September: **The Colorado Fesitval of World Theatre** (719-473-1737; www.cfwt.org) brings world-class theatrical entertainment to the Springs—everything from the comic to the tragic.

CAÑON CITY & THE GOLD RANGE

The main tourist activities in Cañon City are all centered on the Royal Gorge. Folks are traveling up the gorge on the popular Royal Gorge Route train, paddling through the gorge down the Arkansas River, or driving out to the Royal Gorge Bridge to appreciate the 1,000-foot walls from a higher perspective. The tourists you find in town seem to be either on their way to or from one of these activities, or they're just passing through.

Cañon City came into its own as a result of gold being discovered in Cripple Creek. Between 1899 and 1910, most of the downtown was built with the money of wealthy miners who set up house in town. With three railroads serving Cañon City, it was natural that the town would become a regional transportation hub, attracting the wealth of the nearby Gold Range. With the end of mining in the mountains, the town's fortunes waned. Today, the town's main industry is incarceration. There are nine prisons in town, and nearby Florence has another four. And, in fact, the town's most interesting museum is the Colorado Territorial Prison Museum.

The gold that was once found in Cripple Creek made a few people rich, but the boom was over in a few short years. Back in the 1890s, the promise of striking it rich drew many a poor man into the mountains—gold fever they called it. Today Cripple Creek draws people with a different kind of gold fever, gambling. The Old West mining town has been transformed, just as quickly as it was first built. Casinos have taken over the entire downtown. Unlike the glitzy light of Vegas, however, the casinos in Cripple Creek have maintained the town's Old West look and feel. This is definitely gambling Colorado-style.

The town of Victor is just up the road from Cripple Creek. Gold Camp Road, which heads into the mountains west of Colorado Springs, ends up in Victor. This small struggling town has plenty of recreational activities available in the nearby mountains. A number of trails will take you back to old mining sites, and there are plenty of old roads and railroad grades for mountain biking.

GUIDANCE **Cañon City Chamber of Commerce** (719-275-2331 or 1-800-876-7922; www.canoncity.com), 403 Royal Gorge Blvd. The visitor center is located in the historic Peabody House. The house was built in 1880 and was once the home of James Peabody, the 13th governor of Colorado.

Cripple Creek Welcome Center (1-877-858-4653; www.visitcripplecreek.com), 501 E. Bennett Ave. Located right next to the train depot on the east end of town.

More Web sites:

www.downtowncanoncity.com

www.rgcountry.com

www.canoncitycolorado.com

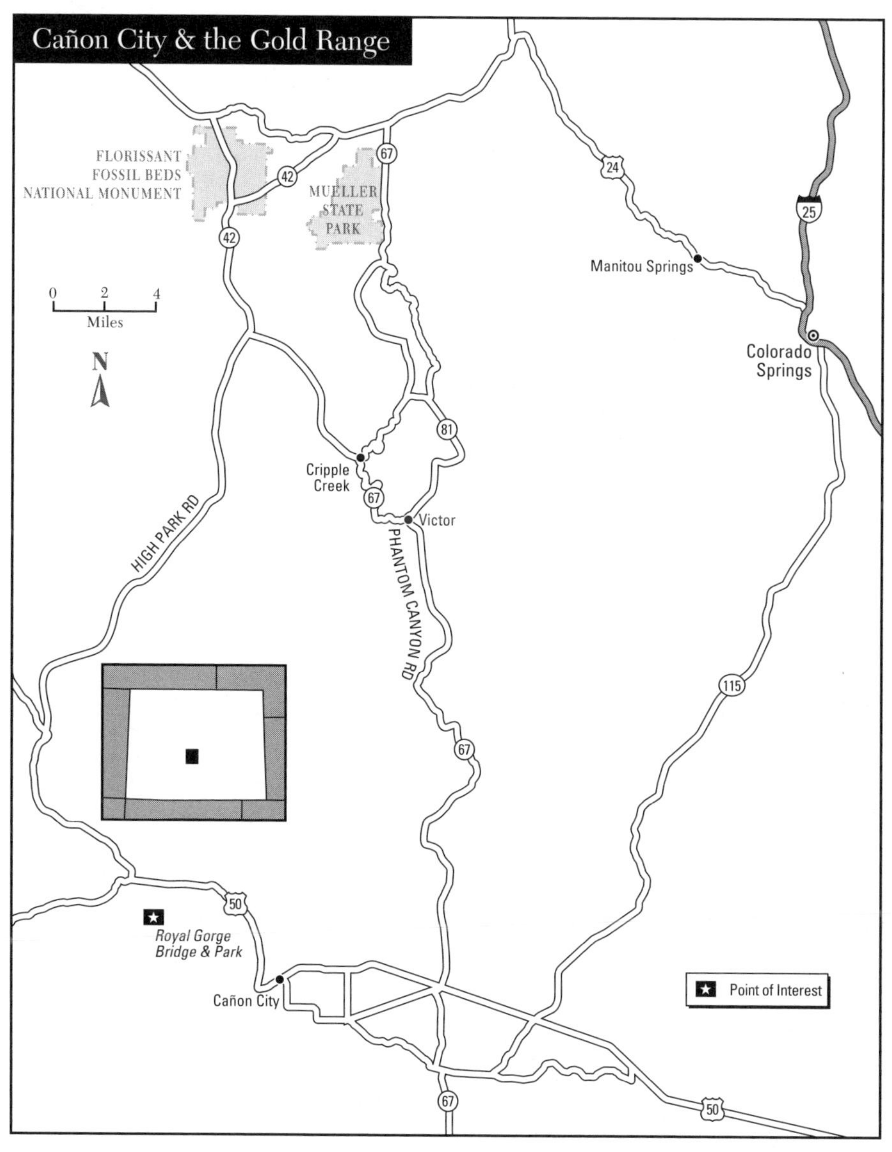

www.cripple-creek.co.us
www.victorcolorado.com

GETTING THERE *By car:* The best way to get to Cañon City and the towns of Cripple Creek and Victor is by car. Parking in Cañon City is easy enough. If you are not in town visiting a casino, you will have to park a couple blocks from downtown in Cripple Creek.

MEDICAL EMERGENCIES **St. Thomas More Hospital** (719-285-2000; www.stmhospital.org), 1338 Phay St., Cañon City, offers 24-hour emergency service.

✷ To See & Do

ATTRACTIONS **Royal Gorge Bridge and Park** (719-275-7507 or 1-888-333-5597; www.royalgorgebridge.com), 4218 Fremont CR 3A, Cañon City. Open year-round; see Web site for seasonal hours. Some locals may call it the "highest suspension bridge in the world to nowhere," but for the 300,000 visitors who come each year to gaze down into the Royal Gorge from a height of 1,053 feet, it's worth the visit. The bridge is an impressive feat of engineering. Built in 1929, it's the highest suspension bridge in the world. And though it's true that the bridge is not a throughway for any traffic, the bridge and the park offer unique ways to experience the Royal Gorge. For example, the Aerial Tram, the longest of its kind in the world, carries guests 1,100 feet above the canyon floor. It offers outstanding views of the gorge and the bridge. Or to explore the gorge from below, you can get to the canyon floor via the park's Incline Railroad. For the kids, there's a mile-long ride on the Silver Rock Railway. In all, there are 21 rides and attractions, including a regular schedule of live entertainment. Adult admis-

ROYAL GORGE BRIDGE

BENNETT AVENUE IN CRIPPLE CREEK

sion $23, seniors $21, and children (4–11) $19. In the off-season, the second ticket is half off.

Buckskin Joe Frontier Town and Scenic Railway (719-275-5149 or 719-275-5485; www.buckskinjoe.com), 1193 CR 3A, Cañon City. Frontier Town open daily in the summer; closed Oct.–April. Royal Gorge Scenic Railway open daily March–Dec. See Web site for hours. The Buckskin Joe Frontier Town is an interesting, if not campy, diversion. This low-scale theme park is set up like an Old West town, complete with gunfights. You can tour the buildings on the main street or grab a bite to eat in the saloon. Down the street is the Royal Gorge Scenic Railway. The train takes guests on a 3-mile, 30-minute loop that runs along the edge of the Royal Gorge. Adult admission to Frontier Town $13 and children (4–11) $11. Adult admission to Royal Gorge Scenic Railway $10 and children (4–11) $9. Adult admission to both town and train $17 and children (4–11) $15.

GAMBLING Cripple Creek has made quite a name for itself as a popular gaming destination. Unlike Blackhawk and Central City, which combined have become a mini-Vegas with all the lights and glam, Cripple Creek has maintained an Old West feel. Storefronts have been preserved so that even when a casino stretches a city block, Bennett Avenue still has the charm of a small mountain town. In a sense, the casinos moved like a hermit crab into the shell of Cripple Creek, and with 17 casinos there are plenty of opportunities here for folks to play away their cash.

♿ **Bronco Billy's Sports Bar and Casino** (719-689-2142; www.broncobillyscasino.com), 233 E. Bennett Ave., Cripple Creek. Bronco Billy's boasts of being a true Colorado-style casino. They have more video poker games than any casino in town. They also have a number of top-notch eateries.

♿ **Double Eagle Hotel and Casino** (719-689-5000; www.decasino.com), 442 E. Bennett Ave., Cripple Creek. The largest casino in town, the Double Eagle has plenty of parking, dining, and gaming.

HISTORIC SITES & MUSEUMS ☂ **Old Homestead House Museum,** 353 Myers Ave. Open daily in the summer 11–4; open weekends until Christmas. This former brothel was the most famous in Cripple Creek. Built in 1896 by madam Pearl DeVere, the house was reputed to have the most beautiful women in town—and the most expensive. The house has been restored and is full of the Victorian touches that were found inside over a hundred years ago. The tour includes the history of Cripple Creek and the Red-Light District.

☂ ♿ **Cañon City Municipal Museum** (719-269-9018), 612 Royal Gorge Blvd. Open in the summer Tue.–Sun. 10–4. The museum looks at the lives of the area's first residents. The complex includes a few buildings, like the 1860 log cabin of Anson Rudd. Admission free.

☂ ♿ **Colorado Territorial Prison Museum** (719-269-3015; www.prison museum.org), 201 N. 1st St. Open daily in the summer 8:30–6; winter Wed.–Sun. 10–5; and spring and fall daily 10–5. Rarely will you get a chance to tour a 19th-century prison. This facility began housing prisoners in 1871. Thirty-two cells are open to the public. The museum offers MP3 and CD tours for individuals looking for a structured approach to the history of the prison. Exhibits include the noose from the last execution by hanging in Colorado, weapons confiscated from inmates, and a gallery of inmate art. Adult admission $7, seniors $6, and youths (6–12) $5.

✐ ☂ ♿ **Dinosaur Depot Museum** (719-269-7150 or 1-800-987-6379; www .dinosaurdepot.com), 330 Royal Gorge Blvd. Hours vary by season; open daily 9–5 in summer. Dinosaur fossils from the late Jurassic Period have been found

COLORADO TERRITORIAL PRISON MUSEUM

HOMESTEAD NEAR FLORISSANT FOSSIL BEDS NATIONAL MONUMENT

in relative abundance around the Cañon City region—in particular in the Garden Park Fossil Area about 12 miles north of town. The Dinosaur Depot Museum exhibits the fossilized remains (as well as replicas) that have been unearthed over the years. The museum provides an excellent paleontological introduction to the area. Adult admission $4, children (4–12) $2, and children under 4 free.

Florissant Fossil Beds National Monument (719-748-3253; www.nps.gov/flfo), 15807 Teller County 1, Florissant. The visitor center is 2 miles south of Florissant on Teller County 1. Open daily 9–5. Tens of thousands of fossils have been found at the Florissant Fossil Beds. The park protects those yet to be found and helps visitors put the known finds in context. The only known fossilized sequoia trunks are found here, as are the fossilized remains of thousands of plants and insects. The park has nature trails, and the park service offers guided tours and interpretive talks. The schedule of tours and talks depends on availability of rangers on any particular day, so call for more information. Admission $3.

✐ ☂ **Mollie Kathleen Mine** (719-689-2466 or 1-888-291-5689; www.goldminetours.com). Located 1 mile north of Cripple Creek on CO 67. Open daily in the summer 9–6; Mar., open Wed.–Sun. 9–5; and Apr. and Oct., open daily 9–5. Closed in the winter. Tours leave every 10 minutes during the busy season and last about an hour. The last tour leaves one hour before close. To enter the Mollie Kathleen Gold Mine, guests descend 1,000 feet into the earth in a man-skip elevator. The mine tour takes you back to the turn of the century, where you can see how hard-rock miners worked. The tour includes a train ride through the mine. Adult admission $15, children (3–12) $10, and children under 3 free.

RAILROADS **Royal Gorge Route** (303-569-1000 or 1-888-724-5748; www.royalgorgeroute.com), 401 Water St., Cañon City. The railroad operates late May–early Oct. The train leaves daily at 9:30, 12:30, 3:30, and 7:00. Few train rides compare with the trip from Cañon City into the Royal Gorge on the Royal Gorge Route Railroad. The scenery is breathtaking. If you want more than just a ride, the railroad has Dinner Trains, Lunch Trains, and Murder Mystery trips. Coach tickets are the most affordable. If you need more of a view, coach passengers can try the open-air observation car. The Vista Dome cars have a curved glass ceiling for unobstructed views. The Lunch Train comes with a three-course gourmet lunch in the vintage dining cars. Adult coach $29.95 and children (3–12) $19.50. Adult Vista Dome $54.95 and children (0–12) $44.50. Adult Lunch Train $69.95 and children (3–12) $49.95.

Cripple Creek & Victor Narrow-Gauge Railroad (719-689-2640; www.cripplecreekrailroad.com), 5th St. and Bennett Ave., Cripple Creek. The railroad runs mid-May–mid-October. There's no better way to get a feel for gold-mining country than to see it being pulled behind a steam locomotive on a narrow-gauge railway. This is how it was done back in the day. The Cripple Creek & Victor Narrow-Gauge Railroad leaves every 40 minutes for a 45-minute, 4-mile round-trip. Adult ticket $11, seniors $10, and children (3–12) $7.

SCENIC DRIVES **Cripple Creek to Victor.** The route to Victor is just 5 miles—head south of town on CO 67. The road is well maintained and pretty wide. It's a short ride with pleasant scenery. Once you get to Victor, there are a couple shops and a restaurant or two where you can grab a bite to eat.

Gold Belt Tour (www.goldbeltbyway.com). This is a Scenic and Historic Byway drive—quite beautiful, though some portions require four-wheel drive (and others a serious dose of fortitude). The byway begins in Florissant and splits into three routes, each eventually terminating in Cañon City. The most laid back,

AERIAL TRAM AT THE ROYAL GORGE

with little gain in elevation, is **High Park Road.** Follow CO 11 south to US 50 and head east to Cañon City. The other two routes take you into Cripple Creek. **Shelf Road** begins a little south of town off CO 67. Following the road will take you straight to Cañon City, but sections of the road are one-lane and four-wheel drive is recommended. CO 67 becomes **Phantom Canyon Road** right past Victor. The road is passable, but it's dirt most of the way. The road takes you to Florence where you can head west on CO 115 back to Cañon City.

✷ Outdoor Activities

GOLF **Shadow Hills Golf Course and Country Club** (719-275-0603; www.golfshadowhills.com), 1232 CR 143, Cañon City. This is a solid course with nice views of the Gold Range to the north. Greens fees $45 for 18 holes.

HIKING, FISHING & RAFTING **Tunnel Drive Trail** is just west of Cañon City off US 50 and Tunnel Drive. The 2-mile trail follows the Arkansas River. Hikers can enjoy passing views of the Royal Gorge Railroad, kayakers and rafters, and occasional wildlife.

The **Skagway Reservoir** is east of Victor. There's a trail to the lake, and the reservoir is a nice spot for some fishing. To get there, take Phantom Canyon Road east of Victor to the first fork. Skagway Road is on the left and will take you to the reservoir and the parking area. The trail is north of the parking area.

Echo Canyon River Expeditions (1-800-590-3246; www.raftecho.com), 45000 US 50 West. Take a trip down through the Royal Gorge or other sections of the Arkansas River. They offer half- and full-day trips. There are also trips that combine rafting with a horseback ride or ride on the Royal Gorge Railway. Half-day trips through the Royal Gorge run $61.

GREEN SPACE Ten miles north of Cañon City is **Red Canyon Park.** This 600-acre park has trails for hiking and biking, as well as picnic areas. The park's unique rock formations are a big draw. To get there, head north on Field Avenue, which turns into Red Canyon Road (CR 9). The park is almost exactly 10 miles north of US 50.

✷ Lodging

HOTELS Cañon City has several hotels and motels. Chains include Holiday Inn Express, Best Western, and Comfort Inn. In Cripple Creek, the **Double Eagle, Gold Rush,** and **Imperial** casinos all have hotel lodging.

Quality Inn and Suites of Cañon City (719-275-8676 or 1-800-525-7727; www.qualityinncanoncity.com), 3075 E. US 50. You won't find mention of many chains in this book, but this Quality Inn has a unique history. Over the years, a lot of movies have been filmed in and around Cañon City, and the hotel has hosted many celebrities. If the rooms are available, guests can sleep in the same rooms that were once used by the likes of John Wayne, Jane Fonda, and Goldie Hawn. That's just to list a few. See the Web site for a complete list with room numbers.

BED & BREAKFASTS **Jewel of the Canyons** (719-275-0378; www.jewelofthecanyons.com), 429 Greenwood Ave., Cañon City. This beautifully restored 1890s Queen Anne has hardwood floors throughout, and the rooms have been tastefully decorated with antique furniture. The B&B has one room and two suites. All have a private bath (though the room's is down the hall a bit). Rooms $89–109.

Carr Manor (719-689-3709; www.carrmanor.com), 350 E. Carr Ave., Cripple Creek. The town's old high school, built in 1897 and 1905, has been converted into this lovely boutique hotel that operates as a B&B. The inn has 14 rooms and suites. They are all attractively decorated—many of the rooms still have the original chalkboards. Amenities include fireplaces, cable TV, and private baths with showers and tubs. Accommodations $100–350.

The Last Dollar Inn (719-689-9113 or 1-888-429-6700; www.lastdollarinn.com), 315 E. Carr St., Cripple Creek. This brownstone structure was originally built in 1898. The inn has six rooms, each with a full private bath. Throughout, the house has been decorated to give guests a sense of the turn of the century, with some rooms more frilly than others. A full country gourmet breakfast is served every morning. Rooms $85–150.

CAMPGROUNDS **Royal Gorge KOA Kampground** (719-275-6116 or 1-800-562-5689; www.koa.com/where/co/06127), 559 CR 3A, Cañon City. Open April 15–Oct. 1. Tent sites are located in the campground's Wilderness Tenting area, a shady lot toward the back of the property. There are also sites for RVs and KOA Kamping Kabins. But that's not all in terms of activities, this campground has mini-golf, go-karts, a giant slide, a Dairy Queen, and a swimming pool. Sites and cabins $26–60.

Royal View Campground (719-275-1900; www.royalviewcampground.com), 9 miles west of Cañon City on US 50, one mile past the entrance to the bridge. The campground has hot showers, laundry facilities, and a swimming pool. There are sites for tents and RVs, and they have small cabins as well. Sites and cabins $27–65.

Lost Burro (719-689-2345 or 1-877-689-2345; www.lostburro.com), 4023 CR 1, Cripple Creek. This campground has 27 tent sites, 24 sites with electricity, and another 6 with full hook-ups. The sites at Lost Burro have plenty of tree cover for shade. There are also hot showers and a dump station. Sites $14–25.

✷ Where to Eat

DINING OUT **Le Petit Chablis** (719-269-3333), 512 Royal Gorge Blvd., Cañon City. Open for lunch Tues.–Fri. 11:30–1:30; dinner Tues.–Thurs. 5:30–8:30 and Fri. and Sat. 5:30–9:30. The menu changes daily at this upscale French restaurant. Le Petit Chablis is located right near town in an older house. The new menu is written on a chalkboard every day in French. (You will have to ask what it says if you don't know French.) Entrées $18–28.

Merlino's Belvedere (719-275-5558; www.belvedererestaurant.com), 1330 Elm Ave., Cañon City. Open in the winter Mon.–Thurs. 11:30–1:30 and 5–8:30; Fri. 11:30–1:30 and 4:30–9; Sat. noon–9; and Sun. noon–

7:30. In the summer, Merlino's Belvedere is the best dining in the area. The focus is on Italian (*belvedere* being a word derived from that language meaning "beautiful view"), but they are also known for exquisite steaks—cut and aged on the premises using only the top 10 percent of Angus beef. The menu also includes such delicacies as frog legs from India and lobster from Australia. Dinner entrées $16–35, lunch $6–7.

♿ **Winfield's** (719-689-5034; www.decasino.com/winfields.htm), 442 E. Bennett Ave., Cripple Creek. Open Fri.–Sun. (and holidays) for dinner 5–10. This upscale restaurant in located in the Double Eagle Casino. The menu is primarily French cuisine and includes steak, lobster, chicken, and lamb. Be sure to call for reservations. Entrées $15–33.

EATING OUT ♿ **The Owl Cigar Store** (719-275-9946), 626 Main St., Cañon City. Open Mon.–Sat. 8–8. Not only does the Owl serve the best burgers in town, they may just be the cheapest. Hamburgers $1.25 and cheeseburgers $1.30.

♿ **Waffle Wagon** (719-269-3428), 1310 Royal Gorge Blvd., Cañon City. Open for breakfast and lunch Wed.–Sun. 6–1. This is a classic diner with a full breakfast menu. For lunch there are burgers and a host of hot sandwiches. Meals $3–4.

BAKERIES & COFFEE SHOPS ♿ **16th Street Café** (719-275-5211), 302A N. 6th St., Cañon City. Open Mon.–Sat. 8–4:30. This bakery and espresso bar serves breakfast and lunch daily. They have fantastic muffins. For lunch there are French baguette sandwiches and pizza.

✷ Entertainment

Thin Air Theatre (719-235-8944; www.thinairtheatre.com) puts on melodrama Wed.–Sun. every week in the summer. The show begins with a sing-along and ends with an olio (a hodgepodge of Vaudeville-style singing, dancing, and comedy). The melodrama itself is always engaging and the cast welcomes the audience's participation. Boos, hisses, cheers, and commentary are all part of the fun. Shows are held at the **Butte Opera House** (www.butteoperahouse.com), 139 E. Bennett Ave., Cripple Creek. Tickets $9–14. Call ahead for reservations because they often sell out.

✷ Special Events

May: **Cañon City Music and Blossom Festival** (719-275-7234), Cañon City. Held the first weekend in May, the festival features a parade, plenty of food vendors, and lots of great music.

June: **Donkey Derby Days** (719-689-3315 or 1-877-858-4653), Cripple Creek. This weekend-long event includes a parade, a donkey race, and the "Gold Stroll" and 1890s-style Barn Dance.

July: **Gold Rush Days** (719-689-2284; www.victorcolorado.com/goldrushdays.htm), Victor. This three-day festival is held the third weekend of July. A lot of musicians come to play, and others come to compete in the Battle of the Bands.

September–October: **Fall Aspen Leaf Tours** (719-689-2169), Cripple Creek. For three weeks, folks can come up to Cripple Creek to celebrate fall. The town offers free Jeep rides into the mountains to see the aspens change color.

UPPER ARKANSAS VALLEY

In the August 2004 issue of *Outside* magazine, Salida, Colorado, was included on their list of "20 Dream Towns." And why not? Salida is a recreational paradise. The Arkansas River, which cuts through the middle of the valley, is where Colorado's white-water enthusiasts come to play. All summer, the river is full of rafts, kayaks, and duckies tackling everything from class I to V rapids. Mountain bikers boast that Salida's mild climate means comfortable riding here year-round. Whereas the mountain towns like Crested Butte stay cold into June, and slickrock country like Fruita is unbearably hot all summer. For hikers, not only are there fifteen 14ers to conquer and hundreds of miles of trails, but the epic Colorado Trail is right there, winding through the Collegiate Peaks (including Mounts Harvard, Yale, and Princeton) along the valley's western boundary.

This recreational spirit extends north to the towns of Buena Vista and Leadville. The town of Buena Vista serves as a kicking-off point for many folks recreating in the valley. One of the most popular rafting trips in the country begins in Buena Vista and heads through Browns Canyon before it hits Salida. Buena Vista is also a place for relaxation and contemplation. It's a small town with a few nice places to stay the night and several exceptional restaurants. Nearby are two hot springs where guests can soak and relax.

Farther north is the town of Leadville. Sitting at 10,430 feet, it is the highest incorporated city in North America. At one time, it was the second largest city in Colorado. During the Silver Boom, fortunes were made in Leadville. It was during this time that the landmark Tabor Opera House and Delaware Hotel were built downtown. Today, just a shadow of the town's former glory remains. Walking up and down Leadville's side streets, you will find many historic Victorian homes. Nearby you can explore the remains of the town's mining industry. While no longer the bustling city it once was, Leadville has several nice restaurants, plenty of lodging, museums galore, and nice little ski area to the south.

GUIDANCE **Leadville/Lake County Chamber of Commerce** (719-486-3900 or 1-888-532-3845; www.leadvilleusa.com), 809 Harrison Ave. Open daily in the summer 9–4. The chamber runs a visitor center at this address.

Buena Vista Chamber of Commerce (719-395-6612; www.buenavistacolorado.org), 343 US 24 S. Open year-round Mon.–Fri. 9–5. In the summers they are

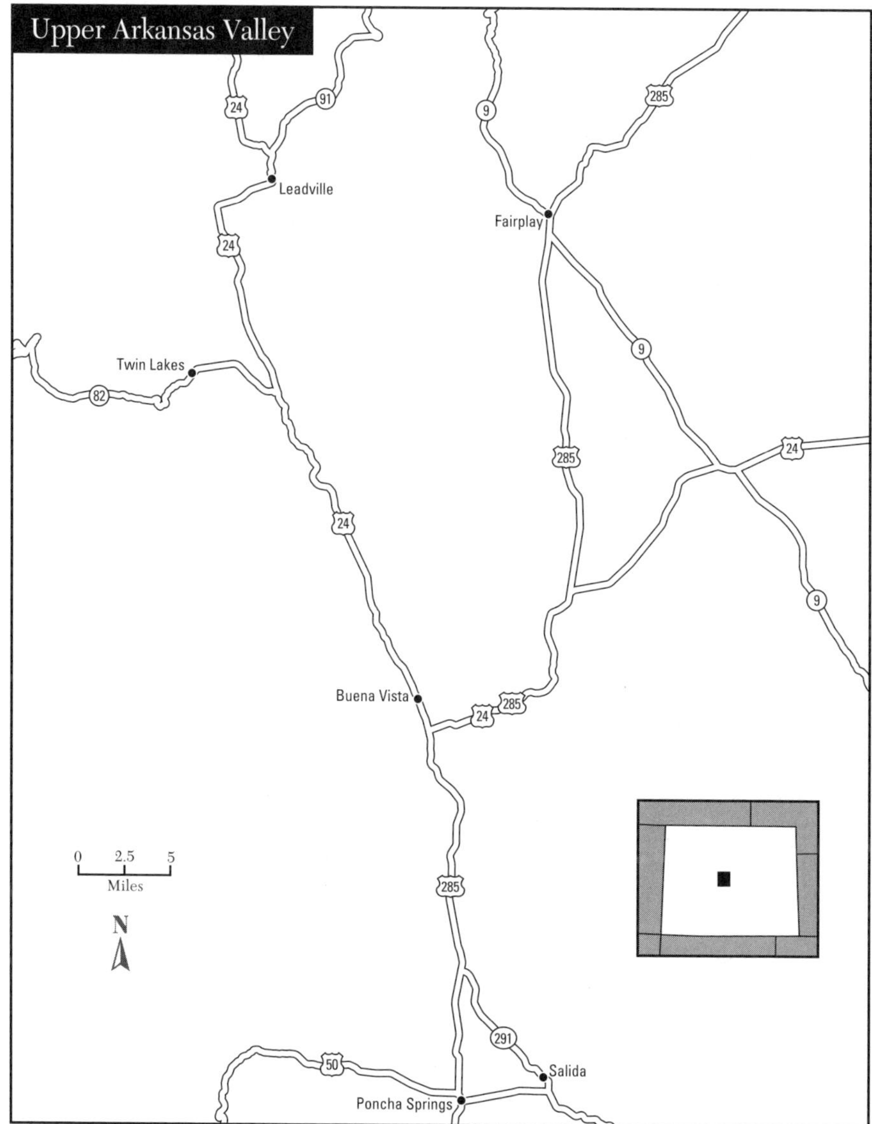

open on weekends. The chamber offices and visitor center are located right on US 24 in an old church, which was originally built in 1879.

Heart of the Rockies Chamber of Commerce (719-539-2068 or 1-877-772-5432; www.salidachamber.org), 406 W. Rainbow Blvd., Salida. The visitor center is open daily in the summer 9–5.

More Web sites:

www.arkansasvalleyliving.com

www.leadville.com

GETTING THERE *By car:* Coming from the west on I-70, get off at US 24 in Minturn (exit 171) and head south. From the east, take CO 91 south at Wheeler Junction (exit 195). Both roads meet in Leadville, at the top of the Upper Arkansas River Valley. Buena Vista and Salida are farther south along the Arkansas River. From Denver, US 285 is a straight shot to Buena Vista. From the southeast, in the area of Pueblo, the best route is US 50 west to Salida.

By air: **Eagle County Regional Airport** (970-524-9490; www.eaglecounty.us/airport), 0871 Cooley Mesa Rd., in Gypsum is the closest commercial airport. Six major airlines have regular flights in and out of the Eagle County Airport.

GETTING AROUND *By car:* A car is your best bet in the Arkansas Valley. If you rent a high-clearance four-wheel-drive vehicle, more of the mountain roads will be open to exploration.

MEDICAL EMERGENCIES **St. Vincent's General Hospital** (719-486-0230; www.svghd.org), 822 W. Fourth St., Leadville. The hospital has a 24-emergency room, and the hospital Web site has information on altitude sickness—a good resource for watching your health in the mountains.

Heart of the Rockies Regional Medical Center (719-539-6661; www.hrrmc.org), 448 E. First St. The medical center has a 24-hour emergency room.

✱ To See & Do

HISTORIC ATTRACTIONS ☂ **Healy House and Dexter Cabin** (719-486-0487; www.coloradohistory.org/hist_sites/healyhouse/H_house.htm), 912 Harrison Ave., Leadville. Open daily May–Sept. 10–4:30. These two houses are some of the earliest in Leadville and tell a little of what life was like when the town was a wealthy, populous center of mining. The Healy House was built in 1878 in the Greek Revival style. It served as a boardinghouse for a time and is decorated with grand Victorian furnishing collected from the area. As the residence of James Dexter, the Dexter Cabin was once a gathering place for the town's rich and powerful. Adult admission $5, seniors $4.50, children (6–16) $3.50, and children under 6 free.

☂ ♿ **Heritage Museum** (719-486-1878), 102 E. Ninth St., Leadville. Open daily in the summer 10–4. The museum houses artifacts from Leadville's early days. There are diaramas illustrating mining life, a scale model of the Ice Palace, and a gallery of works by local artists. Small admission fee.

Matchless Mine (www.matchlessmine.com), 414 W. Seventh St., Leadville. Open daily in the summer 9–5. The story of Horace Tabor and his wife Elizabeth (nicknamed "Baby Doe") is a local legend. One of the Silver Kings, Tabor left his first wife for the much younger Elizabeth McCourt. When the Silver Boom busted, Tabor and Baby Doe were left penniless. All they had was the Matchless Mine, which most everyone believed was tapped out. When Tabor was dying, he told Elizabeth to hold onto the Matchless. For 36 years she lived in a shack near the mine hoping to prove that her husband's faith in the mine was not in vain. She eventually died watching over the mine. Tours of the property include a

ST. ELMO, A GHOST TOWN

peek in the Baby Doe Tabor Museum and a look at the external workings of the mine. Adult admission $4, children (6–12) $1, and children under 6 free.

☂ ♿ **National Mining Hall of Fame** (719-486-1229; www.mininghalloffame.org), 120 W. Ninth St., P.O. Box 981, Leadville, CO 80461. Open daily 11–4. Exhibits include a detailed model of a mining town, complete with model railroad. A series of dioramas illustrates the history of mining, and guests can walk through a section of a reproduction hard-rock mine. The Hall of Fame also boasts a large gift shop and art gallery. Adult admission $7, seniors $6, children (6–12) $4, and children under 6 free.

♿ **Leadville, Colorado & Southern Railroad Co.** (719-486-3936 or 1-866-386-3936; www.leadville-train.com), 326 East Seventh Street. During the busy season (June–Aug.), the railroad leaves the depot twice daily at 10 and 2. The 2.5-hour tour takes passengers into the nearby mountains with views of the Arkansas River valley and the Continental Divide. Adult admission $28.50, children (4–12) $16.50, and children under 4 free.

☂ **Buena Vista Heritage Museum** (719-395-8458; www.buenavistaheritage.org), 506 E. Main St., Buena Vista. Open in the summer Mon.–Sat. 10–5 and Sun. noon–5. Located in the Old Chaffee County Courthouse (completed in 1882), the Heritage Museum houses artifacts from the early years of Buena Vista's history. Admission $3.

HOT SPRINGS The mountains around the Upper Arkansas Valley are home to several hot springs that have been developed and channeled into pools and soaking tubs. Unlike many springs you might find elsewhere in Colorado, the mineral water emanating from the springs in this region is odorless.

LEADVILLE'S MOST FAMOUS COUPLE

In 1956, a new opera by the composer Douglas Moore premiered at the Central City Opera in Colorado. The work was entitled the *Ballad of Baby Doe,* and retold the tragic story of Leadville's most famous couple.

Horace Tabor moved to Colorado in 1859 with his wife and son. They came after hearing of gold in the mountains. Tabor was an ambitious man. He was soon running the general store and post office in Leadville. He played an active role in the community and served for a short time as the town's mayor. In 1878, he agreed to provision two prospectors in return for a portion of whatever profits they might make. Within two months, Tabor's original investment of $17 in equipment and supplies returned to him $10,000, which he quickly invested in other mining endeavors. He soon bough the Matchless Mine, which for a time was the most productive in Leadville.

In 1880, a beautiful young woman of Irish stock came to Leadville. Elizabeth Bonduel McCourt Doe, or "Baby Doe" as she was called, had recently divorced her first husband. Not long after, Baby Doe and Tabor struck up a

♿ **Cottonwood Hot Springs Inn & Spa** (719-395-2102; www.cottonwood-hot-springs.com), 18999 CR 306, Buena Vista. Located 5.5 miles west of town. These lithium hot springs are open daily 9–midnight. In addition to their large natural stone soaking pools, private hot tubs are available for an additional fee. Adult admission $15 and children (under 17) $10.

Mt. Princeton Hot Springs Resort (1-888-395-7799; www.mtprinceton.com), 15870 CR 162, Buena Vista. Pools are open Sun.–Thurs. 9–9 and Fri. and Sat. 9–11. Following Chalk Creek south of Mt. Princeton, the Hot Springs Resort sits nicely between the creek and road. There are three pools—a soaking pool, a cooler lap pool, and an even cooler fun pool with a 300-foot waterslide. The fee is $15 per day.

☂ ♿ **Salida Hot Springs Aquatic Center** (719-539-6738; www.salidapool.com), 410 W. Rainbow Blvd., Salida. Check the Web site for a current pool schedule. This naturally hot mineral water is pumped 5 miles from its source in the mountains to the aquatic center in Salida. The indoor facility is open year-round and features a pool with lanes for swimming laps and a recreational pool. Adult admission $6, seniors $5, children (6–17) $4, and children under 6 $2. Towels, suits, lockers, and showers are all available for an additional fee.

SCENIC DRIVES **Independence Pass** connects Twin Lakes with Aspen, crossing the Continental Divide along the way. It's one of the most scenic routes in the area. The pass is the highest paved path in North America at 12,095 feet. The road, CO 82, is closed in the winter.

relationship, an affair if you will. It seems Tabor and Baby Doe were very much in love, and after divorcing his wife he married Baby Doe officially in 1882. With money in his pocket and an adoring wife, he was able to follow his political ambitions with a vengeance, serving as lieutenant governor of Colorado and as U.S. senator—all the while building opera houses and other monuments to his wealth.

In 1893, with the repeal of the Sherman Silver Purchase Act, Tabor suddenly found himself penniless. Bankrupt, but not without friends, he was appointed to the job of postmaster of Denver. Tabor and Baby Doe's misfortune, however, was not yet over. In 1899, he got appendicitis and died. On his deathbed he made a final request. He asked Baby Doe to hold onto the Matchless Mine, telling her that when silver returned, the mine would restore her fortunes.

Baby Doe took his words to heart and returned to Leadville. She lived in an old storage shack beside the Matchless Mine for 36 years, always believing her beloved Horace was right. She became a recluse, and there is a belief that she may have been suffering from a touch of insanity. She was found in 1935, frozen to death in her shed.

Route of the Silver Kings is the title of a map offered at the Leadville Chamber of Commerce. The map leads you on a self-guided driving tour of Leadville's mining district. Along the way, it tells a little history of each mine. Most roads do not require a four-wheel-drive vehicle.

✷ Outdoor Activities

ALPINE SKIING & SNOWBOARDING **Ski Cooper** (719-486-2277 or 1-800-707-6114; www.skicooper.com), 232 CR 29. Not to be confused with Copper Mountain, Ski Cooper is 10 miles north of Leadville on US 24 (on Tennessee Pass). The ski hill offers 1,200 vertical feet from the base to the summit. There are 26 trails, the longest 1.4 miles. Four hundred skiable acres are served by three lifts. There are another 2,400 acres accessible by snowcat. The ski area has a ski school with instruction for all levels and ages. Adult full-day lift ticket $39, children (6–14) $20, and children under 6 free.

Monarch Ski and Snowboard Area (719-539-3573 or 1-888-996-7669; www.skimonarch.com), 1 Powder Pl., Monarch. Located a little over 21 miles west of Salida on US 50. The chairlifts run 9–4 daily during the ski season. There are no snowmakers here, so the ski area's 54 trails are covered in natural snow. From the summit to the base is a 1,170-foot vertical drop. There are 800 skiable acres here; another 900 available by snowcat. The terrain parks are separated for snowboarders of varying abilities. Adult full-day lift ticket $52, seniors $28, teens (13–15) $32, juniors (7–12) $20, and children under 7 free. The season pass at Monarch gives you access to 10 mountains, including Crested Butte and Loveland.

THE VIEW OF MT. MASSIVE FROM LEADVILLE

Bill's Ski Rentals (719-486-1497; www.billsrentals.com), 131 CO 91, Leadville. Located north of town, the rental shop is the sister store for Bill's Sporting Goods downtown. They rent skis and snowboards, and they sell discounted lift passes to Ski Cooper.

CROSS-COUNTRY SKIING **Piney Creek Nordic Center** (719-486-1750; www.tennesseepass.com/skiing.htm), at the base of the Ski Cooper ski area, 10 miles north of Leadville on US 24. Open daily 9–4:30. Miles of groomed cross-country skiing trails are available with a $10 pass (seniors and children $8). There are routes for all abilities, and the center offers ski rental and private ski instruction as well.

FISHING The **Arkansas River** offers some of the best fly-fishing in Colorado. **Halfmoon Creek** and **Chalk Creek** are also popular spots to float a fly. There are also several lakes that make for a good day out on the water. **Twin Lakes Reservoir** is south of Leadville in the town of Twin Lakes. There is also **Turquoise Lake.** The mountain setting alone makes this lake worth a visit. It's just west of Leadville.

Anglers Junction (719-530-2100 or 1-866-574-2100; www.anglersjunction.com), 845 Oak St., Salida. Located at the junction of US 50 and CO 291, Anglers Junction offers everything an angler could need for a satisfying fly-fishing trip on the Arkansas River. Guided fly-fishing outings can be scheduled for full or half days, and there's an evening float too. A half-day float for one guest is $205 (two guests $240).

ArkAnglers (719-539-4223; www.arkanglers.com), 7500 W. US 50, Salida. This full-service fly shop offers guided tours, fishing gear, and intimate knowledge of local fishing conditions and locations. They also have a shop in Buena Vista (719-395-1796) at 517 US 24 S.

FOUR-WHEELING **Weston Pass** and **Mosquito Pass** were once the main routes to Leadville. Mosquito Pass is the highest auto pass in the United States at 13,986 feet. Both routes have sections that require four-wheel drive.

Buena Vista Jeep Rental (719-395-4418; www.bvjeeps.com), 27899 CR 317, Buena Vista. Rent a Jeep Wrangler or Cherokee and see the mountains without a guide. To get over some of the more remote passes, like Mosquito or Hagerman Pass, you need a four-wheel-drive vehicle, and Buena Vista Jeep Rental rents them for $125/day, up to $780/week.

High Country Jeep Tours (719-395-6111 or 1-866-458-6877; www.highcountryjeeptours.com), 410 US 24 S., Buena Vista. Guests will not need to rent a vehicle or consult a map when they take one of these Jeep tours. Tours include trips to St. Elmo and the Mary Murphy Mine, Mt. Princeton, and Mt. Antero. Adult full-day tour rate $99 and children under 13 $70. Half-day adult $60 and children $45.

GOLF **Mount Massive Golf Course** (719-486-2176; www.mtmassivegolf.com), 259 CR 5, Leadville. This nine-hole public course on the outskirts of Leadville is North America's Highest Golf Course. Greens fees for 9 holes $16–20.

HIKING The Upper Arkansas Valley, between the Collegiate Peaks and the Mosquito Range, has plenty of trails to get you into the mountains. The most noteworthy is the **Colorado Trail.** The trail stretches across the state from Durango to Denver. The section that passes through our region sticks to the west side of the valley. A nice 13-mile trek would be to begin at the trailhead at the west end of Turquoise Lake. Take the trail south until it crosses Halfmoon Road at Emerald Lake.

In Twin Lakes, the Colorado Trail passes along the southern shore of the lakes. Called here the **Interlaken Trail,** the 3-mile route begins at the dam and takes you around the lake to the historic resort town of Interlaken. There are paths here that lead up to Hope Pass if you are looking for more adventure.

In addition to the network of trails, two 14-ers near Leadville offer hikers a chance to put a couple of notches in their belts. **Mt. Elbert** and **Mt. Massive** can each be ascended in a day. Mt. Elbert is an especially juicy conquest because it is the tallest peak in Colorado (14,433 feet). The trailhead for Mt. Elbert is just north of Twin Lakes on CR 24, just past the Lakeview Campground. The route is an 8-mile round-trip from the end of the four-wheel-drive road. The trailhead for Mt. Massive is just beyond the Elbert Creek Campground on Halfmoon Road southwest of Leadville. The round-trip is 13.75 miles.

The Trailhead (719-395-8001; www.thetrailheadcom.com), 707 US 24 N., Buena Vista. Open May–Sept. 8–8, and the rest of the year 9–6 (closed Tuesday). The folks at the Trailhead are an excellent resource for getting familiar with area trails and activities. They offer a full line of equipment for rent, including mountain bikes and camping gear in the summer. And in the winter they rent cross-country and backcountry skis and snowshoes.

MOUNTAIN BIKING Mountain biking is one way to tackle some of the areas tougher back roads. **Mosquito Pass** and **Weston Pass,** which climb the mountains east of US 24, are very popular routes, as is **Hagerman Pass** west of Turquoise Lake. Speaking of the lake, the **Turquoise Lake Trail** runs from the May Queen Campground to the Sugarloaf Dam. The 6.4-mile route is a scenic stretch of trail that overlooks the lake.

The mountains around Salida also boast miles of great mountain biking. The **Monarch Crest Trail** is one of the area's best. There is talk that the government might restrict access, so check with a local shop before heading out. The **Colorado Trail,** another great trail for riding, parallels the Continental Divide from Leadville down to Buena Vista, a bit to the west from Salida. And for a more strenuous ride, try the **Rainbow Trail,** which skirts across the Sangre de Cristo Mountains. You can do a loop that begins and ends in town—ask the folks at Absolute Bikes for route information.

Bill's Sport Shop (719-486-0739; www.billsrentals.com), 225 Harrison Ave., Leadville. This sporting goods store rents bikes.

Absolute Bikes (719-539-9295 or 1-888-539-9295; www.absolutebikes.com), 330 W. Sackett St. Few shops have as much local mountain biking knowledge as these folks. Their Web site has up-to-date trail condition information. They also rent mountain bikes, town cruisers, and trailers for pulling the kids. Full-day trail bike rental $30–50.

PADDLING & RAFTING **Dvorak's Rafting & Kayak** (719-539-6851 or 1-800-824-3795; www.dvorakexpeditions.com), 17921 US 285, Nathrop. Dvorak's offers rafting trips down the Arkansas as well as other rivers in a five-state region—not

KAYAKING THE ARKANSAS RIVER IN SALIDA

including trips down the Rio Grande in Texas and those they lead overseas. Half-day trips for adults run about $50.

Noah's Ark Whitewater Rafting Co. (719-395-2158; www.noahsark.com), 23910 US 285, Buena Vista. The guides take rafters on several stretches of the Arkansas River—the Royal Gorge, the Narrows, Browns Canyon. They also offer rafting and backpacking trips. Rates vary by the trip you schedule but seem to run about $50 for half-day trips and $100 for full-day trips. Children's rates, of course, are a little less.

Twin Lakes Canoe & Kayak Adventures (719-251-9961), 6251 E. CO 82, Twin Lakes. For those yearning to get out on the water, but looking for something different than white-water rafting, Twin Lakes Canoe & Kayak Adventures has canoes and kayaks for rent—perfect for exploring Twin Lakes or Turquoise Reservoir.

GREEN SPACE **Arkansas Headwaters State Park** (719-539-7289; www.parks.state.co.us/parks/arkansasheadwaters), 307 W. Sackett Ave., Salida. Open 24 hours a day. This impressive park is unlike other state parks with a central office and visitor center. The Arkansas Headwaters State Park runs along the Arkansas River from Leadville to Lake Pueblo, a distance of 150 miles. There are six campgrounds and numerous boating access points along the river. Walk-in fee $3; daily vehicle pass $6.

✷ Lodging

HOTELS ((t)) **Delaware Hotel** (719-486-1418 or 1-800-748-2004; www.delawarehotel.com), 700 Harrison Ave., Leadville. The Delaware is fashioned in full-out Victorian style. Each room is different and decorated in antique furnishings. Every available common space has antiques displayed—so much so that the hotel often seems to be an antique gallery. In a very real sense, it is. All the antiques, even those in the rooms, are for sale. All rooms have cable TV. The hotel has no elevator. There's a great restaurant downstairs. Rooms $69–199.

BED & BREAKFASTS ((t)) **The Ice Palace Inn** (719-486-8272 or 1-800-754-2840; www.icepalaceinn.com), 813 Spruce St., Leadville. Built in 1899, this house is full of Victorian charm. The second and third floors are fully carpeted. The suites have jetted tubs and fireplaces. There are fantastic views of the mountains from rooms in the turret. A full gourmet breakfast is served every morning. Remember to bring your slippers, shoes are not allowed past the foyer. Rooms $109–159.

((t)) **The Inn at Buena Vista** (719-395-9293 or 1-877-466-2828; www.innatbuenavista.com) 832 S. Gunnison Ave., Buena Vista. Innkeeper and owner Sandy Schrawder did a fantastic job converting this Baptist church into a high-class B&B. The decorating is contemporary, warm, and comfortable. The Royal Room has a private deck with a spectacular view of the Collegiate Peaks. A full gourmet breakfast is served every morning. The inn offers spa services and has special retreat weekends scheduled throughout the year. Rooms $135–

DELAWARE HOTEL IN LEADVILLE

219. Two-night minimum stay on weekends.

The Tudor Rose (719-539-2002 or 1-800-379-0889; www.thetudorrose.com), 6720 CR 104, Salida. This B&B was built in 1979 as a private residence. It was converted to an inn in 1995. It sits on 37 acres of piñon pine, just 1.5 miles from Salida. The guest rooms are spacious and comfortable. The inn's one suite, the Henry Tudor Suite, has a raised hot tub for two and great views of the mountains. All rooms have TVs and CD players. Free wireless Internet is available in the chalet. A full breakfast is served every morning. Rooms $72–175.

La Roca de Tiza Bed & Breakfast (719-395-8034; www.larocabandb.com), 16420 CR 289A, Nathrop. Located near the Chalk Cliffs west of Nathrop, this small B&B has three rooms. The Piñon Room on the main floor has a private bath with a tub. The other two rooms share a bath with a shower. There are views of Chalk Creek and the cliffs from the Juniper Room. A full "mountain" breakfast is served every morning in the dining room or, if weather permits, on the deck. Rooms $85–165.

CAMPGROUNDS **Sugar Loafin' Campground** (719-486-1031; www.leadville.com/sugarloafin), 303 Hwy. 300, Leadville. This shady campground is located just east of Turquoise Lake. In addition to tent and RV sites, the campground rents out cabins as well. Tent sites $27 and RV sites $30–80.

* Where to Eat

DINING OUT **Tennessee Pass Cookhouse** (719-486-8114; www.tennesseepass.com/cookhouse.htm), Leadville. Groups meet at the base of the Ski Cooper Ski Area (10 miles north of Leadville on US 24) at 5:30 for dinner. As a group they then hike, bike, or Jeep the 1 mile to the cookhouse's remote location in the mountains. In the winter guests hike, snowshoe, or cross-country ski to the cookhouse. Dinner is an elegant, four-course affair. The menu offers a few selections that must be made ahead of time (when you make reservations). Because of the rustic nature of the cookhouse (there is no electricity or running water), the only light is candlelight and heat comes from a woodstove. Dinner $65.

🍸 ♿ **Mothers, a Neighborhood Bistro** (719-395-4443), 414 E. Main St., Buena Vista. Open daily in the summer 8–10, and in winter 8–8. This casually elegant eatery in downtown Buena Vista serves "comfort food and healthy fare." The menu has traditional dishes with added panache, like their gourmet mac & cheese. There is an outstanding wine selection and rustic breads can be ordered by the slice or loaf. Though you order at the counter, this is truly fine dining. In the summer they have outdoor patio seating. Dinner entrées $8.50–12.50.

🍸 ♿ **Amícas** (719-539-5219; www.amicassalida.com), 136 E. Second St., Salida. Open Sun.–Thurs. 11:30–10 and Fri. and Sat. 11:30–11. In the winters they close an hour earlier every day. Wood-oven baked pizza and microbrews are what make this pizzeria/microbrewery the place for dinner on a Friday night (or any night). They have a beer sampler for newcomers looking to find their favorite brew, and both the pizzas and beer can be taken to go. Pizzas $8–10.

Purple Sage Grill (719-530-0285; www.purplesagegrill.com), 14770 US 285, Salida. Open Tues.–Sat. 11–9. The Purple Sage boasts of western food with a global flair. Chef Shelley Long prepares such delights as cowgirl coffee-rubbed ribeye steak and Jamaican pork loin. Be sure to call for reservations. Lunch entrées $7–12 and dinner $15–23.

CHALK CLIFFS SOUTHWEST OF BUENA VISTA

EATING OUT 🍸 ♿ **Grill Bar and Cafe** (719-489-9930; www.grillbarcafe.com), 715 Elm St., Leadville. All the locals will tell you this is the best Mexican food in Leadville. The restaurant started as a boardinghouse. The food was so good that eventually the boarders were kicked out to make room for diners. The green chili is pretty darn good, and diners like to talk about how much they enjoy the margaritas. Dishes $8–15.

"1" ♿ **Bongo Billy's Salida Cafe** (719-539-4261; www.salidacafe.com), 300 W. Sackett Ave., Salida. Open Sun.–Wed. 6:30–9 and Thurs.–Sat. 6:30–11. Open an hour later throughout the summer. The great menu at Bongo Billy's is supplemented by outdoor seating by the river and live music on the weekends. They have a great selection of salads and sandwiches. Bongo Billy's is also a great place to grab a cup of coffee, tea, or your favorite espresso drink. Dishes $5–9.

♿ **First Street Café** (719-539-4759; www.firststreetcafesalida.com), 137 E. First St., Salida. Open Mon.–Thurs. 11–8 and Fri. and Sat. 11–9. The café has been serving Salida since 1985. Some folks will tell you that First Street serves the best burger in town. Others come for the Mexican dishes. And still others simply appreciate the diverse menu and the consistently good food. Lunch dishes $6–10 and dinner $9–20.

BAKERIES & COFFEE SHOPS **The Downtown Bakery & Deli** (719-539-4248), 124 F St., Salida. Open Sun. and Mon. 7:30–noon and Wed.–Sat. 7:30–6. A perfect spot to grab breakfast before a day of rafting or mountain biking.

✱ Selective Shopping

Fabulous Finds Emporium (719-530-0544; www.fabfindsalida.com), 243 F St., Salida. Open daily in the summer, Mon.–Sat. 10–6 and Sun. 1–5. In the fall and winter they close a half hour early during the week. In the spring they're closed on Tuesday. This antiques mall has over 35 vendors and 7,500 square feet of antiques.

✱ Special Events

June: **Blue Paddle FIBArk Whitewater Festival** (www.fibark.com), Salida. FIBArk stands for First in Boating the Arkansas. The festival has all sorts of water events—kayaking competitions and a raft rodeo. There's also live music.

August: **Gold Rush Days** (719-395-6612; www.fourteenernet.com/goldrush), Buena Vista. Burro races, a rubber duck race, and tons of live entertainment punctuate this annual festival. Performers include an impressive array of musicians, as well as storytellers, western dancers, and actors performing melodrama.

August: **Boom Days** (719-486-3900; www.leadvilleboomdays.com), Leadville. The first weekend in August, Leadville celebrates its mining history with a pancake breakfast, parade, and pack burro race. Other activities like mining events and live entertainment round out the weekend.

August: **Leadville Trail 100** (719-486-3502; www.leadvilletrail100.com), Leadville. This mountain bike race covers a hundred miles of technical mountain terrain. Riders will climb over 14,000 feet over the course of the competition. There's also a foot race later in the month.

SAN LUIS VALLEY

Driving west from Walsenburg along US 160, you cross the Sangre de Cristo Range and a wide valley opens up before you. It is 50 miles across the valley floor to the San Juan and La Garita ranges. From north to south, the valley stretches 125 miles. As such, the San Luis Valley is one of the largest valley basins in the country.

Hemmed in by stunning mountain peaks, yet with no peaks of its own, this region is often ignored by the tourists who come to Colorado for Rocky Mountain majesty. If they do come, they are likely here to see the region's biggest attraction, the Great Sand Dunes National Park. These massive dunes rest up against the Sangre de Cristos, northeast of Alamosa.

Since so few people have made the San Luis Valley a vacation destination, there is little tourist infrastructure. There are no boutique hotels, no historic shopping districts, no monthly art walks along the galleries of Main Street. There is no fine dining. This also means that there are no long lines, no crowded streets, no pretentious waiters, and no cheesy tourist trappings.

What the valley does have are a number of small towns that offer true hospitality. Here and there you will find decent small town diners and restaurants. There are also a few quality B&Bs with innkeepers that really go all out for guests. And there are attractions like the Cumbres & Toltec and the Rio Grande Scenic Railroads. For these reasons, the San Luis Valley is prime country for those who want to be near the mountains but enjoy peace and solitude.

The valley is also very popular with hunters and anglers. With several wide rivers and plenty of free-roaming game, it's the perfect spot for a sportsman's vacation.

GUIDANCE **Alamosa County Chamber of Commerce** (719-589-3681; www.alamosa.org), 300 Chamber Dr. Open Mon.–Sat. 8–5. Located in the yellow building that looks like an old train depot, the Alamosa Visitor Center shares an office with the chamber of commerce.

The **Monte Vista Chamber of Commerce** (719-852-2731; www.monte-vista.org) operates a visitor center that is open Mon.–Fri. 8–5. The center is located on Main Street next to the historic Monte Villa Inn.

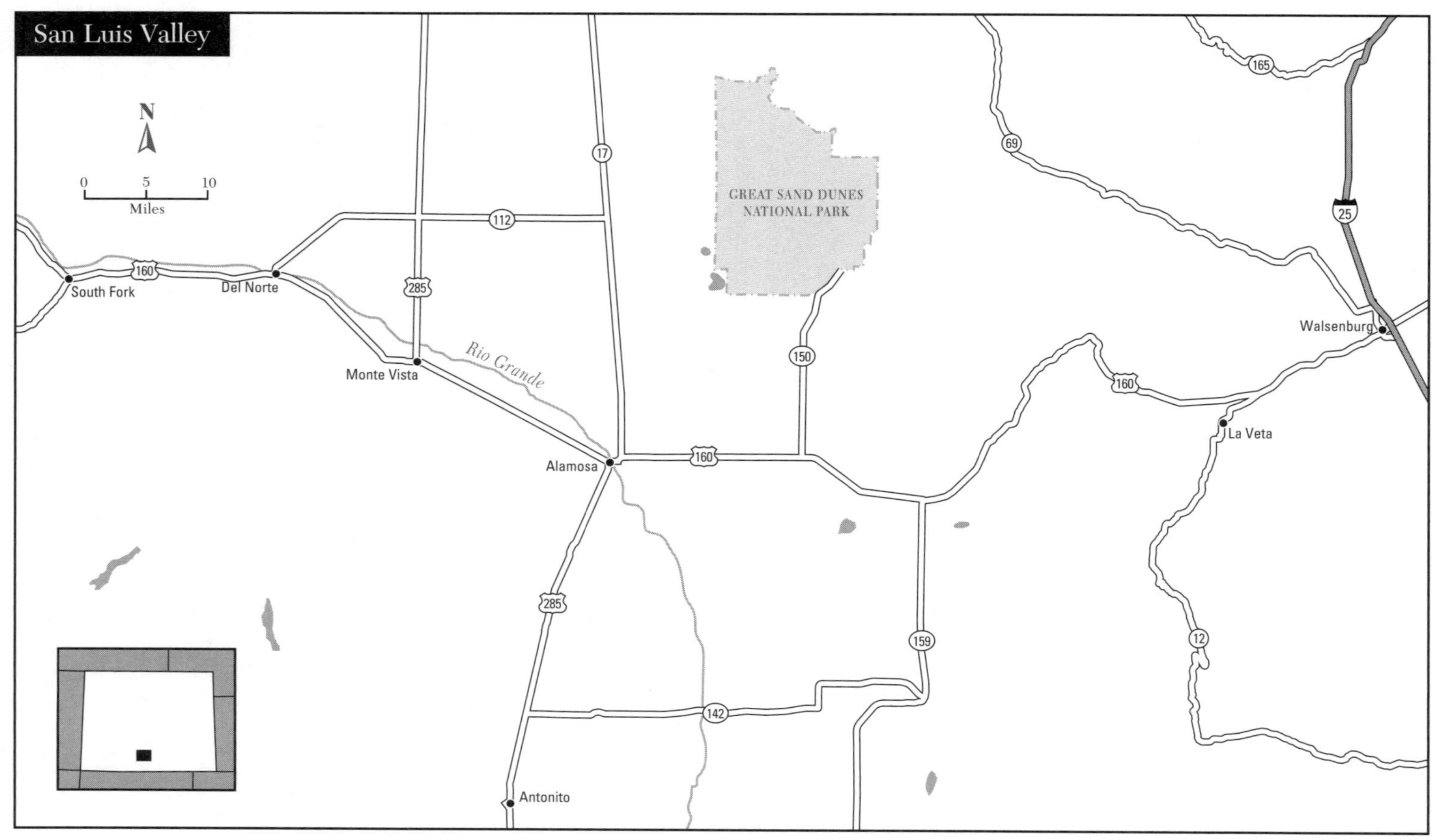
San Luis Valley
N
0
5
10
Miles
GREAT SAND DUNES NATIONAL PARK
South Fork
Del Norte
Monte Vista
Rio Grande
Alamosa
Antonito
Walsenburg
La Veta
160
285
112
17
150
69
165
25
12
159
142

GETTING THERE *By car:* The San Luis Valley is a large stretch of land. The region is cross-cut by US 160, which runs east and west, and US 285, which runs north and south. For some reason, US 285 makes a jog west of Alamosa, and travelers coming from the north will want to follow CO 17.

By bus: **Greyhound** (719-589-4948 or 1-800-231-2222; www.greyhound.com) operates regular service to and from Alamosa from the SLV Van Lines at 8480 Stockton.

MEDICAL EMERGENCIES The following hospitals provide 24-hour emergency service in the San Luis Valley.

San Luis Valley Medical Center (719-589-2511; www.slvrmc.org), 106 Blanca Ave., Alamosa.

Rio Grande Hospital (719-657-2510), 310 CR 14, Del Norte.

✷ To See & Do

Great Sand Dunes National Park and Preserve (719-378-6300; www.nps.gov/grsa), 11500 CO 150, Mosca. Open year-round, 24 hours a day. The Great Sand Dunes are one of Colorado's most spectacular geological features—also one of the state's most unique natural attractions. The dunes seem to rise mystically from the plains. At first dwarfed by the mountains behind, the dunes soon overtake the horizon, towering over the landscape, leaving visitors gawky for a moment in sublime awe.

Thousands of years ago, the San Luis Valley was covered by a shallow lake; it's called Lake Alamosa by those who study and discuss such things. Climatic

GREAT SAND DUNES NATIONAL PARK

change and possible geological events caused the lake to shrink and eventually disappear. A sprawling sand sheet was left behind. Over the years, the sand was blown into a natural pocket against the mountains by the prevailing southwest winds. Storm winds from the opposite direction caused the dunes to rise—the highest up to 750 feet.

For over 11,000 years, the area has attracted human visitors—from the ancient nomadic people who came to hunt the prehistoric bison and mammoths that grazed the nearby plains to the eager park visitors who slather on sunscreen, strap on a CamelBak, and try hoofing to the top of the big dune. In 1932, President Hoover created the Great Sand Dunes National Monument—it was made a national park in 2000.

After paying the entrance fee, begin your tour of the Great Sand Dunes at the visitor center. Exhibits and displays illustrate the natural processes that led to the creation of the dunes. Throughout the day, rangers give informative talks, and there's a bookstore and small art gallery. After tackling the visitor center, most people head down to Medano Creek at the foot of the dunes. If you arrive before July, there will be water enough to cool your feet. This is a nice way to counter the hot sand. After July, the creek dries up until spring. From here, you can begin a walk up the dune or simply sit by the creek in the shade.

Several trails lead into the mountains from the park. With a high-clearance, four-wheel-drive vehicle, you can head up Medano Creek Trail and then hike to Medano Lake. But the best experience of the dunes has to be blazing your own trail to the top and taking in the view. (When Zebulon Pike climbed the one of the taller dunes in 1807, he could see the Rio Grande flowing nearly 30 miles to the southeast.) For those interested in camping on the dunes, a free permit from the visitor center is required. Entrance to the park is $3/person. The Annual Pass only costs $15. It admits the pass holder and all family members in the vehicle into the park for one year.

THE GREAT DUNE

Rio Grande Scenic Railroad (1-877-726-7245; www.alamosatrain.com), 601 State Ave., Alamosa. This rather new scenic railroad takes passengers on two routes. The main full-day trip, the San Luis Express, heads east over the mountains through La Veta Pass, and then stops in La Veta for two hours before heading back. The other trip, the Toltec Gorge Limited, heads south to Antonito, where passengers can connect with the Cumbres & Toltec Scenic Railroad. The train rides on standard gauge rails and uses steam locomotion to transport passengers. Adult round-trip to La Veta $48, seniors $38, and children $33.

♿ **Cumbres & Toltec Scenic Railroad** (1-888-286-2737; www.cumbres toltec.com), 5234 B US 285, Antonito. Trains depart daily from Antonito, Colorado, and Chama, New Mexico. The season runs mid-May–mid-Oct. This is the highest and longest narrow-gauge railroad in the country. The main route is a full-day round-trip to Osier that crosses the Colorado–New Mexico border a number of times as it winds over and through the mountains. Adult coach ticket $62–76 and children (2–11) $31–38. Parlor car fare $115–129 for all ages.

Los Caminos Antiguos Scenic and Historic Byway (www.loscaminos.com). This scenic byway takes travelers around the San Luis Valley. Beginning in Alamosa, the route travels north and then east by the Great Sand Dunes National Park. It then heads south to Fort Garland and San Luis, where it turns west to Cumbres Pass in the southern San Juan Mountains, passing Antonito en route. Along the way, you may see wildlife like golden eagles and pronghorn antelope.

☂ **San Luis Valley History Museum** (719-587-0667; www.museumtrail.org/ SanLuisValleyHistoryMuseum.asp), 306 Hunt Ave., Alamosa. Open daily, June–Oct., 10–4. This museum strives to tell the story of the people who explored and settled the San Luis Valley. From the area's first inhabitants to today's ranchers and farmers, museum exhibits illustrate the region's deep history. Admission free.

GREEN SPACE **San Luis Lakes State Park** (719-378-2020; www.parks.state .co.us/parks/sanluis), P.O. Box 150, Mosca, CO 81146. Open Fri.–Sat. 10–2 and Sun. 1–3. The Sangre de Cristo Range serves as a majestic backdrop to the park's San Luis Lake and Head Lakes. The park offers 4 miles of trails. The landscape is flat, and the trails are accordingly easy going for both hiking and mountain biking. Visitors may also go boating or do some fishing. Daily vehicle pass $6.

✱ Lodging

BED & BREAKFASTS (ı) **The Mansion Bed & Breakfast** (719-852-5151 or 1-877-552-5151; www.the mansionbandb.com), 1030 Park Ave., Monte Vista. This Arts & Crafts mansion was built in 1905, and the inn's four rooms reflect the style of the home. Two rooms have private baths, and the Margaret Brown Room, the more romantic of the two, has a fireplace and claw-foot tub. A full gourmet breakfast is served daily, made from the freshest local ingredients. Rooms $85–110.

(ı) 🐾 **Willow Spring Bed & Breakfast** (719-256-4116; www.willow

THE MANSION IN MONTE VISTA

-spring.com), P.O. Box 500, Moffat, CO 81143. Located halfway between Alamosa and Poncha Springs on CO 17 in Moffat, this B&B began as a hotel in 1910. The inn is decorated throughout with antiques, and guests are served a full breakfast every morning. Children are welcome. Rooms $65.

Cottonwood Inn (719-589-3882 or 1-800-955-2623; www.cottonwood inn.com), 123 San Juan Ave., Alamosa. Close to the Great Sand Dunes, this is one of the nicer places to stay in Alamosa. There are five rooms, each with a private bath. Full-sized breakfast served daily (except in the off-season when guests can enjoy the continental breakfast). Rooms $70–125.

CAMPGROUNDS **San Luis Lakes State Park** (719-378-2020; www .parks.state.co.us/parks/sanluis), P.O. Box 150, Mosca, CO 81146. The campground has 51 sites and a bathhouse with hot showers and modern toilet facilities. After Oct., the campground remains open, but drinking water, electricity, and the dump station remain available. Sites $18 (not including park vehicle pass).

✷ Where to Eat

EATING OUT ♿ **True Grits Steakhouse** (719-589-9954), 100 Santa Fe Ave., Alamosa. Open Mon.–Fri. 4–10, Sat. 11–10, and Sun. 11–9. Folks come for a steak, potato, and salad, but stay for the thematic tribute to John Wayne—his portrait is hung everywhere at True Grits. Dinner $8–20.

Southwest Colorado

4

DURANGO, SILVERTON & THE FOUR CORNERS

PAGOSA SPRINGS & THE SOUTHERN SAN JUANS

TELLURIDE & OURAY

CRESTED BUTTE & GUNNISON

DURANGO, SILVERTON & THE FOUR CORNERS

The story of Durango begins with the railroad. The town was founded in 1880 when General William Palmer, owner of the Denver & Rio Grande Railroad, was refused a spot for his train depot in nearby Animas. By 1882, narrow-gauge rail service had been extended to Silverton, and soon the new town of Durango was busy smelting ores brought down from the mountains. As mining played out in the mountains, the railroad struggled to survive for awhile, and then was closed. The Durango smelter remained busy with uranium for some time after World War II, but the rail line looked like it might be abandoned altogether. A group of individuals lobbied hard for the preservation of the Durango & Silverton Railroad as a tourist attraction and won. It wasn't long before Hollywood took notice and featured the train in a number of movies.

Throughout its history, Durango has catered to tourists. The scenic value of the train ride to Silverton was touted to potential passengers from the beginning. When Mesa Verde National Park was established in 1906, it was yet another attraction that might draw tourists to southwest Colorado.

Today, Durango is established as the region's largest city and continues to flourish. The Animas Riverwalk has opened up the river to pedestrians. The Children's Museum is expanding, and in several years a new museum of wider scope, the Durango Discovery Museum, will be housed in a new complex that will include the town's old Power House. Durango is home to Fort Lewis College (the highest college in North America), the Rocky Mountain Chocolate Factory, and the locally popular Zuberfizz soda company. The biggest industry in town, however, is tourism. Durango serves as a base camp for trips into the Four Corners region as well as a gateway to the mountains. Visitors pour into town to ride the Durango & Silverton Narrow-Gauge Railroad, which makes daily runs to and from Silverton throughout the summer. The Mesa Verde National Park cliff dwellings attract thousands each year. These archaeological sites of the ancient Puebloans have proven to be quite a draw for visitors, and more sites have been found throughout the Four Corners, in the Hovenweep National Monument and the Canyons of the Ancients National Monument.

Durango has also become a recreation center. Hundreds of miles of trails for

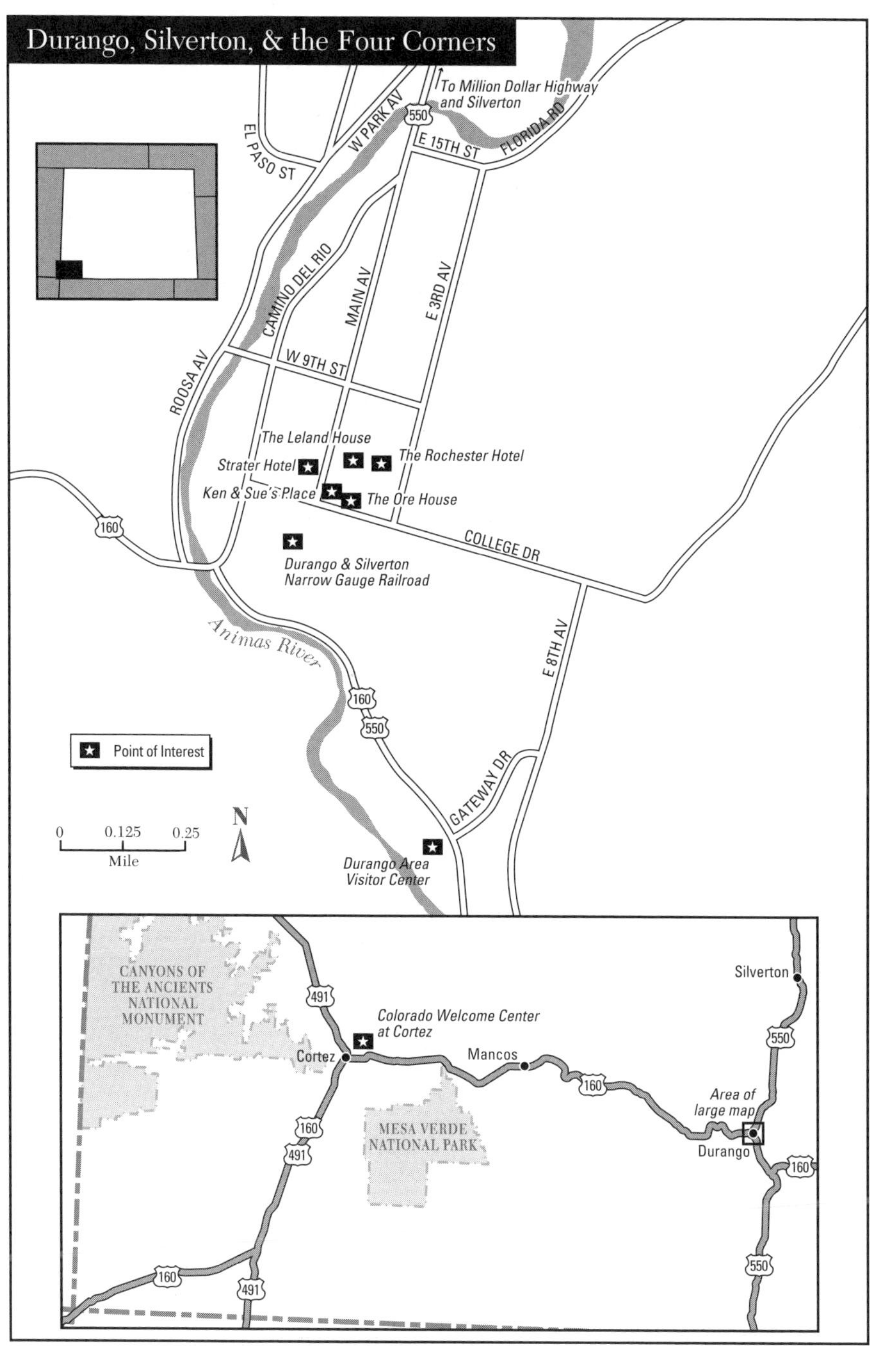

Durango, Silverton, & the Four Corners
To Million Dollar Highway and Silverton
550
W PARK AV
FLORIDA RD
E 15TH ST
EL PASO ST
CAMINO DEL RIO
MAIN AV
E 3RD AV
ROOSA AV
W 9TH ST
The Leland House
Strater Hotel
The Rochester Hotel
Ken & Sue's Place
The Ore House
160
COLLEGE DR
Durango & Silverton Narrow Gauge Railroad
Animas River
E 8TH AV
160
550
Point of Interest
GATEWAY DR
0
0.125
0.25
Mile
N
Durango Area Visitor Center
CANYONS OF THE ANCIENTS NATIONAL MONUMENT
491
Colorado Welcome Center at Cortez
Cortez
Mancos
160
Silverton
550
Area of large map
Durango
160
MESA VERDE NATIONAL PARK
160
491
550
160
491

hiking and mountain biking can be accessed right from town. The Colorado Trail, which begins in Denver, has its western terminus just north of town. And in the winter, Durango Mountain Resort has alpine skiing and snowboarding.

As you read through this chapter, be advised that all the addresses are in Durango unless otherwise indicated.

GUIDANCE **Durango Area Tourism Office** (1-800-525-8855; www.durango.org), 111 S. Camino del Rio. Just as you come into town from the east on US 160 (Camino del Rio), Santa Rita Park will be on your left, along the Animas River. The tourism office/visitor center is there in the park (1-800-463-8726).

Silverton Chamber of Commerce & Visitor Center (970-387-5654 or 1-800-752-4494; www.silvertoncolorado.com), located where US 550 and CO 110 meet. Open daily in the summer 9–6, spring and fall 9–5, and winter 10–4.

Colorado Welcome Center at Cortez (970-565-4048 or 1-800-253-1616; www.mesaverdecountry.com), 928 E. Main St. Open daily in the summer 8–9 and in winter 8–5. The welcome center is operated by the Cortez Chamber of Commerce and the Colorado Tourism office. It provides extensive information for those visiting Colorado, and the staff is able to offer an insider's perspective on visiting Cortez and Mesa Verde National Park. There are walls and walls of brochures, a small bookstore, and clean rest rooms.

More Web sites:

www.durango.com

www.durangodowntown.com

GETTING THERE *By car:* US 160 runs east and west through Durango, terminating in the east in Walsenburg. US 550 runs north and south through town. To the north, US 550 connects with US 50 and continues on to I-70.

By air: The **Durango–La Plata County Airport** (970-247-8143; www.durangogov.org/services/airport.html), 1000 Airport Rd., hosts three major airlines—America West/US Air, United Express, and Delta. Together they provide daily service to and from Denver, Phoenix, and Salt Lake City.

By bus: **Greyhound** operates regular service to and from Durango from the Durango Greyhound station (970-259-2755 or 1-800-231-2222; www.greyhound.com) at 275 E. Eighth Ave.

GETTING AROUND *By bus or trolley:* **Durango Transit** (970-259-5438; www.durangogov.org/RESIDENT/services/transit.html) operates a system of buses and trolleys that cover all of Durango—many run late into the evening.

MEDICAL EMERGENCIES **Mercy Medical Center** (970-247-4311; www.mercydurango.org), 375 E. Park Ave. This hospital operates a 24-hour emergency room.

Durango Urgent Care (970-247-8382; www.durangourgentcare.com), 1800 E. Third Ave. #112. Open daily 9–7. This urgent care facility treats problems that are urgent but not life threatening.

Southwest Memorial Hospital (970-565-6666; www.swhealth.org), 1311 N. Mildred Rd., Cortez. Closer to the Four Corners, this hospital operates a 24-hour emergency room.

✷ To See & Do

EXCURSIONS ♿ **Durango & Silverton Narrow-Gauge Railroad** (970-247-2733 or 1-877-872-4607; www.durangotrain.com), Durango Depot, 479 Main Ave. During the peak summer season the railroad has four trains leaving Durango daily. The train has been used in a number of movies, including *Butch Cassidy and the Sundance Kid.* The 45-mile trek to Silverton runs along the Animas River. The layover in Silverton gives passengers over two hours to roam the town—plenty of time to grab a bite to eat and do some window shopping.

♿ **Bartels' Mancos Valley Stage Line** (970-533-9857 or 1-800-365-3530; www.thestagecoach.com), 4550 CR 41, Mancos. One way to get a feel for the Old West is to take a stagecoach ride. This company will educate visitors on the history of the stagecoach and then take them on a ride through Weber Canyon. There are two-and-a-half-hour lunch and dinner tours in addition the standard one-hour tour. Guests will stop at a log cabin en route for brisket or steak. Adult one-hour tour $45, children (3–11) $22.50.

HOT SPRINGS **Trimble Spa & Natural Hot Springs** (970-247-0111; www.trimblehotsprings.com), 6475 CR 203. Open daily in the summer 8–11; winter (May–June), Sun.–Thurs. 9–10 and Fri. and Sat. 9–11. Back in the day, both Marilyn Monroe and Clark Gable soaked in the Trimble Hot Springs. Today Trimble offers a large swimming pool, hot pools, and a beautifully landscaped picnic area. For the full treatment, consider the spa services, which include a

DURANGO & SILVERTON NARROW-GAUGE RAILROAD

MESA VERDE NATIONAL PARK

Mesa Verde National Park (970-529-4465; www.nps.gov/meve), the park entrance is 10 miles east of Cortez just off US 160. Driving east out of Cortez on the road to Durango, looking to the south, an impressive mesa rises up 2,000 feet from the valley floor. The Spanish called it *Mesa Verde,* or "Green Table." At a glance, there is nothing about Mesa Verde that hints at the secrets the mesa holds.

For 700 years, from the year 600 to 1300, the mesa was inhabited by people who farmed the top of the mesa, hunted its canyons, and over time built their shelters on the cliff walls, hundreds of feet above the canyon floor. The same overhanging cliffs that offered them shelter preserved their dwellings long after they left this place. Most visitors come to see the cliff dwellings, but there are over 4,000 archaeological sites at Mesa Verde that tell the story of this ancient people.

When you get to Mesa Verde, head straight for the Far View Visitor Center. Certain cliff dwellings, like Balcony House and Cliff Palace, are only open to guests on a ranger-guided tour. The visitor center is the only place in the park that sells the tickets for the tours (and it's a long drive back to get tickets if you miss this step). The earlier you can start your day the better; the tours fill up quickly in the summer. No matter when you get there, however, the rangers are very adept at helping guests create an itinerary based on tour availability. The park also maintains a nice bookstore here for more in-depth information on Mesa Verde.

A number of cliff dwellings are only visible from a distance. These are indicated on the park map and by signs and parking areas along the road. There are also mesa-top sites—places where the ancestral Puebloans lived before moving down to the cliffs. Most people, however, come to Mesa Verde to tour the cliff dwellings—to get in and among the ancient walls.

The cliff dwellings open to the public are found on two of the park's mesas. Chapin Mesa is the closest, and it is where you find Cliff House, Balcony House, and Spruce Tree House. Chapin Mesa also has a museum and a snack bar that serves up lunch food. For this reason, most visitors spend their day on Chapin Mesa. Wetherill Mesa is to the west about 20 miles from Chapin by road, which can take up to an hour to drive. It is where you will find Step House and Long House. Visitors park their cars at the Wetherill Mesa information kiosk and take a tram around to the various sites.

Below is a quick summary of the largest and most-visited cliff dwellings:

Cliff Palace is the largest cliff dwelling at Mesa Verde. You will need to take a ranger-guided tour to view the site. Though you only walk 0.25 mile, you will climb five ladders to return to the top of the mesa (they are about 8–10 feet each).

Balcony House is probably the most strenuous of the ranger-led tours. You take the stairs to a ledge below the site and then climb a 32-foot ladder up into the dwelling. To exit the site, you crawl through a 12-foot tunnel that is 18 inches wide at its narrowest point. After that, there are two 10-foot ladders, and a harrowing climb across open rock to get back to the top and the parking lot.

Spruce Tree House is the best preserved of the dwellings, and it is unique in that the kiva roofs have been restored. In the summer, guests tour the dwelling on their own, but in the winter they must take a free ranger-guided tour. The 0.5-mile round trip to the site is not terribly strenuous, but you do climb down and back up 100 feet.

Long House is the second largest cliff dwelling at Mesa Verde. Tours begin at the Wetherill information kiosk where you board the tram. The ranger-guided tour is 90 minutes and boasts of being the park's most in-depth tour. The 0.75-mile hike will take you up two 15-foot ladders, and you will gain 130 feet in elevation on your way back to the tram.

Step House is just a short hike from the Wetherill information kiosk. The 0.75-mile round trip takes you down and back up 100 feet along a winding path. On this self-guided tour, you will get a chance to see a pit house and petroglyphs.

Another option for seeing the park is to sign up for an Interpreted Ranger-Guided Tour at Far View Lodge or Far View Terrace (or call 1-800-449-2288 to make a reservation). The tour includes a lunch and runs about $50.

CLIFF PALACE AT MESA VERDE NATIONAL PARK

number of massage treatments. Adult rate $13/day, seniors $9, children (5–11) $8.50, and children under 5 free.

MONUMENTS & PARKS OF SOUTHWEST COLORADO **Canyon of the Ancients National Monument** (www.blm.gov/co/st/en/nm/canm.html), west of Cortez. A visit to the Canyon of the Ancients should begin at the **Anasazi Heritage Center** (970-882-5600; www.co.blm.gov/ahc), 27501 CO 184, Dolores. This museum is open daily in the summer 9–5, and in the winter 10–4. Admission is $3 for adults; kids under 17 are free. The museum offers visitors the perfect introduction to ancestral Puebloan culture and the canyon. Over 6,000 archaelogical sites have been discovered at the park—many from the ancestral Puebloans, but also a number of more recent Navajo sites. These finds are not recognizable to the average visitor, and their locations are not publicized. For many visitors this makes for a frustrating tour, but visitors who like exploring and the joy of discovery will find it a fun place to visit.

Four Corners Monument (928-871-6647; www.navajonationparks.org/htm/fourcorners.htm), southwest corner of the state, right on US 160. Open daily in the summer 7–8 and in winter 8–5. This is the only place in the U.S. where the boundaries of four states meet in one place. Such a fortuitous alignment cannot be ignored, so in 1912, a cement slab was laid down to mark the spot. Since then a regular granite and brass monument has been erected. Admission is $3 for all ages.

Hovenweep National Monument (970-562-4282; www.nps.gov/hove), McElmo Route, Cortez. The visitor center is open daily 8–5. Tucked inside the Canyon of the Ancients, Hovenweep preserves a large number of ancestral Puebloan structures. The most accessible are part of the Square Tower Group—the largest collection of such sites in the park. A paved trail leads out to an overlook of the site. Continuing on, the path is unpaved and becomes moderately strenuous as it follows the canyon rim. Hikers are rewarded for their efforts with excellent views of all the ruins. A seven-day vehicle pass is $6. If you come in on foot, bike, or motorcycle the fee is $3.

MUSEUMS & HISTORIC SITES ☂ ♿ **Animas Museum** (970-259-2402; www.animasmuseum.org), 3065 W. Second Ave. Open in the summer Mon.–Sat. 10–6 and in winter Tues.–Sat. 10–4. Exhibits and displayed artifacts tell the story of Durango and La Plata County. The museum itself is a bit of history; it's housed in a schoolhouse from 1904. Inside, a classroom has been restored to 1908. The museum also preserves the oldest intact structure in Durango—a cabin built by the blacksmith, C. B. Joy, back in the 1870s. Adult admission $3, children (7–12) $1, and children under 7 free.

National Historic Districts, Durango. Downtown Durango, centered on Main Ave., is a registered historic district. Some of the more noteworthy buildings are the Palace and Statler hotels. A block away, Third Avenue has also been designated as a national historic district. On either side of the tree-lined boulevard you'll find historic homes—many from the Victorian period.

♿ **Old Hundred Mine** (970-387-5444 or 1-800-872-3009; www.minetour.com),

P.O. Box 430, Silverton, CO 81433. The mine is located east of Silverton, so just head out of town on CR 2 and follow the blue and white signs. Open daily in the summer. Tours leave on the hour 10–4. The mine tour takes visitors 1,600 feet underground (it's below 50 degrees in there so dress accordingly). For 50 minutes guides share the history of the mine and demonstrate mining techniques on actual equipment. After the tour, guests can head to the sluice box and pan for gold, silver, and precious stones. Adult admission $16.95, seniors $14.95, children (5–12) $7.95, and children under 5 free if held on lap.

Mayflower Gold Mill Tour (970-387-0294), Silverton; located 2 miles north of Silverton on CO 110, CR 2. Open daily in the summer 10–5. Up until 1991, this facility was used to process precious metals. Guests can tour the mill and see the equipment demonstrated by former employees. Adult admission $6.50, seniors $5.50, and children under 12 free.

Galloping Goose Railroad Museum (970-882-7082), 421 Railroad Ave., Dolores. Open daily in the summer 9–4. This museum celebrates a quirky period of railroad history, when the Rio Grande Southern began using Galloping Geese. These unique vehicles were a hodgepodge combination of old buses and trucks fitted to run on train rails. They usually just pulled one car and were used to transport freight and passengers cheaply. Another museum for railroad buffs would be the **Ridgeway Railroad Museum** (www.ridgwayrailroadmuseum.org) at the Ouray County Fairgrounds in Ridgeway—open on weekends in the summer.

SCENIC DRIVES **San Juan Skyway Byway** (www.byways.org/explore/byways/2101). Durango is a great place to begin one of Colorado's most scenic drives. The San Juan Skyway is a 230-mile loop that heads north from Durango to Ridgway on US 550. It then cuts west on CO 62 to Placerville, then south to Cortez on CO 145, and finally heads back to Durango on US 160. Along the way you'll see some of the state's most stunning scenery.

The stretch of road between Durango and Ouray is known as the Million Dollar Highway. It may have gotten its name from the idea that there was gold ore mixed in with the fill dirt or that it cost a million dollars a mile to build the road over several passes and a gorge. In either case, the trip up to Ouray is at times both breathtakingly beautiful and frighteningly harrowing. Even Colorado natives will admit to some fearful moments on this road, which has stunning drop-offs yet no guardrails.

Along the more westerly route back down to Cortez, the road is easier on the mind, with expansive views of green valleys and white peaks rising above wooded slopes. Part of the byway takes up on a side trip to Telluride.

✷ Outdoor Activities

ALPINE SKIING & SNOWBOARDING **Purgatory at Durango Mountain Resort** (970-247-9000 or 1-800-568-3275; www.durangomountainresort.com), US 550, 28 miles north of Durango. Open daily 9–4. Until 2000, it was called the Purgatory Ski Area, and you will still hear folks call it "Purgatory." The ski area has a vertical drop of 2,029 feet with 1,200 skiable acres. The mountain gets nearly 300 inches of snow, and 250 acres are supplemented with snowmaking. There are 85 runs, most in the intermediate range. There are a host of lessons for kids and adults, beginning and experienced skiers alike. For beginners, the Guaranteed to Green Package promises to get you comfortably skiing on a green run—if not, the next lesson is free. Adult lift ticket $60, seniors $44, "Golden" (70+) $20, students (13–18) $44, and children (6–12) $32.

In the summer, the ski area offers over 50 miles of trails for mountain biking. A single lift up the mountain will cost you $5, but you can use the chairlift all day for $15. They also rent bikes, up to $45 for a whole day.

San Juan Ski Co. (970-259-9671 or 1-800-208-1780; www.sanjuanski.com), 1831 Lake Purgatory Dr. Based at Durango Mountain Resort, the San Juan Ski Co. gives skiers access to 35,000 acres of ungroomed backcountry powder. Guides take skiers out in snowcats and boast that their guests will ski down 8,000–12,000 vertical feet of untouched wilderness wonderland in a day. Food and beverages, as well as use of powder skis and avalanche gear, are included in the cost, which is $290 per person.

Silverton Mountain Ski Area (970-387-5706; www.silvertonmountain.com), P.O. Box 654, Silverton, CO 81433. Silverton Ski Area is the highest in North America. It's also the steepest. As such only advanced and expert skiers are allowed. Guests must be comfortable skiing black-diamond slopes and hiking along a ridgeline for up to 20 minutes. They must also either bring or rent an avalanche beacon, shovel, and probe in order to use the mountain. The ski area offers guided and unguided skiing. There is one chairlift, and with some hiking you can enjoy 3,000-foot vertical drops. Guided skiing $119–129, unguided $49.

Cliffside Ski & Bike (970-385-1461; www.cliffsideski.com), 46825 US 550. This shop can be found about 2.5 miles south of Durango Mountain Resort. They rent equipment for skiers of all skill levels. Skis and boots $15–25.

CROSS-COUNTRY SKIING & SNOWSHOEING There are 200 miles of groomed trails in the Durango area open to cross-country skiers. Hillcrest Golf Course (970-247-1499; www.golfhillcrest.com), 2300 Rim Dr., is on a mesa overlooking Durango and has trails for skiing. **Pine River Valley** (aka Vallecito Nordic Ski Area, 970-884-9782) is a bit farther afield, but open to the public. The trailhead can be found just east of the dam and then north a little ways on the gravel road. Use of the trails is free, but donations are appreciated.

Durango Nordic Center (970-385-2114; www.durangonordic.org/nordic center.htm) at Durango Mountain Resort (see Alpine Skiing & Snowboarding) has over 9 miles of groomed trails for cross-country skiing. They offer instruction and ski rental. The trail fee is $15, or $5 for children and seniors.

FISHING Fishing is good in Durango and the surrounding area. The Animas River runs right through town, and there are plenty of creeks for fly-fishing. To the west in Mancos is Mancos State Park, which has the Jackson Gulch Reservoir—another great spot to cast a line. A great way to get oriented to the Durango fishing scene is to take a trip with a local guide who can show the best the region has to offer.

Animas Valley Anglers (970-259-0484; www.gottrout.com), 264 W. 22nd St. These guides can take you on both floating and wading trips on all the local rivers and creeks. One trip to consider begins with a ride on the Durango-Silverton Narrow-Gauge Railroad into the San Juan National Forest, where anglers are dropped off for a day of fishing. The remote location means fewer people and more fish.

Duranglers (970-385-4081 or 1-888-347-4346; www.duranglers.com), 923 Main Ave. Duranglers offers guide services on all the local rivers—the Animas, Dolores, and Los Pinos. They also take anglers out to the Piedra and San Juan in the east and the Black Canyon of the Gunnison to the north. The shop gives lessons on all aspects of fly-fishing, from building a rod and tying a fly to casting and landing a fish.

GOLF **Dalton Ranch Golf Course** (970-247-7921; www.daltonranch.com), 589 CR 252. This semiprivate course, 6 miles north of Durango, incorporates the Animas River into its design. Greens fees $59–89.

Hillcrest Golf Course (970-247-1499; www.golfhillcrest.com), 2300 Rim Dr. Hillcrest is located north of Fort Lewis College on the mesa overlooking Durango and the Animas Valley. Greens fees $30 for 18 holes.

HIKING A local trails advocacy group, **Trails2000** (www.trails2000.org), publishes a free map of Durango area trails. It is distrubuted through sporting-type shops around town, like Mountain Bike Specialists and Gardenswartz Outdoors on Main Avenue.

The **Colorado Trail** is one of the most significant trails for hikers in the state. Durango is the western terminus of this trail, which stretches northeast to Denver. The trailhead is at the end of Junction Creek Road, west of Durango. Hikers looking for a longer trip can always tackle the entire Colorado Trail—it's only 482.9 miles to Denver.

Close to town, the **Animas Mountain Trail** is a 5-mile loop that climbs 2,000 feet. The hike offers great views of Durango and the Animas Valley. The trailhead and parking area is west off Main Avenue on 32nd Street. Turn north on Fourth Avenue and the parking lot is at the end of the road on the right (you'll have to ignore the one-way sign).

For a leisurely hike in town, follow the **Animas River Trail,** which as the name suggests runs along the Animas River. This paved path begins in Memorial Park at 32nd Street and continues 5 miles to the Mall on S. Camino del Rio (US 160).

Colorado Mountain Expeditions (970-375-1250 or 1-877-600-2656; www.coloradotrailhiking.com), 3635 CR 301. There is no easier way to hike along the Colorado Trail. Colorado Mountain Expeditions offers five-day hiking vacations that include all of your meals, and they even take care of transporting your gear. All you carry is a day pack. The cost for such pampering is $875 per person for each section of the trail.

HORSEBACK RIDING **Buck's Livery** (970-385-2110; www.buckslivery.com), US 550 north at Durango Mountain Resort Ski Area. There is a ride to suit your every inclination at Buck's—trail rides, dinner rides, and backcountry rides, as well as sleigh rides in the winter. They will even take you out hunting and fishing.

Seventy Seven Outfit (970-247-3231; www.77outfit.com), 11374 US 550 S. The guides at Seventy Seven lead day rides and overnight camping trips. They also rent horses if you are looking to ride on your own. Rates vary by the number of people in your party. A two-person day ride is $180 each and a four-person day ride $140 each.

MOUNTAIN BIKING In 1990, the first professional UCI Mountain Bike & Trials World Championships were held in Durango. Seen as a mountain biking mecca of sorts, Durango has more than 2,000 miles of trails, hundreds of which are the ever-coveted singletrack. There are some great downhill sections at Durango Mountain Resort (see Alpine Skiing & Snowboarding for lift information).

A ride closer to town is the **Colorado Trail & Hoffheins Connection.** This 20-mile loop starts at the Colorado Trail trailhead at the end of Junction Creek Road, west out of Durango. Riding up the trail, Hoffheins Connection is just over 600 feet past the Gudy's Rest (an overlook with a bench, placed in honor of Gudy Gaskill, who was a driving force behind the creation of the Colorado Trail). Hoffheins Connection Trail continues on to Lightner Creek Road and US 160, which takes you back to Durango.

Hermosa Creek Trail takes riders from Durango Mountain Resort down to the town of Hermosa—following Hermosa Creek much of the way. The 20-mile trek is smooth downhill singletrack. Though not overly technical, there are some tricky spots. The one-way ride begins 8 miles up Hermosa Park Road behind Durango Mountain Resort.

To spend your entire vacation pedaling, the **San Juan Hut System** (970-626-3033; www.sanjuanhuts.com), P.O. Box 775, Ridgway, operates along a 214-mile route of backcountry roads from Durango to Moab. About every 35 miles, riders crash for the night at one of the huts. The trip takes seven days and six nights and costs $620 per person. In exchange, riders get a sleeping bag and a place to sleep, three meals a day, and trail descriptions and maps.

Pedal the Peaks (970-259-6880; www.pedalthepeaks.biz), 598B Main Ave. These guys rent full suspension and hard-tail mountain bikes. They also know a bit about area trails. Full-day rentals $25–45.

Cliffside Ski & Bike (970-385-1461; www.cliffsideski.com), 46825 US 550. This shop can be found about 30 miles north of Durango. They rent full-suspension and hard-tail mountain bikes. A 24-hour rental is $45.

RAFTING **Durango Rivertrippers** (970-259-0289 or 1-800-292-2885; www.durangorivertrippers.com), 720 Main Ave. Durango Rivertrippers was the first river outfitter licensed by the state. They take guests on rafting trips down the Animas River. With spring runoff, the river sees class IV rapids, which makes for an exciting ride. In the summer, the river levels off and sees rapids up to class III. There are two trips down the Animas: one is two hours and the other a half-day. You can also make the run in a rented inflatable kayak. If you can't get enough of rafting on one of their shorter trips, they offer one-, three-, and six-day trips down the Dolores River, which takes you as far at the Colorado River in Utah. Adult half-day trip with lunch $39, children $28. Adult two-hour trip $25, children $17.

GREEN SPACE **Mancos State Park** (970-533-7065; www.parks.state.co.us/parks/mancos), 42545 CR N, Mancos. Open 24 hours a day. Enclosing the Jackson Gulch Reservoir, the park has camping and trails. The Chicken Creek Trail connects with the Colorado Trail north of Durango. There are other trails here that would make nice short nature walks. There are 5 miles of in-park trails open to biking, hiking, cross-country skiing, and snowshoeing. The reservoir is great for boating and fishing. Daily vehicle pass $6.

San Juan Public Lands Center (970-247-4874; www.fs.fed.us/r2/sanjuan), 15 Burnett Ct. Open Mon.–Fri. 8–4:30. The San Juan National Forest stretches from Dolores in the west all the way to south-central Colorado in the east. North of Durango, most every time you step out of your car, you're standing in the national forest. To learn more about these public lands, check out the bookstore at the Public Lands Center. They have an extensive collection of books and maps on all aspects of enjoying the public lands around Durango and in southwestern Colorado.

✷ Lodging

HOTELS "1" **The Strater Hotel** (970-247-4431 or 1-800-247-4431; www.strater.com), 699 Main Ave. In the hotel's early years, Durango residents would abandon their homes in the winter and stay at the Strater Hotel, which had wood-burning stoves in every room. Built in 1887 by an enterprising young pharmicist, the Strater has been a symbol of Durango's status throughout its history. When Durango saw tough times, the Strater saw tough times. In the 1920s, the hotel was restored to its former glory. As a

STRATER HOTEL

historical site, the hotel's public spaces are used to display antiques and artifacts. The rooms have been modernized and are decorated with subtle Victorian touches. Rooms $105–275.

The Lodge at Tamarron (970-259-2000, 1-800-982-6103, or 1-800-525-0892; www.lodgeattamarron.com), 40292 US 550 N. (18 miles north of Durango). Part of Durango Mountain Resort, the Lodge at Tamarron is perfect for a ski vacation. The lodge has rooms, suites, studios, and lofts—many with kitchens and kitchenettes and beds for larger groups. Some of the accommodations are greater than 1,800 square feet. Rooms are comfortably contemporary. There are indoor and outdoor pools, Jacuzzis, and tennis courts. The lodge also offers a free shuttle to the ski area. Rooms $109–309.

Wyman Hotel and Inn (970-387-5372 or 1-800-609-7845; www.thewyman.com), 1371 Greene St., Silverton. The Wyman was built in 1902 and is on the National Register of Historic Places. As such, it completely complements the Old West feel of Silverton. There are 15 rooms, including suites and various combinations of beds (double queen suites, single queen suites, rooms with king-sized beds, etc.). All the rooms have private baths, several with whirlpool tubs. In addition to the rooms in the hotel, a caboose from the Southern Pacific Railroad has been converted into a honeymoon suite and sits in the neighboring courtyard. A full gourmet breakfast is served every morning, as is an afternoon wine-and-cheese social. Rooms $145–305.

BED & BREAKFASTS **Apple Orchard Inn** (970-247-0751 or 1-800-426-0751; www.appleorchardinn.com), 7758 CR 203. John and Celeste are your hosts at the Apple Orchard Inn—one of the finest B&Bs in Colorado. Casually elegant, upscale, and romantic is how guests describe their stay at the Apple Orchard. There are four guest rooms in the main house and six cottages on the property's 4.5 acres. The yard is

THE WYMAN IN SILVERTON

beautifully landscaped, complete with a meandering stream. Cottages each have private decks, and three have fireplaces. Cottages with whirlpool tubs and private hot tubs are also available. Celeste received culinary training in Europe and prepares a full gourmet breakfast every morning. Dinner is available if arranged in advance. Rooms $90–160 and cottages $110–225.

"1" 🐾 ♿ **The Leland House** (970-385-1920 or 1-800-664-1920; www.lelandhouse.com), 721 E. Second Ave. The Leland House began as an apartment building. Since 1992, it has been a B&B with very spacious accommodations—five queen suites, four queen studios, and the Pittman Suite (essentially a two-bedroom apartment with a full kitchen). Not long after opening the Leland House, the owners, the mother and son team of Diane Wildfang and Kirk Komick, looked across the street at the old Rochester.

Built in 1892, the hotel had deteriorated over the years. Realizing that the rundown building could only hurt business for their side of the street, they decided to buy the hotel and make some renovations. Redesigning the interior, they took the building from a dilapitated hotel with 33 rooms to a comfortable inn with 15 rooms, each with its own bath. Soon the **Rochester Hotel** (www.rochesterhotel.com), at 726 E. Second Ave., was open to the public. Decorated in contemporary cowboy style with Old West Victorian touches, the hotel also has a movie theme with posters and photos from films shot in and around Durango.

The office for both buildings is in the Leland House, but the full gourmet breakfast is served at the Rochester Hotel. So in tune are these two lodgings that if all the doors are open, you can stand at the back of the Rochester Hotel and see clear through the hotel and across the street, through the hallway of the Leland House and out its back door. Suites and studios at the Leland House run $119–349, and rooms at the Rochester Hotel are $119–249.

"1" ♿ **Blue Lake Ranch** (970-385-4537; www.bluelakeranch.com), 16000 CO 140, Hesperus. This B&B has 16 lodging options from the Cabin on the Lake to the Cottage in the Woods to the River House—some can accommodate up to eight guests. The tastefully appointed rooms are complemented by the ranch's natural setting. Suites and cabins $135–375.

✐ 🐾 **Sundance Bear Lodge** (970-533-1504 or 1-866-529-2480; www.sundancebear.com), 38890 CO 184, Mancos. Just minutes from Mesa Verde National Park, the main lodge at Sundance has two rooms. There is a log cabin big enough for a family of four (though just as often it is taken by couples looking for a romantic retreat). The cabin as three decks and a tub and shower lined with river

THE ROCHESTER HOTEL

rocks. The lodge also has a guest house with three bedrooms and two and a half baths. It can be rented as a whole or as two units. Truly a part of the Old West, the neighboring ranch was owned by Louis L'Amour, and a nearby canyon is rumored to have hidden Butch Cassidy when he was running from the law in Telluride. Rooms $99–125, log cabin $150–175, and guest house rooms $125–185 (or $270–289 for the whole house).

Willowtail Springs (970-533-7592 or 1-800-698-0603; www.willowtailsprings.com), P.O. Box 89, Mancos. Willow Springs has three cabins nestled on 60 wooded acres. Depending on the cabin, they can accommodate 4–6 guests. The Bungalow overlooks the lake and features a claw-foot tub and fireplace. The Garden Cottage has views of the La Plata Mountains and the lake and features a fireplace. The Lakehouse has a 40-foot ceiling in the living room, sleeps up to six, and has a TV with satellite and DVD player. All the cabins are homey yet luxuriously appointed with fresh flowers adorning the tables and lush garden landscaping. Wireless Internet is available in the office. Cabins $169–339.

CAMPGROUNDS **Lightner Creek Campground** (970-247-5406), 1567 CR 207. This shady campground along Lightner Creek offers sites for tent camper and RVs. There are also camping cabins for rent as well as two rooms in the main lodge. There's a heated swimming pool, and the creek is open for fishing. This campground is far from the beaten path—a secluded and quiet retreat. Tent sites $26, sites with hook-ups $33–36, and camper cabins $39. Creekside site, add $4; more than two people, add $4 for each extra.

Transfer Park Campground is located north of US 160 on CR 243 east of Durango. Open Memorial Day–Labor Day. With just 25 sites along the Florida River and no showers, just vault toilets and drinking water, Transfer Park doesn't get a lot of traffic. This is a shame as the campground is set in a beautiful spot. This was once the place where horses were unloaded and their cargo transferred to mules for trips into the mountains. Sites $13.

Mancos State Park (970-533-7065; www.parks.state.co.us/parks/mancos), 42545 CR N, Mancos. The park has two campgrounds—32 sites in all. There are vault toilets and drinking water, but no showers. The park also maintains two yurts that are available year-round (heated in the winter). Sites $12 and yurts $60.

RESORTS **Dunton Hot Springs** (970-882-4800; www.duntonhotsprings.com), 52068 W. Fork Rd., Dolores. Quite possibly the most elegant and most unique lodging in Colorado, Dunton Hot Springs began as a ghost town. The town's old buildings were converted into upscale accommodations. There are 11 cabins on the property and a teepee. All but the teepee have private baths. Guests also have use of the Pony Express Stop with its yoga and Pilates studios, the fully stocked library, and the bath house with steam showers and indoor hot springs. And in keeping with the fact that this was a town from the Old West, there's the saloon, which houses a dance hall and kitchen. A full menu of spa services is available. The cost is $250 per person per day.

RAILROAD CARS D&S RailCamp (970-259-3372 or 1-877-872-4607; www.durangotrain.com). For an entirely unique lodging experience, camp in a converted boxcar along the Animas River in the wilderness. The Durango & Silverton Railroad will drop you and your party (with up to six people) along with your very own RV on rails on the Cascade Canyon Wye. The boxcar has bunk beds, kitchen and dining areas, bathroom (with shower), and enough water for a week. Guests are dropped off on Monday and picked up on Friday. A weeklong stay runs $1,600.

✷ Where to Eat

DINING OUT ♿ **Cyprus Cafe** (970-385-6884), 725 E. Second Ave. Open daily for lunch and dinner (hours change seasonally). Located next door to the Leland House in a century-old Victorian, the Cyprus Cafe serves a delicious and innovative menu of Mediterranean cuisine. Guests can eat inside or, in the summer, take their meal on the garden patio. Salads are made of the freshest greens, and the menu includes such entrées as Colorado lamb, pork chop with pine nuts, and vegetarian dishes. Entrées $18–25.

♿ **Ken and Sue's Place** (970-385-1810), 636 Main Ave. Open for lunch Mon.–Fri. 11–2:30. Dinner served daily 5–10. The menu at Ken and Sue's features Southwest-styled dishes with a contemporary flare. Asian influences can be seen in dishes like the ginger-chicken potstickers. Seafood is also a central theme seen even in salads and sandwiches like the ancho-dusted gulf shrimp salad and grilled tuna steak sandwich. Dishes $8–18.

🍸 ♿ **Ore House** (970-247-5707; www.orehouserestaurant.com), 147 E. College Dr. Open nightly 5–11. The Ore House has been Durango's premier steakhouse since it opened in 1972. Located just a block from the train depot, the interior has an old-timey historical feel. The menu includes top sirloin, NY strip, and filets. For seafood, there's everything from Colorado mountain trout to ahi tuna. During the busy season, the Ore House can get a lot of tourist attention, but that hasn't kept it from becoming a local favorite. Dishes $13–37.

Sow's Ear (970-247-3527; www.silverpicklodge.com/sowsear.htm), 48475 US 550 N., Durango Mountain Resort. Guests seated daily for dinner 5–9. This casual dining room has fantastic views of the West Needles Mountains. The menu has several fantastic steak options as well as seafood, chicken, pork chops, and lamb. Reservations recommended on weekends and holidays. Dinner entrées $10–34 and children's menu items $6.

EATING OUT ♿ **Farquarts & Pizza Mia** (970-247-5440), 725 Main Ave. Open daily 10:30–11. This laid-back pizza place also serves burgers and Mexican food. The walls are covered in vintage posters and advertisements, including a banner for the 1990 Mountain Bike Championships, which were held in Durango. For dessert, try the Build-Your-Own S'mores. You roast them right there at the table. Pizzas $11–20.

Francisco's Restaurante y Cantina (970-247-4098; www.franciscorestaurante.com), 619 Main Ave. Open Mon.–Sat. 11–9:30 (or 10) and Sun. 9–9:30. This Mexican restaurant has been family owned since 1968—to stay in business that long, you know they have to be doing something right. The usual fajitas and burritos sit on the menu alongside upscale dishes like steak and jumbo prawns or the maple-mustard-glazed double-cut pork rib chops. Specialty entrées $14–26 and Mexican dinners $9–16.

Olde Schoolhouse Cafe (970-259-2257), 46778 US 550 N. Located just 2 miles south of Durango Mountain Resort. Call for seasonal hours. During the day, the Olde Schoolhouse is the perfect family restaurant. Not only do they have a full menu of gut-pleasers like brats and chicken wings, they may just serve the best pizza in Colorado. After the kitchen closes, the bar takes on a life of its own and becomes a favorite après-ski hangout (or après-bike, après-rock climbing, whatever).

BAKERIES & COFFEE SHOPS ♿

Brickhouse Cafe and Coffee Bar (970-247-3760; www.brickhousecafe.com), 1849 Main Ave. Open Tues.–Sat. 6:30–2 and Sun. 7–1. Located in a historic residence at the north end of Main Avenue, the Brickhouse Cafe serves breakfast and lunch all day. The decorating in the dining area reflects the home's Victorian roots. Everything on the menu, from coffee and lattes to the *huevos rancheros,* can be ordered for take-out or delivery.

BARS, TAVERNS & BREW PUBS 🍸

Lady Falconburgh's Barley Exchange (970-382-9664), 640 Main Ave. Open daily 11–"late night." This local pub proudly serves more than 140 beers, 38 on tap. Inside, the large four-sided bar allows for socialization. They also serve food—the usual pub grub with some southwestern dishes. It has been voted Durango's best pub and is a perennial favorite with locals.

🍸 **Steamworks Brewing Co.** (970-259-9200), 801 E. Second Ave. Open daily at 11. For locally hand-crafted beer, this brewpub is the spot. They serve a nice pub menu that includes oven-fired pizza. When weather permits, there is seating on the patio.

✷ Entertainment

Bar D Chuckwagon Suppers (970-247-5753 or 1-888-800-5753; www.bardchuckwagon.com), 8080 CR 250. Ticket booth opens at 5:30. Dinner served promptly at 7:30. Beef or chicken $18 and steak $28. Children (under 9) $9.

✷ Selective Shopping

Maria's Bookshop (970-247-1438; www.mariasbookshop.com), 960 Main Ave. Open daily 9–9. The bookstore is named after Maria Martinez, a potter of the San Ildefonso Pueblo, whose work inspired the shop logo. This local bookstore has a surprisingly large inventory. The staff is knowledgeable and open to offering reading suggestions.

O'Farrell Hatmakers of Durango (970-259-8822; www.sundancemall.com/ofarrellhats), 399 Camino Iglesia. If paying upwards of $550 sounds like a lot for a cowboy hat, you might just want to stop by to appreciate the craftsmanship that goes into making such a topper. These beaver-felt fur hats are coveted by the western dandy and the hard-working cowpoke alike. *Forbes* magazine named them the best hat-maker in the country back in 2001, and you will see why.

Rocky Mountain Chocolate Factory (970-259-1408; www.rmcf.com), 561 Main Ave. Though you can now find this confectionary all over North America, it all began here on Main in Durango. The factory is now located at 265 Turner Dr. Call and ask about taking a tour.

Toh-Atin Gallery (970-247-8277 or 1-800-525-0384; www.toh-atin.com), 145 W. Ninth St. Open Mon.–Sat. 9–6 and Sun. 10–5. This gallery carries one of the finest selections of Southwest and Native American art in the state.

✷ Special Events

May: **Iron Horse Bicycle Classic** (www.ironhorsebicycleclassic.com), 3777 Main Ave. This annual race pits cyclists against the Durango & Silverton Narrow-Gauge Railroad in a race to Silverton. The train has a shorter route, but it can only go so fast. Bikes can haul downhill, but they have farther to go. For 35 years, the race has been a coveted Memorial Day Weekend event.

June: **Animas River Days** (970-259-3893). The event involves a river parade and lots of fun on the water.

August: **Durango Cowboy Gathering** (www.durangocowboygathering.org). Celebrating the "rich culture and heritage of the American cowboy," the gathering features cowboy poets, musicians, and storytellers. There's even a gun shoot at the Gun Club Range.

PAGOSA SPRINGS & THE SOUTHERN SAN JUANS

For centuries people have been making their way to this spot, west of the mountains along the San Juan River, to soak in the hot sulfur springs. The town's name, Pagosa Springs, comes from the Ute name for this place. *Pagosa* means "healing waters." The water's medicinal quality was confirmed back in the 19th century by U.S. Army physicians, who proclaimed them to be "the most wonderful and beneficial in medicinal effects that have ever been discovered."

There is a definite Southwest feel to Pagosa that you don't find elsewhere in Colorado. It's a laid-back town where people put a premium on enjoying the outdoors and taking time to soak it all in. For some that means literally soaking, whether in a hot tub or just floating in a tube down the San Juan River. For others it means taking advantage of the town's proximity to the mountains and the San Juan Valley, with all the region's opportunities for hiking, mountain biking, and horseback riding.

North and east of Pagosa Springs are the southern San Juan Mountains. In 1890, Nicholas Creede discovered silver in the area (near the Rio Grande River). The town that bears his name, Creede, is the only town in Mineral County. When silver was discovered, the town's population leapt up to 10,000. In a state full of rowdy mining towns, Creede was considered the rowdiest. Some of the Old West's most famous and infamous characters—the likes of Calamity Jane and Bat Masterson—passed through at one time or other.

Farther north is Lake City, which was founded in 1874 as a mining town. Lake City gets its name from nearby Lake San Cristobal, which was formed 800 years ago by the Slumgullion Earthflow—a portion of a nearby mountain sloughed off and blocked the Gunnison River, creating the lake. Today most of Lake City is a National Historic District, with more than 75 buildings from the 19th century. The town is forever remembered as the place where Alferd Packer and his six companions were stranded in the mountains during a harsh winter in 1874. When spring came, only Packer remained. The rest of the party was dead and eaten.

GUIDANCE **Pagosa Springs Chamber of Commerce & Visitor Center** (970-264-2360 or 1-800-252-2204; www.pagosaspringschamber.com), 402 San Juan Dr.

Creede/Mineral Country Chamber of Commerce (719-658-2374; www.creede.com), 1207 N. Main St.

Lake City Chamber of Commerce (970-944-2527; www.lakecity.com), 800 Gunnison Ave.

More Web sites:

www.pagosarocks.com

www.pagosa.com

GETTING THERE *By car:* Pagosa Springs sits on US 160, which stretches east and west across the state. The town is also easily accessible to nearby Santa Fe (just a 150 miles to the south) via US 84. Creede and Lake City are between US 50 and US 160 on CO 149. They are separated by 50 miles and the Continental Divide, but share this region of the San Juans.

By air: The **Durango–La Plata County Airport** (970-247-8143; www.durango gov.org/services/airport.html), 1000 Airport Rd., is only 60 miles to the west. Three major airlines provide daily service to and from Denver, Phoenix, and Salt Lake City.

MEDICAL EMERGENCIES **Pagosa Springs Family Medicine Center** (970-731-4131), 75 S. Pagosa Blvd., Pagosa Springs.

Rio Grande Hospital (719-657-2510), 0310 CR 14, Del Norte. This hospital offers 24-hour emergency care. Del Norte is 37 miles east of Creede on US 160.

✱ To See & Do

Pagosa Hot Springs. One of the first impressions visitors have when coming to Pagosa for the first time is the smell. The town centers on the Pagosa Hot Springs, which are in fact hot sulphur springs. There are two places that offer ways to soak in the springs. The first is the **Springs Resort** (970-264-2284 or 1-800-225-0934; www.pagosahotsprings.com), 165 Hot Springs Blvd. The resort is open daily in the summer 7–11. In the winter it's open until 1 AM on Fri. and Sat. nights. Water from the Great Pagosa Hot Spring, behind the hotel portion of the resort, is piped to the pool area. There are 18 different pools of varying temperatures for your soaking pleasure. The property is well maintained, and each pool has a distinct character of its own. River water mixes in the pools down by the river's edge—some relief if the springs have gotten you overheated. Adult admission $17.25, seniors $14.25, children (2–10) $9, and infants and toddlers free with an adult. Resort hotel guests soak for free.

Another option is the **Spa at Pagosa Springs** (970-264-5910 or 1-800-832-5523; www.pshotsprings.com), 317 Hot Springs Blvd. Open daily 10–10. More therapeutic in nature, the spa has an indoor bath, swimming pool, and a co-ed hot tub. Adult daily rate $8, seniors $6, and children (3–12) $5.

Chimney Rock Archaeological Area (970-883-5359; www.chimneyrockco.org), 3 miles south of US 160 on CO 151. Visitor center open daily mid-May–Sept. 9–4:30. (In the off-season the organization can be reached at 970-264-

PAGOSA HOT SPRINGS

2287.) Guided walking tours leave daily at 9:30, 10:30, 1, and 2. There's an additional tour at noon from mid-June to mid-Aug.

A thousand years ago, the uniqe geological features of this landscape attracted the attention of the ancestral Pueblo people, who came here and lived on the mountain. The archaeological site has over 200 known structures. The Great House, the Great Kiva, and the Ridge House have been uncovered and reconstructed. The community was related to the people of Chaco Canyon in New Mexico, as well as Mesa Verde 100 miles to the west. In fact, it is believed that Chimney Rock was used as a natural observatory for tracking the sun and, most especially, the moon. Were the people here able to signal their counterparts from the summit of Chimney Rock? Take the two-and-a-half-hour tour and find out. Wear good walking shoes. Adult fee $8, children (5–11) $2, and children under 5 free.

North Clear Creek Falls. About halfway between Creede and Lake City is one of Colorado's most beautiful waterfalls. Easy access from the road, no doubt, plays into the fact that it's also one of the state's most photographed waterfalls. A short way up Forest Rd. 510, east off CO 149, you'll find spectacular views of North Clear Creek Falls as it tumbles into a box canyon.

☂ **Underground Mining Museum** (719-658-0811; www.museumtrail.org/CreedeUndergroundMiningMuseum.asp), Forest Rd. 503 #9, Creede. Open daily in the summer 10–4; fall and spring 10–3. This entire museum facility is underground—dug out of solid rock. Exhibits show the tools and methods used throughout the history of mining. Adult admission $5, seniors $4, and children $3.

The Creede Museum (719-658-2374; www.museumtrail.org/creedehistoricmuseum.asp), Rio Grande Railroad Depot (behind Basham Park), Creede. Open daily in the summer 10–4. Located in a historic rail depot, the museum houses a collection of artifacts from Creede and Mineral County. Admission is free.

Silver Thread Scenic Byway (www.byways.org/explore/byways/2116) is a 75-mile stretch of road between South Fork and Lake City, passing through Creede en route. Along the way, you will pass the Slumgullion Earthflow—a continuously moving mass of earth, 4 miles long, that slid down a mountain 700 years ago, damming the Lake Fork of the Gunnison River and creating Lake San Cristobal.

Alpine Loop Scenic Byway is a scenic route through the mountains and passes west of Lake City that requires a four-wheel-drive vehicle. Begin on Alpine Loop Road up to Engineer Pass. The road turns south and crosses Cinnamon Pass on Cinnamon Pass Road heading east back to Lake City. The route also connects up with Ouray or Silverton. The loop will take you through the ghost towns of Sherman and Animas Forks.

✷ Outdoor Activities

ALPINE SKIING & SNOWBOARDING **Wolf Creek Ski Area** (970-264-5639 or 1-800-754-9653; www.wolfcreekski.com), located east of Pagosa Springs, just east of Wolf Creek Pass on US 160, P.O. Box 2800, Pagosa Springs, CO 81147. No ski area in Colorado gets as much snow as Wolf Creek. With 465 inches of the white stuff falling annually, there is no need for snowmaking equipment here. There's an overall 1,604-foot vertical drop, and the longest of the 77 trails stretches 2 miles. The ski area is serviced by seven lifts. Wolf Creek has no on-site lodging,

CHIMNEY ROCK

ALFERD PACKER

In the winter of 1874, Alferd Packer and five other men left the town of Montrose for Gunnison. Though they were advised to wait until spring, the party was anxious to get to their final destination of Breckenridge to start prospecting for gold. Two months later, while people were starting to wonder whatever happened to the six prospectors, Packer emerged from the mountains . . . alone.

There are conflicting stories about exactly where and when Packer was first spotted. It is clear that sometime in April, he was found in the San Luis Valley, spending lots of money that he didn't have when he went into the mountains. His story, at first, was that one by one members of the party died. The remaining members had eaten the dead men in order to survive. The bodies (or at least what remained), he said, could be found along the trail where the men had died.

True or not, few people were buying his story. He was convicted of murder and cannibalism and jailed in Saguache, Colorado. It wasn't long, however, before the bodies of the prospectors were found. They were not strewn along the path as Packer had claimed. Instead, they were found all together on a plateau near Lake City, and it looked like they had all met a violent end. When the authorities went to Saguache to confront Packer with this information, they found he had escaped.

It was nearly 10 years before the law caught up with Packer, who was living in Wyoming under an alias. This time he told another story—how he went out scouting and came back to find one of the party, Shannon Bell, roasting the flesh of the men he had killed with his hatchet. When Shannon Bell charged at him with the hatchet, Packer said he shot him in self-defense.

The new story did not convince anyone either, and Packer was eventually sentenced to 40 years. He was paroled in 1901 and lived the remainder of his life in Littleton, Colorado. He died in 1907, and because of his service during the Civil War was buried in Littleton Cemetary with full military honors.

Now, more than 130 years since that fatal winter, questions about Packer's guilt or innocence still persist. Recent forensic investigations, which involved Packer's gun (found on Cannibal Plateau in Lake City) and the exhumation of Shannon Bell's body, reveal that Packer did indeed shoot Shannon Bell. The other victims had been killed with a hatchet. The evidence, at least, seems to support Packer's second confession.

Guilty or innocent of murder, Alferd Packer, the Colorado Cannibal, remains one of the more colorful characters in Colorado history, and his legend seems to be forever linked to Lake City and the San Juan Mountains.

but there are two concession stands and a cafeteria-style eatery. With an even number of runs for skiers of all abilities, Wolf Creek is good for groups. Adult all-day lift ticket $48, seniors and children $26, and just the beginner lift $19.

HIKING Pagosa Springs and the San Juan Mountains have hundreds of miles of trails for hiking. For a thorough introduction to the area's vast recreational resources, stop by the Pagosa Springs Visitor Center. They have brochures that cover the best area trails.

Piedra Falls Trail is an easy hike to a spectacular waterfall. To get to the trailhead, take Piedra Road 17 miles north to Middle Fork Road. Turn right, drive 2 miles to the first road on your right, E. Toner Road. At the end of the road is where your path begins. Be advised, E. Toner becomes too dangerous to drive in wet weather. It's a short 15- to 30-minute walk to the falls, which you will hear from the start.

Williams Creek Trail offers a more strenuous hike. It's located about 25 miles north of Pagosa Springs—deep into the San Juan Mountains. Take Piedra Road north 22 miles to Williams Creek Road and turn right. The trailhead at the end of the road begins a 14-mile trek to the Continental Divide.

FISHING The San Juan and the Piedra provide miles of river for fly-fishing. The Piedra River is an angler's dream, with 40 miles of canyon water full of wild brown and rainbow trout. In the Pagosa Springs area, there is Echo Lake and Capote Lake. Farther south is the Navajo Reservoir near the New Mexico border. And to the north in Lake City sits Lake San Cristobal.

Let It Fly (970-264-3189; www.flyfishpagosa.com), 1507 W. US 160 #2, Pagosa Springs. The guides at Let It Fly offer full, half-day, and evening tours on area rivers and creeks. Full-day tour $225, half-day $175, and evening $150.

Dan's Fly Shop (970-944-2281; www.dansflyshop.com), 723 Gunnison Ave., Lake City. For nearly five decades Dan has been tying flies and introducing anglers to the best fishing in the San Juans. Through the fly shop, Lake City Angling Services leads guided fishing trips for all level of anglers. The shop has everything you need for a day out on the water, from custom rods to hand-tied flies. Dan also keeps up a fly-fishing museum with vintage equipment and fishing supplies from the Lake City area. Trips should be reserved 4–8 weeks in advance if possible.

GOLF **Pagosa Springs Golf Club** (970-731-4755; www.golfpagosa.com), 1 Pines Club Pl. Located 3 miles west of Pagosa Springs on US 160 at the base of the San Juan Mountains. This golf club has three nine-hole sections (Meadows, Piñon, and Ponderosa) that combine for three 18-hole courses. Greens fees for 18 holes $79 (from May–Oct.); off-season $46.

HORSEBACK RIDING **Astradle a Saddle** (970-731-5076; www.astraddleasaddle.com), P.O. Box 1216, Pagosa Springs, CO 81147. Located 4 miles west of the Wyndham Resort at Pagosa on US 160. This outfitter offers scenic trail rides. Be sure to also ask about their barbeque dinners and winter sleigh rides. One-hour trail rides $30 and two-hour rides $45. The three-and-a-half-hour ride runs $65 (this one climbs 1,500 feet).

RIVER SPORTS **Pagosa Outside** (970-264-4202; www.pagosaoutside.com), 350 Pagosa St. This outfitter is a one-stop shop for outdoor recreation. They lead rafting trips and mountain-biking tours, as well as guided fly-fishing trips through Backcountry Angler. There are several rafting options on the San Juan: half-day trips through Mesa and Montezuma canyons and a two-hour float through town. For a relaxing afternoon, consider renting an inflatable kayak or river tube. Once you float through town, you can jump on the shuttle van (small fee for the whole day) and run the river again. Adult Mesa Canyon trip $59 and children (under 11) $44. Adult Montezuma Canyon trip $65 and children $50. Adult two-hour trip $34 and children $29.

GREEN SPACE **Echo Canyon Lake State Wilderness Area** (www.wildlife.state.co.us), located 4 miles south of Pagosa Springs on US 84. The Echo Canyon Reservoir was built in 1968 to provide a spot for the public to go fishing. The 211-acre lake is used for fishing, boating, hunting, and picnicking. There are often opportunities to view wildlife as well. From the park, you can see the San Juans resting picturesquely to the north.

Navajo State Park (970-883-2208; www.parks.state.co.us/parks/navajo), 1526 CR 982, Arboles. Open 24 hours. The park is located near the New Mexico border along the western shore of Navajo Reservoir. To get there, follow CO 151 south of US 160. Navajo Reservoir has over 15,000 surface acres and stretches 35 miles up the San Juan River. There are some short trails in the park, but the real attraction is the water. For more than a day trip, the park has three campgrounds and two areas set aside with primitive campsites. They also have three cabins for rent. Daily vehicle pass $6.

* Lodging

HOTELS & MOTELS 🐾 ♿ **The Springs Resort** (970-264-4168 or 1-800-225-0934; www.pagosahotsprings.com), 165 Hot Springs Blvd., Pagosa Springs. The accommodations are clean and spacious, but the best feature of the resort is that guests get free access to the resort soaking pools. There is also a spa, salon, and boutique on the premises, which if taken advantage of can make for a very pampered stay. Rooms $149–200, which includes 24-hour access to the springs.

"1" 🐾 ♿ **Matterhorn Mountain Motel** (970-944-2210; www.matterhornmotel.com), 409 Bluff St., Lake City. For a comfortable and affordable stay in Lake City, the Matterhorn is the place. This motel, built in the 1940s, has 12 rooms (six with kitchens) and two cabins—all the accommodations have cable TV. Rooms $85–145.

BED & BREAKFASTS "1" 🐾 **Old Firehouse Bed & Breakfast** (719-658-0212; www.theoldfirehouse.com), 123 N. Main St., Creede. The inn's three rooms and one suite all have a private bath, TV, and DSL Internet access. The rooms are simply decorated in a casually western style—the beds all have beautiful quilts. Not content to simply provide lodging, the Old Firehouse is also a restaurant and ice-cream parlor. Depending on the season, breakfast is served off the menu in the inn's restaurant or is a Continental affair provided in the B&B common area. Rooms $85–110 and suite $110–145.

CAMPGROUNDS **Bruce Spruce Ranch** (970-264-5374; www.brucespruceranch.com), 231 West Fork Rd., Pagosa Springs. Nestled in the mountains, this wooded campground has 32 RV sites (most with full hook-ups), an open tent area, and a mess of cabins. Tent sites $18, RV sites $22, and cabins $48–117.

Pagosa Riverside Campground and Camper Cabins (970-264-5874 or 1-888-785-3234), P.O. Box 268 Pagosa Springs, CO 81147. Located on US 160, 1.3 miles east of US 84. Open Apr.–Nov. This campground sits next to the San Juan River and has plenty of shady sites. For RVs, there are sites with full hook-ups, including cable TV and phone lines. Tent sites $20 and RV sites $27–30.

CABINS & COTTAGES **Cabins at Hartland Ranch** (970-264-1111 or 1-866-377-1115; www.hartlandranch.com), 403 CR 200 (Snowball Rd.), Pagosa Springs. Hartland Ranch has five vacation cabins spread out on 85 acres, each with full kitchen, satellite TV, and Internet. The cabins have one to three bedrooms, and each bedroom has its own bath, fireplace, and TV. The high-ceilinged living rooms offer expansive views. Cabins $175–350.

L-Z Ranch Cabins (970-264-5548; www.lbarzcabins.com), 2244 E. US 160, Pagosa Springs. Two large log cabins, which easily sleep four people, come with full kitchen, bath, and living room area. The genuine rugged charm of these cabins is felt when you see exposed beams or a stone fireplace, but the rustic nature of the lodgings does not extend so far that you can't enjoy modern conveniences like cable TV and kitchen appliances. Cabins $135–145 (for four people).

Where to Eat

DINING OUT ♿ **JJ's Upstream Restaurant** (970-264-9100), 356 E. US 160, Pagosa Springs. Open daily for dinner 4–9. Aside from the fantastic food, the best feature of JJ's is the great patio seating by the river. As it gets dark, lights are used to illuminate the water just beyond the dining area. The menu includes steak, seafood, and your typical American fare. The artichoke dip is really good. From 4–6 PM, they offer an Early Bird Special, but be sure to ask for the Early Bird Menu. Average entrée around $25 (Early Bird entrées $11).

♿ **Antler's Rio Grande Riverside Restaurant** (719-658-2423; www.antlerslodge.com), 26222 CO 149, Creede. Open in the summer daily for dinner at 5. Closed after Sept. The Antler's Rio Grande Lodge is home to their Riverside Restaurant. The menu is known for gourmet appetizers, like hot smoked Pacific salmon rillettes, as well as steak and seafood entrées. Reservations highly recommended.

EATING OUT ♿ **Boss Hogs** (970-731-2626), 157 Navajo Trails Dr., Pagosa Springs. Open daily 11–10. This barbeque joint is known as much for its disjointed decorating as it is for serving great steaks and ribs. The soup and salad bar is always fresh, and the portions are huge. Dinner entrées $13–30.

♿ **The Elkhorn Cafe** (970-264-2146), 438 Pagosa St., Pagosa Springs. Open daily 6–9. Located in downtown Pagosa Springs, the Elkhorn menu is full of classic Mexican food with a touch of Colorado. The green chili finds its way into several dishes and is excellent. Breakfast, lunch, and dinner are all done well here. For dessert, try the stuffed sopapillas. Dishes $6–10.

🍸 ♿ **Kip's Grill & San Juan Room** (719-658-0220; www.kipsgrill.com), 5th and Main St., Creede. Open daily from May–Sept. 11–8. This little cantina serves baja-style tacos, hamburgers, and hot dogs. They also have good margaritas, Colorado microbrews on tap, and Mexican imports on hand. Dinner and lunch dishes $7–10.

✷ Entertainment

♿ **Creede Repertory Theatre** (719-658-2540; www.creederep.org), 124 N. Main St., Creede. In 1966, as the townsfolk of Creede watched the mining industry decline, it was decided that the town needed something to bring in business. They decided to create a theater and sent out a letter to a number of colleges and universities asking talented young theater majors to come to Creede. Twelve students from the University of Kansas answered the call, and the Creede Repertory Theatre was born. Every season, the ensemble cast performs a variety of plays. The quality of theatre in Creede is highly praised locally and nationally. Hundreds audition every year to be part of the cast. Shows are performed in the Old Creede Opera House. The success of the summer season has led to the creation of an extended season that goes through Sept. Tickets $17–26.

TELLURIDE & OURAY

Touring Colorado's mountain towns, folks will notice a pattern to the terrain. In most cases there are two ways in and out of town—the easy way (up the valley) and the hard way (over the mountain). Aspen, for example, is approached from the north by a wide four-lane highway. To the south is the Independence Pass, the highest paved pass in North America. The highway that leads into Telluride is much as you'd expect, perhaps the walls are a bit steep, but the way out is nearly impassable. That doesn't mean there is no way out, but Black Bear Road, which leads west over Black Bear Pass, is so narrow and steep that traffic is only allowed in one direction—down.

The steep walls that surround Telluride add significantly to its scenic beauty, which is enhanced by its old mountain mining town charm. Strict rules have been established on what kinds of buildings can be built in Telluride. They must, it seems, complement the town's historic character and emulate the "old mining town" look. In recent years this translates into either quaint Victorian cottages or larger mill-like structures with steel roofs, and distressed plank exteriors. Interestingly, though Telluride would like to maintain the look of its mining heritage, recent efforts to open an actual small hard-rock mining operation in the nearby mountains have been thwarted on the grounds that the helicopters transporting gear to the mine would put off tourists.

Telluride's story is similar to that of many mining towns. The town began as a mining camp when gold and silver was discovered in 1875. Though thousands came to join in the mining operations, the real boom didn't take off until 1890 when the railroad arrived. As remote mining towns often were, Telluride was rowdy, with plenty of saloons and a thriving red-light district. In 1889, Butch Cassidy robbed his first bank here. In 1891, Telluride made history when Lucien Lucius Nunn called on George Westinghouse and the enigmatic Nikola Tesla to power his mines with electricity. South of Telluride in the town of Ames they constructed a high-voltage generator. In keeping with Tesla's ideas, the generator produced alternating current, and Telluride became the first town in the world to light its streetlamps with alternating current.

Skiing didn't come to Telluride until the 1970s. As an isolated ski town, Telluride was laid back, a haven for hippies who moved in to take advantage of the cheap property rates and fantastic natural surroundings. But money soon

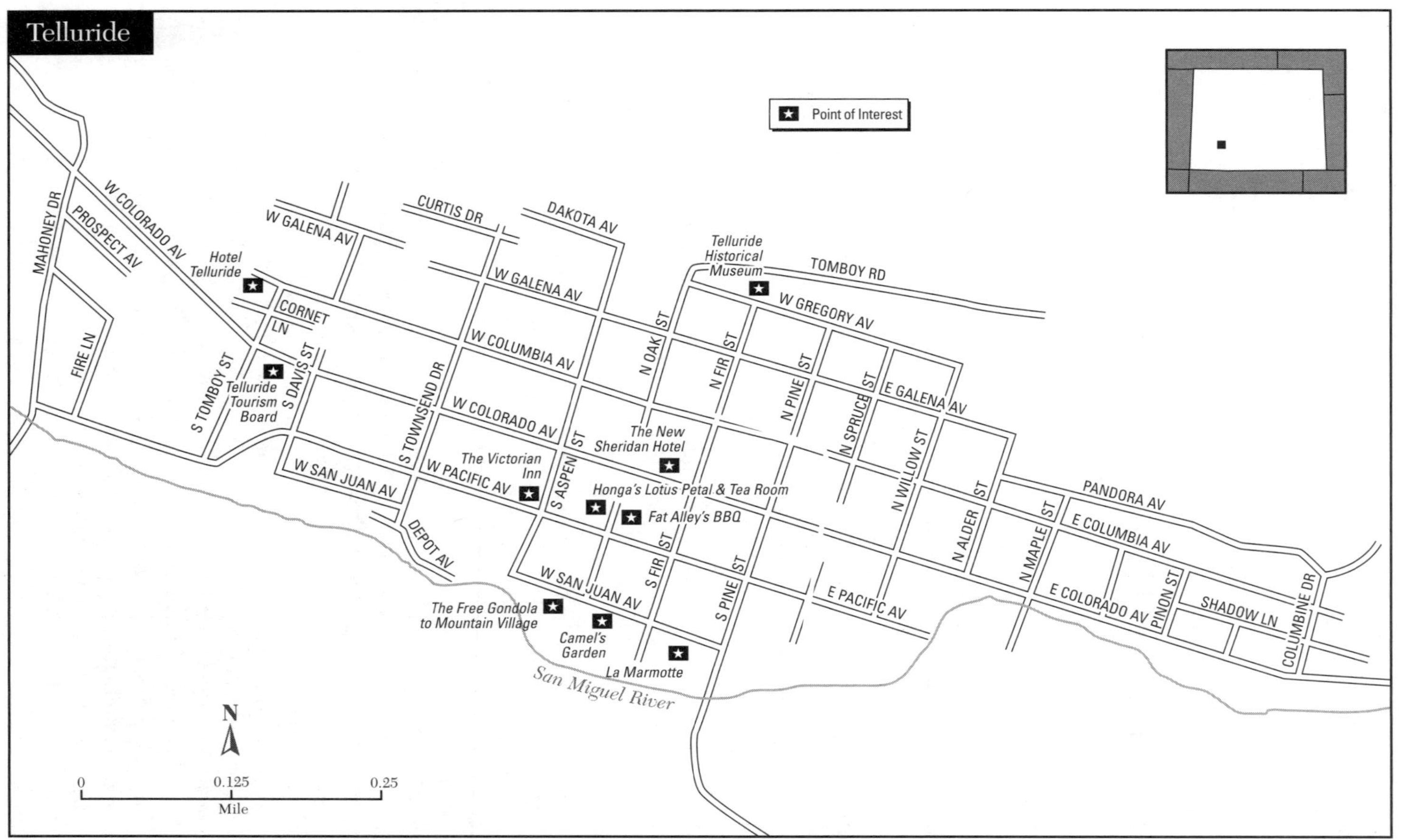
Telluride
Point of Interest
Hotel Telluride
Telluride Tourism Board
Telluride Historical Museum
The New Sheridan Hotel
The Victorian Inn
Honga's Lotus Petal & Tea Room
Fat Alley's BBQ
The Free Gondola to Mountain Village
Camel's Garden
La Marmotte
San Miguel River
MAHONEY DR
PROSPECT AV
W COLORADO AV
FIRE LN
W GALENA AV
CURTIS DR
DAKOTA AV
CORNET LN
S TOMBOY ST
S DAVIS ST
S TOWNSEND DR
W COLUMBIA AV
W COLORADO AV
W PACIFIC AV
W SAN JUAN AV
DEPOT AV
S ASPEN ST
N OAK ST
N FIR ST
S FIR ST
N PINE ST
S PINE ST
N SPRUCE ST
N WILLOW ST
N ALDER ST
N MAPLE ST
PINON ST
TOMBOY RD
W GREGORY AV
E GALENA AV
PANDORA AV
E COLUMBIA AV
E COLORADO AV
E PACIFIC AV
SHADOW LN
COLUMBINE DR
N
0
0.125
0.25
Mile

followed, and after the airport was built in the mid-1980s, Telluride took off. A gondola now takes people up and over the mountain to the ski resort. Mountain Village, on the other side, has become an official town and an entire resort community has risen out of thin air. Because of the region's naturally steep terrain, Telluride offers some hellacious descents. There are also some long, gentle slopes, and the ski area has become a favorite with families.

East of Telluride, over the mountain, sits the little burg of Ouray. Also a mining town at one point, today people come to Ouray to get into the mountains. A couple of companies in town rent Jeeps and take passengers on Jeep tours of the region's spectacular mountain meadows and passes. In the summer, the flowers are fantastic. In the winter, ice climbers come to try their hand at Ouray's ice-climbing park.

Most of the attractions, lodgings, and restaurants listed below are open year-round. Many, however, reduce hours significantly for about six weeks in the spring and fall. Be sure to call ahead during these two off-seasons. Unless otherwise indicated, all addresses are in Telluride.

GUIDANCE **Telluride Tourism Board** (www.visittelluride.com), 630 W. Colorado Ave. Open daily 8–8. The Tourism Board has plenty of literature to guide your stay in Telluride.

More Web sites:

www.telluridevisitorguide.com

www.telluride.com

DOWNTOWN TELLURIDE

GETTING THERE *By car:* Getting to Ouray from the south requires a drive along the Million Dollar Highway up from Durango. From here, Telluride is a short drive north to Ridgeway, and then west on CO 62 and south on CO 145. From Cortez, CO 145 heads northeast in a near-direct route to Telluride.

By air: Both United and Frontier Airlines offer service to and from the **Telluride Regional Airport** (970-728-5313; www.tellurideairport.com), 1500 Last Dollar Rd. # 1.

GETTING AROUND *By bus:* The free **Telluride Bus** (970-728-5700) runs an in-town loop every 20 minutes.

By dial-a-ride: For guests and residents of Mountain Village, free transportation around town can be arranged by calling the **Mountain Village Dial-a-Ride** (970-728-8888). Available daily in the winter 6:30 AM–12:30 AM; summer 7 AM–12:30 AM.

By gondola: Getting from Telluride to nearby Mountain Village is simply the matter of taking a free gondola ride up and over the mountain. The **gondola** (970-728-0588) runs from the north end of Oak Street into the heart of Mountain Village from 7 AM–midnight every day from Nov. 17–Apr. 8 and May 24–Oct. 21.

MEDICAL EMERGENCIES **Telluride Medical Center** (970-728-3848; www.telluridemedicalcenter.org), 500 S. Pacific Ave. The medical center offers 24-hour emergency service.

✷ To See & Do

↑ ♿ **Telluride Historical Museum** (970-728-3344; www.telluridemuseum.com), 201 W. Gregory Ave. Open Tues.–Sat. 11–5 (until 7 on Thurs.) and Sun. 1–5. The local museum is housed in the Old Miner's Hospital Building. Since 1966, the museum has sought to preserve the region's history while providing

FREE GONDOLA TO MOUNTAIN VILLAGE

educational opportunities for the public. The museum has many hands-on exhibits that illustrate Telluride's colorful history—a history that begins with the Ute people who camped and hunted in the area and continues on in the rowdy stories of a Old West mining town. Of particular interest is the replica of the Tomboy Bride Cabin, which shines some light on the life of women around the turn of the century in the mountains of western Colorado. Adult admission $5, seniors and students (6–17) $3, and children under 6 free.

Box Canyon Falls and Park (970-325-7080). Driving south out of Ouray on US 550, the entrance to Box Canyon is at the bend of the first switchback on CR 361. Open May–Oct. 8–7 and 10–10 the rest of the year. A short walk from the parking lot takes you into Box Canyon, across a steel platform, to a very impressive waterfall. The canyon is narrow, yet it seems the rock should not be able to hold in the rushing torrent as it drops 285 feet. So much power within such a tight space is truly sublime. From the steel platform, you can take the stairs to the bottom of the canyon for a different perspective on the falls. Another trail takes you to the top of the canyon where there's an impressive bridge. Adult admission $3, seniors $2.50, and children (6–12) $1.50.

Bachelor-Syracuse Mine Tour (970-325-0220 or 1-800-227-8545; www.bachelorsyracusemine.com), 1222 CR 14, Ouray. Tours leave on the hour daily 9–4 throughout the summer. In June and Aug., the last tour is at 5. Closed July 4th. The hour-long tour at the Bachelor-Syracuse Mine takes you deep into Gold Hill by train to see the workings of an actual gold and silver mine. Afterward, learn how to pan for gold in the stream that runs out of the mine. If you have time, come early in the day and enjoy the all-you-can-eat buffet at the mine's outdoor cafe. Adult tour $16.95 and children (4–11) $8.95.

♿ **Ouray Hot Springs Pool** (970-325-7073), 1200 Main St., Ouray. Summer hours Mon.–Fri. noon–8:45 and Sat. and Sun. 11–8:45. Open year-round, this outdoor pool is fed by the local hot springs. It is divided into three temperature levels—the coolest is cool enough to swim laps. There's also a waterslide. Adult rate $10, seniors and students (7–12) $8, children (3–6) $5, and children under 3 free.

Orvis Hot Springs (970-626-5324; www.orvishotsprings.com), 1585 CR 3, Ridgway. Open daily 9–10. The facility has both indoor and outdoor soaking pools. Outside there's the Island Pond with a waterfall or the Lobster Pot that gets up to 114 degrees. In addition to the indoor pool, there's a private soaking tub that's available to whoever gets to it first. Adult all-day admission $14, children (4–12) $5, and children under 4 free.

Million Dollar Highway is what they call the 75-mile stretch of road between Durango and Ouray. No one is certain where the name came from. Some say it cost a million dollars to build each mile of the highway, which reaches 11,008 feet at Red Mountain Pass. Others say that the dirt used to built the road contained gold ore. Though the moniker is applied to that entire section of US 550, it is the 12 miles south of Ouray that have earned the road its white-knuckle reputation. Along the route old mining operations can be seen on the mountainsides. There are beautiful vistas at every nail-biting turn.

San Juan Skyway Byway (www.byways.org/explore/byways/2101). This 230-mile loop takes you around to Cortez, over to Durango, and back up to Ouray and then Telluride. (See Durango, To See & Do for more information.)

✷ Outdoor Activities

ALPINE SKIING & SNOWBOARDING **Telluride Ski Resort** (970-728-6900; www.tellurideskiresort.com). Lifts run daily during ski season 9–4. From Telluride, the mountain can look a little intimidating—a few lifts heading up from town and all black diamonds coming down. Over on the Mountain Village side, however, the perspective widens considerably. The ski area offers 1,700 skiable acres with an overall vertical drop of 3,530 feet. The longest of the 84 runs is Galloping Goose, a gently sloping 4.6 miles. The number of trails for beginner, intermediate, and advanced skiers is pretty evenly distributed—as are the three terrain parks. For the 2007–2008 ski season, the resort opened eight runs of backcountry-style terrain in Black Iron Bowl. The new runs are accessible by a 10- to 30-minute hike along Prospect Ridge from the top of Lift 12. Adult full-day lift ticket $72, seniors $69, and children (6–12) $52.

Lee's Ski Hill, Ouray. Located east of town on Third Avenue, a free rope tow operates on weekends and during the week in the late afternoon. The short run only drops 75 vertical feet and provides a great opportunity for kids learning the basics of skiing. The hill opens once there's a 9-inch base.

Boot Doctor (970-728-8954 or 1-800-592-6883; www.bootdoctor.com), 650 Mountain Village Blvd. Open daily in the winter 8–7. Located in Mountain Village at the base of the gondola and Lift 4. Boot Doctor primarily makes custom ski boots. They also rent equipment.

CROSS-COUNTRY SKIING & SNOWSHOEING **Telluride Nordic Trails** (970-728-1144; www.telluridenordic.com), Telluride Town Park, 500 E. Colorado Ave. This organization grooms trails for cross-country skiing at Trout Lake, Priest Lake, and Faraway Ranch. They also provide ski lessons and an equipment swap, and they organize an annual Nordic ski race.

TopAten Nordic and Snowshoe Trails (970-728-7517; www.tellurideskiresort.com). Located at the top of Lift 10, the ski and snowshoe area has over 6 miles of groomed trails. There is also a warming tipi and rest rooms. If you don't already have a pass for skiing, you can purchase a passenger lift ticket for Lift 10 for $20—this allows you access to the facilities with Nordic gear and snowshoes.

San Juan Hut System (970-626-3033; www.sanjuanhuts.com), P.O. Box 775, Ridgway. The hut system maintains five backcountry huts that connect Telluride, Ridgway, and Ouray along a route the skirts the Mt. Sneffels Wilderness. A stay at each hut will run $28. There's only room for eight in each hut, so reservations are a must.

Ouray Trail Group (970-325-4288; www.ouraytrails.org), P.O. Box 50, Ouray, CO 81427. The Trail Group publishes a map describing the trails in Ouray County. A branch of the Trail Group, the Ouray County Nordic Council, grooms several miles of trails in the Ouray area for cross-country skiing. Snowshoers are welcome to share the trail but must avoid tramping the set tracks.

MOUNTAIN VILLAGE

FISHING **San Miguel Anglers** (970-728-4477; www.sanmiguelanglers.com), 150 W. Colorado Ave. The San Miguel River flows from out from Telluride to the northwest, where it eventually flows into the Dolores. The guides at San Miguel Anglers lead full- and half-day fishing trips on the San Miguel. They also offer one-on-one fly-fishing instruction. A one-person, half-day trip runs $195 and a full-day trip $260. The per-person rate decreases with each additional guest. Fly-fishing school $300.

RIGS Fly Shop & Guide Service (1-888-626-4460; www.fishrigs.com), 555 Sherman St., Ste 2, Ridgway. The guides at RIGS offer several fly-fishing trips on private sections of the Uncompahgre River. They offer half- and full-day trips as well as fishing instruction. A one-person, half-day trip is $210.

FOUR-WHEELING One of Ouray's biggest activities is four-wheeling through the surrounding mountains. Old mining roads and railroad grades offer unprecedented access to stunning mountain views. In the middle of summer, folks go up to see the wildflowers blooming in the high mountain meadows. There are plenty of reasonably, safe roads to take in the area; Black Bear Road is not one of them. For experienced, mountain-tested four-wheelers, the road is considered a challenge. The road begins at Red Mountain Pass on US 550 and heads up to Black Bear Pass. It then begins a treacherous descent to Telluride, down a mess of steep/narrow switchbacks.

Switzerland of America Tours (970-325-4484 or 1-800-432-5337; www.soajeep.com), 226 Seventh Ave., Ouray. For four-wheel tours, Switzerland of America will take you up into the mountains to explore ghost towns and discover old mining operations or simply gaze upon meadows of wildflowers and scenic waterfalls. Half- and full-day trips are available. For those interested in ditching the driver and taking the wheel themselves, the company also rents Jeep Wranglers. Half-day tours $60, full day $120, and Jeep rental $135–145.

HIKING Telluride is a great town for hikers. Many trails leave right from town. One of the most popular is the trail to Bridal Veil Falls. It's 2.2 miles to the top of the falls, and the hike is moderate to difficult. The trail begins a couple of miles east of town on CO 145, where the asphalt ends.

Telluride Adventures (970-728-4101; www.tellurideadventures.com), 300 S. Mahoney Ave. Among other things, the folks at Telluride Adventures lead guided hiking tours. They lead full- and half-day treks as well as multiday backpacking trips. Half-day hike $100 and full day $125.

HORSEBACK RIDING **Telluride Horseback Adventures** (970-728-9611; www.ridewithroudy.com), 242 Hawn Ln. Roudy Roudebush has a motto: "Gentle horses for gentle people, fast horses for fast people, and for people who don't like to ride, horses that don't like to be rode." Roudy offers trail rides year-round, and in the winter he takes guests on a sleigh ride around the Mountain Village Nordic Ski Area. Rides last from one hour up to a whole day. Call to make reservations.

ICE CLIMBING **Ouray Ice Park** (970-325-4288; www.ourayicepark.com), Uncompahgre Gorge, Ouray. The ice park is located south of town—take CO 361 toward Box Canyon, but stay left at the split. There's parking by the upper bridge. Every year, hundreds of climbers come to Ouray to climb the cliffs at the world's first park devoted soley to ice climbing. The Uncompahgre Gorge was used for ice climbing in the past, but once water from nearby sources was redirected over the cliff walls, the gorge became a real-live attraction. There are 13 different climbing areas, including a Kid's Climbing Park. Because the park is entirely run by the generosity of those who give their time and money to the project, admission is free. However donations are appreciated.

MOUNTAIN BIKING For a gut-busting climb, try the 17-mile route from Telluride to Ouray over Imogene Pass (elevation 13,114 feet). The initial ascent climbs over 4,300 feet. The route is popular with the four-wheel crowd—so if you are heading to the mountains to escape traffic, try another trail.

For a true mountain bike journey, the **San Juan Hut System** (970-626-3033; www.sanjuanhuts.com), P.O. Box 775, Ridgway, operates along a 215-mile route of backcountry roads from Telluride to Moab. About every 35 miles, riders crash for the night at one of the huts. The trip takes seven days and six nights and costs $620 per person. In exchange, riders get a sleeping bag and a place to sleep, three meals a day, and trail descriptions and maps.

Further Adventures (1-800-592-6883; www.furtheradventures.com), 650 Mountain Village Blvd., Mountain Village. This outfitter leads half-, full-, and multiday mountain bike trips all summer for riders of all experience. For beginners, they have the half-day Lizard Head to Galloping Goose ride, which begins with riders being shuttled up to a higher elevation by van and then riding a gentle grade back down to the valley. Prices vary by ride, but a half-day ride for one usually runs about $100. It gets cheaper per person when you add people to your group.

* Lodging

HOTELS **Camel's Garden** (1-888-772-2635; www.camelsgarden.com), 250 W. San Juan Ave. Located kitty-corner to the gondola, the Camel's Garden has 35 rooms, suites, and condos. From the outside, like most buildings in Telluride, the architecture pulls from the town's mining days. Inside, the hotel has a more modern feel. Rooms are furnished in a contemporary style, like Italian marble bathrooms and cherry-oak furniture. Rooms have fireplaces, and most have balconies with a view of town or the mountain. A continental breakfast is served every morning. Accommodations $275–675.

The Hotel Telluride (970-369-1188 or 1-866-468-3501; www.thehoteltelluride.com), 199 N. Cornet St. The spacious rooms at the Hotel Telluride are tastefully decorated with southwestern mountain touches. Luxury is their angle, and they promise guests a wonderful night of rest on their "Incredible Bed," which features 250-thread-count sheets, feather bedding, and a down comforter. A full breakfast is served to guests daily in the Bistro. Rooms $399–936.

The New Sheridan Hotel (970-728-4351 or 1-800-200-1891; www.newsheridan.com), 231 W. Colorado Ave. Located in the heart of Telluride, the original Sheridan opened its doors in 1891. Not long after, it burned to the ground, and the New Sheridan was built (in 1895). For well over a hundred years, the Sheridan has been welcoming guests to Telluride. Today the hotel strives to maintain the building's historic character, and the Victorian style is preserved throughout the hotel. A full breakfast is served daily. The hotel also has a bar (the oldest in Telluride) and a restaurant, the New Sheridan Chop House. Rooms $150–425.

The Victorian Inn (970-728-6601 or 1-800-611-9893; www.tellurideinn.com), 401 W. Pacific Ave. As Telluride continues to grow, finding affordable accommodations in town gets harder and harder. The Victorian

NEW SHERIDAN HOTEL

Inn remains one of the most affordable stays in town. The rooms are spacious and clean. There is no air-conditioning in the summer, but the rooms cool off plenty overnight. A continental breakfast is served every morning. Rooms $79–249.

"1" ♿ **Inn at Lost Creek** (970-729-5678 or 1-888-601-5678; www.innatlostcreek.com), 119 Lost Creek Ln., Mountain Village. The luxurious accommodations at Lost Creek are located in the heart of Mountain Village, an easy walk from the gondola. The lobby is warm and inviting, and the rooms are high-end. Rooms have flat-screen HDTVs, a fireplace, and a large jetted tub. It's a perfect place to rest after a day on the slopes. The inn offers complimentary ski waxing and deburring. Rooms and suites $190–1,895.

"1" ♿ **Beaumont Hotel** (970-325-7000 or 1-888-447-3255; www.beaumonthotel.com), 505 Main St., Ouray. The Beaumont is a quaint hotel with 12 rooms. Each room is uniquely decorated in a style reminiscent of the hotel's Victorian past, but entirely contemporary and tasteful. Rooms, junior suites, and suites are available, all with great views of the surrounding peaks. Rooms and suites $125–350.

BED & BREAKFASTS "1" **Spangler House** (970-325-4944; www.spanglerhouse.com), 520 Second St., Ouray. Innkeepers Jill and Steven Scheu run one of the nicest B&Bs around. The inn has five rooms and one suite, all with their own private bath. The common areas are warm and welcoming, perfectly comfortable after a long day sight-seeing. Amenities include satellite TV, wireless Internet, and a hot tub on the back deck. In the morning Steve cooks up a great breakfast—stuffed French toast, blueberry pancakes, etc. Accommodations $85–170.

"1" ♿ **China Clipper Inn** (970-325-0565 or 1-800-315-0565; www.chinaclipperinn.com), 525 Second St., Ouray. Built in 1995, the China Clipper Inn was intended from the start as a B&B. The inn's exterior in not at all out of place with the historic qualities of Ouray. Inside, the inn's 12 rooms are decorated in a British Colonial style. Many rooms have jetted tubs, fireplaces, decks, and private entrances. The honeymoon suites have fireplaces and Jacuzzi tubs for two. A full breakfast is served daily in the dining room. Rooms $85–210.

CAMPGROUNDS "1" **Ouray KOA** (970-325-4736 or 1-800-562-8026; www.koa.com/where/co/06158), 225 CR 23, Ouray. Open May–Sept. The campground has tent sites and RV sites with electric and full hook-ups. The grounds sit along the Uncompahgre River, and a stream passes through the property. There's a camp hot tub, and every weekend they put on a Texas barbeque with live bluegrass music. Tent sites $27, RV sites $30–38.50, and Kabins $57.50.

✷ Where to Eat

DINING OUT Reservations are recommended.

🍸 ♿ **221 South Oak** (970-728-9507; www.221southoak.com), 221 S. Oak St., Telluride. Open for dinner Mon.–Sat. 6–10. A short walk from the gondola, the restaurant is set in one of the town's historic homes, adding to its intimate charm. The menu is New American cuisine with dishes like grilled swordfish with glass noodles, mushrooms, and tea broth. Chef Eliza Gavin is also the author of *Foreplay: A Book of Appeteasers.* Entrées $24–36.

Y ♿ **Allred's** (970-728-7474; www.allredsrestaurant.com), top of the gondola. Open daily for dinner 5:30–9. Sitting 1,800 feet above Telluride affords fantastic views of the town—its lights a sparkling mass below. Known as much for its contemporary American cuisine and excellent wine list as for the view, Allred's offers fine dining from the top of the free gondola in San Sophia station. Local ingredients of the highest quality go into preparing the menu, which features steak and seafood, as well as elk, lamb, and duck. Dishes $26–36.

Honga's Lotus Petal & Tea Room (970-728-5134), 133 S. Oak St. Open daily for dinner 5:30–10. Pan-Asian cuisine is served in a restored Victorian just off Colorado Avenue. Only the freshest and best ingredients go into their menu, which includes dishes inspired by culinary traditions of Japan, Thailand, and Bali. Fish is flown in daily for their sushi and sashimi. Dishes $8–24.

La Marmotte (970-728-6232; www.lamarmotte.com), 150 W. San Juan Ave. Serving dinner daily with seating beginning at 6. The menu at La Marmotte changes daily, reflecting the availability of fresh local produce. Located in the town's 100-year-old ice house, this rustic French bistro promises an intimate dining experience. Appetizers like yellowfin tuna tartar and hot and cold foie gras with cherry chutney, prepare the way for entrées like sauté of Muscovy duck and seared Alaskan salmon. Dishes $25–40.

♿ **New Sheridan Chop House** (970-728-9700; www.newsheridan.com), 233 W. Colorado Ave. Open daily for dinner 5:30–9. Serving diners in the New Sheridan Hotel since 1895, the Chop House has a reputation for great meals. Steak and seafood top the menu, and the restaurant prides itself on stocking over 125 bottles of excellent wine to complement every entrée. The Chop House also serves a cheese course—three cheeses nightly (selection changes often). Entrées $20–45.

EATING OUT Y ♿ **Chair 8** (970-728-8887; www.chair8.com), 250 W. San Juan Ave. Open daily for lunch and dinner 11–9 and for breakfast Mon.–Fri. 8–11. Located at the base of the gondola and Lift 8, this après-ski destination is retro-loaded with a 1970s feel. The menu in chock full of great American comfort food, all with a gourmet twist—consider the PB&J made with roasted pecan butter, fig jelly, and foie gras. Lunch and dinner dishes $5–12.

Fat Alley's BBQ (970-728-3985), 122 S. Oak St. Open daily 11–10. For barbeque, there's no other restaurant in town. Fat Alley's makes it all—brisket, ribs, pulled-pork sandwiches, and roasted chicken. Sides include coleslaw, potato salad, and sweet potato fries. They also have cheeseburgers and cheesesteak, but how can anyone order a cheeseburger with all that sweet barbeque aroma in the air. Sandwiches $8.50–10 and other dishes $10–20.

Y ♿ **Las Montañas** (970-728-5114; www.lasmontanastelluride.com), 100 W. Colorado Ave. Open in the summer Mon.–Fri. 10–10 and Sat. and Sun. 8–10; in winter, open daily 9–10.

A couple of years back, Las Montañas was one of the newer Mexican restaurants in town, serving a diverse pan-Latino menu. They purchased Telluride's oldest Mexican restaurant and merged both operations at a new location on Colorado Avenue. Today, the menu includes both traditional Mexican dishes (ala Sofio's) and more innovative cuisine. Dinner entrées $16–22.

Y ♿ **The Outlaw Restaurant** (970-325-4366; www.outlawrestaurant.com), 610 Main St., Ouray. The Outlaw Restaurant is nothing if not a classic steakhouse. Always busy, they serve steak, seafood, and a number of highly praised pasta dishes. The wine list has something for most palates. Dishes $16–27. If dining indoors isn't your style, the Outlaw Restaurant and Colorado West Jeep Tours (970-325-4014) will drive you up into the mountains for an Outlaw Mountain Cookout. Call Colorado West for reservations and more information.

BAKERIES & COFFEE SHOPS **Maggie's Bakery & Café** (970-728-3334), 217 E. Colorado Ave. Open Mon.–Fri. 6:30–4 and Sat. and Sun. 7:30–4. Maggie's has a great selection of fresh-baked goods—be sure to try one of their gigantic cinnamon rolls. The cafe serves hot breakfast items and lunch daily.

♿ **Steaming Bean Coffeehouse** (970-369-5575; www.thebean.com), 221 W. Colorado Ave. Open Mon.–Fri. 7–6 and Sat. and Sun. 7:30–6. At the heart of the full menu of coffee drinks is a great cup of joe, made from beans roasted right on the premises. A spare menu of lunch items is served daily—two soups and a special sandwich.

BARS, TAVERNS & BREW PUBS Y ♿ **New Sheridan Bar** (970-728-3911; www.newsheridan.com), 233 W. Colorado Ave. Open daily 3 PM–2 AM. The New Sheridan Hotel boasts the oldest bar in town, looking much as it did over a hundred years ago. This is one of the town's best hangouts, and the après-ski crowd keeps the place busy.

SNACKS ♿ **The Sweet Life** (970-728-8789; www.thesweetlifeinc.com), 115 W. Colorado Ave. Open daily in the summer 11–10 and in winter 11:30–9:30. This 1950s-style parlor serves more than just ice cream. They have smoothies, shakes, and fat-free frozen yogurt. There's also a grill menu with burgers and fries, or you can simply load up on the bulk candy.

* Entertainment

Telluride Repertory Theatre Company (970-728-4539; www.telluridetheater.com), P.O. Box 2469, Telluride, CO 81435. In the summer, the company puts on a three-week run of outdoor productions. In the winter, they retire to the **Sheridan Opera House** (970-728-6363; www.sheridanoperahouse.com), 231 W. Colorado Ave., where they perform Broadway shows. All year-round, Show & Tell play readings are performed throughout town—at bookstores and galleries.

Fly Me to the Moon Saloon (970-728-6666; www.flymetothemoonsaloon.com), 132 E. Colorado Ave. For a regular schedule of live music that includes blues, jazz, funk, bluegrass, and whatever else you can think of, there's no better venue in town.

✷ Selective Shopping

Between the Covers (970-369-0967 or 1-866-728-4504; www.between-the-covers.com), 224 W. Colorado Ave. This little bookstore in downtown Telluride has a great selection of books that cover regional recreation, as well as maps and other resources for travelers.

Wilderness Wonders (970-369-4441 or 1-888-369-4441; www.tonynewlin.com), 126 W. Colorado Ave. Tony Newlin, whose photographs comprise the Wilderness Wonders gallery, strives to let nothing get between his camera and nature in the photos he displays. He uses no filters, artificial light, and no digital manipulation to create his prints. The result is a surprisingly warm and real experience of the wildness and beauty of nature in his work.

✷ Special Events

June: **Telluride Bluegrass Festival** (1-800-624-2422; www.bluegrass.com). Every year thousands gather in Telluride to hear great bluegrass music. The festival has featured the likes of Emmylou Harris and Béla Fleck.

July: **Hard Rock 100** (www.run100s.com/HR). This 100-mile endurance race takes runners on a spectacular loop through the San Juan Mountains.

July: **Telluride Nothing Festival** (www.telluridenothingfestival.com). Throughout the summer, Telluride has some festival or other every weekend—well, every weekend except one. That's when they throw the Nothing Festival. So, for one weekend every summer, locals can forget about the crowds and the hassles and enjoy small-town life because absolutely nothing is going on.

September: **Blues and Brews** (www.tellurideblues.com). For three days, folks come to Telluride to drink microbrews and listen to soulful music.

CRESTED BUTTE & GUNNISON

Somewhat off the beaten path, Crested Butte is the last of the old-school Colorado ski towns. To some extent, the culture here is still governed by ski bums and laid-back hippy types (aka the granola crowd). While Telluride will nix a plan to install a sculpture of an ice climber because it smacks of advertising, the folks in Crested Butte are painting their Victorian cottages every color of the rainbow, and have no qualms about a coffeehouse covered in license plates. Crested Butte may be more relaxed because the actual ski resort, Mount Crested Butte, is 3 miles away. So far, most of the resort development has remained on the mountain.

Once a mining town, Crested Butte did not suffer the fate of other mining towns. Though many got rich from the gold and silver found in the mid-19th century, it was coal (first discovered in 1879) that sustained the community into the 1950s. In the early 1960s, the ski area was developed, and Crested Butte took on a new personality. By the 1970s, hippies had taken over the slopes, and in the summers mountain biking pioneers were riding their fat-tired bikes down the mountainside.

Crested Butte is one of the most scenic spots in the state. It rests at the head of East Valley, a wide gently sloping patch of land that stretches 17 miles south of Gunnison. Mount Crested Butte, at 12,162 feet, stands out noticeably against the sky. The ski mountain in Crested Butte is technically challenging in parts and is closing in on 400,000 annual visitors. The town is surrounded by beautiful scenery. To the north and east is the Maroon Bells Snowmass Wilderness, to the west the Raggeds.

To the south lies Gunnison. This community was here before the mining boom. In 1874, the town was established by farmers and ranchers who had moved to the valley. Gunnison still has an agricultural feel. Many visitors come for the region's recreational activities. In the winter, snowmobiling is a popular activity. In the summer there is plenty of great fishing on area rivers and reservoirs. During hunting season, outfitters take hunters out for deer and elk.

Many folks also use Gunnison a kicking-off point for visits to the Black Canyon of the Gunnison National Park or to enjoy the Curecanti National Recreation Area. South of Gunnison, a day trip will take you into Lake City, and to the east is some excellent whitewater rafting in Salida.

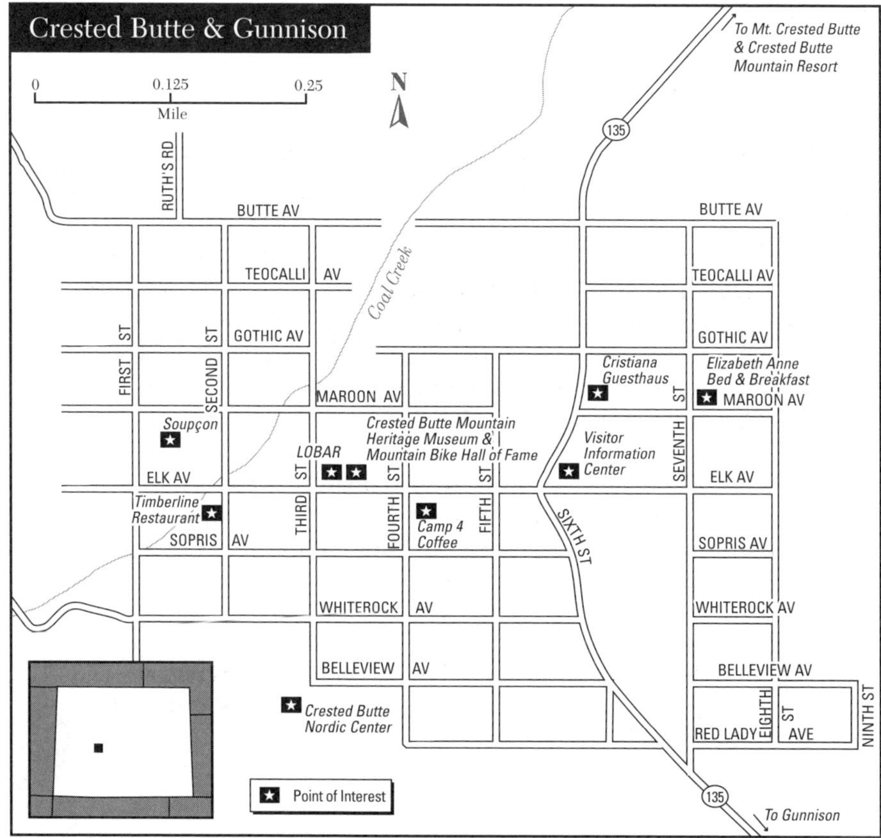

Most of the attractions, lodgings, and restaurants listed below are open year-round. Many, however, reduce hours significantly for about six weeks in the spring and fall. Be sure to call ahead during these two off-seasons. Unless otherwise indicated, all addresses are in Crested Butte.

GUIDANCE **Crested Butte & Mt. Crested Butte Chamber of Commerce** (970-349-6438 or 1-800-545-4505; www.crestedbuttechamber.com), 601 Elk Ave. Open daily 9–5 in summer and winter (Mon.–Fri. 9–5 in the off-season). When you come into town from the south, CO 135 turns into Sixth Street and the visitor center is on your right at the corner of Sixth and Elk. They have all the information you could need, including town maps and trail maps.

Gunnison Chamber of Commerce (970-641-1501; www.gunnison-co.com), 500 E. Tomichi Ave. The Gunnison Chamber offices and visitor center are right on US 50—a couple of blocks east of downtown. They have information on Gunnison as well as Crested Butte.

More Web sites:
www.gunnisoncrestedbutte.com
www.visitcrestedbutte.com

GETTING THERE *By car:* Gunnison is located right on US 50, which begins in Pueblo and meets up with US 70 in the west by Grand Junction. The town is about 200 miles southwest of Denver (about a four-hour drive). The main road to Crested Butte, CO 135, begins in Gunnison and runs 27 miles north to the ski town.

By air: The **Gunnison–Crested Butte Regional Airport** (970-641-2304; www.gunnisoncrestedbutte.com), 711 Rio Grande Ave., Gunnison, sees regular flights from American and United Airlines. Shuttle service to Gunnison and Crested Butte is available through **Alpine Express** (1-800-822-4844; www.alpineexpressshuttle.com), P.O. Box 1250, Gunnison, CO 81230.

GETTING AROUND *By bus:* **Gunnison–Crested Butte RTA** (970-641-5074; www.gunnisonvalleyrta.org) offers bus service between Gunnison and Mt. Crested Butte. Tickets $2 for one-way ride. **Mountain Express** (970-349-7318) is a free bus service that shuttles passengers between Crested Butte and Mt. Crested Butte.

MEDICAL EMERGENCIES **Gunnison Valley Hospital** (970-641-1456; www.gvh-colorado.org), 711 N. Taylor St., Gunnison. The ER is located on the N. Iowa Street side of the hospital—just north of E. Denver Avenue.

✷ To See & Do

⛱ **Crested Butte Mountain Heritage Museum** (970-349-1880), 331 Elk Ave., Crested Butte. Open daily in the summer 10–8 and in winter 10–6. Closed in

THE RIDE UP TO CRESTED BUTTE

MOUNTAIN TOWN BIKE CULTURE

the spring and fall. Mining, ranching, and skiing have all played a key role in the ongoing story of Crested Butte, which is told here with artifacts, exhibits, and historical displays. General admission $3 and children under 12 free.

Mountain Bike Hall of Fame (970-349-6817; www.mtnbikehalloffame.com), 331 Elk Ave., Crested Butte. Same hours as the Crested Butte Mountain Heritage Museum above (they are in the same building). The Mountain Bike Hall of Fame celebrates the history of mountain biking, looking at the continuum of people, places, and events that influenced the creation of the sport. Inductees include pioneers like Joe Breeze and Gary Fisher. For riders, current trail conditions are posted on the Web site. Admission included in the price of the Crested Butte Museum ticket.

West Elk Loop Scenic Byway (www.byways.org/explore/byways/2120). This scenic byway travels through a variety of landscapes, from the high mountain passes outside Crested Butte to the Curecanti National Recreation Area along Blue Mesa Lake. Starting in Gunnison, it heads north along CO 135 to Crested Butte, continuing on over Keebler Pass (9,980 feet) to CO 133. The highway here offers a spur to the north ending in Carbondale. To the southwest, CO 133 catches up with CO 92, which turns south and connects with US 50, which you take back east to Gunnison. The road outside Crested Butte is unpaved.

* Outdoor Activities

ALPINE SKIING & SNOWBOARDING **Crested Butte Mountain Resort** (970-349-2252; www.skicb.com), 12 Snowmass Rd., Crested Butte. Lifts operate daily

BLACK CANYON

Black Canyon of the Gunnison National Park (970-641-2337; www.nps.gov/blca), 102 Elk Creek, Gunnison. The Black Canyon of the Gunnison is one of Colorado's most stunning natural wonders. Throughout the state, the eye is pulled up toward snowy peaks and out to breathtaking vistas. At Black Canyon, however, the eye looks out and down. From the Gunnison River below, the canyon rises 2,722 feet to Warner Point, and at its narrowest span, the canyon is only 1,100 feet wide (40 at the bottom).

South Rim Road offers the best views of the canyon. To get there from US 50, turn north on CO 347 about 15 miles east of Montrose. Begin at the visitor center at Gunnison Point. A short trail brings you down to a spectacular canyon overlook. Inside the visitor center, an impressive log structure in its own right, there's a short video on the canyon and some displays on the history and geology of the park. Along the canyon edge, a number of trails afford a more intimate experience of this impressive landscape. The trails along the top are easy to difficult. Hiking into the canyon, however, is for those in excellent physical condition. There are no trails down to the river, and "hikers are expected to find their own way down and to be prepared for self-rescue."

For more information on the canyon, the Web site has a large collection of videos you can watch covering geology, history, life science, and recreation as it relates to each of the overlooks along the South Rim. Single visit vehicle fee $15. Walk-ins and cyclists (motoring and pedaling) $7.

The **Curecanti National Recreation Area** (970-641-2337 ext. 205; www.nps.gov/cure) offers another vantage point for exploring the canyon region, the Morrow Point Boat Tour. Farther downriver—outside of the towering

9–4. Crested Butte offers skiers a 2,775-foot vertical drop (3,062 for those willing to hike a little). The ski area's 1,167 acres are served by 16 lifts that could conceivably move 20,000 people up the mountain every hour. There are 121 trails, the longest being 2.6 miles, most of which are intermediate level. The DC Canaan Terrain Park has plenty of jumps and about a dozen rail features. There's also a tubing hill for the kids. Adult lift ticket $79, seniors $59.25, children (13–17) $59, and children (7–12) $40. The resort also offers ski and snowboard lessons through their Mountain School. For children's lessons call 970-349-2259 or 1-800-600-7349; for adult lessons 1-800-600-7349 or 970-349-2259.

CROSS-COUNTRY SKIING & SNOWSHOEING **Crested Butte Nordic Center** (970-349-1707; www.cbnordic.org), 620 Second St., Crested Butte. The Nordic center is a nonprofit organization that maintain 31 miles of groomed cross-

cliffs—this 90-minute trip takes you through the upper Black Canyon on a 42-passenger pontoon boat. National Park rangers (or qualified volunteers) lead these guided tours. From Memorial Day to Labor Day, there are two tours daily (except Tues.) at 10 and 12:30. Reservations are required and can be made by calling the number above or by visiting the Elk Creek Visitor Center, 15 miles west of Gunnison. Adult fee $15 and seniors and children (under 13) $7.50.

BLACK CANYON OF THE GUNNISON

country trails around Crested Butte. They also rent gear and lead tours into the Gunnison National Forest. For the complete backcountry ski experience, they book reservations for the Forest Queen Backcountry Hut.

Crested Butte Mountain Resort Snowshoe Tours (970-349-2252; www.skicb.com), 12 Snowmass Rd., Crested Butte. The resort offers moonlight snowshoe tours. You will travel by snowcat to the top of Red Lady Express and hoof it back down to the base. This is a unique way to experience the mountains.

Elkton Cabins (970-349-1815), Elkton, Crested Butte, maintains three cabins for backcountry stays. The cabins have gas cookstoves and woodburning stoves for heat. A backcountry tour to consider would be from Washington Gulch to the cabins. Nightly per-person rate $18–50.

FISHING In addition to the Gunnison River and its three large reservoirs west of

Gunnison, this region has several deep mountain lakes and rocky mountain creeks for fly-fishing.

The East River, for example, starts at Emerald Lake north of Crested Butte and slowly winds its way to Almont. There are great fly-fishing stretches all along its route. Twenty-two miles northeast of Almont, Taylor Reservoir is popular with anglers as well. Though the location is somewhat remote, the **Taylor Park Marina** (970-641-2922; www.taylorparkmarina.com), at 21700 CR 742, Almont, rents out boats and fishing equipment. They sell bait and even have a deli and grill. Check out the Web site—people pull huge fish out of this lake.

Dragonfly Anglers (970-349-1228 or 1-800-491-3079; www.dragonflyanglers.com), 307 Elk Ave., Crested Butte. The guides at Dragonfly offer walk-and-wade as well as float trips. They take anglers on all the area rivers, including the Black Canyon of the Gunnison (part of a multiday trip). Two-person, half-day trips $275–325.

Willowfly Anglers (1-888-761-3474; www.3riversoutfitting.com), 130 CR 742, Almont. This Orvis-endorsed outfitter offers guided fishing trips from spring into fall. There are several kinds of trips you can make, from walk-and-wade trips to fly-fishing or spin-fishing float trips. They even offer a full-day mountain lake option. Two-person, half-day trips $130–265.

GOLF **The Club at Crested Butte** (970-349-6127; www.theclubatcrestedbutte.com), 385 Country Club Dr., Crested Butte. Golf is just one of the many activities.

Dos Rios Country Club (970-641-1482), 501 Camino Del Rio, Gunnison. Two rivers wind through the 18-hole regulation course at Dos Rios. This is a semi-private course. Greens fees $25–65.

HIKING For the ultimate hiking trip, consider walking to Aspen. This day-long hike, up through West Maroon Pass, is facilitated by a network of old roads and trails. The route is about 10.5 miles, not including the distance from the towns to their respective trailheads. You can arrange to have **Dolly's Mountain Shuttle** (970-349-2620) drive you back to Crested Butte for only $50/person. For those walking from Aspen, the shuttle can also pick you up at the trailhead and drive you the 11 miles back to Crested Butte.

Colorado Backcountry (970-349-0800; www.alpinemeadowshiking.com), P.O. Box 1745, Crested Butte. This guide service offers a complete menu of hiking options, from full- and half-day trips to sunrise runs and evening strolls to all-out backcountry wilderness adventures. For longer hikes, they offer gourmet lunches and day-pack rental. See the Web site for a complete list of guided mountain tours.

Alpineer (970-349-5210 or 1-800-223-4655; www.alpineer.com), 419 Sixth St., Crested Butte. Open daily 9–6. This shop sells and rents backcountry gear. They are also an excellent resource for learning about area trails and hikes.

HORSEBACK RIDING **Fantasy Ranch Horseback Adventures** (970-349-5425 or 1-888-688-3488; www.fantasyranchoutfitters.com), 29 Whiterock, Crested Butte. This outfitter offers true horseback adventures. The Ride and Flight of Your Life trip takes guests on a beautiful ride over East Maroon Pass on the way to Aspen. They then return to Crested Butte via airplane. Of course, they also offer day rides and short rides in summer and winter.

MOUNTAIN BIKING One day back in 1976, the good folks of Crested Butte were visited by a bunch of ne'er-do-wells out of Aspen. These gentleman had ridden their motorcycles up over Pearl Pass and down to Crested Butte and spent the evening drinking at the local bar boasting of their unsurpassable feat of derring-do. Back then CB had even more of a laid-back hippy vibe than now, but the sight of Aspenites bragging it up in their watering hole was too much to take. The next day a group set off from Crested Butte, up the Pearl Pass Trail—on their bicycles. They had to spend the night on the mountain, but the next day they arrived in Aspen to thumb a well-deserved nose at their motorized counterparts. Every September the feat is repeated with the Pearl Pass Tour to Aspen. It is the oldest continuous mountain biking event in the world.

Mountain biking has deep roots in Crested Butte. The trails in the surrounding country are not just plentiful and challenging; they are legendary. For a solid introduction to area trails and rides, be sure to stop by one of the local shops or sign up for a guided tour with a bike outfitter.

To get a feel for the place, ask about the **Lower Loop,** a pleasant trail that begins at the Peanut Mine northwest of town. You can begin in town and there are some alternate trails up to the mine. For a more challenging ride, one with spectacular views, try **Trail #403**—a trail for experienced riders in good physical condition. Beginning in Washington Gulch, you climb and cross over to Gothic Road, which takes you back to town.

Crested Butte Mountain Guides (970-349-5430 or 1-800-455-2307; www.crestedbutteguides.com), 416 Sopris Ave., Crested Butte. This outfitter leads guided tours of all the area's classic rides—Trail #401, Lower Loop, etc. Full-day tour for 1–2 riders $250.

Crested Butte Ski and Bike Shop (1-800-301-9169; www.crestedbuttesports.com), 35 Emmons Loop, Crested Butte. The shop sells, rents, and repairs skis and bikes. For mountain biking, the shop rents the full-suspension Cannondale Prophet—a fine bike by any standard. Full 24-hour rental $40.

GREEN SPACE **Curecanti National Recreation Area** (970-641-2337 ext. 205; www.nps.gov/cure), 103 Elk Creek, Gunnison. Three reservoirs along the Gunnison River form the heart of this recreation area east of the Black Canyon of the Gunnison. The main entry point, the Elk Creek Visitor Center, is 15 miles west of Gunnison off US 50. The park offers all sorts of recreational activities, from boating and fishing to hiking and camping. Combined with the bordering national park, the area offers 75,000 acres for you to explore. Single visit vehicle fee $15. Walk-ins and cyclists (motoring and pedaling) $7.

✷ Lodging

HOTELS **Grand Lodge Crested Butte** (970-349-8000 or 1-888-823-4446; www.grandlodgecrestedbutte.com), 6 Emmons Loop. This high-end, full-service hotel is located right next to the ski lifts. Amenities include a year-round heated indoor/outdoor pool, hot tub, and steam room. There's on-site dining at the Woodstone Grille, Woodstone Deli, and Woodstone Lounge. The hotel offers a variety of accommodations, from simple guest rooms to suites and condos. The rooms are spacious and tastefully decorated. Rooms and suites $99–209.

Crested Butte Retreat (970-349-1658; www.crestedbutteretreat.com), 39 Whetstone Rd. This elegant, high-end "boutique mountain lodge" sits on the mountainside above Mt. Crested Butte, just 300 yards from the ski runs. With only 10 rooms, the retreat has an intimate and relaxing feel. They serve a hearty continental breakfast that includes to-order items like pancakes and omelettes. Rooms $115–445.

Elk Mountain Lodge (970-349-7533 or 1-800-374-6521; www.elkmountainlodge.net), 129 Gothic Ave. The lodge features 19 individually decorated rooms, each with a private bath and cable TV. Five of the rooms have balcony views of the Elk Mountains. Lodge amenities include the Lodge Bar, which is open every evening until 10 or 11, a large indoor hot tub, and a continental breakfast served daily during ski season. Rooms $120–160.

Cristiana Guesthaus (970-349-5326 or 1-800-824-7899; www.cristianaguesthaus.com), 621 Maroon Ave. The Guesthaus is a lot like a B&B—a residence with three rooms for guests. The rooms are simply decorated and comfortable, and the hospitality from the innkeepers memorable. There is a hot tub on the deck with views of the mountains, and in the summer, the rock garden is quite beautiful. A continental breakfast is served daily. Rooms $70–110.

Nordic Inn (970-349-5542 or 1-800-542-7669; www.nordicinncb.com), 14 Treasury Rd. Located in Mt. Crested Butte, within walking distance of the ski area, the Nordic Inn has a variety of affordable rooms, many with kitchenettes. Amenities include cable TV and a continental breakfast. Rooms $82–196.

Water Wheel Inn (970-641-1650 or 1-800-624-1650; www.waterwheelinnatgunnison.com), P.O. Box 882, Gunnison, CO 81230. Located 2 miles west of Gunnison on US 50. The innkeeper, Dr. Jim Valenzuela, sees the Water Wheel as a home base for visitors looking to take on all the activities the Gunnison area has to offer. To that end, the inn has fostered relationships with area outfitters and can help you plan any number of trips, from hunting to snowmobiling, horseback riding, and fishing. To help guests make a good start to the day, the continental breakfast, which includes cereals, bagels, and waffles, is supplemented with fresh biscuits and hot gravy. The property is an old-school hotel, but as a new owner, Dr. Valenzuela has been making a ton of changes. Rooms along the back have beautiful views of the neighboring Dos Rios Golf Course. Rooms $59–160.

BED & BREAKFASTS **Elizabeth Anne Bed & Breakfast** (1-

888-745-4620; www.crested-butte-inn.com), 703 Maroon Ave. Within walking distance of Elk Avenue and downtown, all five rooms at the Elizabeth Anne are comfortable and homey. They each have full, private baths, and wireless Internet is available throughout the inn. Dogs are welcome. They claim they serve "the best gourmet breakfast anywhere," and judging from the way guests go on about the food, they might just be right. Rooms $110–205.

CABINS & COTTAGES **Pioneer Guest Cabins** (970-349-5517; www.thepioneer.net), 2094 Cement Creek Rd. Established in 1939, the Pioneer Guest Cabins offer eight log cabins nestled in the heart of the Gunnison National Forest along Cement Creek. The first four cabins were built in the 1920s to house skiers who came to tackle the Pioneer ski area. They really resonate with a sense of history. The other four cabins were built in the 1960s and are just as charming. In the winter, gas heat keeps the cabins warm, and the beds are stocked with flannel sheets and down comforters. They all have kitchens, a bathroom, and can sleep larger parties. Cabins $109–159.

✷ Where to Eat

DINING OUT 🍸 **LOBAR** (970-349-0480; www.thelobar.com), 303 Elk Ave., Crested Butte. Open daily at 5:30 PM. Located under the Company Store at Elk and Third, LOBAR specializes in sushi, with fresh fish flown in six days a week. The menu was recently expanded with dishes like grilled lobster and Kobe beef.

Soupçon (970-349-5448; www.soupconrestaurant.com/main.php), 127A Elk Ave., Crested Butte. Open Mon.–Sat. for dinner. There are two nightly seatings at 6 and 8:15. This French bistro, housed in a very American log cabin, serves an ever-changing menu of French/American cuisine. Reservations highly recommended. Dishes $31–50.

🍸 ♿ **Timberline Restaurant** (970-349-9831; www.timberlinerestaurant.com), 201 Elk Ave., Crested Butte. Open daily for dinner 5:30–10. The upscale, contemporary menu at Timberline has distinctly western touches. New York strip sits alongside Colorado rack of lamb and Rocky Mountain trout. More formal dining upstairs is complemented by a casually elegant bistro and bar downstairs. Dishes $14–42.

♿ **Garlic Mike's** (970-641-2493; www.garlicmikes.com), 2674 CO 135 N., Gunnison. This Italian restaurant north of Gunnison is the finest place in town for dining. The traditional Italian menu includes some gems like the New York strip steak carbonara. Entrées $14–25.

EATING OUT **Izzy's** (970-349-5630), 218 Maroon Ave., Crested Butte. Breakfast and lunch daily 7–2. Izzy's is tucked into an alley off Elk Avenue. They serve a great breakfast—bagels, French toast, and latkes are all favorites. For lunch there's fresh-made soups and sandwiches.

Secret Stash (970-349-6245; www.thesecretstash.com), 21 Elk Ave., Crested Butte. Open daily for dinner at 5. For pizza, there's no better place in town. The Secret Stash also has pretty good buffalo wings. After your meal, you might just want to sit back and take in the restaurant's funky atmosphere. Pizzas $13–20.

♿ **Paradise Café** (970-349-6233), 303 Elk Ave., Crested Butte. Open daily for breakfast 7–11 and lunch 12–3. The breakfast burritos, skillets, and *huevos rancheros* make this one of the best places in town for a hearty breakfast. For lunch there's a decent selection of sandwiches, salads, and soups. The service is quick, friendly, and accommodating. Dishes $6–10.

Donita's Cantina (970-349-6674), 330 Elk Ave., Crested Butte. Dinner served daily at 5:30. For classic Mexican dining, Donita's has good food, hearty portions, and affordable prices. Dishes $8–18.

🍸 ♿ **Trough Restaurant** (970-641-3724) 37550 US 50, Gunnison. When locals head out for a good meal and perhaps a drink, they head to the Trough, 2 miles west of Gunnison on US 50. The sign is kind of small, so it's easy to miss. They serve great steak, chicken, and seafood.

BAKERIES & COFFEE SHOPS

♿ **Camp 4 Coffee** (970-349-5148; www.camp4coffee.com), 402½ Elk Ave., Crested Butte. Outside, Camp 4 is covered with old license plates. Inside, they serve one of the best cups of coffee in town. Roasted locally, the coffee is served at restaurants all over Crested Butte. Sledgehammer is one of their most popular blends. You might even want to buy a pound of beans for your own Crested Butte experience at home.

BARS, TAVERNS & BREW PUBS 🍸

The Eldo (970-349-6125), 215 Elk Ave., Crested Butte. Open daily 3–2. The Eldo (short for "El Dorado") has a motto: A sunny place for shady people. They have nine beers on tap and a great selection of bottled brews. Pool table, TVs, and live music make this a great bar for just hanging out.

THE LEGENDARY COFFEEHOUSE CAMP 4 COFFEE

✷ Entertainment

Crested Butte Music Festival (970-349-0619; www.crestedbuttemusic festival.com), 308 Third St. Every year in the month of July, Crested Butte is alive with the sound of music. The music festival puts on a concert every night—chamber musicians, big bands, and bluegrass pickers all take the stage throughout the month.

✷ Selective Shopping

Paragon Gallery (970-349-6484), 132 Elk Ave., Crested Butte. The gallery is a co-op of over a dozen local artists. Jewelry, pottery, stained glass, paintings, and sculpture by some of the most talented artists from Crested Butte and Gunnison are on display.

✷ Special Events

February: **Crested Butte Winter Carnival** (970-349-4950), Crested Butte. In the winter, the town is all about skiing. The carnival features a Big Air ski and snowboard jump contest (downtown, no less) and a Nordic ski race.

February: **U.S. Extreme Freeskiing Championships** (www.skicb.com/winter-activities-adventure-freeskiing.html), Crested Butte. This annual event brings in extreme skiers from around the country.

June: **Fat Tire Bike Week** (1-800-545-4505; www.ftbw.com), Crested Butte. In the summer, the town is all about mountain biking. Events include a chainless descent down Keebler Pass, the Clunker Crit, and a whole mess of freaks on bikes.

July: **Crested Butte Wildflower Festival** (970-349-2571; www.crestedbuttewildflowerfestival.com), 409 Second St. Every year at the height of summer, the meadows and mountains around Crested Butte erupt into full bloom—wildflowers everywhere. Events include nature hikes, horseback rides, and four-wheel-drive rides into the mountains. There is live music, plenty of food, and art on display.

September: **Pearl Pass Tour to Aspen** (www.mtnbikehalloffame.com), Crested Butte. This ride commemorates the legendary Pearly Pass conquest of 1976.

Vinotok (970-641-4742), Crested Butte. Before the snow starts falling, the town of Crested Butte comes out and makes merry. Everyone's complaints are written down and stuffed in the "grump," which is burned at festival's end.

Eastern Colorado 5

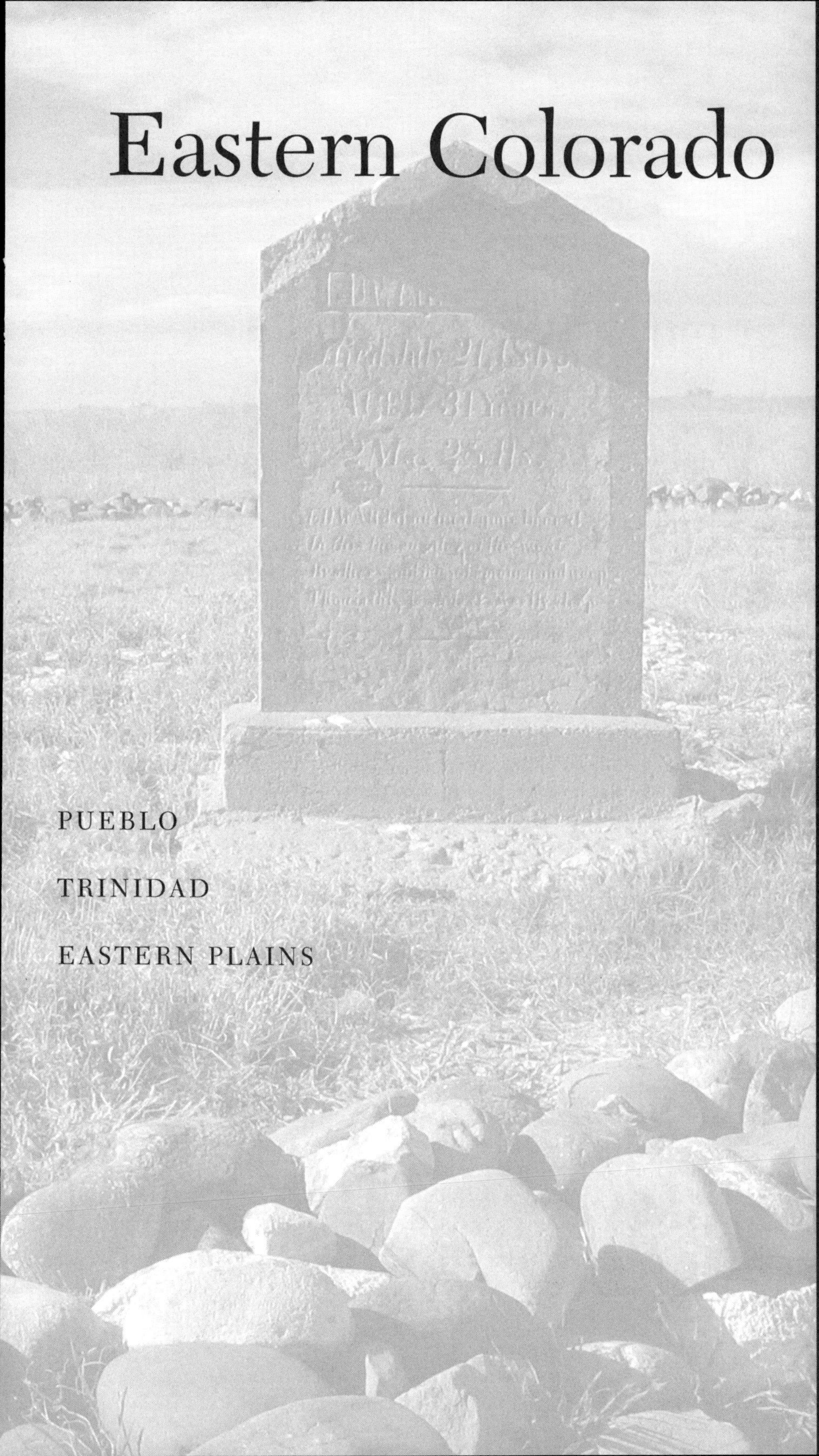

PUEBLO

TRINIDAD

EASTERN PLAINS

PUEBLO

Though often overshadowed by Colorado Springs to the north, Pueblo is the largest city in the southeast region of the state. With over 100,000 residents, Pueblo is a thriving community. Annual events like the Colorado State Fair and the Chile & Frijoles Festival are big draws, as is Lake Pueblo State Park. The fair alone is Colorado's biggest event—drawing nearly half a million people to Pueblo over 11 days every summer. Part mini-metropolis and part college town, Pueblo offers all the conveniences of a big city with distinctly small-town charm. This is no truer than when you visit the Union Avenue Historic District, the City Zoo, or any one of Pueblo's great restaurants.

As the southernmost city along Colorado's Front Range, Pueblo offers easy access to the mountains in the west and the state's southeastern plains. In a matter of hours, you can be driving up to view the Royal Gorge outside Cañon City or buying fresh cantaloupe from a roadside stand in Rocky Ford in the east. Closer to town, you are within minutes of museums, a zoo, and Lake Pueblo State Park.

Two waterways meet in the heart of Pueblo. For centuries, the confluence of the Arkansas River and Fountain Creek, just east of the Rockies, has been a natural place for people to meet, make camp, or trade goods. In 1706, Juan de Ulibarri, a Spanish captain leading a small expedition out of Santa Fe, crossed the Arkansas River and set up camp, becoming the first recorded European to visit the site of present-day Pueblo.

When Zebulon Pike and his men made their way up the Arkansas River in 1806, they built a small log stockade on the site. Pike then set off on a side trip north to see if he could summit a surprisingly high mountain peak he had seen on the horizon. Though he gave up the attempt and declared the mountain inaccessible, Pikes Peak still bears his name.

In 1842, legendary mountain man Jim Beckwourth built a trading post here. He was joined by a number of settlers, and they called the settlement Fort Pueblo. On Christmas day, 1854, a drunk settler opened the fort to a group of Utes and Apaches. Led by Tierra Blanca, the natives killed nearly everyone inside.

Gold and silver were found in the nearby mountains in the late 1850s. The subsequent rush of settlers established Fountain City, which was later absorbed into Pueblo.

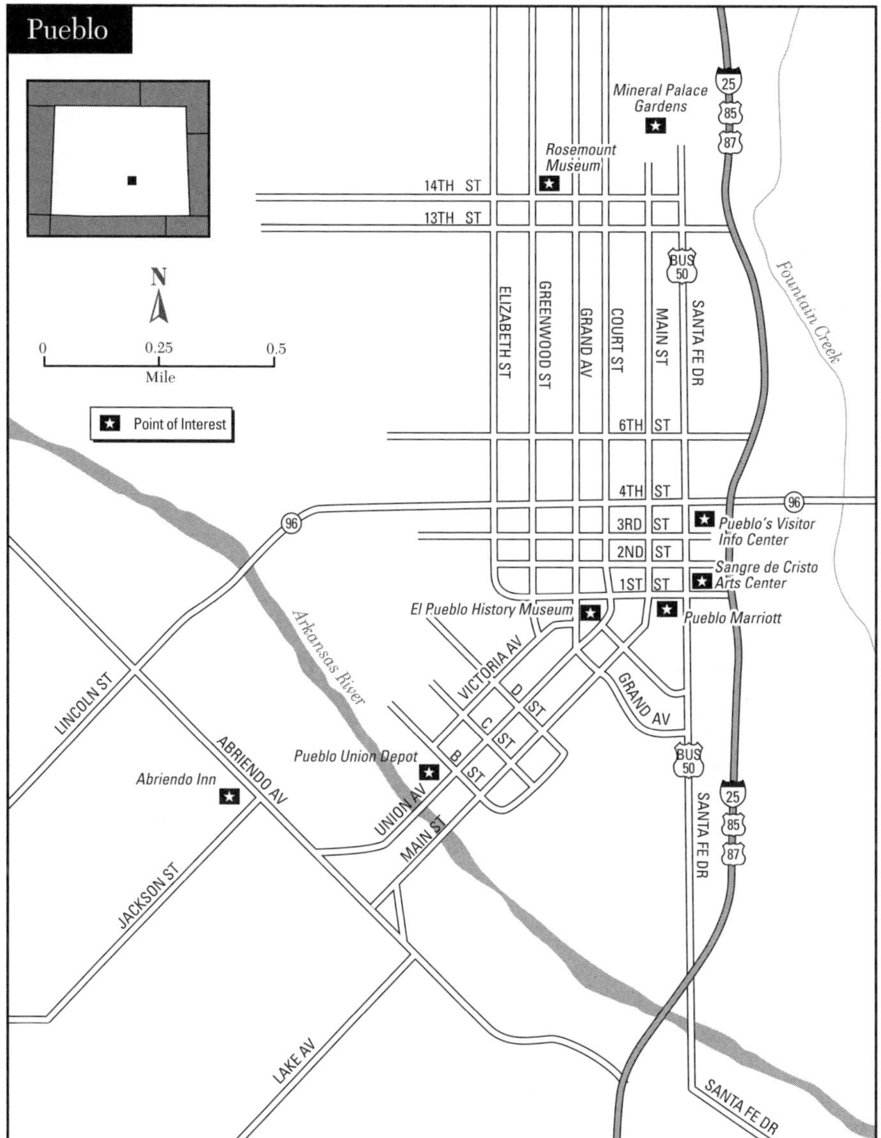

Since its formal inception in 1860, Pueblo has had many ups and downs. In 1872, the Denver & Rio Grande Railroad came to town bringing more prosperity to the region. Colorado Coal & Iron Company built the town's first blast furnace in 1881, and coal mining and steel production remained the driving force behind Pueblo's economy into the 20th century. All this industry brought an influx of immigrants—a legacy that lives today in Pueblo's surprising cultural diversity.

On the evening of June 3, 1921, a sudden downpour, 10 miles west of Pueblo, caused the Arkansas River to rise. Rainfall 30 miles to the north had the same effect on Fountain Creek. When the two swollen streams met in downtown Pueblo, the result was disaster. The Great Flood of 1921 wiped out a third of the businesses in Pueblo and killed hundreds of people.

It took decades for downtown Pueblo to recover from the flood. In the 1980s, the idea for a Union Avenue Historic District was born. As shops and restaurants began to move back to Union Avenue, Pueblo began an ambitious riverwalk project downtown: the Historic Arkansas Riverwalk of Pueblo. Millions of dollars have been pumped into building a park around the old Arkansas River channel (after 1921 the river was rerouted south of town). The riverwalk serves as the perfect backdrop for a number of Pueblo's festivals.

There are a higher percentage of Hispanics in Pueblo than in other cities in Colorado. And over the years, other immigrant groups have made Pueblo their home. As a result, Pueblo has unmatched cultural resources. Many of these are highlighted by the Sangre de Cristo Arts Center. They can also be seen in the town's many Italian and Mexican restaurants.

The town's largest tourist attraction today is the Pueblo Reservoir at Lake Pueblo State Park. The lake pulls in over a million visitors each year.

GUIDANCE **Greater Pueblo Chamber of Commerce** (719-542-1704 or 1-800-233-3446; www.pueblochamber.org and www.destinationpueblo.com), 302 N. Santa Fe Ave., P.O. Box 697, Pueblo CO 81003. The chamber of commerce office is several short blocks north of the Union Avenue Historic District. At this location, the chamber maintains Pueblo's Visitors Information Center, which is open Mon.–Fri. 8–5 and some Saturdays 10–2.

More Web sites:

www.seepueblo.com

www.puebloguidebook.com

www.gopueblo.com

www.pueblo.us

GETTING THERE *By car:* If you're coming from the north or south, I-25 is your best bet. The interstate follows the Front Range and passes through Denver, Colorado Springs, and Pueblo on its way to Santa Fe, Albuquerque, and points south. From the east and the west, US 50 winds its way across the state, from Grand Junction in the west to Kansas in the east. If you take this two-lane highway, be aware that speed limits are lower in populated areas, and stoplights are not uncommon.

By air: The most accessible airport to Pueblo is the **Colorado Springs Airport** (719-550-1972; www.flycos.com), about 45 miles to the north. Every year, it seems, more cities have direct flights in and out of Colorado Springs. If you're not renting a car, shuttle service from Colorado Springs can be arranged with **Shuttle Service of Southern Colorado** (719-545-9444 or 1-877-545-9435), 215 S. Victoria Ave. #B. However, if you are renting a car and are willing to drive a little farther, be sure to check prices for flights to Denver. The **Denver International Airport** (1-800-AIR2DEN; www.flydenver.com) is about 120 miles north of Pueblo (a good two-hour drive), but it's often cheaper to land in Denver and drive the rest of the way.

By train: There is no rail service to Pueblo, although **AMTRAK** (1-800-872-7245; www.amtrak.com) has train terminals in Denver to the north and Trinidad to the south. From both locations, you can take their Throughway bus service directly to Pueblo (see below for bus depot information).

By bus: **Greyhound** operates regular service to and from Pueblo from the **Pueblo Bus Depot** (719-543-2775 or 1-800-231-2222; www.greyhound.com), which is located near I-25, north of US 50 at 1080 Chinook Ln.

GETTING AROUND *By car:* The best way to get around town is by car. Aside from the usual rush-hour traffic on the interstate and major cross streets, Pueblo is a great town for driving. Interstate 25 runs north and south through town, and it's the quickest way to travel from one side of town to another. Retail businesses are plentiful around I-25, which is especially helpful if you have a sudden need to visit a Barnes & Noble or a Wal-Mart (both located near the intersection of I-25 and US 50 along with every other retail convenience you would expect). Exit 98B for 1st St. is the quickest route for getting to the old Union Avenue Historic District. Three blocks north of 1st Street, you can pick up CO 96 (here it is also called 4th Street). Following CO 96 to the west will take you just north of the Colorado State Fairgrounds, right by the Pueblo Zoo on your way out to Lake Pueblo State Park. Unless you are in town to go to the State Fair, parking is rarely a problem (and even then it's not bad).

By bus: The city operates a transit system that can get you almost anywhere in Pueblo. The **Pueblo Transit** (719-553-2727; www.pueblo.us/transit) Web site has a map of bus fares, routes, and schedules.

MEDICAL EMERGENCIES If you are in need of medical attention, two main hospitals serve the Pueblo area. Both facilities offer 24-hour emergency medical treatment.

St. Mary–Corwin Medical Center (719-560-4000 or 1-800-228-4039; www.stmarycorwin.org), 1008 Minnequa Ave.

Parkview Medical Center (719-584-4000; www.parkviewmc.org), 400 W. 16th St.

✷ To See & Do

MUSEUMS ✐ ☂ ♿ **Buell Children's Museum** (719-543-0130; www.sdc-arts.org/bcc.html), 210 N. Santa Fe Ave. Open Tues.–Sat. 11–4. Once you visit the Buell Children's Museum, you will understand why *Child* magazine rated it as the second best children's art museum in the country in 2002. Your kids will have a blast exploring hands-on, interactive exhibitions, making their own art in the Artrageous Studio, or visiting the Magic Carpet Theater where they can watch a play or perform themselves. For the even younger set, the Buell Baby Barn is full of activities for children under four. The museum isn't just about art either; plenty of exhibitions focus on science and history. There's always something new going on, so be sure to check the Web site for current exhibits and activities. The Buell Children's Museum is part of the Sangre de Cristo Arts and Conference Center (see Entertainment). Adult admission $4 and children $3.

✐ ☂ ♿ **El Pueblo History Museum** (719-583-0453; www.coloradohistory.org/hist_sites/Pueblo/Pueblo.htm), 301 N. Union Ave. Open Tues.–Sat. 10–4. If you are interested in the history of southeastern Colorado, a great place to start is at the El Pueblo History Museum, located in the heart of Pueblo, just north of the Union Avenue Historic District. The museum features an adobe trading post and plaza from the 1840s, as well as the archaeological excavation for El Pueblo's original trading post. Permanent exhibits walk visitors through Pueblo's history, from the region's earliest inhabitants up to the present. There's a wealth of history to explore, including artifacts from early American Indian inhabitants and the armor and weapons of French and Spanish explorers. Also, the museum building also houses the Frontier Pathways Scenic and Historic Byways Information Center (see Scenic Drives). Adult admission $4; seniors, children, and students $3; and children 5 and under free. On Saturday, all children 12 and under are free.

♿ **Pueblo Railway Museum** (for tours, call 719-251-5024 or 719-295-1517; for the office, call 719-544-1773; www.pueblorailway.org), located adjacent to the Pueblo Union Depot on B St., at the south end of the Union Avenue Historic District. The museum has several tracks in the coach yard behind the Union Depot, and more tracks running along the Riverwalk, where you can see vintage railroad equipment like a 100-year-old red wooden caboose. The museum also offers smaller indoor exhibits across the street from Union Depot in the Southeastern Colorado Heritage Center. Admission is free; donations appreciated.

PUEBLO UNION DEPOT

ROSEMOUNT MUSEUM

☂ ♿ **Rosemount Museum** (719-545-5290; www.rosemount.org), 419 W. 14th St. (at Grand Ave.). Open Tues.–Sat., from 10 until the last tour at 3:30. The most impressive feature of Rosemount, the Victorian mansion built by the Thatcher family in 1893, is that nearly everything you find inside is original to the home. Walking into the 37-room mansion is like walking back in time. The entrance hall features a grand Tiffany chandelier, and turning toward the staircase, visitors will see the large stained-glass window that memorializes the Thatcher's two young children, who did not live to see Rosemount completed. Also on the main floor in the drawing room, you can see and listen to a unique Steinway player piano. Upstairs, as you go from room to room, you will find that different wood was used for the woodwork—mahogany, oak, cherry, maple. There's quite a lot of history in each room, and tours of the 24,000-square-foot home take about an hour. Adult admission $6, seniors (60+) $5, children (6–18) $4, and children 5 and under free. Also located on the property, is the **Carriage House Restaurant at Rosemount** (see Eating Out).

✐ ☂ ♿ **SteelWorks Museum of Industry & Culture** (719-564-9086; www.cfisteel.org), 215 Canal St. Open Mon.–Sat. 10–4. Located on the south side of town, the museum is housed in the old Colorado Fuel and Iron Corporation headquarters. The museum commemorates Pueblo's past as a major steel producer. Exhibits illustrate the history of mining, labor issues, steel production, and the specific role played by the Colorado Fuel and Iron Company in Pueblo and the region. Adult admission $3, children (4–12) $2, and children under 4 free.

ZOOS ♿ **Pueblo Zoo** (719-561-9664; www.pueblozoo.org), City Park, 3455 Nuckolls Ave. Summer hours (Memorial Day–Labor Day) Mon.–Sat. 9–4 and

Sun. 12–4; winter hours Mon.–Sat. 9–4 and Sun. noon–4. This 25-acre zoo, located in Pueblo's City Park is home to 325 animals, representing 121 species. Right off the bat, you will notice that this is a small city zoo, but considering its size, there is a lot to see and do. As you walk through the various exhibits, you will see animals from nearly every region of the world. There are lions from Africa, bears from Asia, and kangaroos from Australia. There are also river otters from Colorado, as well as a slew of small mammals, birds, and snakes. Be sure the kids don't miss Pioneer Farm, where they can feed and pet some of the animals. Adult admission $6, seniors (65+) $5.25, children (3–12) $3.50, and children 2 and under free.

HISTORIC SITES **Union Avenue Historic District** (719-543-5804; www.seepueblo.com), centered around Union Avenue; the Historic District begins at 1st Street in the north and ends at B Street in the south. In 1886, the three burgs that made up Pueblo consolidated. The resulting boom made Union Avenue into a thriving center of business. In 1921, disaster struck when the nearby rivers flooded—over 11 feet of water flowed through the city. The district took years to recover from the destruction. In the 1980s, there was a push to renew the old downtown with projects like the city's fabulous Riverwalk. As a result, the Union Avenue Historic District has been turned upside-down as numerous shops and restaurants have sprung up, making this a great place to spend an afternoon. Throughout the district, there are nearly 40 plaques that tell the history of various buildings. Area merchants can provide you with a self-guided walking tour. Throughout the year, numerous events are held, from car shows to art walks—see the Web site for a complete listing. Parking is free, though limited to two hours during shopping hours. (See Entertainment, Selective Shopping, and Where to Eat for places to see and things to do.)

Historic Arkansas River Riverwalk of Pueblo (see Parks, Green Space).

SCENIC DRIVES **The Frontier Pathways Scenic and Historic Byways** (719-583-8631; www.frontierpathways.org), 301 N. Union Ave. (located in the El Pueblo Historic Museum). This drive will take you up and through the Wet Mountains southwest of Pueblo. It's a beautiful drive. Head west from Pueblo on CO 96, about 55 miles to the town of Westcliffe. Return by a southern route, backtracking 15 miles on CO 96 to CO 165, through Fairview and Colorado City, and then north on I-25.

✷ Outdoor Activities

CYCLING **Pueblo River Trails System** (see Parks, Green Space). This 35-mile network of paved trails is open to cyclists and walkers. The trails follow the Arkansas River and Fountain Creek, connecting trails as far west as Lake Pueblo State Park with downtown Pueblo and the University of Southern Colorado in the north. Cyclists must always yield to pedestrian traffic.

GOLF Because of the climate, Pueblo golf courses claim to offer more playable days a year than most others courses in the state. More information about

Pueblo's three golf courses—current greens fees, dress codes, etc.—can be found online at www.golfinpueblo.com.

Desert Hawk Golf Course at Pueblo West (719-547-2280), 251 S. McCulloch Blvd. Open year-round. Located in Pueblo West south of US 50. Greens fees are less than $30.

Elmwood (719-561-4946), City Park, 3900 Thatcher Ave. Open year-round. This course is located adjacent to the Pueblo City Park. Greens fees are under $30.

Walking Stick (719-584-3400), 4301 Walking Stick Blvd. Open year-round. This course was given a four-star rating by *Golf Digest* and is considered one of Colorado's best. The course offers some beautiful landscape features unique to Pueblo. Given all the hype, greens fees are still reasonable, under $30. The course also maintains a pro shop and restaurant. There is a dress code.

Hollydot (719-676-3341 or 1-866-307-2792; www.hollydotgolf.com), 55 N. Parkway, Colorado City. Just a quick 20-mile drive south of Pueblo brings you to Hollydot—a fine golf course, with views of the Wet Mountains. You can play nine holes on their West Course or a full 18 on the Gold Links Course. It is by far one of the most affordable courses in southeast Colorado. Prime weekend rates for 18 holes will cost you $25 (or $36 with a cart). Monday, Tuesday, and Wednesday are the best deal with an 18-hole round running $15 (or $26 with cart). Kids under 18 pay only $4 for nine holes.

PADDLING **Pueblo Whitewater Park.** Located on the Arkansas River between Union Avenue and 4th Street, this half-mile stretch of water has been designed with eight drops separated by large pools. The resulting hydraulic action makes this the perfect playground for kayakers. For more information, contact **Pueblo Paddlers** (www.pueblopaddlers.com), P.O. Box 1482, Pueblo CO 81002, or stop by and talk with the guys at **Edge, Ski, Paddle, and Pack** (719-583-2021; www.edgeskiandpaddle.com), 107 N. Union Ave.

PUEBLO'S WHITEWATER PARK

SWIMMING The city maintains several pools at parks around Pueblo—**City Park** and **Mineral Palace Park** are particularly nice (see Parks, Green Space). If you like a more natural experience, you can swim the Arkansas River at **Rock Canyon Swim Beach** (see Lake Pueblo State Park under Parks, Green Space).

GREEN SPACE PARKS **City Park** (719-566-1745), 800 Goodnight Ave. Not only is City Park home to the Pueblo Zoo, it is a great place for recreation of all sorts. The park has a disc-golf course, horseshoe pits, tennis courts, softball fields, a swimming pool, and lakes stocked for fishing. There are even two bocce courts, built to international standards. The park is adjacent to the city golf course, Elmwood (see Outdoor Activities, Golf). One of the park highlights that visitors should not miss is a ride on the City Park Carousel—originally built in 1911.

Lake Pueblo State Park (719-561-9320; www.parks.state.co.us/parks/LakePueblo), 640 Pueblo Reservoir Rd. One of the area's biggest attractions is Lake Pueblo State Park, which hosts over 1.5 million visitors every year. In the summer, this part of the country gets pretty hot, often in the triple digits—the 4,500-acre Pueblo Reservoir offers a welcome respite from the heat.

A highlight of the park is the **Rock Canyon Swim Beach** (719-564-0065). Since the lake is primarily surrounded by short prairie grass, the park has provided numerous shaded picnic areas for groups and individuals. The Rock Canyon Swim Beach is no exception. There are also facilities for changing and showering—with lockers for storing your stuff. In addition to the large sandy beach, there's a five-story waterslide, bumper boats, and paddleboats. Be aware, it costs an extra $1 per person to get into the Rock Canyon Swim Beach (plus a little extra for the waterslide and boats). Also note that pets are not allowed.

LAKE PUEBLO

Two separate marinas serve boaters on Lake Pueblo. The **North Shore Marina** (719-547-3880; www.noshoremarina.com), 1 N. Marina Rd., has over 600 boat slips. It also maintains a Ship's Store where you can get everything you need for a day on the lake, from food and gear to fishing licenses. The **South Shore Marina** (719-564-1043; www.thesouthshoremarina.com), 600 Pueblo Reservoir Rd., has 370 boat slips. It has a store for boaters as well. Both offer services for maintaining, repairing, and winterizing your boat.

In addition to swimming and boating, the parks boast of 348 picnic spots, 401 campsites, 18 miles of trails for hikers and bikers, and 16 miles of trails for horseback riding. The longest of the hiking trails is the Dam Trail, which is over 16 miles long and connects all the major sections of the park. The tree-lined Pueblo River Trail follows the Arkansas River and is a relatively easy walk. The Arkansas Point Trail is less than a mile and leads to the bluffs, where you can get a panoramic view of the reservoir. Stop at the park's visitor center for trail maps and other information. The visitor center is open Mon.–Fri. 8–4. In addition to information, they offer a store where you can buy guidebooks and fishing licenses.

A fee is required to visit the park. You can purchase a day pass for $6. If you plan on making trips to other Colorado state parks, you might want to pick up an annual pass for $60.

If you simply want to see Lake Pueblo in all its grandeur, but don't have the time or inclination to get a day pass and wander around the park, there's an overlook that is easily accessed from US 50. Heading west on 50, turn south on S. Purcell Boulevard. The road gets narrower as you go, and it eventually turns into S. Liberty Point Boulevard where it dead-ends at a small parking lot. You will find yourself on the bluffs that overlook the north side of the park. This is Liberty Point Outlook. Park and take the short hike to the outlook where the view is spectacular. The trail is paved and not at all strenuous, and the view is well worth the detour.

Mineral Palace Park (719-545-5319), 1600 N. Santa Fe Ave. A greenhouse now stands on the original site of Pueblo's Mineral Palace, which opened in 1891 to showcase Colorado's rich mineral wealth and celebrate the state's mining industry. Unfortunately, the building was demolished in 1942. Today, Mineral Palace Park is known for its spectacular gardens and annual flower displays. It is also a great place to cool off in the summer—the park's large shady trees are perfect for picnicking, and the community pool has a waterslide for the kids.

Pueblo Mountain Park and the **Mountain Park Environmental Center** (719-485-4444; www.hikeandlearn.org), 9161 Mountain Park Rd., Beulah. Far outside the city limits, about 30 miles southwest on CO 78, the City of Pueblo owns and maintains a park at the base of the Wet Mountains, just outside Beulah. Pueblo Mountain Park was created by the city in 1918, making it Pueblo's first outdoor recreation facility. A visit to the park is a great day trip, especially if you want to get closer to the mountains and enjoy hiking. There are several miles of trails; a few connect to those in neighboring San Isabel National Forest. Trail maps are available at the Mountain Park Environmental Center. In addition to maps and general visitor information, the MPEC offers various activities throughout the year. Be sure to check their Web site for a schedule of guided nature hikes.

NATURAL EDUCATION **The Greenway and Nature Center** (719-549-2414; www.gncp.org), 5200 Nature Center Rd. Adjacent to Lake Pueblo State Park, just east along the Arkansas River, the Greenway and Nature Center is located in Rock Canyon. There are miles of trails for horseback riding or cycling. Bikes can be rented from their bike shack (719-251-9312). This is also the home of the **Raptor Center of Pueblo** (719-549-2327). Open 11–4 every day but Mon. Admission is free. Looking after injured birds of prey is the main mission of the Raptor Center. Birds too injured to be released back into the wild stick around to help educate visitors about these birds and their way of life.

WALKS ♿ **Historic Arkansas Riverwalk of Pueblo** (719-595-0242; www.puebloharp.com). The 26-acre Riverwalk complex is located in downtown Pueblo between D Street and Grand Avenue, easily accessible from Main Street. Though not big enough for a day-long hike, the Riverwalk is perfect for an afternoon or evening stroll. Begin with a walk around Lake Elizabeth at the HARP's west end and then make your way past Kelly Falls. Hidden among the landscaping are little bronze statues of wildlife—animals, insects, even a bronze fish leaping in a side stream. Water from the Farley/Reilly Fountain cascades down water steps to the river, while Confluence Fountain is lit up at night so spectators can see the jets shooting water over 50 feet in the air.

The Daily Grind operates a coffee stand if you are in need of refreshment, and all of Union Avenue's fine dining is within easy walking distance. If you want to get out on the water, paddleboats can be rented at the boathouse on Lake Elizabeth (719-595-1589). The one-person boat is $6 for half an hour; the two- to four-person boat is $10 for half an hour. See the Web site for hours. You could also take a ride on the HARP excursion boat—narrated rides take about 20 minutes. Adult admission $5, seniors and military $4, children (3–12) $3, and kids under three ride free.

The HARP's amphitheater is often used for summer concerts and festivals, so be sure to check out the Web site to see what events are planned for when you're in town.

Pueblo River Trails System. Connecting up with trails in the Lake Pueblo State Park, the Pueblo River Trail follows the Arkansas River to where it meets Fountain Creek and heads upstream, eventually jogging over to CSU-Pueblo. There are some side trails that take you around Runyon Lake and connect the system with the Historic Arkansas Riverwalk of Pueblo downtown. Maps are available on the **Pueblo Parks and Recreation** Web site (www.pueblo.us/parks).

✱ Lodging

If you are looking for your favorite hotel chain, Pueblo most likely has it. A gamut of hotels runs alongside I-25, north of exit 101—the majority right on Elizabeth Street. The Pueblo Chamber of Commerce can provide you with a complete list.

HOTELS ♿ **Pueblo Marriott** (719-542-3200 or 1-800-228-9290; www.marriott.com), 110 W. 1st St. Right off the interstate and only blocks from Pueblo's historic downtown area, the Pueblo Marriott is very conveniently located for exploring Pueblo. The hotel offers all the amenities you would expect at a Marriott—cable TV, pay-per-view, restaurant, pool, etc. Rooms and suites $100–170.

BED & BREAKFASTS **Abriendo Inn** (719-544-2703; www.abriendo inn.com), 300 W. Abriendo Ave. This B&B, located within walking distance of the Union Avenue Historic District, is one of the best things going in Pueblo. In fact, many consider it the best B&B in Colorado. Once inside, you will see what all the fuss is about. The inn maintains 10 guest rooms, all of which are located on the second or third floors. Antique furniture graces the common rooms and guest rooms, and considering the emphasis on maintaining a "period" feel, the decorating is pleasantly contemporary. The inn's amenities include free wi-fi Internet access, an around-the-clock supply of snacks, and afternoon tea. Each room has a private bath, air-conditioning, and cable TV. Some rooms feature whirlpool baths—especially pleasant when the weather is a bit chilly. Every morning, Kate Zamora serves a fabulous gourmet breakfast. The menu changes regularly, but beer bread toast is always available, a favorite of guests. Rooms $59–145.

The Edgar Olin House (719-544-5727; www.olin-house.com), 727 W. 13th St. Three rooms are available at this B&B, and like the rest of the house, they are decorated in grand Victorian style. "Victorian" always brings to mind images of heavy curtains and lots of lace, but the innkeepers did not go overboard when it came to decorating. In fact, the atmosphere is downright comfortable. Amenities include a full gourmet breakfast, afternoon tea, and, in the summer, a chance to enjoy the inn's flower garden. Rooms all have a private bathroom, air-conditioning, refrigerator, and TV with DVD player (a large collection of DVDs available). The Judge Coulter Room is particularly attractive with its Jacuzzi for two. Rooms $69–149.

CAMPGROUNDS **Lake Pueblo State Park,** (719-561-9320; www.parks.state .co.us/parks/LakePueblo), 640 Pueblo Reservoir Rd. The state park maintains 401 campsites divided into three campgrounds. The Northern Plains Campground is to the north of the park, near the North Marina. The campground offers electrical and non-electrical sites, and group camping is available. All the sites at the Juniper Breaks Campground are non-electrical. On the south side of the park is the Arkansas Point Campground, located near the South Marina. This campground is all electrical sites. All sites have a fire pit and covered picnic table (shade is a lifesaver in the summer). Electrical sites have some extra amenities like flush toilets and showers (bring coins for the shower). They also have dump stations and laundry facilities.

All of the sites at Juniper Breaks, as well as some at Arkansas Point, are open for off-season camping (Oct. 1–Apr. 1). Shower and laundry facilities, however, are closed during the off-season. You can reserve campsites online (follow the links on the park Web site) or by calling 1-800-678-2267. Sites $8–22.

Pueblo KOA (719-542-2273 or 1-800-562-7453; www.koakampgrounds .com/where/co/06161), 4131 I-25 N., exit 108 off I-25. For recreation, the campground has a heated pool and a "jumping pillow." There are facilities for all sorts of campers—you can park your RV, pitch your tent, or rent one of their Kamping Kabins. Rates run from $20 for a basic site up to $70 for their Super Site.

Pueblo South/Colorado City KOA (719-676-3376 or 1-800-562-8646; www.koakampgrounds.com/where/co/06105), 9040 I-25 South, exit 74 off I-25. Located about 20 miles south of Pueblo, this campground has a heated pool, hot tub, and a mini-golf course. Rates run from $20 for a basic site up to $70 for their Super Site.

✷ Where to Eat

Throughout its history, people from around the world have made their way to and through Pueblo. Spanish-speaking folks have been here since the region was considered the territory of Spain. Later, Italians and other immigrants made their way to Pueblo to find work in the booming mining and steel industries. Nowhere is this rich heritage as readily evident as when you look for a place to eat in Pueblo. The city serves up great Italian and Mexican cuisine, and there are plenty of classic American steakhouses and burger joints. While a lot of the action is centered on the downtown area, be sure to get in your car and see what's cooking around the city as well.

DINING OUT **La Renaissance** (719-543-6367; www.larenaissance restaurant.com), 217 E. Routt Ave. Open Mon.–Sat., evenings 5–9. The property alone is worth a meal at La Renaissance, which makes its home in a restored Presbyterian church, originally built in 1886. The church interior's exposed beams and stuccoed walls complement a menu that is also traditional—steak, seafood, and chicken are mainstays. If you like ribs, be sure to try their Incomparable Baby Back Pork Ribs, which are outstanding. Entrées $15–20 (a little more for the chef's selection and the bigger cuts of prime rib, a little less for the veggie plate).

EATING OUT **Angelo's Pizza Parlor And-a-Moré** (719-545-3400; www.angelos-pizza.com), 223 S. Union Ave. Open Sun.–Thu. 11–10 and Fri. and Sat. 11–11. This is the place to go for pizza if you are downtown (they also have a location on the north side of town at 1110 US 50 W.). I love the interior brick walls and movie posters; the place has a fun vibe. Pizzas $7 (up to $20 for their specialty creations). Sandwiches and other Italian entrées $6–8.

Cactus Flower (719-545-8218), 4610 N. Elizabeth St. Open Mon.–Sat. 11–10 and Sun. 11–9. Often cited as the best place for Southwest cuisine in Pueblo. Great atmosphere—local artists have their work displayed throughout. Entrées $8–12.

Carriage House Restaurant at Rosemount (719-543-4192; www.rosemountrestaurant.com), 419 W. 14th St. Lunch is served Tues.–Sat. from 11AM to 2 PM; afternoon tea, Tues.–Sat. 1:30–2; and dinner, Fri. and Sat. "by reservation or chance." Ron Charlton has been the chef and proprietor of the Carriage House Restaurant at Rosemount since 2003. His menu includes entrées like Chicken Piccata and Alfredo Pacifica, and the lunch menu has a fantastic selection of sandwiches. The ambience is pleasant and particularly festive around the holidays. Lunch $10–14; afternoon tea $14 (tea and tour $18); and dinner $15–18.

♿ **Gold Dust Saloon** (719-545-0741), 217 Union Ave. This is a great place to grab lunch when you're downtown. For a saloon it has a surprisingly bright and airy interior. In addition to burgers and fries, they serve a variety of excellent sandwiches.

Do-Drop-In (719-542-0818), 1201 S. Santa Fe Ave. Open Mon.–Sat. 6 AM–10 PM and Sun. 6 AM–9 PM. Ask around and Puebloans will tell you some of the best pizza in town is found at the Do-Drop-In. The crust is thick and sweet. There are plenty of televisions if you need to keep an eye on a game. The TVs and the game room turn out to be nice distractions while you wait—since everything is made from scratch, it can take some time to get your food. Entrées $12–20.

BAKERIES & COFFEE SHOPS ♿ **The Daily Grind** (719-561-8567), 209 S. Union Ave. Open Mon.–Fri. 7 AM–11 PM, Sat. 8–11, and Sun. 8–6. The Daily Grind's baristas pour a complete menu of hot and cold drinks. They also have bagels, Danishes, and doughnuts as well as cheese cake and fantastic brownie bars. The priciest drink is $4.50—snacks generally in the $2 range.

♿ **Hopscotch Bakery** (719-542-4467; www.hopscotchbakery.com), 333 S. Union Ave. Open Mon.–Fri. 7–5:30 and Sat. 8–4. Proprietors Mary Oreskovich and Richard Warner opened the Hopscotch Bakery in 2005. Until recently, they ran what was the best little restaurant in Pueblo, the Steel City Diner. The lunch menu at the bakery maintains the couple's commitment to using quality, locally grown products to create great food. Definitely try their salad of mixed field greens. Lunch about $6.

BARS, TAVERNS & BREW PUBS 🍸 ♿ **Shamrock Brewing Company** (719-543-9974; www.shamrockbrewing.com), 108 W. 3rd St. Open Mon.–Thurs. 11–midnight, Fri. and Sat. 11–1 AM, and Sun. 10–11. This pub has been around for more than 40 years. They brew their own beer, including a chili beer that's a bit on the spicy side.

🍸 ♿ **Phil's Radiator Service and Beer Garden** (719-584-2671), 109 E. C St., Pueblo (within the Union Street Historic District). Open daily 4 PM–2 AM. You simply have to love a bar located in an old garage. Inside, Phil's Radiator Service offers pool. Outside in the beer garden, they often have live music throughout the summer. Located right downtown, the bar is a favorite with the younger set.

✵ Entertainment

Pueblo Symphony (719-545-7967) 2200 Bonforte Blvd. Every year on the Saturday before the Fourth of July, the Pueblo Symphony provides music for Pueblo Riverwalk—a show that is punctuated by a fireworks display. The orchestra's season runs from late fall to late spring.

Sangre de Cristo Arts and Conference Center (719-295-7200; www.sdc-arts.org), 210 N. Santa Fe Ave. Whether you are interested in music, theatre, dance, or the visual arts, the Sangre de Cristo Arts Center has it all. The Children's Playhouse Series

PHIL'S RADIATOR SERVICE AND BEER GARDEN

has performers that the whole family can enjoy. Festive Fridays brings various bands to Pueblo every week throughout the summer. The Center even has a ballet theatre. Tickets for most events are very reasonably priced. While you're there, take the kids to the Buell Children's Museum (see To See & Do) or visit their art galleries.

I-25 Speedway (719-542-2277), 400 Gobatti Pl. If you are interested in auto racing, Pueblo's I-25 Speedway is located north of town at exit 108. The quarter-mile track is a favorite for racing late model Grand Prix cars.

Colorado State Fair and Rodeo (1-800-876-4567; www.coloradostatefair.com). A highlight of the Colorado State Fair is the annual rodeo. (For more information, see Colorado State Fair, Special Events.)

✷ Selective Shopping

There are a number of great shops in Pueblo's Union Avenue Historic District.

A Blast from the Past Antiques (719-546-6647; www.abftpa.com), 123 S. Union Ave. This shop specializes in antiques from the 1950s through the 1970s. A great place to celebrate 20th-century pop culture.

Aladdin's Antique Mall (719-545-2851; www.aladdinsmall.com), 118 and 120 S. Union Ave. A number of antiques vendors show off their goods at this 7,500-square-foot facility.

Somewhere in Time at 220 S. Union Ave. and **Somewhere in Time Too** at 105 S. Union Ave., have a great selection of 19th- and early 20th-century antiques. If you like ornate, plush Victorian furniture, both of these places will keep your attention.

Kushnir Furniture (719-543-5804), 216 S. Union Ave. Antique technology buffs will love this place. In addition to a small stash of antique furniture, they have quite a few antique radios on hand, as well as old record players, TVs, and movie projectors.

John Deaux Art Gallery (719-545-8407), 221 S. Union Ave. Sells paintings and sculptures by Colorado artists.

Pueblo Southwest Trading Co. (719-542-4998 or 1-800-224-3047; www.puebloswtradingco.com), 104 S.

Victoria Ave. Just a block west of Union Avenue, this shop specializes in southwestern home décor—everything from furniture to accessories.

✷ Special Events

♿ ✐ *August:* **Colorado State Fair** (719-561-8484 or 1-800-876-4567; www.coloradostatefair.com), 1001 Beulah Ave. The Colorado State Fair has been a Pueblo institution since 1872, making it older than Colorado itself. It was originally billed as the Southern Colorado Agricultural and Industrial Association. The fair takes place at the end of summer—the 11-day event always closes out on Labor Day. It is clearly the biggest annual event in Pueblo. In fact, with nearly half a million people making their way from around the state to take part in the festivities, it's the biggest annual event in Colorado.

You can take in such competitive events as the rodeo, pig racing, and the Mutton Busting competition (where kids compete to stay seated on rambunctious sheep). There are various livestock and agricultural contests every day. Or you can enjoy carnival rides, firework shows, and concerts.

The main gate is on Prairie Avenue, between Tulane and Purdue streets. There are also gates on Arroyo and Beulah avenues. Tickets can be picked up on your way into the fair for $5 during the week, or $8 Fri.–Sun. For cheaper admission, check out the Colorado State Fair Web site for a list of Discount Days—on certain days they offer discounts for different groups (like military personnel or seniors)—and for the general public, various corporate sponsors also run deals for cheaper tickets.

Beulah Outdoor Arts and Crafts Show. Beulah is 25 miles southwest of Pueblo on CO 78. For more than 50 years now, they have hosted an annual arts and crafts festival. Over a hundred vendors will display their wares against the backdrop of the gorgeous Beulah Valley. The fair is usually held in early August.

✐ *September:* **Chile & Frijoles Festival** (1-800-233-3446), downtown Pueblo. Held every year in mid-September, the Chile & Frijoles Festival celebrates the region's agricultural produce, in particular chilies and pinto beans. Additionally, various artists and craftspeople use this opportunity to display their work. Competitions during the festival include the Best Bean Dip in Pueblo, the Holy Frijoles cooking contest, and a jalapeno eating contest. There's also a farmer's market, plenty of food vendors, and live entertainment.

TRINIDAD

The historic section of downtown Trinidad, with its brick-paved streets, old buildings, restaurants, and art galleries, seems tailor-made for tourists. The old Santa Fe Trail once ran down Main Street, and today this section of the trail has been made a National Historic District, called the Corazon de Trinidad (the "heart of Trinidad").

Trinidad sits at the most natural place for a town. Nearby is the confluence of the Purgatoire River and Raton Creek. To the southeast looms Fishers Peak. At an altitude of 9,627 feet, it is the highest point in the U.S. east of I-25. To the west lies the fertile Purgatoire River Valley, and to the east the plains of southeast Colorado.

For centuries, various people have called this region home. The first settlers of European decent were Gabriel Gutierrez and his nephew, who in 1859 built a cabin here. Strategically located on the Santa Fe Trail, by 1861 the town of Trinidad had become an important stop for travelers.

Over the years, Trinidad has had its share of colorful characters. Old West legends like Doc Holliday and Billy the Kid walked the streets. In the 1880s, Bat Masterson served as marshal in Trinidad. Even Wyatt Earp made his way to Trinidad for a time. Later during the heydays of coal mining, Mother Jones came to town to help organize the union.

Today the town is more settled, but no less colorful. In 1969, Dr. Stanley Biber performed his first sex-change operation in Trinidad. Soon people had dubbed the town, the "Sex Change Capital of the World."

With a thriving arts community and a growing number of galleries, Trinidad is becoming a travel destination in its own right. You might hear Trinidad called "the little Santa Fe." To some extent that is the feel here, but it ignores the unique character of this distinctly Colorado town, a character well worth experiencing.

GUIDANCE **Colorado Welcome Center at Trinidad** (970-641-2983), 309 Nevada Ave., also houses the **Trinidad and Las Animas County Chamber of Commerce** (719-846-9285; www.trinidadchamber.com). The folks behind the counter are locals who are eager to tell you about their town. They are a great source of information—they know if it has been snowing near Cuchara Pass, and they can recommend a great place for lunch. As one of the state welcome centers, they have brochures for every major attraction in Colorado.

More Web sites:

www.historictrinidad.com

www.trinidadco.com

www.exploresoutheastcolorado.com

GETTING THERE *By car:* If you're coming from the north or south, I-25 is your best bet. The interstate follows the Front Range and passes through Trinidad on its way to Santa Fe, Albuquerque, and points south. From the east, US 350 cuts down from US 50 in La Junta.

By air: The most accessible airport to Trinidad is the **Colorado Springs Airport** (719-550-1972; www.flycos.com), about 130 miles to the north.

By train: **AMTRAK** (1-800-872-7245; www.amtrak.com) has a terminal in Trinidad, and the Southeast Chief makes a stop here on its way to Los Angeles.

By bus: **Greyhound** (719-846-7271 or 1-800-231-2222; www.greyhound.com) has a stop in Trinidad. Check the Web site for route information and tickets.

GETTING AROUND *By foot:* With the number of historic buildings and the brick-paved streets, Trinidad is great for walking.

By trolley: **Trinidad Trolley** (719-846-9843 ext. 133), 309 Nevada Ave. Open daily 10–3, and free. The Trinidad Trolley leaves the parking lot of the Colorado Visitor Center at the top of every hour (last tour at 3). As you tour the town, you get on and off along the way to explore various attractions.

MEDICAL EMERGENCIES **Mt. San Rafael Hospital** (719-846-9213; www.msrhc.org), 410 Benedicta Ave. Located on Trinidad's east side, the facility offers 24-hour emergency medical treatment.

✷ To See & Do

MUSEUMS ☂ ♿ **Trinidad History Museum** (719-846-7217; www.coloradohistory.org), 300 E. Main St. Open daily May–Sept. 10–4. In the off-season, the museum is open "pending staff availability." They suggest you call for hours. The museum complex includes the Baca House, Bloom Mansion, and the Santa Fe Trail Museum (312 E. Main St.). In addition to the beautifully preserved buildings, the Baca House and Bloom Mansion also have impressive gardens for visitors to tour. Adult admission $6, seniors $5, students and children (6–12) $3, and kids under 6 free. Tickets can be bought at the museum bookstore or the Santa Fe Trail Museum.

☂ ♿ **A. R. Mitchell Memorial Museum and Gallery** (719-846-4224; www.mitchellmuseum.com), 150 E. Main St. Open May–Sept., Tues.–Sun. 10–4. A. R. Mitchell was a prolific artist who was adept at capturing cowboy life. He grew up on a homestead west of Trinidad and rose to fame painting covers for Western pulp magazines. Today, an impressive collection of his work is found in this museum, which also displays the work of other Western artists, including painters and photographers—there's even a collection of Spanish colonial folk art.

Louden-Henritze Archaeology Museum (719-846-5508; www.trinidadstate.edu/museum), 600 Prospect at Trinidad Junior State College. Open Mon.–Thurs. 10–3. This museum takes a deeper look at the region's history. Exhibits include geological formations, fossils, and a dinosaur track exhibit. Kids will get a kick out seeing the mammoth tusks and other Ice Age animal bones. Free admission.

Old Firehouse No. 1 Children's Museum (719-846-8220 or 719-846-2024), 314 N. Commercial St. Open summers Mon.–Fri. 11–3. This museum strives to teach guests about Victorian Trinidad from a child's point of view. Kids love the hands-on exhibits, 1900s classroom, and vintage fire truck. Free admission.

HISTORIC SITES **El Corazon de Trinidad.** This is a 6.5-mile section of Trinidad's downtown historic district. It's also a National Historic Landmark District. There are historical markers around town telling the story of individual people and places important to Trinidad. Guidebooks are also available for sale at the Carnegie Public Library, 202 N. Animas, or at any of the museums in town, that will guide you on a walking tour of the district.

Ludlow Monument. In 1914, fighting broke out between the Colorado National Guard and striking coal miners. The tent colony in which the miners and their families were living was burned to the ground. Later, two women and 11 children were found in a cellar beneath one of the tents, dead from asphyxiation. In addition, two union leaders were killed. The event was called the Ludlow Massacre, and union organizers put out a call to arms. For 10 days, skirmishes were fought between miners, mine companies, and the National Guard. Fighting stopped when President Wilson sent in federal troops. The massacre is com-

A HISTORIC LOCOMOTIVE

memorated at the Ludlow Monument. Next to the monument is a cellar door that leads down to the place where the women and children died.

GUIDED TOURS **Colt Ranch** (719-845-0353: www.coltranch.com), 10,000 CR 43.6. Jim Colt will take you via stagecoach to the old mining town of Primero. The town was active from 1901 to 1933. Though the buildings are gone, there is enough left to give your imagination a boost as you explore this unique ghost town. Call for tour information and to make tour reservations.

SCENIC DRIVES **The Santa Fe Trail Scenic and Historic Byway** (www.santafetrailscenicandhistoricbyway.org). The Santa Fe Trail runs across the entirety of southeast Colorado, from Kansas to New Mexico, but there is an 80-mile stretch along US 350 that is a particularly nice drive. Starting in La Junta, US 350 winds through the Comanche National Grasslands on its way to Trinidad. The prairie is marked with small canyons and low buttes—much more scenic than endless fields of corn. There are several places where you can stop and make a short hike to see the old ruts left by countless wagons traveling the Santa Fe Trail.

Scenic Highway of Legends (www.huerfanocounty.org/os/shol.htm). This scenic drive begins in Trinidad and follows CO 12 west up the Purgatoire River Valley, through the Cuchara Pass into the Cuchara Valley. Just outside La Veta it connects with CO 160 and ends at I-25. Along the way you pass by the historic Coke Ovens in Cokedale. Before you enter Stonewall, there's a bridge on the right over the Purgatoire River with a house on it—an interesting sight. The geological feature from which Stonewall gets its name stretches out on both sides of the road and is worth a stop. From here the terrain becomes more rocky and pronounced as you climb to Cuchara Pass. Be sure to stop in Cuchara—it's a good place to stop for a bite to eat.

✷ Outdoor Activities

GOLF **Trinidad Las Animas County Municipal Golf Course** (719-846-4015; www.trinidadgc.com), 1417 Nolan Dr. This nicely kept municipal course has great views of the Sangre de Cristo Mountains. The course was built in 1915 and is the fourth oldest course in Colorado. Eighteen holes $21–23.

Grandote Peaks Golf Club (719-742-3391 or 1-800-457-9986; www.grandotepeaks.com), 5540 CO 12, La Veta. Graced by great mountain views with the Cuchara River running through, there is no better course in the area. Grandote Peaks was named one of top three courses in Colorado by *Golf Digest.* Eighteen holes $45–65.

SKATEBOARDING **Trinidad Skate Park** (www.trinidadskatepark.com), 1415 Beshore Ave. Open daily 8–10. If you are looking for a unique diversion, and enjoying skateboarding, the Trinidad Skate Park is just the place. The park is 15,000 square feet, and the variety built into the park's design will keep even the most avid boarder from getting bored. Access is free.

DOWNTOWN CUCHARA

GREEN SPACE **Trinidad Lake State Park** (719-846-6951; www.parks.state.co.us/parks/trinidadlake), 32610 CO 12, Trinidad. Open 24 hours a day, the park is just a short drive from Trinidad. Anglers come to Trinidad Lake for the great fishing for rainbow and brown trout, walleye, and bluegill. Hikers will find a number of excellent paved and unpaved trails—the more adventurous taking the Reilly Canyon Trail to the old town of Cokedale and Reilly Canyon. There are 9 miles of trails for mountain biking and number paved trails for the roadies. Daily park pass $6.

Lathrop State Park (719-738-2376; www.parks.state.co.us/parks/lathrop) 70 CR 502, Walsenberg. Open daily 5–10. Fishing open 24 hours. This is Colorado's oldest state park. Two lakes, Horseshoe and Martin, and several ponds make Lathrop a great spot for fishing. The lakes are stocked with everything from rainbow trout to northern pike. There's even a children's fishing pond for the young'uns. Biking is popular on the 3-mile Cuerno Verde Trail, and there's a 9-hole course for golfers. Daily park pass $6.

✷ Lodging

There are numerous places to hole up for a night or two in Trinidad as well as in the little towns along the Highway of Legends. Stonewall, Cuchara, and La Veta have their share of inns, B&Bs, and remote properties with rental cabins. The addresses listed below, however, are all in Trinidad unless otherwise noted.

HOTELS Trinidad has a view of the usual chain hotels—Quality Inn, Holiday Inn, Best Western, Super 8—all located near I-25.

BED & BREAKFASTS **Chicosa Canyon Bed & Breakfast** (719-846-6199; www.chicosacanyonbb.com), 32391 CR 40. Twelve miles northwest of Trinidad, the Chicosa Canyon B&B has two guest rooms and a cabin that sleeps four. The secluded 64-acre property has trails for hiking and horseback riding. If you are traveling with horses, overnight stabling is available. Rooms $110–120 and cabin $160.

Tarabino Inn (719-846-2115 or 1-866-846-8808; www.tarabinoinn.com), 310 E. 2nd St. This tastefully decorated B&B is located two blocks off Main Street in Trinidad. The inn has four rooms. The Walnut Suite has its own private bath. The Chestnut Suite has a detached private bath. Both the West and East Gable Rooms share a bath. A full breakfast is served daily 8–9. A continental breakfast is available before and after this time. Rooms have cable TV and a VCR. Rooms $84–129.

Colt Ranch (719-845-0353; www.coltranch.com), 10,000 CR 43.6. West of Trinidad, the Colt Ranch offers more than just a B&B. Visitors come for chuckwagon dinners, Dutch oven classes, and tours of area mining towns. However, lodgers are not lost in the fray with all these activities. Rooms are in keeping with the Western ranching theme. A full gourmet breakfast is provided every morning. Lunches and dinners are available at an additional cost. They have three rooms in the main house and the upstairs of the carriage house sleeps four. There is a tipi and shepherd's wagon for a more rustic experience when the weather permits. Rooms $155, Carriage House $250, and tipi and shepherd's wagon $100.

THE SPANISH PEAKS FROM TRINIDAD

Inn at the Spanish Peaks Bed & Breakfast (719-742-5313; www.innatthespanishpeaks.com), 310 E. Francisco St., La Veta. There are three rooms, all with unique themes—the Costa Rica Suite with wicker furniture, the St. Andrews Suite with a golfing theme, and the Colorado Suite with heavy log accents. All the rooms have private baths and decks. There is wireless DSL, but the inn does not have phones or televisions in order to promote a peaceful stay, removed from distractions. Rooms $95–140.

CAMPGROUNDS **Trinidad Lake State Park** (719-846-6951; www.parks.state.co.us/parks/trinidadlake), 32610 CO 12. The 62 campsites at Trinidad Lake sit on a ridge 150 feet above the reservoir. The park is somewhat wooded and many sites offer shade. A number of the sites are available for winter camping. Amenities include flush toilets, showers, and laundry facilities (all available May 1–Oct. 15). Many sites have electrical hook-ups. Sites $14–18.

Lathrop State Park (719-738-2376; www.parks.state.co.us/parks/Lathrop) 70 CR 502, Walsenberg. Located north of Trinidad, west of Walsenberg, Lathrop has 103 campsites. Amenities include vault and flush toilets, pay showers, and laundry facilities. Many sites have electrical hook-ups. A number of sites are open throughout the winter, as are the flush toilet and shower facilities. Sites $12–18.

CABINS & COTTAGES **Yellow Pine Ranch** (719-742-3528; www.yellowpine.us), 15880 CO 12, Cuchara. Open May–Oct. Yellow Pine Ranch has nine cabins and a lodge for rent. The cabins sleep 2–8, depending on the unit. The lodge sleeps 12–15. They all have a full kitchen, and none has a TV or telephone. The ranch offers horseback riding for adults and children 7 and older throughout the summer. Cabins $85–155. The main lodge is $500.

✱ Where to Eat

DINING OUT **Rino's Italian Restaurant & Steakhouse** (719-845-0949), 400 E. Main St. Open for lunch Wed.–Fri. 11–2 and dinner Wed.–Sun. 5–9. I am not sure if Rino's is better known for its menu or the singing waiters. Yes, they really sing, and with gusto, but this in no way detracts from the casually elegant atmosphere and fine Italian dining. The menu includes Italian standards as well as a full selection of seafood. Lunch $5–10 and dinner $10–25. Reservations for dinner are recommended.

Timbers Restaurant (719-742-3838), 23 Cuchara Rd., Cuchara. Open all summer Tues.–Fri. 5–9 and Sat. 11–9. Sun. lunch buffet 11–3 and Sun. dinner buffet 5–9. Nestled on the main strip of Cuchara, just off the Highway of Legends, Timbers is the best spot in Cuchara for fine dining. It has a fantastic menu of steak, chicken, and fish. And musicians are regularly engaged to provide live entertainment. The bar serves a bar menu all day. Reservations are recommended for the restaurant.

EATING OUT **Black Jack's Saloon, Steakhouse & Inn** (719-846-9501; www.blackjackssaloon.com), 225 W. Main St. Open for lunch Tues.–Sat. 11–3 and for dinner Mon.–Thurs. 4–9 and Fri.–Sat. 4–10. Located right downtown, Black Jack's has everything you could need for a stop in Trinidad. In addition to the excellent steakhouse, there's an authentic Old West saloon and a five-room inn. For lunch, this might be the best place in town to grab a burger. Lunch $6–9 and dinner $10–26.

Mission at the Bell (719-845-1513), 134 W. Main St. Open Mon.–Thurs. 11–8 and Fri. and Sat. 11–9. Located in the basement of the Bell Block, you will be surprised how open and bright this place is—especially during the day when skylights let in some sun. They serve authentic Mexican food—they make their own red and green chili—and meals run $6–9.

Nana and Nano's Monteleone's Deli and Pasta House (719-846-2696), 418 E. Main St. Open Tues.–Wed. 10:30–6 and Thurs.–Sat. 10:30–7. This is the best place for Italian in Trinidad. Everything is made from scratch, and like the Italian restaurants in Pueblo, you can expect to wait a bit for your food. Ahhh, but it's worth it. Great sauces, lots of different pasta dishes, and the classic meatballs and Italian sausage. Sandwiches $4–6 and entrées $6–11.

Yesterday's Pizza (719-845-8640), 512 San Juan St. Open Mon.–Thurs. 11–8:30, Fri.–Sat. 11–10, and Sun. noon–8:30. Every college town has to have a great pizza place. The students at Trinidad State Junior College have Yesterday's Pizza. From pizzas to lasagna, everything is made with best ingredients. Carryout and delivery only; free delivery in Trinidad on orders over $10.

BARS, TAVERNS & BREW PUBS 🍸

Trinidad Brewing Company (719-846-7069; www.trinidadbrewingcompany.com), 516 Elm St. Open Mon.–Sat. 11–11. Known primarily for their handcrafted beer, the menu is worthy of attention too. From buffalo burgers to great salads, the pub keeps guests both quenched and satisfied. Various bands and an Open Mic Night provide regular live music.

🍸 ♿ **The Dog Bar & Grill** (719-742-6366), 34 Cuchara Ave., Cuchara. Open Sun.–Thurrs. 11–10-ish and Fri. and Sat. 11–midnight. Any evening in Cuchara, you will find the Dog Bar your best bet for refreshment and some live entertainment. On a summer night, the place can get so full that crowds pour out onto the front porch. If the bustling scene inside gets to be too much, there's an outside seating area away from the music and dance floor.

✷ Entertainment

Southern Colorado Repertory Theatre (719-846-4765; www.scrtheatre.com) performances at the Massari Theater, corner of State and Broom, on the college campus. See the Web site for a complete schedule of summer shows.

✷ Selective Shopping

Corazon Gallery (719-846-0207), 149 E. Main St. Open Mon.–Sat. 10–5 and Sun. noon–4 (in winter, Mon.–Sat. 10–4.) This is Trinidad's local artist co-op, showcasing work from a number of artists from the southeast Colorado region.

First Street Gallery (719-846-1441 or 1-866-846-1441; www.trinidadarts.org), 150 E. 1st St. Open Apr.–Dec. Tues.–Sat. 10–3. The gallery stages nine openings a year with the purpose of promoting regional and contemporary art.

✵ Special Events

June: **Santa Fe Trail Days Festival** (Trinidad Chamber of Commerce 719-846-7021 or 1-866-480-4750), downtown Trinidad. Every year Trinidad hosts this festival, which has something for everyone—live music, great food, a car show, a petting zoo, even a chili cook-off. And to celebrate the Santa Fe Trail, there are reenactments and "living history" activities.

August: **Trinidad Round-Up and the Las Animas County Fair** (719-846-7021 or 719-846-6881), 2100 N. Linden Ave. Starting a few days before and going through the Labor Day weekend, this fair is a highly anticipated regional event. There are the usual livestock shows, a carnival, and, of course, the rodeo.

Trinidaddio Blues Festival (719-846-3000 ext. 21 or call the Trinidad Chamber at 719-846-9285; www.trinidaddio.com), Central Park. The Trinidaddio Blues Festival made its appearance in 1998, and it continues to be a popular event every year. General admission $20, children (6–12) $5, and children 5 and under free.

EASTERN PLAINS

The region east of the mountains, from I-25 to the Kansas border, is essentially a long, flat stretch of land—much to the chagrin of first-time visitors driving into Colorado from the east, hoping to leave behind the endless prairies when they hit the state line. For many travelers, the eastern plains don't readily come to mind when making a list of desirable Colorado travel destinations. There are no tourist towns, no revived historic districts with art-gallery-lined streets. There are no ski hills, and celebrity sightings are rare. The plains, however, have a strong appeal to different travelers for various reasons.

For the purposes of this book, the region is divided into the northeast and southeast plains. The northeast is that area around I-70 and north. The other major throughway here is I-76, which connects Denver to Nebraska. The southeast section is cut by US 50, which for a time follows the old Santa Fe Trail and runs from Pueblo to Kansas.

The northeast plains are primarily farming country, with more ranching to the north. Ranchers first brought their livestock out this way in the late 19th century. Later, sheep were brought in to graze the plains. Eventually settlers came here to homestead and farm the land. For years people farmed or ranched, and they prospered. When larger companies began buying up farmland, the days of the family farm were numbered. Where many small farming communities thrived now sit virtual ghost towns. Today the biggest towns in the northeast are found along I-76—Fort Morgan and Sterling being the biggest.

Fort Morgan is best known for being Glenn Miller's hometown. Though Miller was born in Iowa, he went to high school here, and every year they celebrate with the Glenn Miller Festival. Science fiction fans may be interested to know that Fort Morgan is also the burial place of Philip K. Dick, author of *Do Androids Dream of Electric Sheep?* and *The Man in the High Castle.*

Sterling is the first big town you hit coming in from Nebraska on I-76. The story of Sterling is tied closely with the railroad. In 1881, the few settlers in the area heard the Union Pacific Railroad was planning on pushing down their way. So they offered the railroad some land with the understanding that a town would be established around a train stop there. So Sterling was born. Today, the railroad yard is an unavoidable symbol of downtown. Right off the highway you will find the Sterling Tourist Information Center, which has information on all of

Colorado, and farther from the highway there are a bunch of fast-food joints on Main Street.

The southeast plains are a paradise for nature lovers—especially the birdwatchers who come a long way to see the lesser prairie chicken and the annual migration of the snow goose. Some people come to hike into Picketwire Canyonlands to view 150-million-year-old dinosaur footprints—the longest set of fossilized dinosaur tracks in the world. Others simply come for the quiet—for the plains have a certain majesty that can't be compared to the mountains in the west.

The old Santa Fe Trail once passed right through the heart of southeast Colorado—roughly following US 50 from the east and then heading southwest with US 350. Though the Trail has lain unused for over a century, you can find clues to its past all over the place. There are still places where you can find ruts left by countless wagons, driven by pioneers and traders as they made their way back and forth across the plains. Forts along the way served as way stations, where travelers could stock up on supplies and hear news from the frontier or back home. Bents Old Fort, a National Historic Site, lies just outside La Junta.

The Arkansas and Purgatoire rivers, which meet just outside Las Animas, define the region. Tapping into that resource with irrigation ditches in the 1870s transformed the region's agricultural potential, giving Colorado some of its most productive farming land. Today, the area towns boast of prized produce, like Rocky Ford's famous cantaloupes.

The main towns lie along US 50. La Junta, Las Animas, and Lamar are the largest and hold the greatest potential for finding a good place to eat and put up for the night. Each of these towns also has historic sites that make for great touring.

BENT'S OLD FORT

La Junta began as a small settlement next to the railroad track that ran east and west along the Arkansas River. The town was made official in 1881. For years it served as a place for farmers and ranchers to get their produce to market via the railroad. Agriculture is still a big deal. Just east of town, you can get a feel for life on the plains in the 1840s at Bent's Old Fort National Historic Site. Or you can visit the Koshare Indian Museum and Kiva in town, which celebrates the Native American culture and is the home of the Koshare Indian Dancers.

Las Animas was founded in 1869 at the confluence of the Arkansas and Purgatoire rivers. In the town's early days, it was a center of commerce. Famous pioneer and mountain man Kit Carson lived in Boggsville before moving to nearby Fort Lyons, where he died. You can get a sense for the old town at the Boggsville National Historic District 2 miles south of Las Animas. The man is commemorated at the Kit Carson Museum.

Lamar, founded in 1886, was named after the Secretary of the Interior under Grover Cleveland, Lucius Quintius Lamar. With this name, the townsfolk hoped to secure their town as the location for a new land office—the strategy worked. For many years the town was booming as people streamed in from the east looking to claim free land. Big Timbers Museum in Lamar can teach you a lot about those days and frontier life in general. You can also learn about the Japanese-American internment camp that used to operate nearby.

GUIDANCE

Northeast Plains

Colorado Welcome Center at Julesburg (970-474-2054), exit 180 off I-25. Open daily in the summer 8–6. Coming into Julesburg out of Nebraska, you may feel like you haven't quite gotten to Colorado yet, but this is it. A statue out front commemorates the riders who made the Pony Express possible.

Fort Morgan Area Chamber of Commerce (970-867-6702 or 1-800-354-8660; www.fortmorganchamber.org), 300 Main St., Fort Morgan. Open Mon.–Fri. 8–5.

Sterling and Logan County Chamber of Commerce (970-522-5070 or 1-866-522-5070; www.logancountychamber.com), 109 N. Front St., Sterling. Located in the town's historic Union Pacific Depot. Sterling also has a great Colorado Tourist Information Center right off I-76.

Colorado Welcome Center at Burlington (719-346-5554). The welcome center has its own on and off ramp, just west of exit 438. Open daily in the summer 8–6. The state welcome centers have all the information you need for researching lodging and activities for a trip to Colorado. The staff is also well versed on local happenings and attractions.

More Web sites: www.northeastcoloradotourism.com

Southeast Plains

La Junta Chamber of Commerce (719-384-7411; www.lajuntachamber.com), 110 Santa Fe Ave., La Junta. The LJCC Web site has a rather complete list of area museums and attractions as well as links of interest for tourists.

COLORADO WELCOME CENTER IN JULESBURG

Las Animas/Bent County Chamber of Commerce (719-456-0453), 332 Ambassador Thompson Blvd., Las Animas. Though there's no official visitor center, the chamber office has brochures on area attractions.

Colorado Welcome Center (719-336-3483) and the **Lamar Chamber of Commerce** (719-336-4379; www.lamarchamber.com) both reside at 109A E. Beech St., Lamar. The welcome center is staffed by locals who can answer your questions and give you a free state map. Outside, you can't miss the 18-foot-tall statue commemorating the women who traveled west along the Santa Fe Trail—the Madonna of the Trail Monument.

More Web sites:

www.exploresoutheastcolorado.com

www.santafetrailscenicandhistoricbyway.org

GETTING THERE *By car:* Driving to Colorado from the east side of the country, people will often ask if you are taking the northern route or the southern route. By this they mean I-80 or I-70, respectively. Of course, as you come across I-80, you will veer southwest in Nebraska on I-76. These two interstates, 70 and 76, are your main routes through the region.

To get to the southeast plains take I-25 to US 50, which runs east, eventually into Kansas. From the south, you can break off from I-25 in Trinidad and take US 350, which runs northeast to La Junta and US 50.

By air: The closest airport in the northeast is the **Denver International Airport** (1-800-AIR2DEN; www.flydenver.com). Renting a car you will find you are close to both I-70 and I-76. The **Colorado Springs Airport** (719-550-1972;

www.flycos.com) is your best bet for flying into the southeast.

By train: **AMTRAK's** (1-800-872-7245; www.amtrak.com) California Zephyr (Chicago to San Francisco) makes stops in Fort Morgan and Denver. The Southwest Chief runs from Chicago to Los Angeles, making stops at stations in La Junta and Lamar.

By bus: **Greyhound** (www.greyhound.com) operates regular service along I-70 (there is a stop in Limon) and I-76 (stops at Fort Morgan, Sterling, and Brush). There is also regular service to and from Pueblo from the **Pueblo Bus Depot** (719-543-2775 or 1-800-231-2222; www.greyhound.com), which is located near I-25, north of US 50 at 1080 Chinook Ln. From there you can travel east along US 50 and southeast to Springfield.

GETTING AROUND *By car:* Since towns are few and far between, you will need a car to get around the southeast plains.

By foot: To really experience the immensity of the plains, you have to get out of the car and do a little hiking. Remember that it gets awfully hot here in the summer, so drink lots of water.

MEDICAL EMERGENCIES

Northeast Plains

These facilities offer 24-hour emergency medical treatment.

Colorado Plains Medical Center (970-867-3391; www.coloradoplainsmedicalcenter.com), 1000 Lincoln St., Fort Morgan.

East Morgan County Hospital (970-842-6200), 2400 W. Edison, Brush. Located just east of Fort Morgan.

Southeast Plains

The facilities listed below offer 24-hour emergency medical treatment. Also, be aware that there are facilities in nearby Pueblo and Trinidad as well.

Arkansas Valley Regional Medical Center (719-384-5412; www.avrmc.org), 1100 Carson Ave., La Junta.

Prowers Medical Center (719-336-4343; www.prowersmedical.com), 401 Kendall Dr., Lamar.

Southeast Colorado Hospital (719-523-4501; www.sechosp.org), 373 E. 10th Ave., Springfield.

✷ To See & Do

HISTORIC SITES–SOUTHEAST PLAINS ✐ ♿ **Bent's Old Fort National Historic Site** (719-383-5010; www.nps.gov/beol), 35110 CO 194 E., La Junta. Open daily in summer (June–Aug.) 8–5:30, and daily the rest of the year 9–4. Guided tours at 10:30 and 1. The quarter-mile walk from the parking area to the fort is an easy stroll. If you are unable to walk the path, a shuttle is available. Adults (13+) $3, children $2, and children 5 and under free.

✐ **Boggsville National Historic District** (719-456-2748), 2 miles south of Las

Animas on CO 101. Admission and tours are free. There are three RV sites, tent camping sites, tipis to rent, full bathrooms, and showers for campers.

The Sand Creek Massacre National Historic Site (719-383-5051; www.nps.gov/sand), 910 Wansted St., Eads (park office). The park office is in town, but the park itself is located east of Eads on CR W. (Take CO 96 east to CR 54; head north to CR W where the road Ts. Turn east and go 1.3 miles to the park entrance.) Open Fri.–Sun. 9–4. The Sand Creek Historic Site opened to the public in the summer of 2007, with rangers giving "history talks" three times a day. On November 29, 1864, Col. John Chivington led 800 soldiers in an attack upon an encampment of unarmed Native Americans at nearby Sand Creek. The colonel ordered his men to, "Kill and scalp all, big and little." When the "battle" was over, nearly 200 Indians had been slain—mostly elderly men, women, and children. The park commemorates this atrocity and tries to put the event in historical context.

MUSEUMS–NORTHEAST PLAINS ☂ ♿ **Fort Morgan Museum** (970-542-4010; www.ftmorganmus.org), 414 Main St., Fort Morgan. Open Mon. 10–5, Tues.–Thurs. 10–8, Fri. 10–5, and Sat. 11–5. The Fort Morgan Museum preserves and commemorates pieces of Fort Morgan history, from archaeological artifacts found on local digs to the Hillrose Soda Fountain that closed in the 1970s. Admission is "by donation."

☂ ♿ **Old Town Museum** (719-346-7382 or 1-800-288-1334), 420 S. 14th St., Burlington. Open year-round Mon.–Sat. 9–5 and Sun. noon–5. This 6½-acre complex offers visitors a chance to tour a number of historic buildings. There's a sod house and an old jailhouse. There's even a saloon complete with a piano player and dancing girls. Throughout you will find artifacts from the turn of the

KIT CARSON COUNTY CAROUSEL AND MUSEUM

GENOA TOWER AND MUSEUM

century—there are plenty of cars and old tractors. In the summer they have entertainment and ice cream and wagon rides. Adult admission $6, seniors $5, children 12–17 $4, children 3–11 $2, and kids under 3 free.

Kit Carson County Carousel & Museum (719-348-5562; www.kitcarsoncountycarousel.com), 815 15th St., Burlington. Open Memorial Day–Labor Day 1–8. Recently completed, the Kit Carson County Carousel now has a fantastic museum. Though the museum is small, a lot is presented, and presented well. Visitors can see how carousel horses are made or learn how the organ works. Rides on the carousel cost just a quarter. Museum admission $1 (under 9 free).

Overland Trail Museum (970-522-3895; www.sterlingcolo.com/dept/plr/museum.php) 210533 CR 26.5, Sterling. Open Apr.–Oct., Mon.–Sat. 9–5 and Sun. 1–5; Nov.–Mar. Mon.–Sat. 10–4. This is a museum and an entire village of pre-1915 structures. The museum is housed in a fieldstone building from 1936 and commemorates the many people who traveled the Overland Trail, which was a spur off the Oregon Trail that ran east and west across Nebraska. Would-be gold miners and pioneers made the Overland Trail the most traveled road in the world from 1862 to 1868. Adult admission $2.

Genoa Tower and Museum (719-763-2309), 30121 Frontage Rd., Genoa. Open daily 8–8. To call the Wonder Tower in Genoa a museum is a bit of a stretch. It is, however, a confusingly preserved piece of Americana—a tourist trap along the lines of the world's largest pancake and the ubiquitous Mystery Spot. For a dollar you can tramp through a collection of junk like you've never seen and climb to the top for a view of six states. (Really? Six states?) On your way out you can test your wits and try to identify a tool or gadget from years past. If you guess right, they will refund the dollar you paid for admission. All and all, it's an experience to remember. Admission $1.

MUSEUMS–SOUTHEAST PLAINS ☂ ♿ **Koshare Indian Museum and Kiva** (719-384-4411; www.kosharehistory.org), 115 W. 18th St., La Junta. Open daily in summer 10–5 (open until 9 when they have a show); in winter, open daily noon–5, except Mon. and Wed. open 5–9. Back in 1933, a group of Boy Scouts gathered together to form an Indian club. They began performing Native American dances. Soon the Koshare Indian Dancers, as they were named, gathered quite a following—inspiring boys from various troops to work hard and meet the requirements of becoming Koshare Dancers themselves. Their celebration of native culture culminated in the creation of the Koshare Indian Museum and Kiva, which reportedly houses one the world's finest collections of Native American art and artifacts. The Koshare Indian Dancers are still around today and regularly perform in the Kiva. Adult admission $4, seniors and students $3, and children under six free.

☂ **Otero Museum** (719-384-7500), 706 W. Third St., La Junta. Open in summer (June–Sept.) Mon.–Sat. 1–5. Open by appointment in the off-season. Several historic buildings make up the Otero Museum complex, which strives to preserve the history of La Junta and Otero County. There's the blacksmith shop and the old-time grocery. They also have the requisite schoolhouse—in this case a log cabin replica of the first schoolhouse in Otero County. Among the many artifacts, of particular interest is the 1865 stagecoach, built in Concord, New Hampshire. Admission free.

☂ ♿ **Big Timbers Museum** (719-336-2472; www.bigtimbers.org), 7515 W. US 50, Lamar. Open Tues.–Sat. 1–5. The museum is named after the giant cottonwood trees that once lined the Arkansas River near Lamar. The area was once a spot where Native Americans camped for the winter. The everyday lives of past residents of southeast Colorado are chronicled by the artifacts such as agricultural tools used by early pioneers. The museum also tells the story of nearby Camp Amache, a World War II internment camp.

☂ **Kit Carson Museum** (719-456-2507), Corner of Ninth and Bent, Las Animas. Open daily in the summer noon–4. Kit Carson is a little bit of a local hero of sorts, but the museum is not just about the famous pioneer. This museum focuses on the lives of people who lived in Bent County from the time of Carson up to World War II. There are a number of buildings on the property, including the first city jail in Las Animas and a one-room schoolhouse.

SCENIC DRIVES **The Santa Fe Trail Scenic and Historic Byway** (www.santafetrailscenicandhistoricbyway.org). The drive begins in Trinidad and follows US 350 up to La Junta and then US 50 east to Lamar. Along the way you will pass close to various historical sites and markers that track the history of the Santa Fe Trail.

Pawnee Pioneer Trails. This scenic and historic byway takes you across the Pawnee National Grasslands with views of the Pawnee Buttes. The trip is a great introduction to the beauty of shortgrass prairie. The trail starts in Sterling (and

Fort Collins, the two legs meeting in Raymer), and then makes its way west to Ault. The route follows some back roads, so stop by the Sterling Tourist Information Center for a map and directions.

✸ Outdoor Activities

BIRDWATCHING **Bent's Bird Sanctuary** (719-456-0011), 10950 E. US 50, Las Animas. There are feeding stations, and a number of trails wind through the sanctuary, which is located right behind the Bent's Fort Inn. You can purchase bird feed in the hotel lobby.

John Martin State Park (719-829-1801; www.parks.state.co.us/parks/John MartinReservoir), 30703 CR 24, Hasty. Nearly 400 species of birds can be found around the John Martin Reservoir and nearby Lake Hasty. In the winter, the area is a regular roosting place for bald eagles.

Comanche National Grasslands (719-523-6591), 27162 US 287, Springfield. The lesser prairie chicken is pretty unique to southeast Colorado. At one time, the bird thrived in this region's prairies. As the prairies were tilled under for farmland, the lesser prairie chicken population dropped. But the restoration of prairie in the Comanche National Grasslands has helped stabilize bird numbers. Every year, from Mar. to June, male prairie chickens perform an elaborate courtship ritual for the females. Year after year, they return to the same display grounds, called leks. You need to reserve a spot to view this annual event—the number of cars and people allowed out to view the display grounds is limited, and you must follow certain rules in order to participate. Call the Grasslands office for more information.

FISHING **John Martin Reservoir and Lake Hasty** (719-829-1801; www.parks.state.co.us/parks/JohnMartinReservoir), 30703 CR 24, Hasty. People fishing the reservoir have caught everything from walleye and bass (largemouth and smallmouth) to bluegill and catfish. Lake Hasty has many of the same species but is also stocked with rainbow trout.

Queens State Wildlife Area, 15 miles south of Eads on US 287. There are a number of lakes in the wildlife area for fishing. The Nee Noshe, Nee So Pah, and Nee Grande Lakes, as well as Upper and Lower Queens reservoirs, offer anglers a chance at landing a variety of species like catfish, walleye, and largemouth and smallmouth bass.

HIKING **Pawnee Grasslands.** See Green Space, Parks.

Picketwire Canyonlands. See Green Space, Parks.

Vogel Canyon. See Green Space, Parks.

GREEN SPACE

Northeast Plains

Bonny Lake State Park (970-354-7306 or 1-800-678-2267; www.parks.state.co.us/parks/bonnylake), 32300 YC Rd. 2, Burlington. Open daily 5–10. The park is just north of I-70, not terribly far from the Kansas border. The main draw here is the reservoir, Bonny Lake, which offers visitors a chance to do some fishing, boating, jet skiing, swimming, and other water sports. They also have trails for hiking and, in the winter, cross-country skiing. The reservoir is about 1,900 acres and is home to walleye and bass. Daily park pass $6.

Jackson Lake State Park (970-645-2551; www.parks.state.co.us/parks/jackson lake), 26363 CR 3, Orchard. Open 24 hours a day. The park is located 20 miles northwest of Fort Morgan. Some of the biggest attractions at Jackson Lake are the excellent swimming beaches. The lake is relatively shallow, so it warms up nicely. Visitors also take advantage of the other water sports—fishing, boating, jet skiing. It is a popular park with hunters as well. There are some trails for hiking and biking. Daily park pass $6.

North Sterling State Park (970-522-3657; www.parks.state.co.us/parks/north sterling), 24005 CR 330, Sterling. Visitor center open daily 8–4:30. Park open 24 hours, no day use after 10 PM. Over 3,000 acres of water make this a great get-away in the summer. Trails for mountain biking and hiking and opportunities to swim, boat, and fish attract thousands of guests to North Sterling annually. Daily park pass $6.

Pawnee National Grassland and Pawnee Buttes (970-295-6600; www.fs.fed .us/r2/arnf), 2150 Centre Ave., Bldg. E, Fort Collins. The offices for the Pawnee Grassland are in Fort Collins, but the grassland itself is farther north. The Pawnee Buttes are well worth the drive into the country. They sit alone on the plains, rising 250 feet above the prairie floor. To get there, take CO 14 to CR 103, head north to Keota and follow the signs to the parking area. Once you are there, it's a level 1.5-mile walk to the buttes. There are other trails in the Pawnee Grassland, so stop by the offices in Fort Collins for maps and more information.

Southeast Plains

John Martin State Park and Lake Hasty (719-829-1801; www.parks.state.co .us/parks/johnmartinreservoir), 30703 CR 24, Hasty. East of Las Animas, the Arkansas River was dammed to create John Martin Reservoir. Below the dam is the well-stocked Lake Hasty. This is a popular park for boaters, anglers, and birdwatchers. Lake Hasty has a swim beach, the only one in the park. Hikers can get some exercise walking Red Shin Trail, a 4.5-mile hike that ends at a marker for the Santa Fe Trail. Daily park pass $6.

Comanche National Grasslands. The nearly 420,000 acres of shortgrass prairie that make up the Comanche National Grasslands are fairly inhospitable. It is a dry region and the days are either very hot or very cold. The delicate balance that allowed the prairie to thrive in these conditions was tipped by years of ranching and farming. By the time of the Dust Bowl years, the prairies were no longer viable for agriculture. So in 1938, the government started buying back the land. The grasslands are found primarily in two areas, just south of La Junta and just south of Springfield.

Picketwire Canyonlands and Dinosaur Tracks. Take CO 109 south of La Junta 13 miles to CR 802. Head west 8 miles and turn south on CR 25. After 6 miles, you will find the Corral Parking Area. The paleontological jewel of southeast Colorado is found here at Picketwire Canyonlands: over 1,300 dinosaur footprints, Native American rock art, early Hispanic settlements, and a historic ranch. The tracksite is considered the largest in North America.

Vogel Canyon. The directions to the Vogel Canyon parking lot are pretty simple. Head north of La Junta 13 miles on CO 109. There's a sign there directing you to turn west on CR 802 (also known as Vogel Canyon Road). After 1.5 miles, turn south on 505A and go another 1.5 miles to the parking lot. Four different trails provide the best way to explore the sandstone canyon. The Canyon Trail is particularly exciting—several spurs get you close to the canyon walls, where you can see Native American rock art, some nearly 800 years old. The Overlook Trail is handicapped accessible. The gravel path leads along the top of the canyon and lets you see a good bit of the scenery. Just as at Picketwire Canyonlands, you may stumble upon the ruins of some old building, which makes a hike here that much more interesting. The trails are not just used for hiking, but horseback riding and mountain bike riding as well.

✷ Lodging

Southeast Plains

HOTELS The pickings are mighty slim when it comes to hotels in southeast Colorado. Your best places to stay are closer to I-25 in Pueblo or Trinidad. There are Best Westerns in Las Animas (719-456-0011; 10950 E. US 50) and Lamar (719-336-7753; 1301 N. Main St.), but reviews are mixed. There is also a Holiday Inn Express in La Junta (719-384-2900; 27994 Frontage Rd.).

Mid-Town Motel (719-384-7741), 215 E. Third St., La Junta. Located near the main drag, the Mid-Town Motel offers clean (though somewhat dated) rooms at extremely affordable rates. If you are looking for a place to crash for the night, you won't be disappointed. Rates $40–50.

BED & BREAKFASTS **The Finney House** (719-384-8758), 608 Belleview Ave., La Junta. This beautifully restored 1899 Victorian home is a jewel, located in a quiet neighborhood close to downtown. Four rooms are available, and if you are looking for a longer stay, one room even has its own kitchen. The owner/innkeeper Shirley Flock serves a fine gourmet breakfast, and dinner is available (just be sure to set it up with Shirley in advance). Rates $70–85.

3rd Street Nest Bed & Breakfast (719-336-5217; http://home.bresnan.net/~3rdstnestbb), 304 S. Third St., Lamar. Just a couple blocks from downtown Lamar, the 3rd Street Nest has two rooms. During the week, innkeeper Jane Felter maintains a "Super Continental" breakfast and prepares a gourmet breakfast on weekends. Cable TV in each room. Both rooms have a private bath, though the Garden Room's bath is in the hall. There's a garden hot tub out back. Lavender 'n' Lace Suite (with whirlpool tub) $65–75. The Garden Room $60–70.

CAMPGROUNDS **Boggsville National Historic District** (719-456-2748), 2 miles south of Las Animas on CO 101. You can camp at Boggsville. They have three RV sites, tent camping sites, tipis to rent, full bathrooms, and showers for campers. (See To See & Do, Historic Sites for more information on the historic side of things at Boggsville.)

John Martin State Park (719-829-1801; www.parks.state.co.us/parks/JohnMartinReservoir), 30703 CR 24, Hasty. The state park maintains 213 campsites divided into two campgrounds. The Lake Hasty Campground is east of the John Martin Dam next to Lake Hasty. The site is rather wooded, offering nice shade in the summer. Fifty-four of the campground's 109 sites are open year-round. All are wired for electricity. The campground has flush toilets and showers (bring coins for the shower). They also have dump stations and laundry facilities. The Point Campground is more open than Lake Hasty, as it is surrounded by the reservoir on three sides with desert prairie to the north. Camping facilities here are a little more rustic. Three sets of vault toilets serve the 104 sites, which run $8–22.

Northeast Plains

BED & BREAKFASTS **The Old Library Inn** (970-522-3800; www.oldlibraryinn.com), 210 S. Fourth St., Sterling. This library was built in the 1920s, and it has been transformed into a simple, elegant B&B. The inn has three rooms, each with a private bath—one even has a large whirlpool tub. Throughout the inn you see reminders that this was once a library. On weekdays, there is a continental breakfast, and a full breakfast is prepared on weekends. Rooms $85–130.

"1" **Craig Ranch Bed & Breakfast and Horse Hotel** (719-775-2658; www.craigranchbandb.com), 50452 CR 23, Limon. Five rooms. Start your day with a hearty, country breakfast. Savor light, fluffy pancakes with fried apples, eggs, bacon, juice, coffee, and tea. Or satisfy your appetite with homemade muffins, jams, jellies, and granola. They also offer tours of the ranch—a great way to get a feel for life in eastern Colorado. Rates $80.

"1" ♿ **Claremont Inn** (719-348-5125 or 1-888-291-8910; www.claremontinn.com) 800 Clairmont, Stratton. This B&B calls itself "an oasis on the Colorado Plains." In many respects they are right—lodging of this caliber is not found for miles. And just as you can charge a mint for water in the desert, the rates here are pretty high-falutin. You will not, however, be disappointed by your stay. You might even want to plan on staying over on one of their special weekends, where you can take cooking classes, enjoy a murder mystery, or simply sweep your beloved away for a romantic getaway. Rates $150–250.

CAMPGROUNDS **Jackson Lake State Park** (970-645-2551; www.parks.state.co.us/parks/jacksonlake), 26363 CR 3, Orchard. Many of the park's 260 campsites are open year-round. Rest rooms, showers, and laundry facilities are located conveniently throughout the campground. Sites $14–18.

North Sterling State Park (970-522-3657; www.parks.state.co.us/parks/northsterling), 24005 CR 330, Sterling. The three campgrounds at North Sterling have a total 191 sites. Electric hook-ups are available. Rest rooms, showers, and laundry facilities are located conveniently to each campground. Sites $14–18.

"1" **Limon KOA** (719-775-2151 or 1-800-562-2129; www.koacolorado

.com), 575 Colorado Ave., Limon. Hook-ups include electrical, telephone, and cable TV. There is a camp swimming pool, and the campground rents bikes for those who want to take a ride. In addition to RV and tent sites, they also have one- and two-room Kabins for rent.

Bonny Lake State Park (970-354-7306 or 1-800-678-2267; www.parks.state.co.us/parks/bonnylake), 32300 YC Rd. 2, Burlington. There are 191 sites with a combination of flush and vault toilets. Showers and laundry facilities are also available. Sites $14–18.

* Where to Eat

EATING OUT ♿ **Stroh's Inn** (970-867-6654), 901 W. Platte Ave., Fort Morgan. The most popular item at the Stroh's Inn is their prime rib sandwich, which is served on cheese bread. The menu is chock full of comfort food.

♿ **TJ Bummer's Kitchen** (970-522-8397; www.buffalohillscampground.com/bummers.htm), 203 Broadway St., Sterling. Open daily 6–9 in the summer. Bummer's is probably the best place in town to grab a bite in Sterling. They are known for their down-home cooking and generous portions. As their tagline reads: "Not Fancy, Just Friendly."

♿ **Hog's Breath Saloon** (719-384-5089), 808 E. Third St., La Junta. The name may sound intimidating, ill conceived, or just plain humorous, but the Hog's Breath is one of the best places in town for family dining. In addition to the usual American dishes—their rib eye special is pretty tasty—they have some unusual items. For an appetizer try the snake eggs, which are bacon-wrapped jalapenos stuffed with cream cheese. Burgers start at $6 and dinner entrées run $10–15 (up to $20 for the lobster tail).

* Entertainment

Koshare Indian Dancers. See Koshare Indian Museum and Kiva under To See & Do, Museums.

* Special Events

February: **High Plains Snow Goose Festival and Nature Arts and Crafts Fair** (www.lamarchamber.com/goose/index.htm), Lamar. Celebrating the annual migration of the snow goose, the city of Lamar has also planned an annual arts and crafts fair that allows artists who try to capture the beauty of nature a chance to show their stuff.

August: **Kit Carson County Fair** (719-346-7382 or 1-800-288-1334; www.kitcarsoncounty.org/~perry/index), 815 15th St., Burlington. First week in Aug.

Arkansas Valley Fair (719-254-7723; www.arkvalleyfair.com), 800 N. Ninth St., Rocky Ford. The first Arkansas Valley Fair was back in 1878, and it's the oldest continuous annual fair in Colorado. The fair has the usual events—truck and tractor pulls, rodeo events, and even a demolition derby. Ticketed events $5–10 for adults and $3 for children under 12.

INDEX

B

D

E

F

G

H

I

J

K